NEET Foundation

Cell Biology

Workbook and Activity Sheets for Students of High School

Chandan Sukumar Sengupta

Creative Commons Series

NEET Foundation Cell Biology

Chandan Sukumar Sengupta

ISBN: 9798886676587

This Book is dedicated to fellow asirants of Pre Medical Entrance Examinations.

Contents

Foreword ... vii

Chemistry of Life ... ix

Points to Remember ... xi

Introduction ... xiii

1. Cell : The Unit of Life ... 1
   - Plasma Membrane ... 3
   - Endomembrane System ... 7
   - Plastids ... 14
   - Mitochondria ... 18
   - Nucleus and Chromosomes ... 24
   - Special Study Cell Wall ... 38
   - Review of Studies A ... 41
   - Review of Studies B ... 58
   - Test Paper I ... 70
   - Test Paper II ... 76
   - Test Paper III ... 84
   - Test Paper IV ... 87
   - Test Paper V ... 89
   - Test Paper VI ... 91
   - Test Paper VII ... 93
2. Cell Cycle ... 101
   - Worksheet 1 ... 101
   - Worksheet 2 [unsolved] ... 104
   - Worksheet 3 ... 105
   - Worksheet 4 ... 106
   - Worksheet 5 ... 107
   - Worksheet 6 ... 108
3. Chemical Basis of Genes ... 113
4. Regulations of Genes ... 123
5. Mendelism and Inheritence ... 127

Test Papers 129
- Review 1 129
- Review 2 130
- Review 3 131
- Review 4 133
- Review 5 136
- Review 6 143
- Review 7 153
- Worksheet 1 157
- Worksheet 2 165
- Worksheet 3 173
- Worksheet 4 174
- Worksheet 5 176
- Worksheet 6 179
- Worksheet 7 180
- Worksheet 8 182
- Worksheet 9 183
- Term End Assignment....184
- Evaluation 2 192
- Evaluation 3 201
- Evaluation 4 213

Foreword

Preparation for any examination or for any targated entrance requires planning. Such kind of specific planning requires proper understanding of the content areas and related framework of curriculum. All kinds of examinations have a definite pattern of questions and proper settings of content areas specified for designing test papers. Students are expected to attend that definite pattern of questions for gaining a desirable score.

Things to be avoided while preparing for an examination:

a. Fear is our enemy. It hampers the intellect. That is why one should not allow oneself to be trapped in fear.
b. Overlooking any content areas may not give adequate mastery of any subject. One should go on exploring minute details of the content areas meant for the test.
c. Indulgence in so many topics cannot give mastery of any subject. One should avoid unwanted indulgence in subject areas which are not relevant.
d. Overconfidence is another problem which hampers the growth of skills. Students gaining higher score in a small group may not be capable of gaining such mastery in any higher group. That is why one should not get inflicted with overconfidence.
e. Small things which are often neglected by a student may put the fellow in trouble. Small and easy questions often become challenging.

Assets of a Student:

a. Books, exam papers, previous year papers, quality guidance of teachers and good associations are very importane assets.
b. One should keep all sorts of information properly arranged and indexed.
c. All schedules of a student meant for the preparation for the test should be maintained properly.
d. One should maintain confidence upon oneself. Such confidence will enhance skill of the individual and equip the mind and intellect with readiness.
e. Regularity of study is another important factor that makes the student contented.
f. Quick recap of syllabus is most important for preparing oneself for higher challemges.
g. Regular classroom study along with some higher challenges will make the ward fit for higher level examinations.

There are several other factors which can be considered before moving on for preparing oneself for some higher challenges. None of the parts of content areas duly prescribed for a test should be avoided. Prpeparation for any exam does not mean limiting oneself up to the final content area duly prescribed for the test. Grasping through some higher level content areas may also equip oneself for the test. Studies related to cell and molecular biology, for an example, should not be limited only up to the level of the specified classroom. It should have some higher level inputs in it.

One should go on analyzing the patterns of test paper, model papers and other references for giving extra touch to the preparatory efforts. One should go on examining updates periodically for making oneself acquainted with changes of different types.

Working in a group will give additional advantage as such kinds of association will equip the student with doubt clearing initiatives. Grou discussion will also increase the levels of confidence of the fellow student.

Merely learning without getting involved in regular practice cannot bring fruitful results of desired type. We must go on practicing test papers regularly for removing our doubts.

Questions are there without respective answers. It can be obtained from the source. There exists a plan of fulfilling dual purpose of the effort. These sets can be utilized to engage a student for working out the possible outputs without being inflicted primarily with answers.

If answers are provided alongside the questions then the material will fulfill half of the purpose. It cannot contingent for overcoming the problems and also cannot facilitate in skill enhancement efforts.

Set of questions can be used for the purpose of assessing skill acquisition process and also can be assigned to the ward by parents and guides.

It is not mandatory to go through all sets of problems, but not to skip any of the problems is recommended for assuring the perfect skill acquisition.

Science is the evergrowing field of knowledge. Most of the human activities depend directly or indirectly on the proposals of science. It also increases the basic understanding of a person regarding the day to day events and related concerns. We can even describe most of the daily events on the basis of our scientific observations.

Whenever we come across any new events then our mind start recollecting different ideas related to our knowledge base. We also start correlating the reported events for assuring applicability of such knowledge base. Some of the events from our daily life often strike our mind differently. Why tooth pastes are basic in nature? Why room cleaners are acidic? Why metallic copper cannot react with salt solution of iron, zinc or sodium? Other such questions of particular types can be advanced to ascertain the need of intensive studies of the related areas of science for making oneself adequately equipped for accepting some higher challenges.

This activity book can provide an ample scope of learning to the fellow learners which are needed for improving their skills and competences related to science and technology. Extended worksheets and self evaluation modules can be used for assessing the progress of the individual learner. Chapters are grouped on the basis of their inter-relations. These are also grouped on the basis of their subject areas.

Learning by doing will be the best approach of acquiring skills in the field of Science and Technology. One can move through experience sharing to enhance one's skills and competence related to science and technology. Learning with understanding is a participatory process of interaction through which information flows from experts to the learners. It is also a process of sharing experiences and concerns. It will equip both the learners and facilitators in enhancing their skills of participatory learning.

Chemistry of Life

It is an established fact that all the life forms are made up of cells and cells are the building blocks of life, as a cell can perform all sorts of metabolic and regulatory functions, as a cell can give birth to new cells, as cells often get specialised for performing different types of coordinated functions to provide an ease of living to organisms. Amoeba, being a unicellular organism, can perform the same digestive functions just like that of human beings.

Cell is made up of different smaller components, which remain housed in various compartments as per need; all such components are combinations of some complex molecules (we coin a common word biomolecules to refer all such complex molecules). Some of such complex molecules are Carbohydrates, fats, proteins, vitamins, nucleic acids and other hybrid molecules; some are complex polysomes and some are complex polypeptide chains. Both saturated and unsaturated organic molecules participate in manufacturing different types of biomolecules.

Most of the biomolecules are endogenous (synthesised by the living organism) and some like carbohydrate, proteins, fats, vitamins and minerals are exogenous too (taken up by organisms in different forms). Some of the biomolecules are very simple and some (like proteins, fats, DNA and RNA) are oligomers or polymers. Nucleoside, for an example, is formed by attaching a nitrogen base to ribose or deoxyribose sugar. Nitrogen bases include include cytidine (C), uridine (U), adenosine (A), guanosine (G), and thymidine (T). Phosphorylation of nucleoside gives birth to a nucleotide. Ribonucleotides (A, U, G and C along with ribose sugar) can take part in forming RNA; deoxyribonucleotides (A, T, G and C along with deoxyribose sugar) joins to form single stranded or double stranded DNA molecule. DNA double helix structure along with A – T and G – C pairing is proposed by Watson and Crick. Due to adequate stability of this structure the molecule is qualified to accept the role of genetic material. RNA on the other hand got specialisation due to presence of an extra OH group; polymorphism of this molecule provided an extra advantage to living form to maintain different types of folding and anastomosing to make the molecule capable of giving birth to different types of complex molecules, such as tRNA, mRNA, rRNA, snRNA and severall other structures.

Monosaccharides, being the simple sugar, contains both aldehyde and ketone group in their structure.

Hexose, pentose, heptose, fructose, galactose etc. are some examles of mnosaccharides. Sucrose, maltose and lactose are disaccharides in which two monsaccharides join to form the molecule having linkage of two sugar molecule. In this way polysaccharides having linkage of several monoosaccharides are also made. Oligosaccharides having combination of 3 to 10 monomers; and large polysaccharides having combination of more than 10 monomers are also there in the living cell for fulfilling various purposes.

Lipids, being a fally acid ester, act as basic building block for membranes of different organelles and the membrane of a cell. Another important function erformed by fat molecules is storage of energy for future use, such as triglyceride. Lipid molecule consists of a hydrophilic head and hydrophobic tail (may be two or three in number). Head part can have variations; such as oligosaccharide head in glycolipids, phosphate linkage in phospholipids or STEROL linkage in steroids (example cholesterols).

Amono acids, the monomer used in the formation of polypeptide chain, contain both amino group and carboxylic groups in their molecule. Sequence of amino acids to be incorporated in a polypeptide chain is determined by gene sequences housed in the genetic material. Genetic information is first transcribed in nucleus, and then the messenger molecule (mRNA) along with protein factory (the Ribosome) translates the information to make the desired polypeptide chain. It is also observed that cellular components interact in a definite fashion to manufacture specific types of proteins on the basis of the genetic information duly evolved. Here lies the key of variations which makes an organism different from the other. Protein molecules get modified and folded differently to form secondary, tertiary and quarternary structures. Protein block without any attachment of cofactor, substrate or inhibitor group is called apoenzyme. Cofactors to be incorporated in the apoenzyme can be inorganic or organic; which forms coenzyme (a functional enzyme). Isoenzymes or isozymes are combinations different parts of structural units; they are either product of different genes or different roducts of alternative splicing. Fetal haemoglobin is an example of isoform of non-enzymatic protein which is also developmentally regulated.

Just like enzymes, which works as a chemical regulator in a cell, hormones also work as a coordinator, inducer, motivator or inhibitor of cellular functions by regulating different molecular level activities. Insulin, for an example, works to regulate level of glucose in blood. Thyroxine produced in thyroid gland is an iodenised derivative of amino acid tyrosine. Hormones released by adrenal cortex have several vital roles to play: glucocorticoids play a role in metabolism of glucose and regulating stress; mineralocorticoid plays a role in regulating filtration of blood in kidney.

Several examles can be advanced to show the diversified situation in which biomolecules play vital role in ensuring life process of a living cell; such molecules also regulate different mechanisms in which cells respond to the immediate exterior environment. Some amino acids (ten in number) are called essential amino acids as they are not synthesised in our body.

***

Points to Remember

1. An improved model of the structure of cell membrane was proposed by Singer and Nicolson (1972) widely accepted as fluid mosaic model. According to this, the quasi-fluid nature of lipid enables lateral movement of proteins within the overall bilayer. This ability to move within the membrane is measured as its fluidity.
2. The membrane is selectively permeable to some molecules present on either side of it. Many molecules can move briefly across the membrane without any requirement of energy and this is called the passive transport.
3. Water may also move across this membrane from higher to lower concentration. Movement of water by diffusion is called osmosis.
4. Polar molecules cannot pass through non-polar lipid bilayer. Such molecules and ions molecules are transported across the membrane against their concentration gradient, i.e., from lower to the higher concentration. (Energy dependent Active Transport). Example: $Na^{=}$/ $K^{=}$ pump.
5. Algae have cell wall, made of cellulose, galactans, mannans and minerals like calcium carbonate, while in other plants it consists of cellulose, hemicellulose, pectins and proteins. The cell wall of a young plant cell, the primary wall is capable of growth. Such growth gradually diminishes as secondary layer of cel wall develops. Cell wall of Monera contain Peptidoglycan, another chemical which makes it distinctly different than compared to cell walls of eukaryotes.
6. Middle lamella is a layer having calcium pectate as a principal composition, which holds or glues the different neighbouring cells together in plant body. Plasmodesmata ensures linkage of such neighbouring cells and ensures passage of chemicals from one cell to the other.
7. The endomembrane system include endoplasmic reticulum (ER), golgi complex, lysosomes and vacuoles. Due to lack of co-ordinations and functional integrity other organelles are not considered as members of endomembrane system.
8. Two distinct zones: luminal (inside ER) and extra luminal (cytoplasm) compartments are the results of the networked arrangement of ERs.
9. Lipid-like steroidal hormones are synthesised in SER (in animalcells).
10. The Golgi cisternae are concentrically arranged near the nucleus with distinct convex (cis or the forming face) and concave (trans or maturing face). These sites remain inter-connected, but differ considerably. It is the site of synthesis of glycol-proteins and glycolipids. A number of proteins synthesised by ribosomes duly embedded on the endoplasmic reticulum are modified in the cisternae of the golgi apparatus before they are released from its trans face in the form of secretory vesicles.
11. All types of hydrolytic enzymes (hydrolases – lipases, proteases, carbohydrases) optimally active at the acidic pH remain packed inside lysosomes.
12. Single membrane bound vacuoles (tonoplasts) are of common occurrence in plant cells. In Amoeba, Paramoecium and other Protists the contractile vacuole is important for osmoregulation and excretion. In many cells, as like those formed in protists, food vacuoles are formed by accommodating food particles inside vacuoles.
13. Being the site of aerobic respiration, he two membranes have their own specific enzymes associated with the specialised function. The mitochondrial matrix also possesses single circular DNA molecule, a few RNA molecules, ribosomes (70S) and the components required for the synthesis of proteins. These organelles divide by fission.
14. Chloroplasts (contains green pigment chlorophyll), chromoplasts (contains pigments other than green; fat soluble carotenoid pigments like carotene, xanthophylls and others) and leucoplasts (having no colour distinction; also modified for storage of food) are three distinct types of plastids.

15. Amyloplasts store carbohydrates (starch), e.g., potato; elaioplasts store oils and fats; aleuroplasts store proteins.
16. Number of chloroplast varies: 1 per cell of the Chlamydomonas, a green alga to 20-40 per cell in the mesophyll.
17. A number of organised flattened membranous sacs called the thylakoids, are present in the stroma. Such thylacoids are arranged in stacks (grana); different stroma lamellae connecting the thylakoids of the different grana remain associated. Chlorophyll pigments are present in the thylakoids. The ribosomes of the chloroplasts are smaller (70S).
18. Ribosomes (a membraneless organelle) are observed for the first time as dense article by George Palade (1953. Two subunits of 80 S ribosomes are 60 S and 40 S while that of 70 S ribosomes are 50 S and 30 S. Here 'S' (Svedberg's Unit) stands for the sedimentation coefficient.
19. A network of filamentous proteinaceous structures consisting of microtubules, microfilaments and intermediate filaments present in the cytoplasm (cytoskeleton) is responsible for providing definite shape to a cell.
20. Individual unit of cilia and flagella have a core called the axoneme, which possesses a number of microtubules running parallel to the long axis. The axoneme usually has nine doublets of radially arranged peripheral microtubules, and a pair of centrally located microtubules (9 + 2 arrangement; a distinct feature of eukaryotes). Each unit emerge from centriole-like structure called the basal bodies.
21. A pair of cylindrical structure (centriole) are encircled by amorphous pericentriolar materials to form centrosome. Central part (hub) and peripheral spookes (triplets) are made up of proteins. This organelle plays a vital role during cell division by taking part in spindle formation. Basal body of cilia and flagella are also made up of centrioles. Spikes get arrangements over the basal body.
22. Being the central part of a cell (eukaryotic) nucleus accommodates genetic materials. Chromatin contains DNA and some basic proteins called histones, some non-histone proteins and also RNA. A single human cell has approximately two metre long thread of DNA distributed among its forty six (twenty three pairs) chromosomes.
23. All the proteins are synthesised by an organism on the basis of genetic information provided by the DNA housed in the nucleus; they provide a template deending upon which cellular translator instruments make the polypeptide chains of different types to meet cellular and extra cellular demands.
24. Nitrogen bases are the key components of nucleotides, which make up the entire collection of genetic materials in living organisms; such kind of stable structure makes the molecule qualified for playin the role as genetic material. DNA is more stable than RNA which makes the molecule suitable as genetic material of eukaryotes.
25. Genetic code specifies a definite type of amino acid to be translated in the polypeptide chain; it is also a key to bring variation in organisms.
26. Expression of any phenotypic character in an organism depends upon the combination of contrasting alleles of the single set of genes (as evident in genotype of an organism). Genes always pass on from parent to offspring without becoming distorted or altered by any means.
27. Expression and reglation of genes is absolutely a cellular activity which resides on the function of regulator, inducer and terminator segments of genes. Individual genes get transcribed individually in eukaryotes and are transcribed collectively in prokaryotes (like bacteria).
28. Code sequence embedded in a gene can be altered because of mutations (point mutation, insertion of code, frame shift mutation etc.).
29. Series of mutation often develops a new mating type; hence can be considered as a switching on process of organic evolution.

Introduction

This book is meant primarily for fellow aspirants of different competitive examinations, pre-medical entrance examinations and other pre-board qualifying examinations. Maximum number of questions is to be covered through this publication; for that purpose also only relevants points from different content areas were taken up. Some of such areas might have a prominent presence. While dealing all the parts of this book one should remain aware of the fact that this book cannot be considered as a textbook. It can have a wider horizon of the coverage of content areas, which a textbook can rarely provide; it has also application oriented approach. The world of living organisms evolved gradually from single celled primitive organisms to multicellular and complicated organisations of modern age. The term eukaryotes (from the greek-true nucleus) have linear structures of DNA (which often takes a dense and compact structure called chromosomes during cell division). These are associated with chromosomal proteins called histone protein. These chromosome are found in the cell's nucleus, which is separated from the rest of the expanded zone of cytoplasm by a nuclear membrane. Eukaryotes also have a mitotic apparatus (various cellular structure that participate in a type of nuclear division called mitotis). Evidence from paleobotany indicates that the first eukaryotic cells appeared on earth approximately two billion yrs ago. These cells evolved from prokaryotic organism by a process of intracellular symbiosis. The structure of these newly developed cells was so versatile that eukaryotic microorganism soon spread out into available habitats and adopted greatly diverse styles of living to withstand harsh climate.

Only certain eukaryotes are small enough to fall into the scope of microbiology; the protozoa, fungi and algae. The fungi, algae, and protozoa are the eukaryotic microorganism evolved along three distinct lines of nutrient requirements, cellular architectures and energy acquisition. The fungi absorb nutrients from host or are parasitic or saprophytic in nature. The algae carry out photosynthesis with the help of hotosynthetic pigments to form cellular ATP. Protozoa acquire nutrients and energy through ingestion of organic compounds (holozoic mode of nutrition) often using phagocytosis to bring nutrients into the cell.

Analysis of similarities and differences of different micro-organisms and their cellular components will rovide us a general template depending upon which we can analyse the situation of other instances; while doing so we can even equip desired skills of opting comparative study of biology in general.

Cytology, the subject area which deals with structure and function of a cell, is the key area of discussion in this volume of publication. Genetics, being the science of inheritance, is another faculty which deals with flow of genetic information from one generation to the other. Due to involvement different cellular components in both the streams of studies (both cytology and genetics) it would be better if we discuss aspects related to both of the fields of studies jointly.

Cytopathology tests are also called smear test which often involves preparation of glass microscope slides by using smear sample being sread upon the surface of glass. Some of the prominent areas of the study of cytopathology are listed depending upon the examination of virtually all body organs and tissues:

Gynecologic cytology – concerning the female reproductive tract

Urinary tract cytology – concerning the ureters, urinary bladder and urethra. See Urine cytology.

Effusion cytology – concerning fluids collections, especially within the peritoneum, pleura and pericardium

Breast cytology – principally concerning the female breast

Vaginal cytology - principally concerning non-human mammals

Thyroid cytology – concerning the thyroid gland

Lymph node cytology – concerning lymph nodes

Respiratory cytology – concerning the lungs and airways

Gastrointestinal cytology – concerning the alimentary tract; Soft tissue, bone and skin cytology

Kidney and adrenal cytology; Liver and pancreas cytology; Central nervous system cytology

Eye cytology; Salivary gland cytology.

Cell Biology is the branch of study which deals with structure, function and propagation of living cells and other related components at different levels of organisation. It also enables us to analyse similarities and differences of different components of a cell; similar analysis paves a way for better understanding of the facts related to transmission of genetic information from one cell to the other. The extended branch of cell biology can accommodate different consideration of genes and inheritance; for that purpose the term "Cytogenetics" is duly coined. Cellular and molecular basis of inheritance is the branch of biology which confers adequate development of the studies related to gene and inheritance after Mendel (the father of Genetics). Scope of discussion related to genes, inheritance and Mendelism is based on all such modern studies duly made by scholars and scientists time to time.

Main purpose of the study of cytogenetics is to integrate the understanding related to different structural and functional units of cells along with their role in ensuring perfect expression of genes. Such kinds of integrated approaches paved a way for us to design the chemical process duly involved in expression of genes at different levels. It also enabled us to trace out different reasons involved in revalence of several genetic disorders in a population.

Studies related to switching on, switching off and suppression of gene expressions also enabled us to find out chances of variations which might have brought series of changes in an organisms to make the organisms ultimately a distinct mating type; a distinct group which can be considered as a unique mating type; moving finally towards giving birth to development of such organisms into a new secies. It was the tenure of Mendelian studies during which flow of individual genes were considered as independent of the other irrespective of their locations on the collective gene pool. Later on the concept of linked gene, suppressed gene, newly developed gene, lethal gene and several other complex combinations came in the field of studies to confer the complex mechanisms of transfer of genes from one generation to the other.

Linked genes remain associated so closely that they transmit from arents to offsrings without getting separated during the rocess of reductional division or even without forming any intermediate new variant type. Studies related to factors influencing exression and transmission of genetic information is also a key to develop proper understanding of the ways and means of inheritance which often develops under the influence of the chemically active segments of the gene pool.

***.

1. Cell : The Unit of Life

Cell, being the unit of life, is capable of conducting all the basic functions of a living forms; some can have specialised functions and some are capable of performing all kinds of metabolic and reproductive functions. Nearly every dynamic function in your body depends on proteins. There exists different kinds of chemicals in a cell which ensures different types of functions; some of the energy giving nutrients , such as carbohydrates and fats, are responsible for meeting energy requirement of a cell; molecules like proteins take part in constructive and regulatory functions; chemicals like nucleic acids play a role in maintaining and propagating genetic information from one generation to the other; chemicals like vitamins and minerals work as body protecting entity. A protein is a polymer of small molecular building blocks called amino acids. Of all of molecules of cellular organisations and extra cellular entities, proteins are structurally and functionally the most elaborate and varied. We have different proteins in our body meant for different types of specialised activities. Their most important role is as enzymes, the chemical catalysts that speed and regulate virtually all chemical reactions in your cells; as hormones, to induce or inhibit certain functions of cellular components; as building blocks, like those of histone octameres to construct and protect genetic materials.

On the basis of numbers of cells an organism may be unicellular or multicellular. It may be pprokaryotic or eukaryotic on the basis of presence or absence of organelles. Such organism may be plant or animal on the basis of types of outer coverings and other parts of cells.

Cells even vary on the basis of their role as they can play in the living body; nerve cells, for an example, remain involved in transmitting impulse in the living body. A cell is often called a structural and functional unit of life because of its capabilities of performing all the life process independently. It rarely relies upon any foreign agents for any kind of functional regulations. They simply get specialised in higher organisms for defining their specific role on the basis of their scope in the tissue system with which they remain associated. Such specialisations become materialised in due course of time during the process of development. It is even clear from various aspects of life process that a cell can successfully give birth to another cell of identical type through the process of equational division (mitosis). Organisms produce germ cells by the process of reductional cells division (meiosis).

Size of a cell also varies from few microns to a metre. Some prokartotic cells of bacteria are the smallest ones.

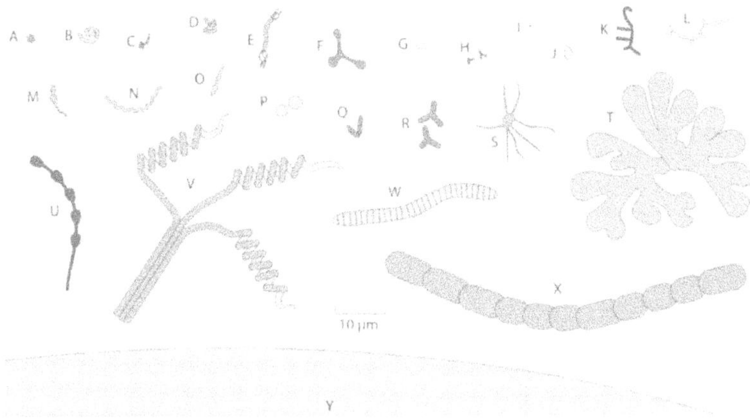

[Figure representing various types of cells plotted on the basis of their size.]

Cells of some types often remain freely in the connective fluid (like blood) with a clear distinction of their functions and the type of roles they definitely play in the action site. Blood cells of vertebrate are such type of divergent functional unit. White blood cells look after the protection of the body from foreign particles and the red blood cell remain responsible for the transport of respiratory gases, like oxygen and carbon dioxide.

They are more special in terms of their different sizes and appearance of their nucleus. In some cases the cell remains anucleated (Red Blood Cells of Human Beings).

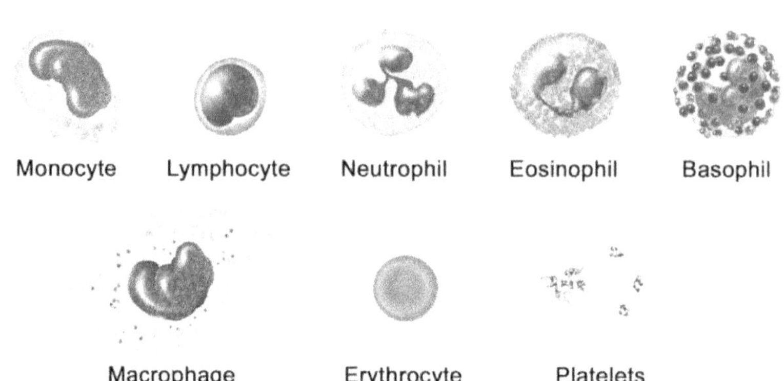

Variations often observed regarding number of nucleus present in a cell. It may be anucleated, nucleated, binucleated or polynucleated. Skeletal muscle of mammals is an example of such type of polynucleated cell.

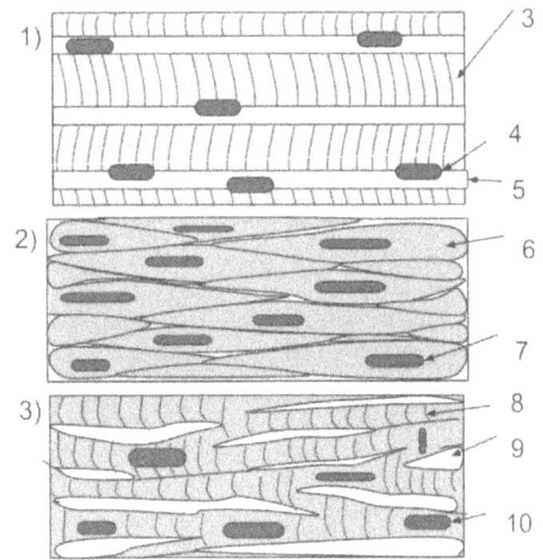

[Figure : 1) Skeletal muscle cells are long tubular cells with striations (3) and multiple nuclei (4). The nuclei are embedded in the cell membrane (5) so that they are just inside the cell. This type of tissue occurs in the muscles that are attached to the skeleton. Skeletal muscles function in voluntary movements of the body. 2) Smooth muscle cells are spindle shaped (6), and each cell has a single nucleus (7). Unlike skeletal muscle, there are no striations. Smooth muscle acts involuntarily and functions in the movement of substances in the lumens. They are primarily found in blood vessel walls and walls along the digestive tract. 3) Cardiac muscle cells branch off from each other, rather than remaining along each other like the cells in the skeletal and smooth muscle tissues. Because of this, there are junctions between adjacent cells (9). The cells have striations (8), and each cell has a single nucleus (10). This type of tissue occurs in the wall of the heart and its primary function is for pumping blood.]

There are several other features related to structure and function of a cell. The entire discussion and related practice materials are represented in this handbook for enhancing the basic understanding of the fellow aspirant. Several thematic areas related to cell and molecular biology will be discussed afterwards.

Plasma Membrane

The plasma membrane (the cell membrane) forms a flexible boundary between the living cell and its surroundings. For a structure that separates life from nonlife, this membrane is amazingly thin. It would take a stack of more than 8,000 plasma membranes to equal the thickness of a page of this book. Each phospholipid is composed of two distinct regions—a head with a negatively charged phosphate group and two nonpolar fatty acid tails. Phospholipids group together to form a two-layer sheet called a phospholipid bilayer.

The phospholipids' hydrophilic heads face outward, exposed to the aqueous solutions on both sides of a membrane. Their hydrophobic tails point inward, mingling together and shielded from water. Embedded in this lipid bilayer are diverse proteins, floating like icebergs in a phospholipid sea. Electron micrograph showing the three-layered (trilaminar) structure of the plasma membrane of an erythrocyte after staining the tissue with the heavy metal osmium. Osmium binds preferentially to the polar head groups of the lipid bilayer, producing the trilaminar pattern. The outer edge of a differentiated muscle cell grown in culture showing the similar trilaminar structure of both the plasma membrane (PM) and the membrane of the sarcoplasmic reticulum (SR), a calcium-storing compartment of the cytoplasm.

For describing structural speciality of plasma membrane Singer and Nicolson proposed the fluid mosaic model.[1]

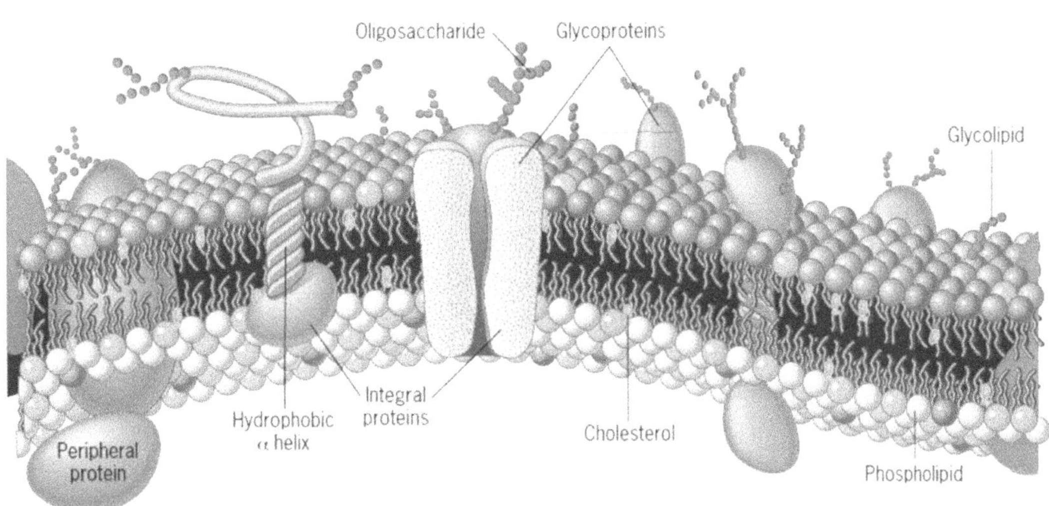

Fig: Structure of Plasma Membrane: Portion of a plasma membrane showing the same basic organization as that proposed by Singer and Nicolson. The external surface of most membrane proteins, as well as a small percentage of the phospholipids, contain short chains of sugars, making them glycoproteins and glycolipids. Those portions of the polypeptide chains that extend through the lipid bilayer typically occur as α helices composed of hydrophobic amino acids. The two leaflets of the bilayer contain different types of lipids as indicated by the differently colored head groups. The outer leaflet may contain microdomains ("rafts") consisting of clusters of specific lipid species.

The ratio of lipid to protein in a membrane varies, depending on the type of cellular membrane (plasma vs. endoplasmic reticulum vs. Golgi), the type of organism (bacterium vs. plant vs. animal), and the type of cell

[1] *The fluid-mosaic model proposed in 1972 by S. Jonathan Singer and Garth Nicolson of the University of California, San Diego. In the fluid-mosaic model, which has served as the "central dogma" of membrane biology for more than three decades, the lipid bilayer remains the core of the membrane, but attention is focused on the physical state of the lipid.*

(cartilage vs. muscle vs. liver). For example, the inner mitochondrial membrane has a very high ratio of protein/lipid in comparison to the red blood cell plasma membrane, which is high in comparison to the membranes of the myelin sheath that form a multilayered wrapping around a nerve cell. The inner mitochondrial membrane contains the protein carriers of the electron-transport chain, and relative to other membranes, lipid is diminished. Being amphipathic in nature membrane lipids contain both hydrophilic and hydrophobic regions. Most membrane lipids contain a phosphate group, which makes them phospholipids. Because most membrane phospholipids are built on a glycerol backbone, they are called phosphoglycerides. A less abundant class of membrane lipids, called sphingolipids, are derivatives of sphingosine, an amino alcohol that contains a long hydrocarbon chain. Sphingolipids consist of sphingosine linked to a fatty acid by its amino group. Cholesterol, as evident from certain animal cells, is absent from the plasma membranes of most plant and all bacterial cells. These molecules are oriented with their small hydrophilic hydroxyl group toward the membrane surface and the remainder of the molecule embedded in the lipid bilayer. Depending on the species and cell type, the carbohydrate content of the plasma membrane ranges between 2 and 10 percent by weight. More than 90 percent of the membrane's carbohydrate is covalently linked to proteins to form glycoproteins; the remaining carbohydrate is covalently linked to lipids to form glycolipids.

Transmembrane proteins pass entirely through the lipid bilayer and thus have domains that protrude from both the extracellular and cytoplasmic sides of the membrane. Some integral proteins have only one membrane-spanning segment, whereas others are of multispanning types. Peripheral proteins are placed entirely outside the lipid bilayer, placed on either the cytoplasmic or extracellular side, yet are associated with the surface of the membrane by forming some noncovalent bonds. Lipid anchored proteins are covalently linked to a lipid molecule that is situated within the bilayer. Several large families of membrane proteins contain an interior channel that provides an aqueous passageway through the lipid bilayer. The linings of these channels typically contain key hydrophilic residues at strategic locations. Maintenance of membrane fluidity is an example of homeostasis at the cellular level. If the temperature of a culture of cells is lowered, the cells respond metabolically. The initial "emergency" response is mediated by enzymes that remodel membranes, making the cell more cold resistant. Remodeling is accomplished by (1) desaturating single bonds in fatty acyl chains to form double bonds, and (2) reshuffling the chains between different phospholipid molecules to produce ones that contain two unsaturated fatty acids, which greatly lowers the melting temperature of the bilayer.

Because lipids provide the matrix in which integral proteins of a membrane are embedded, the physical state of the lipid is recognised as an important determinant of the mobility of integral proteins. The demonstration that integral proteins can move within the plane of the membrane was a cornerstone in the recommendation of the fluid-mosaic model. Cells can be induced to fuse with one another by making the outer surface of the cells "sticky" so that their plasma membranes adhere to one another. Cells can be induced to fuse by addition of certain inactivated viruses that attach to the surface of plasma membrane, by adding a specific compound (like polyethylene glycol), or by a giving a mild electric shock. This mechanism has played an important role in the field of medical science and is currently used in an invaluable technique to prepare specific antibodies. The plasma membranes of many cells possess a fibrillar network, or "membrane skeleton," consisting of peripheral proteins situated on the cytoplasmic surface of the membrane. A certain proportion of a membrane's integral protein molecules are either tethered to the membrane skeleton or otherwise restricted by it.

We consider plasma membrane as a selectively permeable structure as it allows passage of some specific molecules and rejects passage of some other molecules directly through lipid bilayer. The substance, to be allowed to move across membrane, must be present at higher concentration on one side of the membrane than the other, and the membrane must be permeable to the substance. A membrane may be permeable to a given solute either (1) because that solute can pass directly through the lipid bilayer, or (2) because that solute can traverse an aqueous pore that spans the membrane. Small non-polar molecules (like oxygen) can have an easy movement through lipid bilayer (direct diffusion). One simple measure of the polarity (or nonpolarity) of a substance is its partition coefficient, which is the ratio of its solubility in a nonpolar solvent, such as octanol or a vegetable oil, to that in water under conditions where the nonpolar solvent and water are mixed together. Comparatively small molecules manage an easy passage through lipid bilayer without experiencing much obstacles. Water molecules move from a region of lower solute concentration to a region of higher solute concentration. When a cell is placed into a hypotonic solution, the cell rapidly gains water by osmosis and swells; in hypertonic solution cell shrinks. If a plant cell is placed into a hypertonic medium, its volume shrinks as the plasma membrane pulls away from the surrounding cell wall, a process called plasmolysis; as a result lants lose support and wilt.

Cell membranes contain ion channels, that is, openings in the membrane that are permeable to specific ions. Most ion channels are highly selective in allowing only one particular type of ion to pass through the pore. The diffusion of ions through a channel is always downhill (from a state of higher energy to a state of lower energy). neurotransmitters, such as acetylcholine, act on the outer surface of certain cation channels, while cyclic nucleotides, such as cAMP, act on the inner surface of certain calcium ion channels.

The binding of the solute to the facilitative transporter on one side of the membrane is thought to trigger a conformational change in the protein, exposing the solute to the other surface of the membrane, from where it can diffuse down its concentration gradient. Facilitative transporters are specific for the molecules they transport, discriminating, for example, between D and L stereoisomers. Both enzymes and transporters exhibit saturation-type kinetics. Unlike ion channels, which can conduct millions of ions per second, most facilitative transporters can move only hundreds to thousands of solute molecules per second across the membrane. A gradient favoring the continued diffusion of glucose into the cell is maintained by phosphorylating the sugar after it enters the cytoplasm, thus lowering the intracellular glucose concentration. Humans have at least five related proteins (isoforms) that act as facilitative glucose transporters. Active transport depends on integral membrane proteins that selectively bind a particular solute and move it across the membrane in a process driven by changes in the protein's conformation. Endergonic movement of ions or other solutes across the membrane against a concentration gradient is coupled to an exergonic process, such as the hydrolysis of ATP, the absorbance of light, the transport of electrons, or the flow of other substances down their gradients. Active transport drives the movement of ions in only one direction. It is the Na/K-ATPase that is responsible for the large excess of Na^+ions outside of the cell and the large excess of K^+ions inside the cell. The sodium–potassium pump is found only in animal cells. This protein is thought to have evolved in primitive animals as the primary means to maintain cell volume and as the mechanism to generate the steep $Na^+$and K^+gradients that often play a key role in the formation of impulses in nerve and muscle cells. The epithelial lining of the stomach also contains a P type pump, the H^+/K^+-ATPase, which secretes a solution of concentrated acid into the lumen of stomach.

Some of the functions of plasma membrane is pointed out as follows:

(1) An example of membrane compartmentalization in which hydrolytic enzymes (acid hydrolases) are sequestered within the membrane-bounded vacuole.

(2) As a site of enzyme localization: The fixation of CO_2 by the plant cell is catalyzed by an enzyme that is associated with the outer surface of the thylakoid membranes of the chloroplasts.

(3) As a selectively permeable barrier: Water molecules are able to penetrate rapidly through the plasma membrane, causing the plant cell to fill out the available space and exert pressure against its cell wall.

(4) Solute transport: Hydrogen ions, which are produced by various metabolic processes in the cytoplasm, are pumped out of plant cells into the extracellular space by a transport protein located in the plasma membrane.

(5) Transfer of information from one side to another (signal transduction): In this case, a hormone (e.g., abscisic acid) binds to the outer surface of the plasma membrane and triggers the release of a chemical message (such as IP3) into the cytoplasm. In this case, IP3 causes release of Ca^{2+} ions from a cytoplasmic warehouse.

(6) Cell–cell communication: Openings between adjoining plant cells, called plasmodesmata, allow materials to move directly from the cytoplasm of one cell into its neighbors.

(7) Energy transduction: The conversion of ADP to ATP occurs in close association with the inner membrane of the mitochondrion.

Evaluate Understanding

1. What types of integral proteins would you expect to reside in the plasma membrane of an epithelial cell that might be absent from that of an erythrocyte? How do such differences relate to the activities of these cells?

2. Many different types of cells possess receptors that bind steroid hormones, which are lipid-soluble molecules.Where in the cell do you think such receptors might reside? Where in the cell would you expect the insulin receptor to reside? Why?

3. When the trilaminar appearance of the plasma membrane was first reported?

4. Suppose you were planning to use liposomes in an attempt to deliver drugs to a particular type of cell in the body, for example, a fat or muscle cell. Is there any way you might be able to construct the liposome to increase its target specificity?

5. How is it that, unlike polysaccharides such as starch and glycogen, the oligosaccharides on the surface of the plasma membrane can be involved in specific interactions? How is this feature illustrated by determining a person's blood type prior to receiving a transfusion?

6. Trypsin is an enzyme that can digest the hydrophilic portions of membrane proteins, but it is unable to penetrate the lipid bilayer and enter a cell. Because of these properties, trypsin has been used in conjunction with SDS–PAGE to determine which proteins have an extracellular domain. Describe an experiment using trypsin to determine the sidedness of proteins of the erythrocyte membrane.

7. Why plasma membrane is considered as selectively permeable membrane?

8. Suppose you were culturing a population of bacteria at 15^0C and then raised the temperature of the culture to 37^0C.What effect do you think this might have on the fatty acid composition of the membrane? on the transition temperature of the lipid bilayer? on the activity of membrane desaturases?

9. What is the difference between a two-dimensional and a three dimensional representation of a membrane protein? How are the different types of profiles obtained, and which is more useful? Why do you think there are so many more proteins whose two-dimensional structure is known?

10. How would you expect the concentrations of solute inside a plant cell to compare to that of its extracellular fluids? Would you expect the same to be true of the cells of an animal?

Endomembrane System

Membrane bound cell organelles like Endoplasmic Reticulum, Glgi aaratus, vesicles, Lysosomes and peproxysomes jointle participate along with Nuclear envelope to form Endomembrane System of a cell. This system provide different compartments to the living cell to be used for conducting different chemical reactions without getting influenced by another experiments. It is also a path remain involved in tracing out a secretory path for the living cell.

The peripheral Endoplasmic Reticulum that extends from the nuclear envelope is comprised of both a polygonal network of tubules and flat, stacked membrane cisternae close to the nucleus. The stacked cisternae are covered with ribosomes for the synthesis, import, and folding of membrane, luminal, and secreted proteins. The rough ER contains specialized receptors and channels that transfer proteins synthesized by ribosomes in the cytoplasm across ER membranes. Inside the ER lumen, newly synthesized proteins are exposed to a dense meshwork of chaperones and other modifying enzymes (estimated to be 200 mg/mL) that catalyze their folding and assembly before letting them move up to Golgi apppparatus through vesicles. Both soluble and transmembrane proteins are exported from the ER at sites called ER export domains. These tubulovesicular membranes lack ribosomes and bud off vesicle intermediates for delivery to the Golgi apparatus. The ER surface forming the inner nuclear envelope (which faces the nucleoplasm) contains specialized proteins that interact with the nuclear lamina and chromatin. Peroxisomes, lipid droplets, and the Golgi apparatus all depend directly or indirectly on the ER for their biogenesis and maintenance. During peroxisome biogenesis, the ER provides the initial scaffold for recruiting core components involved in peroxisomal protein import. The smooth ER, composed of tubular elements lacking ribosomes, is dedicated to enzyme pathways involved in drug metabolism (hepatocytes), steroid synthesis (endocrine cells), or calcium uptake and release. The cytochrome P450 family of heme containing membrane proteins resides in the smooth ER. Cells dedicated to the manufacturing, customisation, storage, and regulated secretion of proteins (such as exocrine cells and activated B cells) are rich in rough ER. Smooth ER is abundant in endocrine cells that often remain involved to synthesize steroid hormones and in muscle cells fulfilling their requirement to store and release Ca^{2+} to control contraction.

All soluble and membrane proteins destined for ER translocation using the cotranslational pathway contain a hydrophobic “leader” sequence that serves as a recognition signal for ensuring direction to the ER membrane. N-terminal leader sequences (termed signal sequences) are typically 15 to 35 amino acids long and contain a hydrophobic core of at least 6 residues. For many membrane proteins, the first transmembrane segment (a hydrophobic stretch of 16 to 25 residues) serves as a signal sequence. Secretory proteins and soluble parts of membrane proteins move through the translocon pore into the ER lumen. Transmembrane domains of integral membrane proteins leave the translocon pore through the lateral gate to enter the hydrophobic environment of the lipid bilayer. Transmembrane proteins are categorized as type 1, type 2, or polytopic species depending on the orientation of their transmembrane domains across the lipid bilayer. This orientation is established during translation of mRNA into the corresponding polypeptide chain and maintained as the protein moves to its final destination in the cell during the process of budding and fusion events. Type 2 transmembrane proteins use a transmembrane domain in the middle of the polypeptide as an internal signal sequence. Polytopic proteins that span the membrane multiple times (Example: ion channels and carriers) use multiple stop-transfer signals, none of which are cleaved by signal peptidases.

Most proteins synthesized in association with the ER are glycoproteins with covalently attached carbohydrates. One class of oligosaccharides is added to asparagine residues during translocation of the protein into the ER. Sometimes proteins with signal sequences fail to translocate into the ER and are mislocalized to the cytoplasm. This can happen if there are mutations in the signal sequence, certain stresses, or intrinsic inefficiencies in their translocation. Lipids are processed and repared for further use in smooth ER. Pumps using ATP hydrolysis as their energy source redistribute lipids across the membrane bilayers of the Golgi apparatus and plasma membrane. Final step of cholesterol manufacturing is accomplished in ER leading to cholesterol take place in the ER, but cholesterol is not a resident ER lipid and is rapidly exported to post-ER membranes, including the plasma membrane, where it participate in the lipid bilayer to constitutes up to 50% of the lipid content of the bilayer. Synthesis and degeneration of enzymes involved in rocessing of cholesterol is regulated by a feedback mechanism. Ceramide (the backbone of all sphingolipids) begins its synthesis through sequential condensation of the amino acid serine with two fatty acids on the cytoplasmic face of ER membranes.

Distinct compartments of the secretory pathway provide protective environments to synthesize, fold, assemble, and modify membrane and secretory proteins before they are exposed on the cell surface. Eukaryotic cells have the capacity to store secretory proteins in membrane compartments; allowing the cell to regulate the release of proteins from the cell surface in response to internal or external signals. Membranes with distinct lipid compositions allow for specialized functions in the various compartments. The lipid composition of the ER is favorable for folding of transmembrane proteins. Ordered, flexible arrays of cholesterol and sphingolipids in the plasma membrane are mechanically stable and make the layer impermeable to water-soluble molecules. Cargo proteins next fold and are sorted and concentrated within membranebound carrier vesicles for transport to the next compartment. The vesicular tubular carriers (VTCs) that bud from the ER are destined for fusion with membranes of the Golgi apparatus. Golgi apparatus secures its position as a major site of processing bio-molecules before letting them to move towards trans-vesicles for the purpose of secretion. The flow of cargo and lipid forward through the secretory system toward the plasma membrane (anterograde traffic) is balanced by selective retrograde traffic of cargo proteins and lipids back toward the ER for the purpose of re-utilisation of the processed molecules. The ER produces cholesterol and glycerophospholipids while the Golgi apparatus synthesizes glycosphingolipids and sphingomyelin.

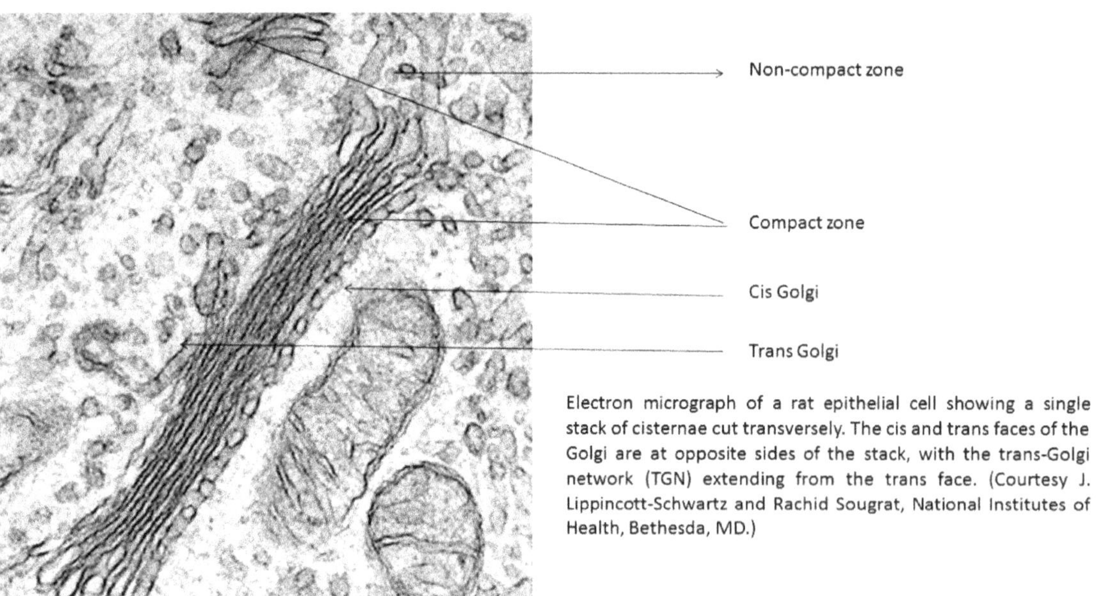

Electron micrograph of a rat epithelial cell showing a single stack of cisternae cut transversely. The cis and trans faces of the Golgi are at opposite sides of the stack, with the trans-Golgi network (TGN) extending from the trans face. (Courtesy J. Lippincott-Schwartz and Rachid Sougrat, National Institutes of Health, Bethesda, MD.)

Fig: Various components of Golgi complex.

Cargo molecules use three distinct modes of transport out of the ER: bulk flow, signal-mediated sorting, and partitioning within the lipid bilayer. Many membrane proteins partition into the bilayer of transport carriers based on their collective physicochemical properties without the help of specific sorting signals or receptors.

Plasma membrane proteins, having long transmembrane helices, partition into the thicker membranes of transport vesicles. ER-resident proteins with shorter transmembrane domains are retained in the thinner bilayer of the bulk ER for ensuring maintenance of regularity and integrity of the organelle.

Some sort of structural polarisation is also evident from the special type of orientations of Golgi lamellae, cesterns and vesicles; cis and trans vesicles differ considerably; forming and maturing faces of Golgi have several differences. Stacks of Golgi cisternae in animal and plant cells all exhibit a cis-to-trans polarity reflecting the passage of cargo through the organelle. Proteins and lipids from the ER enter the cis face (entry face) of the stack. After passing through the stack of cisternae, cargo leaves from the trans face at the opposite side of the stack. Membrane sorting and transport activities of the Golgi are high at the cis and trans faces and within the tubular-vesicular elements (non-compact zone) that interconnect the stacks.

The size, appearance, and even existence of the Golgi apparatus depend on the amount and rate of movement of secretory substances through the secretory pathway.[2] None of membrane proteins are peprmanent members of Golgi apparatus as they regularly join and exit the organelle while following different secretory pathways. In that context this organelle is a dynamic one. Being the chief function, most cell-surface proteins and lipids and secreted proteins are glycosylated (incorporation of glucose molecules in protein and fat molecules). Their glycans participate in numerous biological functions, including inter cellular and cell–matrix interactions, intracellular and intercellular trafficking, and different types of cell signaling. During cell division this cell organelle, along with all of its components, disassembles in many eukaryotic cells and then reassembles during interphase. After growing by simple addition of monosaccharide units, many oligosaccharides are modified by enzymes that add phosphate, sulfate, acetate, or methyl groups or isomerize specific carbons. Enzymes present in this organelle also add oligosaccharides to the hydroxyl groups of serine and threonine residues of selected proteins, such as proteoglycans, heavily glycosylated proteins in secretory granules, and the extracellular matrix.

Glycosyltransferases add specific sugar residues to glycans, while glycosidases remove specific sugar residues. All these enzymes[3] are type II transmembrane proteins with a short cytoplasmic amino terminal domain followed by a transmembrane segment and catalytic luminal domain within the Golgi cisternae. These, and pther enzymes present in the cell organelle, also mark specific proteins for transport to lysosomes by phosphorylating the 6-hydroxyl of mannose. This modification is the sorting signal that directs lysosomal enzymes to mannose 6-phosphate receptors in the trans-Golgi apparatus for targeting to lysosomes. These enzymes also load noncovalently associated cholesterol and phospholipids onto high-density and low-density lipoproteins for secretion by liver cells into the blood.

Some of the prominent mechanisms of endocytosis include phagocytosis, macropinocytosis, clathrin-mediated endocytosis, caveolae-dependent, uptake, and nonclathrin/noncaveolae endocytosis. All the protrusions or invaginations of the plasma membrane that are accomplished during these diverse endocytic processes require coordinated interactions between a variety of protein and lipid molecules that dynamically link the plasma membrane and cortical actin cytoskeleton housed inside the cell in the form of a widespread network. If any solid organic cluster of molecules or living forms are trapped inside a living cell (as evident during the process of Phagocytosis duly performed by amoeboid cells) both the plasma membrane and internal membranes contribute to make a phagocytic cup. Internal membranes from recycling endosomes, late

[2] *The yeast Saccharomyces cerevisiae has a poorly developed Golgi apparatus because secretory transport is normally too fast for elaborate Golgi structures to accumulate. Conditions that slow transport of moolecules out of the Golgi apparatus in yeast cells lead to the Golgi apparatus enlarging and rearranging into compact stacks similar to those seen in most animal and plant cells.*

[3] *There are more than 200 enzymes involved in processing of macromolecules inside Golgi apparatus. They jointly participate in manufacturing glycoproteins and glycolipids.*

endosomes, and possibly endoplasmic reticulum (ER) contribute to the phagocytic cup by fusing with the plasma membrane in a process called focal exocytosis. When secretory lysosomes fuse at the forming phagocytic cup, they release cytokines that contribute to inflammation; an immune response. Many cells ingest extracellular fluid in large endocytic structures called macropinosomes. Growth factors or other signals stimulate actin-driven protrusions of the plasma membrane in the form of ruffles. It is induced by activation of plasma membrane receptors.

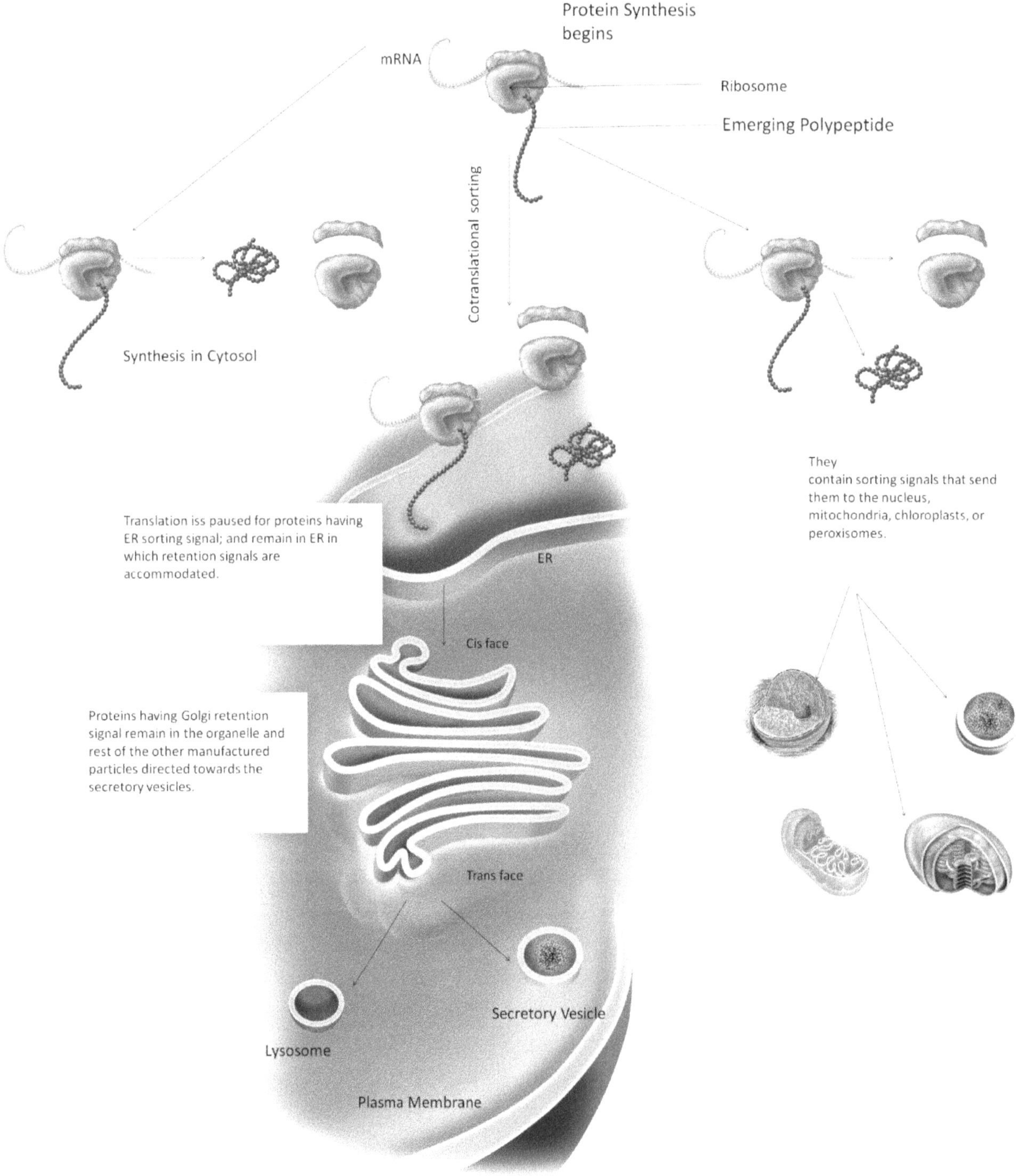

Fig: Involvement of Endomembrane System in synthesis and secretion of protein molecules.

Removal of these same receptors from the cell surface by macropinocytosis down-regulates their signaling activity. Constitutive macropinocytosis allows cells to take up molecules from the medium. Endocytosis regulates the strength or duration of signalling most simply by controlling the number of receptors available in the plasma membrane for activation by ligands. When such endocytosis occurs nonuniformly across the cell, localized signaling emerges. One example of this is at the leading edge of migrating cells. Lysosomes, the major digestive organelles present in a living cell, contain at least sixty distinct hydrolytic enzymes; including proteases, peptidases, phosphatases, lipases, phospholipases, glycosidases, sulfatases, and nucleases. Lysosomal hydrolases are tagged in the Golgi apparatus with mannose-6-phosphate groups on their N-linked oligosaccharides. Mannose-6- phosphate receptors in the trans-Golgi network employed to divert the tagged hydrolases to endosomes and lysosomes for accelerating further actions. Cytoplasmic substrates are delivered to lysosomes by dedicated autophagosomes and by direct capture from the cytoplasm in a process termed autophagy; the structure involved in materialising such process is called autophagosome. Long-lived cytosolic proteins and integral membrane proteins circulating within the secretory and endosomal systems are degraded by lysosomes, whereas short-lived cytoplasmic proteins and endoplasmic reticulum (ER) membrane proteins are degraded by the proteasome. Macroautophagy (involves engulfment of large portion of cytoplasm), microautophagy, and chaperonemediated autophagy are processes leading to the breakdown of cytoplasmic constituents within lysosomes; a key function leading towards implementation of cellular homeostasis.

Revision Works.

1: ………………………………. seems to be one of the mechanisms used by these proteins to shape the lipid bilayer into a tubule. Additionally, they also appear to use a wedge-like structural motif that causes the membrane to curve. These two classes of proteins are redundant, since the overexpression of one protein can compensate for the lack of the other protein.

2. Which of these is true about the endoplasmic reticulum?
A.Dependent on the cytoskeleton B.Made of tubular cisternae that are 100 nm in diameter
C.Is contiguous with the plasma membrane and therefore ideal for protein secretion
D.All of the above

3. Which of these is a function of smooth endoplasmic reticulum?
A.Synthesis and secretion of steroid hormones
B.Maintenance and regeneration of the plasma membrane
C.Storage and release of Ca2+ ions D.All of the Above

4. Which of these is true about the functions of proteins that stabilize the structure of the endoplasmic reticulum?
A.Translocons are important in maintaining the curvature of cisternae
B.DP1/Yop1p group of proteins can create oligomers that form a scaffold and stabilize the curved regions of the ER
C.Reticulons are capable of forming wedge-like structures that insert themselves into the plasma membrane and anchor the ER D.All of the Above

5. Which of the following is NOT a function of the endoplasmic reticulum?

A.Creating and folding proteins B.Creating new lipid molecules for the cellular membrane
C.Modifying chemicals that will be secreted from the cell
D.Transcribing DNA into mRNA

6. Which of these is true about the rough endoplasmic reticulum?
A. Crucial for synthesizing proteins that are secreted from the cell
B. Important during lactation and the production of milk
C. Studded with ribosomes and polysomes
D. All of the above

7. Which of these molecular mechanisms is directly involved in proper protein folding in the ER?
A. Binding of Signal Recognition Particles to a nascent polypeptide
B. Translocons on the ER membrane C. Glycosylation and binding of molecular chaperones
D. All of the above

8. Which of these proteins is involved in anterograde transport from the rough ER to the Golgi apparatus?
A. Ubiquitin and the proteasome B. CNR/CXT chaperone proteins
C. COPII D. All of the above

9. Which of these is true about the smooth endoplasmic reticulum?
A. Dependent on the intermediate filaments of the cytoskeleton
B. Made of tubular cisternae that are 100 nm in diameter
C. Interaction with mitochondria influences a number of its functions D. All of the above

10. Which of these is a function of smooth endoplasmic reticulum?
A. Synthesis and secretion of steroid hormones
B. Maintenance and regeneration of the plasma membrane
C. Storage and release of Ca2+ ions D. All of the above

11. Which of these proteins influence the calcium store of smooth ER?
A. Receptor expression enhancing proteins (REEPs)
B. Ryanodine receptors and Inositol-1,4,5-trisphosphate receptors
C. Reticulons and DP1 D. All of the above

12. What is Lysosomal Storage Disease?

13. What is the mechanism by which most LSDs occur?
A. The lysosomes are too small to contain the large molecules that they normally can break down.
B. Enzymes are not packaged into the lysosomes in the Golgi apparatus correctly.
C. Deficiency in one hydrolytic enzyme in lysosomes leads to a buildup of large molecules, eventually killing the cell.
D. The phospholipid bilayer of lysosomes does not form correctly, so the lysosomes cannot contain the necessary enzymes.
14. Elaborate different components of Endomembrane System along with their functions.

Key : 1 : Oligomerization; 2 : C; 3: D; 4: D; 5: D;

6: D is correct. The rough endoplasmic reticulum plays an important role in synthesizing proteins destined for secretion from the cell. Therefore, it is studded with ribosomes and polysomes, which are translating mRNA containing the code for these proteins. This process is particularly important during lactation since milk contains a number of proteins that sustain a baby during the initial months.

7: C is correct. Of the three options, only glycosylation and the binding of molecular chaperones plays a role in protein folding within the ER. The binding of SRPs to a growing polypeptide chain and the presence of translocons on the ER membrane are important aspects of protein synthesis. However, these components of protein synthesis are not directly involved in the polypeptide reaching its correct 3-D shape or native structure.

8: C is correct. Ubiquitin-mediated proteasomal degradation of proteins is an important part of the quality control mechanism within the cell for disposing of misfolded proteins. Similarly, the CNR/CXT system and other molecular chaperones are also part of the mechanisms within the rough ER to ensure that polypeptides fold into their correct formation. Once this process is complete, however, it is COPII proteins that are involved in the anterograde transport of vesicles carrying cargo towards the Golgi from the endoplasmic reticulum.

9: C is correct. The interaction of smooth ER with mitochondria not only influences its functions in carbohydrate and lipid metabolism but also plays an important role in integrating the signals of the entire cell and inducing apoptosis under certain conditions. While the formation of the endoplasmic reticulum is dependent on the cytoskeletal machinery of the cell, particularly microtubules, the importance of intermediate filaments is not very clear. The ER is made of tubular cisternae and two-dimensional sheets. However, the diameter of cisternae rarely exceeds 60 nm. In yeast, they are even smaller, with a diameter of about 30 nm.

10. D is correct. The SER forms a three-dimensional polygonal network across the cell and is often made of cisternae. It contains a number of enzymes involved in sterol and steroid hormone synthesis. Its role in the creation of cholesterol and phospholipid makes it important in the generation and maintenance of the plasma membrane and the entire endomembrane system. It also stores and releases calcium – a function that is particularly important in excitable cells.

11. B is correct. REEPs, reticulons and DP1 are involved in stabilizing the curved structure of ER tubules. However, it is ryanodine receptors and inositol-1,4,5-trisphophate receptors that influence its calcium store.

12. LSDs usually occur when a person is deficient in one enzyme that breaks down large molecules like proteins or lipids. Because the enzyme is lacking, the large molecules cannot be broken down, and they eventually build up within the cell and kill it.

13. C is correct. Most lysosomal storage disorders occur when a person is deficient in a single hydrolytic enzyme. With low/no enzyme activity, the molecule that the enzyme is supposed to act on does not get broken down, and large molecules accumulate in the cell. Eventually, too many large molecules build up in the cell and it dies.

14. Different components of Endomembrane system

1. Nuclear envelope: Double membrane that surrounds the nucleus
2. Endoplasmic reticulum: Protein secretion and sorting; Glycosylation; Lipid synthesis
Metabolic functions and accumulation of Ca2+
3. Golgi apparatus: Protein secretion and sorting; Glycosylation
4. Lysosome/vacuoles: Degradation of organic molecules; Storage of organic molecules;
Accumulation of water (plant vacuoles)
5. Peroxisomes: Breakdown of toxic molecules such as H_2O_2; Breakdown and synthesis of organic molecules
6. Plasma membrane: Uptake and excretion of ions and molecules; Cell signalling; Cell adhesion

***

Plastids

Plastids are a double membrane bound cell organelle responsible for storage of food, pigmentation of some body parts of organisms and helping autotrophs in making their food. We can find them easily in some pprotists and all types of plants. Green pigment bearing plastids are called chloroplastids. They have capabilities of trapping solar radiation. During photosynthesis, relatively low-energy electrons are removed from a donor compound and converted into high-energy electrons using the energy absorbed from light. These high-energy electrons are then employed in the synthesis of reduced biological molecules, such as starch and oils. It is likely that the first groups of photoautotrophs, which may have dominated Earth for two billion years, utilized hydrogen sulfide as their source of electrons for photosynthesis, carrying out the overall reaction where (CH_2O) represents a unit of carbohydrate.

$$CO_2 + 2\,H_2S \quad \text{(presence of light)} \quad = \quad (CH_2O) + H_2O + 2\,S$$

There are numerous bacteria living today that carry out this type of photosynthesis. Over a long period of evolution, the symbiotic cyanobacterium was transformed from a separate organism living within a host cell into a cytoplasmic organelle, the chloroplast. As the chloroplast evolved, most of the genes that were originally present in the symbiotic cyanobacterium were either lost or transferred to the plant cell nucleus. chloroplasts arise by fission from preexisting chloroplasts; or their nonpigmented precursors (proplastids). Chloroplast is housed inside a sac like membrane bound disc like structure called thylacoid; stack of thylacoids form a unit called granum; all the grana provides reaction site for light facilitated reactions. The light-absorbing reactions of photosynthesis occur in large pigment–protein complexes called photosystems. Two types of photosystems are required to catalyze the two light absorbing reactions utilized in oxygenic photosynthesis. One photosystem, photosystem II (PSII), boosts electrons from an energy level below that of water to a midway point. The other photosystem, photosystem I (PSI), raises electrons from a midway point to an energy level well above that of $NADP^+$.

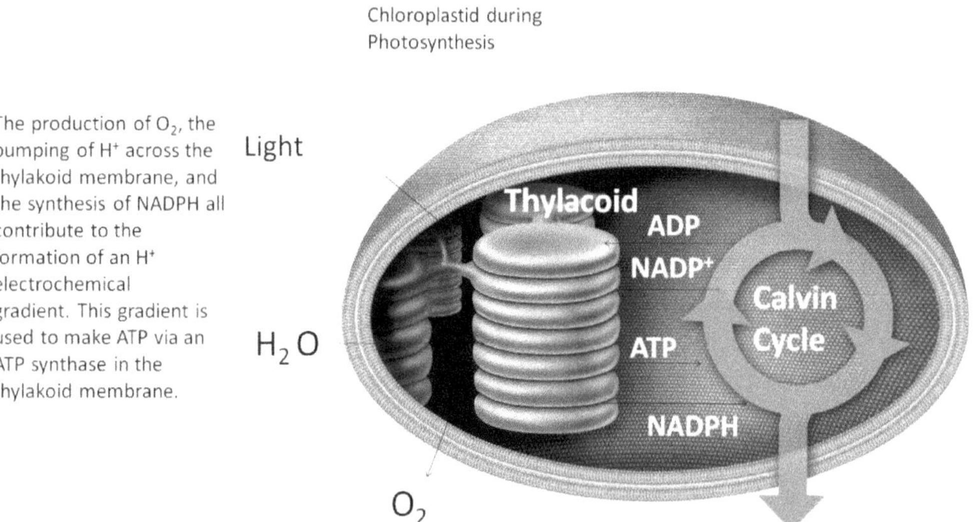

Fig: Diagram displaying phases of reactions taking place inside Chloroplastid of a living cell.

The two photosystems act in series one after the other. The two types of photosystems in plants, as well as those of photosynthetic bacterial cells, exhibit marked similarities in protein composition and overall architecture. Photosystem II uses absorbed light energy for two interrelated activities: removing electrons from water and generating a proton gradient.

The synthesis of ATP in chloroplasts is achieved by a chemiosmotic mechanism called photophosphorylation, which is similar to the oxidative phosphorylation used to make ATP in mitochondria. In chloroplasts, ATP synthesis is driven by the flow of H^+ from the thylakoid lumen into the stroma via ATP synthase. The light reactions produce an H+ electrochemical gradient in which more H+ is in the thylakoid lumen and less in the stroma.

The gradient is generated in three ways:

1. The splitting of water places H+ in the thylakoid lumen.

2. The movement of high-energy electrons along the ETC from photosystem II to photosystem I pumps H+ into the thylakoid lumen.

3. The formation of NADPH consumes H+ in the stroma.

The steps of the light reactions of photosynthesis produce three chemical products: O_2, NADPH, and ATP:

1. O2 is produced in the thylakoid lumen by the oxidation of water by photosystem II. Two electrons are removed from water, producing 2 H^+ and 1/2 O_2. The two electrons are transferred to P680 molecules.

2. NADPH is produced in the stroma using high-energy electrons that are first boosted to a higher energy level in photosystem II and then are boosted a second time in photosystem I. Two high-energy electrons and one H+ are transferred to $NADP^+$ to produce NADPH.

3. ATP is produced in the stroma via ATP synthase that uses an H^+ electrochemical gradient.

Calvin cycle uses more ATP than NADPH.

How can plant cells avoid making too much NADPH and not enough ATP?

In 1959, Daniel Arnon discovered a pattern of electron flow that is cyclic and generates only ATP. Arnon termed the process cyclic photophosphorylation because (1) the path of electrons is cyclic, (2) light energizes the electrons, and (3) ATP is made via the phosphorylation of ADP. Due to the path of electrons, the mechanism is also called cyclic electron flow. The energy may be transferred among multiple pigment molecules until it is eventually transferred to a special pigment molecule designated P680, which is located within the reaction center of PSII. The P680 pigment is so named because it can directly absorb light at a wavelength of 680 nm. However, P680 is more commonly excited by resonance energy transfer from a chlorophyll pigment in the light-harvesting complex. In either case, when an electron in P680 is excited, the molecule is designated P680*. The light-harvesting complex is also called the antenna complex because it acts like an antenna that absorbs energy from light and funnels that energy to P680 in the reaction center.

A high-energy (photoexcited) electron in a pigment molecule is very unstable. It may abruptly release its energy by giving off heat or light. Unlike the pigments in the light-harvesting complex that undergo resonance energy transfer, P680* can actually release its high-energy electron and become P680+. The role of the reaction center is to quickly remove the high-energy electron from P680* and transfer it to another molecule, where the electron is stable. This molecule is called the primary electron acceptor (see Figure 8.11). The transfer of the electron from P680* to the primary electron acceptor is remarkably fast.

Review:

Q. Describe the roles of the lightharvesting complex, P680, and the primary electron acceptor during the absorption of light energy by photosystem II (PSII). At which step is the light energy captured?

ANSWER Light-harvesting complex: The role of the light-harvesting complex is to absorb light. Because it is composed of many pigment molecules (chlorophylls and β-carotene), the light-harvesting complex is the most likely place for visible light to be absorbed. When a pigment molecule absorbs light, an electron is boosted to a higher energy level, and that energy is transferred via resonance energy transfer to P680.

P680: The role of P680 is to provide a link between the lightharvesting complex and the primary electron acceptor. Although P680 can directly absorb light, P680 is far more likely to gain energy from the light-harvesting complex, which converts it to P680*. The high-energy electron of P680* is then transferred to the primary electron acceptor.

Primary electron acceptor: The role of the primary electron acceptor is to capture the light energy. The high-energy electron of P680* is unstable. However, when it is transferred to the primary electron acceptor, the electron becomes stable, meaning that it will not drop down to a lower energy level. As O_2 builds up in a leaf, rubisco adds O_2 instead of CO_2 to RuBP. A two-carbon product of this reaction is then broken down in the cell. This process is called photorespiration because it occurs in the light (photo) and consumes O_2 and releases CO2 (respiration). But unlike cellular respiration, it uses ATP instead of producing it; and unlike photosynthesis, it yields no sugar. Photorespiration can, in fact, drain away as much as 50% of the carbon fixed by the Calvin cycle.

Q. Why C4 plants are so named?

C4 plants are so named because they first fix CO2 into a four-carbon compound. When the weather is hot and dry, a C4 plant keeps its stomata mostly closed, thus conserving water. It continues making sugars by photosynthesis using the Pathway.

Q. What are CAM plants?

Ans: A second photosynthetic adaptation has evolved in pineapples, many cacti, and other succulent (water-storing) plants. Called CAM plants, these species are adapted to very dry climates. A CAM plant conserves water by opening its stomata and admitting CO_2 only at night. CO_2 is fixed into a four-carbon compound, which banks CO_2 at night and releases it during the day. Thus, the Calvin cycle can operate, even with the leaf's stomata closed during the day.

Q. What are the sites of carbon fixation and Calvin cycle in C4 plants?

Ans: In C4 plants, carbon fixation and the Calvin cycle occur in different types of cells. In CAM plants, these processes occur in the same cells, but at different times of the day.

Q. Point out similarities in between C3, Cr and CAM plants.

Ans: CAM, C4, and C3 plants all eventually use the Calvin cycle to make sugar from CO_2. The C4 and CAM pathways are two evolutionary adaptations that minimize photorespiration and maximize photosynthesis in hot, dry climates. Electrons shuttle from photosystem II to photosystem I, providing energy to make ATP, and then reduce NADP+ to NADPH. Photosystem II regains electrons as water is split and 02 released.

During photophosphorylation, the electron transport chain located in the membrane of thylacoid pumps H^+ into the thylakoid space. The concentration gradient drives H^+ back through ATP synthase, powering the synthesis of ATP.

Evaluate

1. What are grana in chloroplasts made of?

A. Outer membrane-bound proteins B. Stacks of inner membrane structures

C. Chlorophyll D. All of the above

2. Which of these is NOT a function of a chloroplast stroma?

A. Stress response B. Intracellular signaling

C. Release of high energy electrons upon interaction with photons D. All of the above

3. What are the steps involved in Calvin Cycle?

4. What are the other methods of carbon fixation evolved in plants growing in hot and dry climate?

5. Which of the following terms best describes the filamentous algae Spirogyra, which use light energy to convert CO_2 and H_2O to sugars and other organic molecules, and release O_2 as a by-product? Are such organisms thought of as producers or consumers of the biosphere? (Explain your answer.)

a. heterotrophs; producers b. photoautotrophs; producers

c. chemoheterotrophs; consumers d. chemoautotrophs; consumers

6. Most scientific experts agree that climate change is already occurring and has potentially catastrophic consequences for all of life on Earth. The Paris Agreement of 2015 represented a global consensus on the need to reduce greenhouse gas emissions. However, in 2017 the United States announced its intention to withdraw from the Agreement in 2020. Go online to research and summarize the main agreements reached in this historic global climate accord and the U.S. government's reasons for withdrawing. What roles do you think scientists, politicians, and citizens will need to play to cut emissions and limit global warming?

Ans 1. B is correct. Grana are made of stacks of thylakoids, that are formed by invaginations of the inner membrane in chloroplasts. While chlorophyll exists as a part of the photosystems that harness light energy, grana are more than just aggregates of pigments.

Ans 2. C is correct. The release of high energy electrons is purely a function of reaction centers in thylakoids. Though the stroma are involved in providing protons during the electron transport chain, they are not directly involved in the release of high energy electrons. The stroma has been implicated in both stress response and in intracellular signaling, through the formation of finger-like protrusions.

Ans 3. The steps of the Calvin cycle include carbon fixation, reduction, release of G3P, and regeneration of RuBP. Using carbon from CO_2, electrons from NADPH, and energy from ATP, the cycle constructs G3P, which is used to build glucose and other organic molecules.

Ans 4. In C3 plants, a drop in CO_2 and rise in O_2 when stomata close divert the Calvin cycle to photorespiration. C4 plants and CAM plants first fix CO_2 into four-carbon compounds that provide CO_2 to the Calvin cycle even when stomata close on hot, dry days.

Ans 5. Option b is correct; They manufacture their food in presence of sunlight and never depend upon any other organisms for obtaining nutrients.

***

Mitochondria

Mitochondria, being the energy manager of a cell, remains associated with metabolism of nutrients for the purpose of liberating energy currency (ATP). Being a double membrane structure the membranes of the mitochondrion divide the organelle into two aqueous compartments, one within the interior of the organelle, called the matrix, and a second between the outer and inner membrane, and called the intermembrane space. The matrix has a gel-like consistency owing to the presence of a high concentration (up to 500 mg/ml) of water-soluble proteins. The outer membrane is composed of approximately 50 percent lipid by weight and contains a specific mixture of enzymes involved in such diverse activities as the oxidation of epinephrine, the degradation of tryptophan, and the elongation of fatty acids. The inner membrane contains more than 100 different polypeptides and has a very high protein/lipid ratio (more than 3 : 1 by weight, which corresponds to about one protein molecule for every 15 phospholipids). A series of invaginated membranous sheets, called cristae, can be located in the inner membrane.The inner membrane is virtually devoid of cholesterol and rich in an unusual phospholipid, cardiolipin (diphosphatidylglycerol). Cardiolipin plays an important role in facilitating the activity of the proteins involved in ATP synthesis. mitochondria possess their own genetic material and the machinery to manufacture their own RNAs and proteins. This nonchromosomal DNA encodes a small number of mitochondrial polypeptides (for example, 13 in humans) that are tightly integrated into the inner mitochondrial membrane along with polypeptides encoded by genes residing in the genes housed in nucleus.

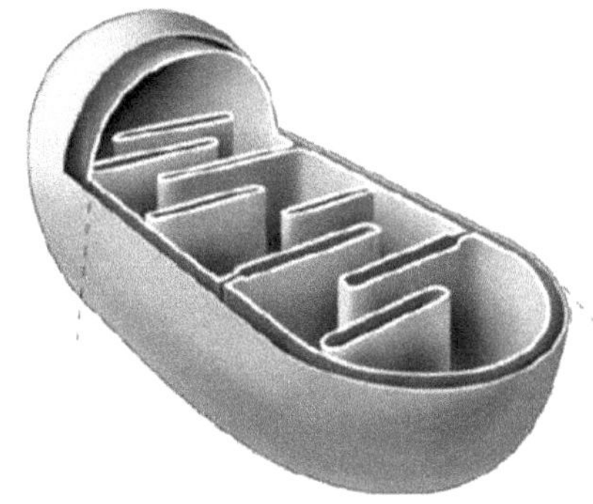

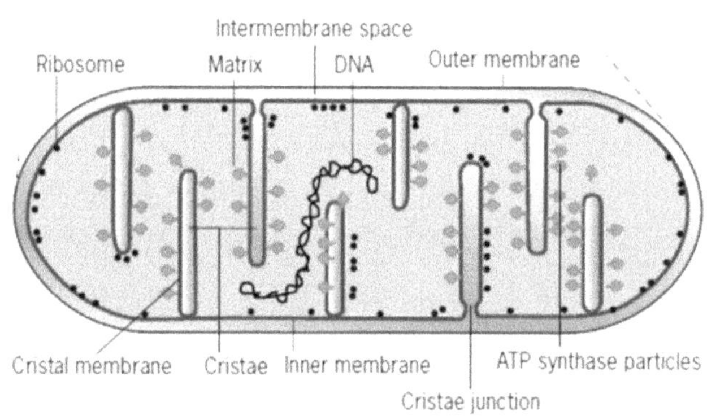

Fig: Diagram of a Mitochondrion: showing the threedimensional internal structure (top) and a thin section.

Functional specialisation of different enzyme complexes made the organelle competent enough in metabolising glucose molecules and other organic moolecules completely for the purpose of releasing ATPs. The reactions of glycolysis generate pyruvate and NADH in the cytosol. In the absence of O_2, the pyruvate is reduced by NADH to lactate (or another product of fermentation, such as ethanol in yeast). The NAD———————————— formed in the reaction is reutilized in the continuation of glycolysis. In the presence of O_2, the pyruvate moves into the mitochondrial matrix (facilitated by a membrane transporter), where it is decarboxylated and linked to coenzyme A (CoA), a reaction that generates NADH.The NADH produced during glycolysis donates its high-energy electrons to a compound that crosses the inner mitochondrial membrane. The acetyl CoA passes through the TCA cycle, which generates NADH and $FADH_2$. The electrons in these various NADH and $FADH_2$ molecules are passed along the electron-transport chain, which is made up of carriers that are embedded in the inner mitochondrial membrane, to molecular oxygen (O_2). The energy released during electron transport is used in the formation of ATP. If all of the energy from electron transport were to be utilized in ATP formation, approximately 36 ATPs could be generated from a single molecule of glucose.

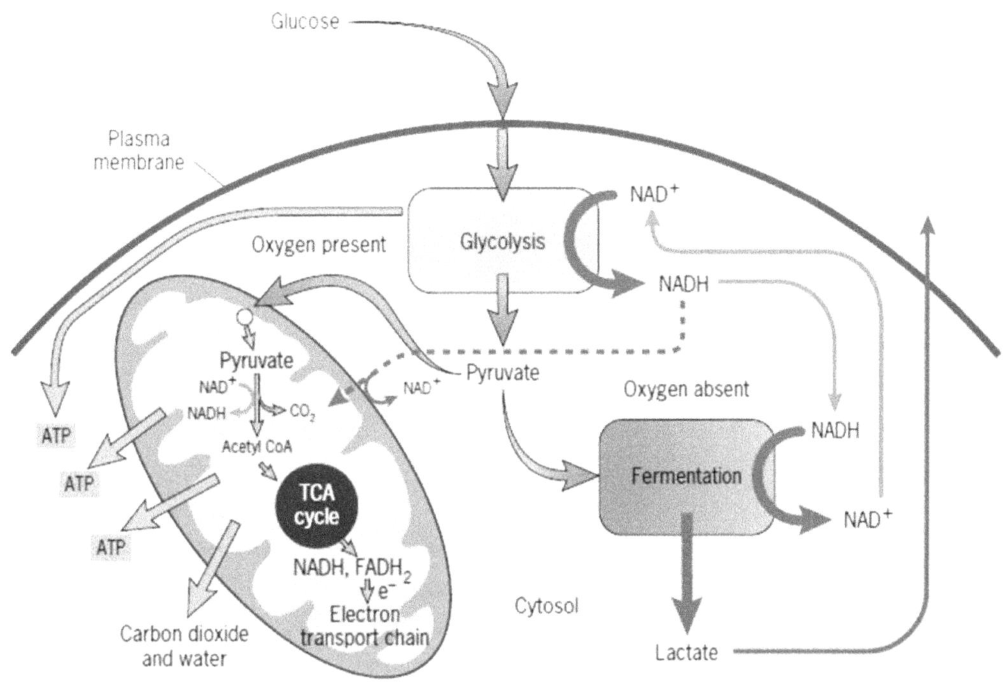

Fig: A schematic diagram showing function of mitochondria.

Mitochondria utilize an ionic gradient across their inner membrane to drive numerous energy-requiring activities, most notably the synthesis of ATP.When ATP formation is driven by energy that is released from electrons removed during substrate oxidation, the process is called oxidative phosphorylation.

The electron-transport chain contains five types of membranebound electron carriers: flavoproteins, cytochromes, copper atoms, ubiquinone, and iron-sulfur proteins. Flavoproteins consist of a polypeptide bound tightly to one of two related prosthetic groups, either flavin adenine dinucleotide (FAD) or flavin mononucleotide (FMN). Cytochromes are proteins that contain heme prosthetic groups. The iron atom of a heme undergoes reversible transition between the Fe^{3+} and Fe^{2+} oxidation states as a result of the acceptance and loss of a single electron. Ubiquinone (UQ , or coenzyme Q) is a lipid-soluble molecule containing a long hydrophobic chain composed of five-carbon isoprenoid units.

The respiratory chain, as embedded in mitochondrial membrane, consists of four complexes of electron carriers and two other carriers (ubiquinone and cytochrome c) that are independently disposed. Electrons enter the chain from either NADH (via complex I) or $FADH_2$ (a part of complex II). Electrons are passed from either complex I or II to ubiquinone (UQ), which exists as a pool within the lipid bilayer. Electrons are subsequently passed from reduced ubiquinone (ubiquinol) to complex III and then to the peripheral protein cytochrome c, which is thought to be a little bit mobile in nature. Electrons are transferred from cytochrome c to complex IV (cytochrome oxidase) and then to O_2 to result formation H_2O.

.

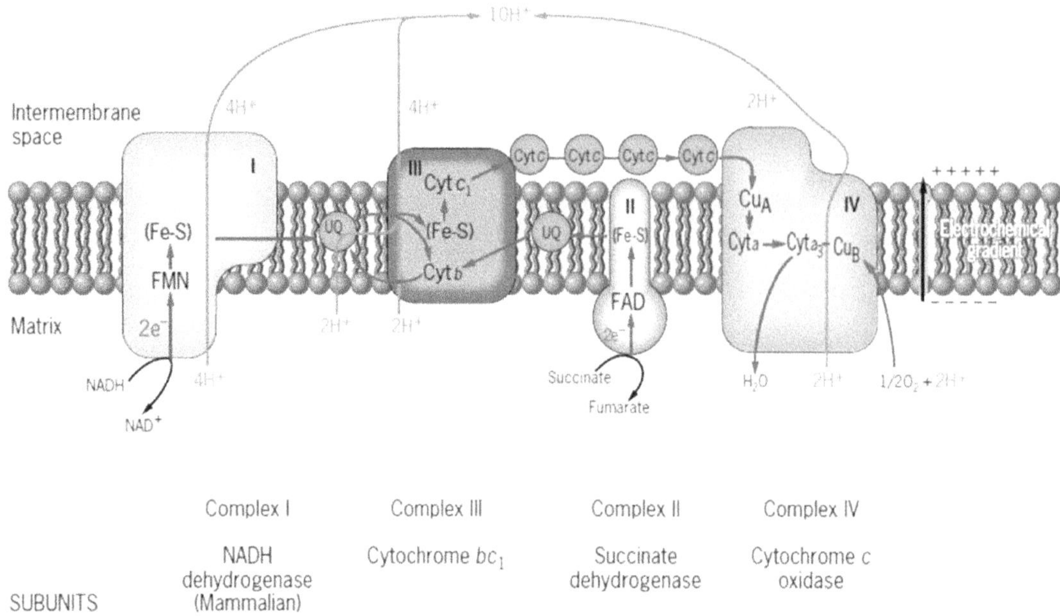

Fig: Diagram showing different parts of Electron Transport System

Chemiosmosis is the process where the energy generated from the proton gradient is used to produce ATP. The transfer of electrons in the ETC is coupled with the translocation of the proton (H^+) which develops a proton gradient. The movement of H^+ ions down their electrochemical gradient activates the ATP synthase enzyme which will catalyze the phosphorylation of ADP forming ATP molecule.

Review:

1: Of the five types of electron carriers, which has the smallest molecular mass? Which has the greatest ratio of iron atoms to electrons carried? Which has a component that is located outside the lipid bilayer? Which are capable of accepting protons and electrons and which only electrons?

2. Why do some electron transfers result in a greater release of energy than other transfers?

3. Which is NOT a reason why mitochondria are thought to have evolved from free-living bacteria?

A. Mitochondria have their own DNA.
B. Mitochondria reproduce through binary fission.
C. Mitochondrial DNA is inherited matrilineally.
D. The genome is similar to that of bacterial DNA.

4. Which is a function of mitochondria?

A. Regulating metabolism
B. Producing ATP
C. Storing calcium
D. All of the above

5. Which is NOT a reason why mitochondria are thought to have evolved from free-living bacteria?

A. Mitochondria have their own DNA.
B. Mitochondria reproduce through binary fission.
C. Mitochondrial DNA is inherited matrilineally.
D. The genome is similar to that of bacterial DNA.

6. Where is the mitochondrial matrix located?

A. Within the inner membrane
B. Between the inner and outer membrane
C. Inside the mtDNA
D. In the intermembrane space

7. For one molecule of Glucose Kreb's cycle will produce ....

8. The synthesis of ATP from ADP and P

a. stores energy in a form that can drive cellular work. b. involves the hydrolysis of a phosphate bond.

c. transfers a phosphate, priming a protein to do work. d. is an exergonic process.

9. What couples the electron transport chain to ATP synthesis?

10. Cellular respiration involves three main stages. Where and in which stages is CO2 produced within the cell?

11. For each glucose molecule processed, what are the net molecular products of glycolysis?

12. During glycolysis, how many total substrate-level phosphorylation reactions occur per molecule of glucose?

13. How many CO_2 and ATP molecules have been produced after stages 1 and 2 (per one molecule of glucose)?

14. What is the total number of NADH and $FADH_2$ molecules generated during the complete breakdown of one glucose molecule to six molecules of CO_2?

Answer Key.

4. D is correct. All of the above are functions of mitochondria. Mitochondria also have roles in apoptosis, cell signaling, and thermogenesis.

5. C is correct. While it is true that mtDNA is inherited from the mother, it is not a reason why mitochondria are thought to have evolved from bacteria that had an endosymbiotic relationship with cells. It is inherited this way because sperm do not contain mitochondria. Choices A, B, and D suggest that mitochondria have similarities to, and evolved from, bacteria.

6. A is correct. The matrix is a space enclosed by the mitochondrion's inner membrane. Choices B and D both refer to the intermembrane space, which is the space between the two membranes.

7. for every 1 pyruvate molecule added, the Krebs cycle will produce:

2 molecules of CO_2 3 molecules of NADH 1 molecule of $FADH_2$ 1 molecule of GTP

8. option a is true; ATP is called energy currency of cell.

9. As electrons are passed down the energy staircase, the electron transport chain also pumps hydrogen ions (H+) across the inner mitochondrial membrane into the narrow intermembrane space. The result is a concentration gradient of H+ across the membrane. In chemiosmosis, the potential energy of this concentration gradient is used to make ATP.

10. Pyruvate oxidation and the reactions of the citric acid cycle complete the breakdown of glucose to carbon dioxide. The CO_2 we exhale is generated in the mitochondria of cells during this stage of cellular respiration.

11. Two molecules of pyruvate, two molecules of ATP, and two molecules of NADH.

12. Four substrate-level phosphorylation reactions occur for each molecule of glucose: two during step 6 and two during step 9.

13. Six CO_2 are produced and 4 ATP (two in glycolysis and two in the citric acid cycle)

14. 10 NADH: 2 from glycolysis, 2 from the oxidation of pyruvate, and 6 from the citric acid cycle; and 2 FADH2 from the citric acid cycle. (double the output after the sugar-splitting step of glycolysis.)

Diagram of TCA Cycle

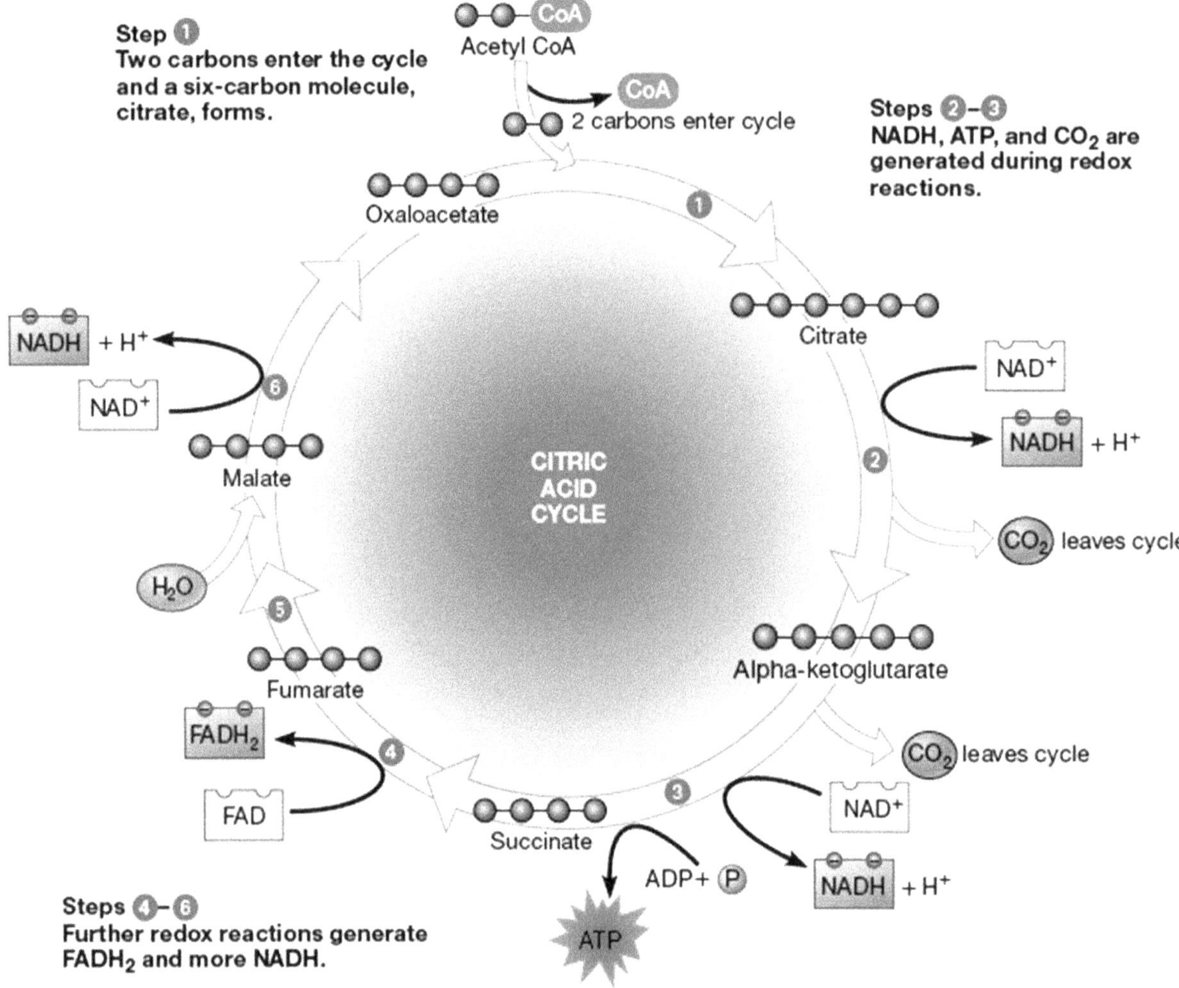

Q. The initial study discussed identified brown fat in less than 10% of the patients whose scans were analyzed. The second study identified brown fat in 96% of participants. What accounts for this difference in research results?
Solution: Brown fat was activated and thus identified in response to the cold temperature treatment of the second study.

Q. Explain where O_2 is used and CO_2 is produced in cellular respiration.
Solution: O2 accepts electrons at the end of the electron transport chain. CO2 is released during the oxidation of intermediate compounds in pyruvate oxidation and the citric acid cycle.

Q. What causes muscle soreness after intense exercise?
Solution: One common type of fermentation (lactic acid fermentation) takes place in muscle bands. Our muscle cells and certain bacteria can regenerate NAD+ by this process; it can be observed that NADH is oxidized back to NAD^+ as pyruvate is reduced to lactate. Muscle cells can switch to lactic acid fermentation when the need for ATP outpaces the delivery of O_2 via the bloodstream. The lactate that builds up in muscle cells was thought to cause the muscle soreness that occurs a day or so after intense exercise.

Q. A glucose-fed yeast solution is introduced to a vat designed for the production of a special solution. However, the technician fails to secure the lid correctly. What would be the outcome of the finished solution?
Solution: The alcohol would not find an anaerobic environment required for fermentation and would be alcohol-free. Also, without the presence of alcohol, the solution would accumulate a large volume of yeast.

Q. Mitochondria in brown fat cells are different from mitochondria in other cells and allow most of the energy to be released as heat. Which part of cellular respiration is different in these mitochondria?

a. glycolysis b. citric acid cycle

c. electron transport chain d. The coupling of ATP synthesis with the H+ gradient

Q. The poison cyanide binds to an electron carrier within the electron transport chain and blocks the movement of electrons. When this happens, glycolysis and the citric acid cycle soon grind to a halt as well. Why do you think these other two stages of cellular respiration stop? (Explain your answer.)

a. They run out of ATP. b. Unused O2 interferes with cellular respiration.

c. They run out of NAD+ and FAD. d. Electrons are no longer available.

Q. ATP synthase enzymes are found in the prokaryotic plasma membrane and in the inner membrane of a mitochondrion. What does this suggest about the evolutionary relationship of this eukaryotic organelle to prokaryotes?

Q. From which single molecule of the citric acid cycle is NADH, CO2, and ATP produced?

a. alpha-ketoglutarate b. citrate c. pyruvate d. succinate

Q. Which of the following molecules is an intermediate for the synthesis of proteins, carbohydrates, and fats during cellular respiration?

a. acetyl CoA b. glycerol c. glyceraldehydel-3-phosphate d. glucose

Oidative Phosphorylation:

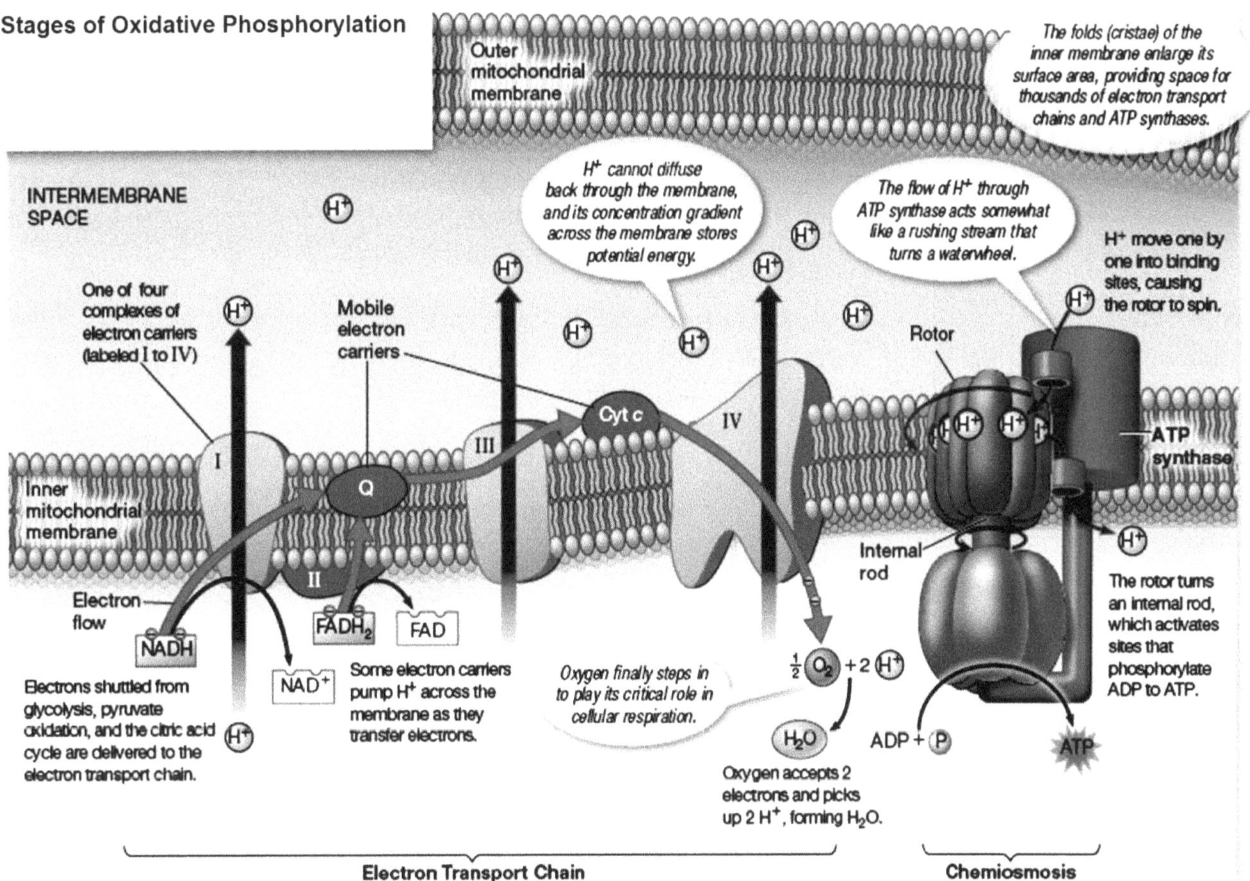

Nucleus and Chromosomes

Chromosomes are enormous DNA molecules that can be propagated stably through countless generations of dividing cells. Nucleus, especially in eukaryotes, accommodate all the chromosomes inside a double membrane bound compartmentalised structure to pprotect genetic materials from adverse impacts of hydrolytic enzymes. In addition to the genes, only three classes of specialized DNA sequences are needed to make a fully functional chromosome: (a) a centromere, (b) two telomeres, and (c) an origin of DNA replication for approximately every 100,000 base pairs (bp). Centromeres regulate the partitioning of chromosomes during mitosis and meiosis. Telomeres protect the ends of the chromosomal DNA molecules and ensure their complete replication.

Each mitotic chromosome consists of two sister chromatids (corresponding to the two copies of the replicated DNA) that are held together at a waist-like constriction called the centromere. The centromeric substructure that binds microtubules and directs the movements of chromosomes during mitosis is called kinetochore. The centromere is defined by specific DNA sequences plus proteins that bind to them, although epigenetic factors also play a key role. Structure of chromosome and allied functional specialities can be discussed in detail in another unit devoted to elaborate the cell cycle. The continuous DNA fiber of each chromosome is packaged into many hundreds of thousands of nucleosomes linked in series. The nucleosome core particle is disk-shaped, with DNA coiled in a left-handed superhelix around an octamer of core histones. This octamer consists of a central tetramer composed of two closely linked H3:H4 heterodimers, flanked on either side by two H2A:H2B heterodimers. nucleosomal chromatin resembles a string of 10 nm diameter beads with linker DNA extended between adjacent nucleosomes. Each nucleosome in chromosomes is typically associated with approximately 200 base pairs of DNA. Subtracting 166 base pairs for two turns around the histone octamer leaves 34 base pairs of linker DNA between adjacent nucleosomes.

Chromatin has traditionally been categorized into two main classes based on structural and functional criteria. Euchromatin contains almost all genes, both actively transcribed and quiescent. Heterochromatin is transcriptionally repressed and is generally more condensed than euchromatin.

The inactivated X

Chromosome forms a discrete patch of heterochromatin at the nuclear periphery known as the Barr body. Because most genes carried on the inactivated X chromosome become transcriptionally silent, females with two X chromosomes have the same levels of X chromosome-linked gene expression as males with a single X chromosome.

Loops are clearly seen in lampbrush chromosomes during meiotic prophase in oocytes of many species. These loops are sites of intense transcriptional activity as oocytes stockpile huge stores of the components needed for rapid cell divisions during early development of the fertilized egg. Similar loops are present in the giant polytene chromosomes found in some tissues of Drosophila larvae. Each polytene chromosome consists of more than 1000 identical DNA molecules packed side-by-side in precise linear register. Stress or stimulation of gene expression by hormones causes certain bands to lose their compact shape and puff out laterally. Each puff is composed of hundreds of identical, actively transcribed chromatin loop domains.

Members of the SMC protein family have several important roles in chromosome dynamics. The name derives from their roles in the structural maintenance of chromosomes. SMC proteins are components of multiprotein complexes, such as condensin and cohesin, that are essential for mitotic chromosome architecture, the regulation of sister chromatid pairing, DNA repair and replication, and the regulation of gene expression.

Condensin I regulates the timing of chromosome condensation and has an essential role in changing the genome organization from TADs to a brush-like array of loops as chromosomes form during entry of cells into mitosis. Condensin II apparently drives the compaction of the chromosome loops along the sister chromatid axes.

The kinetochore is a button-like structure embedded in the surface of the centromeric chromatin of most eukaryotic mitotic chromosomes. When thin sections of centromeres are examined by electron microscopy, the kinetochore often appears to have several layers. The inner kinetochore is embedded in the surface of the centromere and is composed of a specialized form of chromatin. The outer kinetochore consists of an outer plate with a fibrous corona on its outer surface. It is also observed that chromosomes tend to occupy discrete regions within the nucleus called chromosome territories. The boundaries of adjacent territories, where more actively transcribed regions are generally located, overlap with one another such that approximately 40% of each territory intermingles with adjacent territories. The chromatin of these overlapping regions tends to be less compact than in the rest of the territory, and is referred to as the interchromosomal domain. Most RNA transcription and processing are thought to occur within this domain.

Structures associated with RNA transcription and processing are found at up to 10,000 sites spread throughout the typical mammalian nucleus as well as in a few more prominent domains. The dispersed sites likely correspond to structures called perichromatin fibrils. The diffuse staining probably corresponds to splicing factors associated with perichromatin fibrils at dispersed sites. Most speckles correspond to clusters of interchromatin granules, particles 20 to 25 nm in diameter distributed throughout the interchromosomal domain.

Cajal bodies have a coiled fibrous substructure. First identified by electron microscopy, up to 10 of these structures are seen in transformed cells. They are usually absent from nontransformed normal cells. They contain the human autoantigen p80-coilin and survival of motor neurons (SMN) protein, which is encoded by the gene mutated in spinal muscular atrophy, a severe, inherited, human, muscular wasting disease. They are involved in small nuclear ribonucleoprotein (snRNP) and small nucleolar ribonucleoprotein (snoRNP) assembly and in maturation of telomerase (which also contains an RNA component).

Nucleolus, the site of rRNA transcription, is also the site of processing of several other noncoding RNAs, including the RNA component of the signal recognition particle. It plays an important role in helping organize the genome during interphase, as well as in regulating the stability of p53, a critical transcription factor that is involved in regulating the cell cycle, particularly when DNA damage occurs.

PML bodies are thought to enhance gene repression by serving as assembly sites for certain transcriptional co-represser complexes. They also appear to be targeted during viral infections. Fusion of the marker protein PML to the α-retinoic acid receptor is often found in acute promyelocytic leukemia (hence the name PML), in which the PML bodies appear highly fragmented.

Polycomb groups are defined as concentrations of the DNA repair-associated protein 53BP1. Also known as PIKA (polymorphic interphase karyosomal association) and OPT (Oct1/PTF/transcription) domain. These domains may be up to 5 μm in diameter during G1 phase, but their morphology and number vary across the cell cycle. They appear to correspond to sites of DNA damage during mitosis that arise as a result of incomplete DNA replication during S-phase.

Nuclei of rapidly growing transformed cells typically have one to 10 prominent Cajal bodies. These structures are absent from most nontransformed (normal) cells. Most mammalian cells have one to five nucleoli, which are specialized regions 0.5 to 5.0 µm in diameter surrounding transcriptionally active ribosomal RNA (rRNA) gene clusters. Nucleoli are the sites of most steps in ribosome biogenesis, from the transcription and processing of rRNA to the initial assembly of ribosomal subunits. Fibrillar centers of nucleolus contain concentrations of rRNA genes, together with RNA polymerase I and its associated transcription factors. Actively transcribed ribosomal genes are found near the border between the fibrillar centers and a dense fibrillar component that surrounds them. Several nucleolar proteins and RNA polymerase I remain bound at NORs (Neucleolar Organising Regions) as cells enter and exit mitosis but most nucleolar proteins coat the surface of the mitotic chromosomes forming a peri-chromosomal layer. a wide variety of nucleolar components assemble into particles termed prenucleolar bodies that associate with the NORs in a process requiring transcription of the rRNA genes.

Nuclear pore complexes and the associated pore membrane bridge both nuclear membranes and provide the primary route for communication between the nucleus and cytoplasm during interphase. Chromatin interactions with nuclear pores can have both positive and negative effects on gene expression. In mammalian cells, the chromatin near pores appears less condensed (less heterochromatic) than most chromatin adjacent to the lamina. Several hundred integral membrane proteins are associated with the inner nuclear membrane, often in in a tissue specific manner. Of these, the lamin B receptor, LAP2 (lamina-associated protein 2), emerin, MAN1, SUN1, and SUN2 have been characterized in detail. Some inner nuclear membrane proteins bind lamins to help anchor the lamina polymer to the membrane and many can interact with chromatin. Nuclear pore complexes have a scaffold consisting of three stacked rings each with eightfold symmetry. Cytoplasmic and nuclear rings flank a prominent spoke ring that is intimately associated with the pore membrane linking the inner and outer nuclear membranes. The nuclear ring is anchored to the nuclear lamina. A less-prominent fourth luminal ring surrounds the pore membrane in the NE lumen. Approximately 30 core proteins, called nucleoporins, are present in multiples of eight copies.

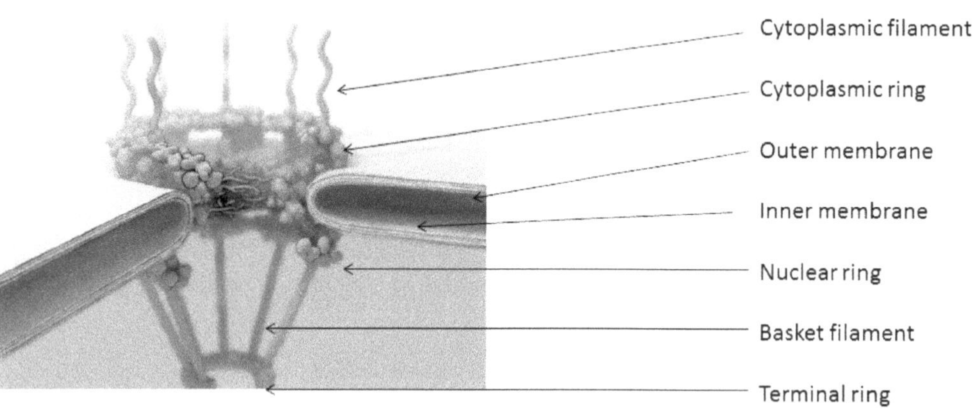

Fig: Diagram of a Nuclear Pore Complex.

Integral proteins of the inner nuclear membrane enter the nucleus by diffusion in the plane of the membrane. Proteins that are imported into the nucleus bear a nuclear localization sequence (NLS), also called a nuclear localization signal, that is recognized by specific carrier proteins called transport receptors. Nuclear components are transported into the nucleus while components that function in the cytoplasm are transported out. This means that each carrier picks up its cargo on one side of the nuclear envelope and deposits it on the other. mRNA is exported as very large mRNP complexes that begin to assemble during RNA processing with binding of the transcription export (TREX) complex to the mRNA. These mRNP complexes dock on the inner surface of the pore, where they are subjected to quality control by the exosome and other surveillance activities. Incorrectly processed mRNAs are degraded. Correctly processed mRNAs are guided through the nuclear pore by a dimeric transport receptor. Nuclear trafficking is often regulated by phosphorylation near the NLS[4] on the cargo. Phosphorylation adjacent to a basic NLS inhibits nuclear import. This provides a mechanism to regulate the ability of a particular cargo to enter the nucleus in response to cell cycle. Many proteins exported from the nucleus bear a nuclear export sequence (NES) that is recognized by transport receptors related to those used for nuclear import.

Regulation of Genes

Proteins called transcription factors (TFs) turn genes on or off by binding to DNA regulatory sequences associated with sequences encoding the protein or RNA product of the gene. The paradigm of this level of regulation is the bacterial repressor that controls expression of genes required for lactose metabolism in Escherichia coli. In eukaryotes, such factors are numerous (about six percent of human genome). They are also quite diverse, binding to a wide range of DNA regulatory sites.

Synthesis of RNA by RNA polymerases is a cyclic process that can be broken down into three sets of events: initiation, elongation, and termination. RNA polymerase binds to the chromosome near the beginning of the gene, forming a preinitiation complex at a sequence termed a promoter.

Concluding Remarks

Before a cell divides, it must accurately replicate the vast quantity of genetic information embedded chemically in its DNA. Because the two strands of a DNA double helix are complementary, each strand can act as a template for the synthesis of the other. DNA replication, in that specific context, produces two identical, double-helical DNA molecules, enabling genetic information to be copied and passed on from a cell to its daughter cells and from a parent to its offspring without letting any of the segment off the track or off the template; some recombinations and realignment of their sequences can be a case.

• During replication, the two strands of a DNA double helix are pulled apart at a replication origin to form two Y-shaped replication forks. DNA polymerases at each fork produce a new complementary DNA strand on each parental strand. In that way DNA polymerase replicates a DNA template with remarkable fidelity, making only about one error in every 107 nucleotides copied; accuracy of such level is made possible by a proofreading process in which the enzyme corrects its own mistakes as it moves along the DNA segment housed in that position of chromatin.

• Only the leading strand at the replication fork can be synthesized in a continuous fashion. On the lagging strand as DNA polymerase synthesizes new DNA in only one direction. DNA is synthesized in a discontinuous backstitching process, producing short fragments of DNA that are later joined together by DNA ligase. DNA polymerase is incapable of starting a new DNA chain from scratch. DNA synthesis is primed by an RNA

[4] *Proteins that are imported into the nucleus bear a nuclear localization sequence (NLS), also called a nuclear localization signal, that is recognized by specific carrier proteins called transport receptors.*

polymerase called primase, which makes short lengths of RNA primers that are then elongated by DNA polymerase. These primers are subsequently erased and replaced with DNA in due course of progression of the activity.

• DNA replication requires the cooperation of many proteins that form a multienzyme replication instrument that copies both DNA strands as it moves along the double helix.

• In eukaryotes, telomerase (a special enzyme) replicates the DNA at the ends of the chromosomes.

• The rare copying mistakes that escape proofreading are dealt with by mismatch repair proteins, which increase the accuracy of DNA replication to one mistake per 109 nucleotides copied.

• Damage to one of the two DNA strands, caused by unavoidable chemical reactions, is repaired by a variety of DNA repair enzymes that recognize damaged DNA and excise a short stretch of the damaged strand. The missing DNA is then resynthesized by a repair DNA polymerase, using the undamaged strand as a template.

• If both DNA strands are broken, the double-strand break can be rapidly repaired by nonhomologous end joining. Nucleotides are lost in the process, altering the DNA sequence at the repair site.

• Homologous recombination can flawlessly repair double-strand breaks using an undamaged homologous double helix as a template. Highly accurate DNA replication and DNA repair processes play a key role in protecting organisms from the uncontrolled growth of somatic cells; which in due course of time can cause cancer.

Struture of DNA

Structure of DNA

Character of a Genetic Material: For a molecule to serve as the genetic material, it must exhibit four crucial characteristics: replication, storage of information, expression of information, and variation by mutation. Replication of the genetic material is one facet of the cell cycle and as such is a fundamental property of all living organisms. Once the genetic material of cells replicates and is doubled in amount, it must then be partitioned equally—through mitosis—into daughter cells. The genetic material is also replicated during the formation of gametes, but is partitioned so that each cell gets only one-half of the original amount of genetic material—the process of meiosis. Although the products of mitosis and meiosis are different, these processes are both part of the more general phenomenon of cellular reproduction.

Expression of Stored Genetic Information: The initial event in this flow of information is the transcription of DNA, in which three main types of RNA molecules are synthesized: messenger RNA (mRNA), transfer RNA (tRNA), and ribosomal RNA (rRNA). Of these, mRNAs are translated into proteins, by means of a process mediated by the tRNA and rRNA. Each mRNA is the product of a specific gene and leads to the synthesis of a different protein. The chemical information in mRNA directs the construction of a chain of amino acids, called a polypeptide, which then folds into a protein (the Central Dogma of molecular genetics. Some viruses contain an RNA core rather than a DNA core. In these viruses, it appears that RNA serves as the genetic material—an exception to the general rule that DNA performs this function. In 1956, it was demonstrated that when purified RNA from tobacco mosaic virus (TMV) was spread on tobacco leaves, the characteristic lesions caused by viral infection subsequently appeared. Thus, it was concluded that RNA is the genetic material of this virus.

Nucleotides: DNA is a nucleic acid, and nucleotides are the building blocks of all nucleic acid molecules. Sometimes called mononucleotides, these structural units consist of three essential components: a nitrogenous base, a pentose sugar (a 5-carbon sugar), and a phosphate group. There are two kinds of nitrogenous bases: the nine-member double-ring purines and the six-member single-ring pyrimidines. Two types of purines and three types of pyrimidines are commonly found in nucleic acids. The two purines are adenine and guanine, abbreviated A and G. Three pyrimidines are cytosine, thymine, and uracil, abbreviated C, T, and U, respectively. The chemical structures of A, G, C, T, and U are shown in Figure 10–7(a). Both DNA and RNA contain A, C, and G, but only DNA contains the base T and only RNA contains the base U. Each nitrogen or carbon atom of the ring structures of purines and pyrimidines is designated by an unprimed number. Note that corresponding atoms in the two rings are numbered differently in most cases. The pentose sugars found in nucleic acids give them their names. Ribonucleic acids (RNA) contain ribose, while deoxyribonucleic acids (DNA) contain deoxyribose. If a molecule is composed of a purine or pyrimidine base and a ribose or deoxyribose sugar, the chemical unit is called a nucleoside. If a phosphate group is added to the nucleoside, the molecule is now called a nucleotide. Nucleosides and nucleotides are named according to the specific nitrogenous base (A, T, G, C, or U) that is part of the molecule. If the base is a purine, the N-9 atom is covalently bonded to the sugar; if the base is a pyrimidine, the N-1 atom bonds to the sugar. In deoxyribonucleotides, the phosphate group may be bonded to the C-2', C-3', or C-5' atom of the sugar.

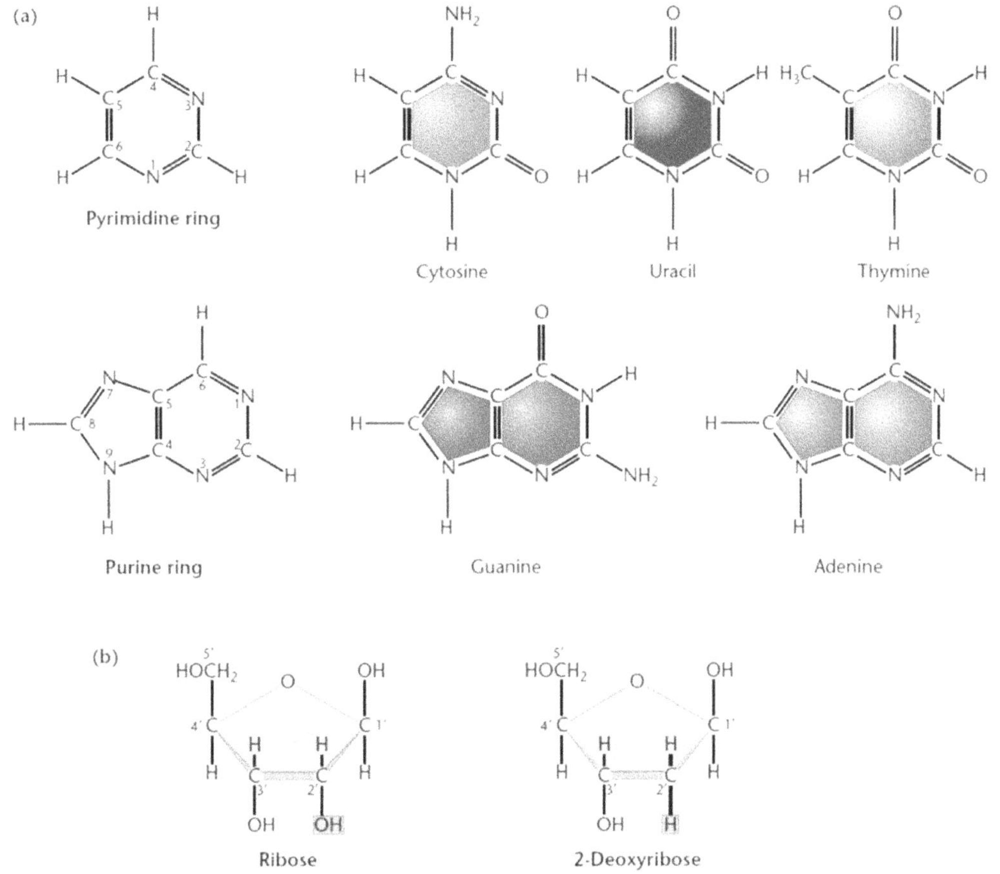

(a)

Pyrimidine ring

Cytosine

Uracil

Thymine

Purine ring

Guanine

Adenine

(b)

Ribose

2-Deoxyribose

The triphosphate form is significant because it serves as the precursor molecule during nucleic acid synthesis within the cell. In addition, adenosine triphosphate (ATP) and guanosine triphosphate (GTP) are important in cell bioenergetics because of the large amount of energy involved in adding or removing the terminal phosphate group. Each structure has a C-5' end and a C-3' end. Two joined nucleotides form a dinucleotide; three nucleotides, a trinucleotide; and so forth. Short chains consisting of up to approximately 30 nucleotides linked together are called oligonucleotides; longer chains are called polynucleotides. Long polynucleotide chains account for the large molecular weight of DNA and explain its most important property—storage of vast quantities of genetic information.

In 1953, James Watson and Francis Crick proposed that the structure of DNA is in the form of a double helix. Their model was described in a short paper published in the journal Nature. In a sense, this publication was the finish of a highly competitive scientific race. Watson's book The Double Helix recounts the human side of the scientific drama that eventually led to the elucidation of DNA structure.

Findings of Chargaff:

1. The amount of adenine residues is proportional to the amount of thymine residues in DNA.
2. The sum of the purines (A + G) equals the sum of the pyrimidines (C + T).
3. The percentage of (G + C) does not necessarily equal the percentage of (A + T).

Main features of the Double Helix model of DNA proposed by Watson and Crick.

1. Two long polynucleotide chains are coiled around a central axis, forming a right-handed double helix.
2. The two chains are **antiparallel**; that is, their C-5′-to- C-3′ orientations run in opposite directions.
3. The bases of both chains are flat structures lying perpendicular to the axis; they are "stacked" on one another, 3.4 Å (0.34 nm) apart, on the inside of the double helix.
4. The nitrogenous bases of opposite chains are *paired* as the result of the formation of hydrogen bonds; in DNA, only A " T and G ,C pairs occur.
5. Each complete turn of the helix is 34 Å (3.4 nm) long; thus, each turn of the helix is the length of a series of 10 base pairs.
6. A larger **major groove** alternating with a smaller **minor groove** winds along the length of the molecule.
7. The double helix has a diameter of 20 Å (2.0 nm).

Arrangement of the components in double helix DNA molecule produces the major and minor grooves along the molecule's length. Furthermore, a purine (A or G) opposite a pyrimidine (T or C) on each "rung of the spiral staircase" in the proposed helix accounts for the 20-Å (2-nm) diameter suggested by X-ray diffraction studies. The specific A " T and G , C base pairing is described as complementarity and results from the chemical affinity that produces the hydrogen bonds in each pair of bases.

Svedberg Coefficient: Different RNAs are distinguished according to their sedimentation behavior in a centrifugal field and by their size (the number of nucleotides each contains). Sedimentation behavior depends on a molecule's density, mass, and shape, and its measure is called the Svedberg coefficient (S). While higher S values almost always designate molecules of greater molecular weight, the correlation is not direct; that is, a twofold increase in molecular weight does not lead to a twofold increase in S.

rRNA, mRNA and tRNA

Ribosomal RNA usually constitutes about 80 percent of all RNA in an E. coli cell. Ribosomal RNAs are important structural components of ribosomes, which function as nonspecific workbenches where proteins are synthesized during translation. The various forms of rRNA found in prokaryotes and eukaryotes differ distinctly in size.

Messenger RNA molecules carry genetic information from the DNA of the gene to the ribosome. The mRNA molecules vary considerably in size, reflecting the range in the sizes of the proteins encoded by the mRNA as well as the different sizes of the genes serving as the templates for transcription of mRNA. While Table 10.4 shows that about 5 percent of RNA is mRNA in E. coli, this percentage varies from cell to cell and even at different times in the life of the same cell.

Transfer RNA, accounting for up to 15 percent of the RNA in a typical cell, is the smallest class (in terms of average molecule size) of these RNA molecules and carries amino acids to the ribosome during translation. Because more than one tRNA molecule interacts simultaneously with the ribosome, the molecule's smaller size facilitates these interactions.

Q . DNA having more percentage of G C pairs requires higher temperatures to denature completely.

Because G , C base pairs have one more hydrogen bond than do A T pairs, they are more stable under heat treatment. Thus, DNA with a greater proportion of G C pairs than A T pairs requires higher temperatures to denature completely. When absorption at 260 nm is monitored and plotted against temperature during heating, a melting profile of the DNA is obtained.

Q. Which of the following statement is not correct?

A. Although both proteins and nucleic acids were initially considered as possible candidates for genetic material, proteins were initially favored.

B. By 1952, transformation studies and experiments using bacteria infected with bacteriophages strongly suggested that DNA is the genetic material in bacteria and most viruses.

C. Although initially only indirect observations supported the hypothesis that DNA controls inheritance in eukaryotes, subsequent studies involving recombinant DNA techniques and transgenic mice provided direct experimental evidence that the eukaryotic genetic material is DNA.

D. Only DNA serves as the genetic material in some bacteriophages as well as some plant and animal viruses.

E. As proposed by Watson and Crick, DNA exists in the form of a right-handed double helix composed of two long antiparallel polynucleotide chains held together by hydrogen bonds formed between complementary, nitrogenous base pairs.

F. The second category of nucleic acids important in genetic function is RNA, which is similar to DNA with the exceptions that it is usually single stranded, the sugar ribose replaces the deoxyribose, and the pyrimidine uracil replaces thymine.

Ans: Option D;

Q. (a) Based strictly on your scrutiny of the transformation data of Avery, MacLeod, and McCarty, what objection might be made to the conclusion that DNA is the genetic material? What other conclusion might be considered?

(b) What observations, including later ones, argue against this objection?

Solution: (a) Based solely on their results, it may be concluded that DNA is essential for transformation. However, DNA might have been a substance that caused capsular formation by directly converting nonencapsulated cells to cells with a capsule. That is, DNA may simply have played a catalytic role in capsular synthesis, leading to cells displaying smooth type III colonies.

(b) First, transformed cells pass the trait onto their progeny cells, thus supporting the conclusion that DNA is responsible for heredity, not for the direct production of polysaccharide coats. Second, subsequent transformation studies over a period of five years showed that other traits, such as antibiotic resistance, could be transformed. Therefore, the transforming factor has a broad general effect, not one specific to polysaccharide synthesis. This observation is more in keeping with the conclusion that DNA is the genetic material.

Q. If RNA were the universal genetic material, how would it have affected the Avery experiment and the Hershey–Chase experiment?

Solution: In the Avery experiment, digestion of the soluble filtrate with RNase, rather than DNase, would have eliminated transformation. Had this occurred, Avery and his colleagues would have concluded that RNA was the transforming factor. Hershey and Chase would have obtained identical results, since 32P would also label RNA but not protein. Had they been using a bacteriophage with RNA as its nucleic acid, and had they known this, they would have concluded that RNA was responsible for directing the reproduction of their bacteriophage.

3. A quest to isolate an important disease-causing organism was successful, and molecular biologists were hard at work analyzing the results. The organism contained as its genetic material a remarkable nucleic acid with a base composition of A = 21 percent, C = 29 percent, G = 29 percent, U = 21 percent. When heated, it showed a major hyperchromic shift, and when the reassociation kinetics were studied, the nucleic acid of this organism reannealed more slowly than that of phage T4 and E. coli. T4 contains 10^5 nucleotide pairs. Analyze this information carefully, and draw all possible conclusions about the genetic material of this organism, based strictly on the preceding observations. As a test of your model, make one prediction that if upheld would strengthen your hypothesis about the nature of this molecule.

Solution: First of all, because of the presence of uracil (U), the molecule appears to be RNA. In contrast to normal RNA, this one has base ratios of A/U = G/C = 1 , suggesting that the molecule may be a double helix. The hyperchromic shift and reassociation kinetics support this hypothesis. In the kinetic study, since none of the nucleic acid segments reannealed more rapidly than bacterial or viral nucleic acid, there is no repetitive sequence RNA. Furthermore, the total length of uniquesequence DNA is greater than that of either phage T4 (10^5 nucleotide pairs) or E. coli. A prediction might be made concerning the sugars. Our model suggests that ribose rather than deoxyribose should be present. If so, this observation would support the hypothesis that RNA is the genetic material in this organism.

Q. What observations are consistent with the conclusion that DNA serves as the genetic material in eukaryotes? List and discuss them.

Ans: The early evidence would be considered indirect in that at no time was there an experiment, like transformation in bacteria, in which genetic information in one organism was transferred to another using DNA. Rather, by comparing DNA content in various cell types (sperm and somatic cells) and observing that the action and absorption spectra of ultraviolet light were correlated, DNA was considered to be the genetic material. This suggestion was supported by the fact that DNA was shown to be the genetic material in bacteria and some phages. Direct evidence for DNA being the genetic material comes from a variety of observations including gene transfer, which has been facilitated by recombinant DNA techniques.

Q. What might Watson and Crick have concluded had Chargaff's data from a single source indicated the following?

	A	T	G	C
%	29	19	21	31

Why would this conclusion be contradictory to Wilkins's and Franklin's data?

Ans: Because in double-stranded DNA, A=T and G=C (within limits of experimental error), the data presented would have indicated a lack of pairing of these bases in favor of a single-stranded structure or some other non-hydrogen-bonded structure. Alternatively, from the data it would appear that A=C and T=G, which would negate the chance for typical hydrogen bonding since opposite charge relationships do not exist. Therefore, it is quite unlikely that a tight helical structure would form at all. In conclusion, Watson and Crick might have concluded that hydrogen bonding is not a significant factor in maintaining a double-stranded structure.

Q. Main difference between DNA and RNA.

Three main differences between RNA and DNA are the following:

(1) uracil in RNA replaces thymine in DNA,

(2) ribose in RNA replaces deoxyribose in DNA, and

(3) RNA often occurs as both single- and partially doublestranded forms, whereas DNA most often occurs in a double-stranded form.

Q. What component of the nucleotide is responsible for the absorption of ultraviolet light? How is this technique important in the analysis of nucleic acids?

Review of Studies

Q. Why is binary fission classified as asexual reproduction?

Solution: Because the genetically identical offspring inherit their DNA from a single parent.

Q. Why do fully-grown human cells continue to divide?

Solution: To continually renew and repair tissues and to produce gametes for reproduction.

Q. When does a chromosome consist of two identical chromatids?

Solution: When the cell is preparing to divide and has duplicated its chromosomes but before the duplicates actually separate

Q. Identify different stages of cell division as displayed in the following diagram.

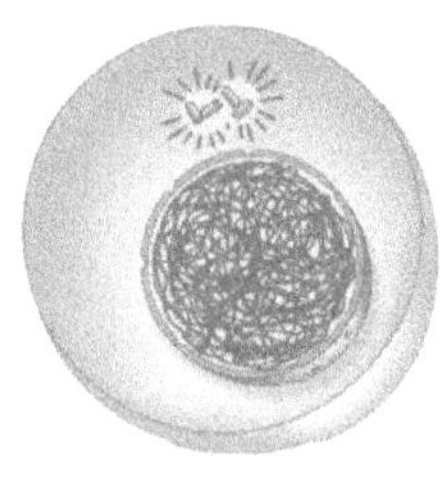
I

II

III

IV

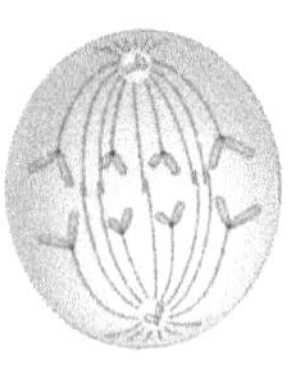
V

VI

Solution: All the stages indicate different phases of Mitosis.

Q. A researcher treats cells with a chemical that prevents DNA synthesis from starting. This treatment would trap the cells in which part of the cell cycle?

Solution: G1.

Q. How would the cells undergoing mitosis be different during metaphase and prophase?

Solution: Chromosomes would be condensed in both phases but only aligned during metaphase.

Q. Contrast cytokinesis in animals with cytokinesis in plants.

Solution: In animals, cytokinesis involves a cleavage furrow in which contracting microfilaments pinch the cell in two. In plants, it involves formation of a cell plate, a fusion of vesicles that forms new plasma membranes and new cell walls between the cells.

Q. Compared with a control culture, the cells in an experimental culture are fewer but much larger in size when they cover the dish surface and stop growing. What is a reasonable hypothesis for this difference?

Solution: The experimental culture is deficient in one or more growth factors.

Q. What is Cell Cycle Control System?

Solution: The cell cycle control system is a set of molecules that both triggers and coordinates key events in the cell cycle. The cell cycle is not like a row of falling dominoes, with each event causing the next one in line. During mitosis, for example, metaphase does not automatically lead to anaphase. Certain specialised proteins of the cell cycle control system must trigger anaphase to begin.

Q. At which stage of Cell Cycle do the chromosomes exist as duplicated sister chromatids?

Solution: G2 and M checkpoints of Cell Cycle.

Q. What is Malignant Tumor?

Solution: A malignant tumor is a mass of abnormally reproducing cells that can spread into neighboring tissues and invade other parts of the body, with the potential to displace normal tissue and interrupt organ function as it grows.

Q. What is metastasis?

Solution: A few tumor cells may enter the blood and lymph vessels and thereby move to other parts of the body, where they may proliferate and form new tumors. The spread of cancer cells beyond their original site is called metastasis.

Q. Why do cancer cells divide more rapidly than normal cells?

Solution: They do not respond to the normal signals that regulate the cell cycle.

Q. Do pairs of homologous chromosomes carry the same genes?

Solution: Yes, they have the same genes but may have different versions of those genes.

Q. How many autosomes are found in a human sperm cell? How many and which sex chromosomes?

Solution: 22 autosomes plus either an X or Y sex chromosome.

Q. Identify different stages of cell division as displayed in the following diagram.

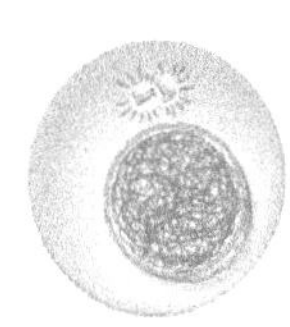

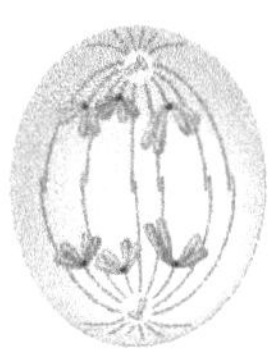
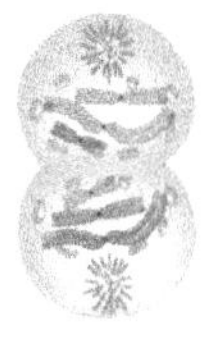

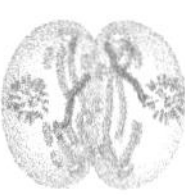

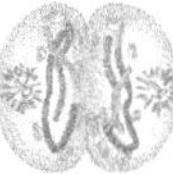

Solution: All the stages of cell division represent Meiosis (A reductional Cell Division).

Q. The Australian kangaroo has a diploid number of 16. How many chromosomal combinations are possible for gametes formed by meiosis?

Solution: 256; 2n = 16, so n = 8. ^{2n} = 256; therefore, 256 chromosomal combinations are possible for gametes formed by meiosis.

Q. If you were to examine a chromosome from one of your gametes, is it likely to look exactly like that same chromosome from one of your skin cells?

Solution: No, each chromosome probably looks like a cut-and-paste hybrid of segments derived from a pair of homologous chromosomes.

Q. A gene encoding one of the proteins involved in DNA replication has been inactivated by a mutation in a cell. In the absence of this protein, the cell attempts to replicate its DNA. What would happen during the DNA replication process if each of the following proteins were missing?

A. DNA polymerase	B. DNA ligase
C. Sliding clamp for DNA polymerase	D. N uclease that removes RNA primers
E. DNA helicase	F. P rimase

Answer: A. Without DNA polymerase, no replication can take place at all. RNA primers will be laid down at the origin of replication.

B. DNA ligase links the DNA fragments that are produced on the lagging strand. In the absence of ligase, the newly replicated DNA strands will remain as fragments, but no nucleotides will be missing.

C. Without the sliding clamp, the DNA polymerase will frequently fall off the DNA template. In principle, it can rebind and continue, but the continual falling off and rebinding will be time-consuming and will greatly slow down DNA replication.

D. In the absence of RNA-excision enzymes, the RNA fragments will remain covalently attached to the newly replicated DNA fragments. No ligation will take place, because the DNA ligase will not link DNA to RNA. The lagging strand will therefore consist of fragments composed of both RNA and DNA.

E. Without DNA helicase, the DNA polymerase will stall because it cannot separate the strands of the template DNA ahead of it. Little or no new DNA will be synthesized.

F. In the absence of primase, RNA primers cannot begin on either the leading or the lagging strand. DNA replication therefore cannot begin.

Q. Discuss the following statement: "The DNA repair enzymes that fix deamination and depurination damage must preferentially recognize such damage on newly synthesized DNA strands."

Answer: DNA damage by deamination and depurination reactions occurs spontaneously. This type of damage is not the result of replication errors and is therefore equally likely to occur on either strand. If DNA repair enzymes recognized such damage only on newly synthesized DNA strands, half of the defects would go uncorrected. The statement is therefore incorrect.

Q. Explain how nondisjunction could result in a diploid gamete.

Solution: Chrosomes, as evident from different stages of normal cases of cell division, get equally distributed to newly developed cells during cell division. There is an occasional mishap, called a non-disjunction, in which the members of a chromosome pair fail to separate. After a nondisjunction, one gamete receives two of the same type of chromosome and another gamete receives no copy of that chromosome. A diploid gamete would result if the nondisjunction affected all the chromosomes during one of the meiotic divisions.

Q. Which of the following statements are correct? Explain your answers.

A. A bacterial replication fork is asymmetrical because it contains two DNA polymerase molecules that are structurally distinct.

B. O kazaki fragments are removed by a nuclease that degrades RNA.

C. The error rate of DNA replication is reduced both by proofreading by DNA polymerase and by DNA mismatch repair.

D. In the absence of DNA repair, genes are unstable.

E. N one of the aberrant bases formed by deamination occur naturally in DNA.

F. C ancer can result from the accumulation of mutations in somatic cells.

Q. Discuss the following statement: "Primase is a sloppy enzyme that makes many mistakes. Eventually, the RNA primers it makes are disposed of and replaced with DNA synthesized by a polymerase with higher fidelity. This is wasteful. It would be more energy-efficient if a DNA polymerase made an accurate copy in the first place."

Answer : Although the process may seem wasteful, it is not possible to proofread during the initial stages of primer synthesis. To start a new primer on a piece of single stranded DNA, one nucleotide needs to be put in place and then linked to a second and then to a third, and so on. Even if these first nucleotides were perfectly matched to the template strand, they would bind with very low affinity, and it would consequently be difficult to distinguish the correct from incorrect bases by a hypothetical primase with proofreading activity; the enzyme would therefore stall. The task of the primase is to "just polymerize nucleotides that bind reasonably well to the template without worrying too much about accuracy." Later, these sequences are removed and replaced by DNA polymerase, which uses newly synthesized (and therefore proofread) DNA as its primer.

Q. Which of the following statements are correct? Explain your answers.
A. A bacterial replication fork is asymmetrical because it contains two DNA polymerase molecules that are structurally distinct.

B. O kazaki fragments are removed by a nuclease that degrades RNA.

C. T he error rate of DNA replication is reduced both by proofreading by DNA polymerase and by DNA mismatch repair.

D. In the absence of DNA repair, genes are unstable.

E. N one of the aberrant bases formed by deamination occur naturally in DNA.

F. C ancer can result from the accumulation of mutations in somatic cells.

Answer:
A. False. Identical DNA polymerase molecules catalyze DNA synthesis on the leading and lagging strands of a bacterial replication fork. The replication fork is asymmetrical because the lagging strand is synthesized in pieces that are then stitched together.

B. False. Only the RNA primers are removed by an RNA nuclease; Okazaki fragments are pieces of newly synthesized DNA on the lagging strand that are eventually joined together by DNA ligase.

C. True. With proofreading, DNA polymerase has an error rate of one mistake in 107 nucleotides polymerized; 99% of its errors are corrected by DNA mismatch repair enzymes, bringing the final error rate to one in 109.

D. True. Mutations would accumulate rapidly, inactivating many genes.

E. True. If a damaged nucleotide also occurred naturally in DNA, the repair enzyme would have no way of identifying the damage. It would therefore have only a 50% chance of fixing the right strand.

F. True. Usually, multiple mutations of specific types need to accumulate in a somatic cell lineage to produce a cancer. A mutation in a gene that codes for a DNA repair enzyme can make a cell more liable to accumulate further mutations, thereby accelerating the onset of cancer.

Special Study Cell Wall

Structure of Plant Cell wall

It is derived from the living protoplast.

It consists of the middle lamella, primary cell wall, plasmodesmata, secondary cell wall, and pits.

Middle lamella

After the cytokinesis, it is the first-formed layer.

It is present in between the two adjacent cells.

It is made up of calcium and magnesium pectate.

It helps to join the two adjacent cells.

Primary cell wall

It is the first formed cell wall.

It is present in the inner side of the middle lamella.

It is the thin and permeable layer that can be expanded.

Cutin and cutin waxes are present in some epidermal cells of the leaf and stem. It makes the primary cell wall impermeable.

It is formed before the growth and development of the cell.

It is made up of matrix and microfibrils.

Matrix is made up of water, hemicelluloses, pectin, lipids, and proteins.

Microfibrils are embedded in the gel-like matrix.

The primary cell wall of the plant is made of cellulose.

In the fungi, chitin makes the primary cell wall, and in bacteria murein makes it.

Primary cell wall forms the only cell wall in the immature meristematic and parenchymatous cells.

Plasmodesma (plural: plasmodesmata)

Plasmodesmata are cytoplasmic or protoplasmic bridges present in the primary cell wall of adjacent cells.

They form a protoplasmic continuum called symplast.

They transfer cytoplasmic materials among adjacent cells.

Secondary cell wall

The secondary cell wall is situated inner to the primary cell wall.

This is the thick layer, permeable, and cannot be expanded.

It forms after the growth and development of the cell.

It is present in the cells of the thick-walled dead tissue of the plant. Eg: Cells of sclerenchyma, tracheids, and vessels.

It is differentiated into the outer layer (S1), middle layer (S2), and inner layer (S3).

Each layer is made up of a matrix and microfibrils.

The chemical composition of the matrix is almost similar to the matrix of the primary cell.
Microfibrils of the secondary cell wall is made up of cellulose and lignin.
Some chemicals like suberin, silica, wax, resins, oils, etc. are also deposited in the secondary cell wall.
Pits
In the secondary cell wall, pits are the unthickened areas or depressed areas.
A pit consists of a pit cavity or pit chamber and pit membrane.
The pit membrane consists of the primary cell wall and middle lamella.
The pit membrane is permeable.
So pit helps in rapid translocation of materials between two adjacent cells.

Tertiary cell wall: In some plant cells, there is the presence of another cell wall beneath the secondary cell wall. It is known as the tertiary cell wall.
The morphology, chemistry, and staining properties of the tertiary cell wall are different from the primary and secondary cell walls.
In the tertiary cell wall, xylan is also present in it.

Cell Wall of Gram Negative Bacteria
The Cell wall of the Gram-Negative Bacteria is very complex as compared to that of Gram-Positive Bacteria. Combined with the major role of the outer membrane of the cell, with a layer of peptidoglycan, its functional properties are complex, and here is a description of the cell wall and its functional parts.

The cell wall of gram-negative bacteria is complex having a thin layer of the peptidoglycan layer of 2-7nm and a thick outer membrane of 7-8nm thick.
Microscopically, there is a space that is seen between the cell membrane and the cell wall, known as the periplasmic space made up of periplasm. However it is found in both Gram-negative and Gram-positive bacteria, but in gram-negative the periplasmic space is larger.

Cell Wall of Gram Negative Bacteria
It is also known as murein, making up 90% of the bacterial cell wall content.
Its major role is to provide shape and maintain cell wall strength and rigidity.
It is a high-quality polymer made up of two identical sugar derivates, named N-acetylglucosamine and N-acetylmuramic acid and a chain of L- amino acids and three distinct D- amino acids that are rarely found in proteins i.e D-glutamic acid, D-alanine, and meso-diaminopimelic, which protect the cell wall from attack by peptidase enzymes.
The D-amino acids and the L-amino acids connect to the N-acetylmuramic acid, L-amino acid specifically the L-lysine can replace the meso-diaminopimelic acid.
This interconnection od peptidoglycan subunit makes the peptidoglycan Strong to maintain the bacterial shape and integrity, with the ability to be elastic and stretch.
The peptidoglycan is also permeable allowing molecules to move in and out of the bacterial cell.

Teichoic Acid: This is a fortified wall made up copolymers of glycerol.
It is water-soluble making up to 50% of the total dry weight of the bacterial cell wall.
It is either directly connected to the peptidoglycan, covalently or to the cell membrane (lipoteichoic acid). The direct link to the peptidoglycan in by the 6-hydroxyl N-acetylmuramic acid.
It is negatively charged and they extend to the peptidoglycan surface, giving the bacterial cell wall a negative charge.
It also contributes to maintaining the structure of the cell wall.
It is completely absent in gram-negative bacteria.

Lipid : They have a thin layer of lipids below the peptidoglycan, of about 2-5%, which functions to anchor the bacterial cell wall

Functions of plant cell wall

It provides mechanical support as the skeletal framework in the plant.
It protects the inner components of the cell from mechanical injuries.
It is permeable to the water and solutes. It is the presence of the water-filled channels which allows the free diffusion of water and water-soluble substances. Eg: gas, salt, sugar, hormones.[5]
It prevents entry of the pathogenic agents inside the cell acting as the first line of defense.
When the cell is kept in the hypotonic solution, it prevents the osmotic bursting of the cell.
In the cell wall, cutin, wax, silica, and suberin is present which reduces the rate of transpiration.
The cell wall of root hairs helps in the absorption of sap from the soil.
Walls of tracheids and vessels help in the conduction of sap.
Middle lamella helps to join the adjacent cells.
Plasmodesmata help in the transfer of cytoplasmic materials among adjacent cells.

Cell wall in the defense mechanism

During the infection, oligosaccharides elicitors can be released.
These substances can be released from the host plant's cell wall i.e DAMPs (Damage-associated Molecular patterns) or they can be from the pathogen cell wall i.e PAMPs (Pathogen-associated Molecular patterns).
It occurs during the process of degradation.
In the plasma membrane, immune receptors are present which receive these elicitors.
It then activates the defense responses of DAMP or PAMP-triggered immunity.

[5] *Presence of Water filled channels ensure permeability; primary cell wall and pit membrane exhibit permeability in a better way than compared to secondary and tertiary layers.*

Review of Studies A

1. Glycolysis produces ATP by

a. phosphorylating organic molecules in the priming reactions.

b. the production of glyceraldehyde 3-phosphate.

c. substrate-level phosphorylation.

d. the reduction of NAD^+ to NADH.

2. What is the role of NAD^+ in the process of cellular respiration?

a. It functions as an electron carrier.

b. It functions as an enzyme.

c. It is the final electron acceptor for anaerobic respiration.

d. It is a nucleotide source for the synthesis of ATP.

3. What is the importance of fermentation to cellular metabolism?

a. It generates glucose for the cell in the absence of O_2.

b. It oxidizes NADH to NAD^+ during electron transport.

c. It oxidizes NADH to NAD^+ in the absence of O_2.

d. It reduces NADH to NAD^+ in the absence of O_2.

4. The link between electron transport and ATP synthesis

a. is a high-energy intermediate like phosphoenol pyruvate.

b. is the transfer of electrons to ATP synthase.

c. is a proton gradient. d. depends on the absence of oxygen.

5. A chemical agent that makes holes in the inner membrane of the mitochondria would

a. stop the movement of electrons down the electron transport chain.

b. stop ATP synthesis. c. stop the citric acid cycle. d. All of the choices are correct.

6. Yeast cells that have mutations in genes that encode enzymes in glycolysis can still grow on glycerol. They are able to utilize glycerol because it

a. enters glycolysis after the step affected by the mutation.

b. can feed into the citric acid cycle and generate ATP via electron transport and chemiosmosis.

c. can be utilized by fermentation.

d. can donate electrons directly to the electron transport chain.

7. When a hibernating animal uses its stored fat to power basic body functions (e.g., breathing), it is
a. converting kinetic energy to potential energy.
b. converting kinetic energy to chemical energy.
c. converting potential energy to kinetic energy.
d. converting chemical energy to potential energy.

8. During certain stages of cellular respiration, electrons are transferred from glucose molecules to a molecule called nicotinamide adenine dinucleotide (NAD+). In this example,
a. glucose is oxidized and NAD+ is reduced.
b. glucose is reduced and NAD+ is oxidized.
c. both glucose and NAD+ have gained protons.
d. glucose has gained protons and NAD+ has lost protons.

9. Where is the energy stored in a molecule of ATP?
a. Within the bonds between nitrogen and carbon
b. In the carbon-to-carbon bonds found in the ribose
c. In the phosphorus-to-oxygen double bond
d. In the bonds connecting the two terminal phosphate groups

10. The molecule ATP is less stable than ADP + Pi because
a. the negatively charged phosphates repel each other.
b. the positively charged phosphates repel each other.
c. ATP is much larger than ADP and Pi.
d. the adenine in ATP is charged.

11. Cells use ATP to drive endergonic reactions because
a. ATP is the universal catalyst.
b. energy released by ATP hydrolysis makes ΔG for coupled reactions more negative.
c. energy released by ATP hydrolysis makes ΔG for coupled reactions more positive.
d. the conversion of ATP to ADP is also endergonic.

12. Which of the following statement cannot be accepted as a true statement?

a. Deoxyribonucleic acid (DNA) and ribonucleic acid (RNA) are polymers composed of nucleotide monomers. Cells use nucleic acids for information storage and transfer.

b. Nucleic acids are nucleotide polymers. Nucleic acids contain four different nucleotide bases. In DNA these are adenine, guanine, cytosine, and thymine. In RNA, thymine is replaced by uracil.

c. DNA stores genetic information. DNA exists as a double helix held together by specific base pairs: adenine with thymine and guanine with cytosine. The nucleic acid sequence constitutes the genetic code.

d. RNA has many roles in a cell. RNA is made by copying DNA. RNA carries information from DNA and forms part of the ribosome. RNA can also be an enzyme and due to non-stability it cannot take a role of genetic material. It can affect gene expression while obtaining copies of genetic information from DNA and providing the same to ribosome.

13. How is a polymer formed from multiple monomers?

a. From the growth of the chain of carbon atoms

b. By the removal of an —OH group and a hydrogen atom

c. By the addition of an —OH group and a hydrogen atom

d. Through hydrogen bonding

14. Why are carbohydrates important molecules for energy storage?

a. The C—H bonds found in carbohydrates store energy.

b. The double bonds between carbon and oxygen are very strong.

c. The electronegativity of the oxygen atoms means that a

carbohydrate is made up of many polar bonds.

d. They can form ring structures in the aqueous environment of a cell.

15. Plant cells store energy in the form of _________, and animal cells store energy in the form of ___________.

a. fructose; glucose

b. disaccharides; monosaccharides

c. cellulose; chitin

d. starch; glycogen

16. Which carbohydrate would you find as part of a molecule of RNA?

a. Galactose

c. Ribose

b. Deoxyribose

d. Glucose

17. A molecule of DNA or RNA is a polymer of

a. monosaccharides.

c. amino acids.

b. nucleotides.

d. fatty acids.

18. What makes cellulose different from starch?

a. Starch is produced by plant cells, and cellulose is produced by animal cells.

b. Cellulose forms long filaments, and starch is highly branched.

c. Starch is insoluble, and cellulose is soluble.

d. All of the choices are correct.

19. What monomers make up a protein?

a. Monosaccharides c. Amino acids

b. Nucleotides d. Fatty acids

20. A triglyceride is a form of _______ composed of ___________.

a. lipid; fatty acids and glucose b. lipid; fatty acids and glycerol

c. carbohydrate; fatty acids d. lipid; cholesterol

21. You can use starch or glycogen as an energy source, but not cellulose because

a. starch and cellulose have similar structures. b. cellulose and glycogen have similar structures.

c. starch and glycogen have similar structures. d. your body makes starch but not cellulose.

22. Which of the following is NOT a difference between DNA and RNA?

a. Deoxyribose sugar versus ribose sugar b. Thymine versus uracil

c. Double-stranded versus single-stranded d. Phosphodiester versus hydrogen bonds

23. Which part of an amino acid has the greatest influence on the overall structure of a protein?

a. The ($—NH_2$) amino group b. The R group

c. The (—COOH) carboxyl group d. Both a and c are correct.

24. A mutation that alters a single amino acid within a protein can alter

a. the primary level of protein structure. b. the secondary level of protein structure.

c. the tertiary level of protein structure. d. All of the choices are correct.

25. Two different proteins have the same domain in their structure. From this we can infer that they have

a. the same primary structure. b. similar function.

c. very different functions. d. the same primary structure but different functions.

26. What aspect of triglyceride structure accounts for their insolubility in water?

a. The COOH group of fatty acids

b. The nonpolar C—H bonds in fatty acids

c. The OH groups in glycerol

d. The C=C bonds found in unsaturated fatty acids

27. The spontaneous formation of a lipid bilayer in an aqueous environment occurs because

a. the polar head groups of the phospholipids can interact with water.

b. the long fatty acid tails of the phospholipids can interact with water.

c. the fatty acid tails of the phospholipids are hydrophobic.

d. Both a and c are correct.

28. A bacterial cell that can alter the composition of saturated and unsaturated fatty acids in its membrane lipids is adapted to a cold environment. If this cell is shifted to a warmer environment, it will react by

a. increasing the amount of cholesterol in its membrane.

b. altering the amount of protein present in the membrane.

c. increasing the degree of saturated fatty acids in its membrane.

d. increasing the percentage of unsaturated fatty acids in its membrane.

29. What variable(s) influence(s) whether a nonpolar molecule can move across a membrane by passive diffusion?

a. The structure of the phospholipids bilayer

b. The difference in concentration of the molecule across the membrane

c. The presence of transport proteins in the membrane

d. All of the choices are correct.

30. Which of the following does NOT contribute to the selective permeability of a biological membrane?

a. Specificity of the carrier proteins in the membrane

b. Selectivity of channel proteins in the membrane

c. Hydrophobic barrier of the phospholipid bilayer

d. Hydrogen bond formation between water and phosphate groups

31. How are active transport and coupled transport related?

a. They both use ATP to move molecules.

b. Active transport establishes a concentration gradient, but coupled transport doesn’t.

c. Coupled transport uses the concentration gradient established by active transport.

d. Active transport moves one molecule, but coupled transport moves two.

32. A cell can use the process of facilitated diffusion to

a. concentrate a molecule such as glucose inside a cell.

b. remove all of a toxic molecule from a cell.

c. move ions or large polar molecules across the membrane regardless of concentration.

d. move ions or large polar molecules from a region of high concentration to a region of low concentration.

33. Cells use ATP to drive endergonic reactions because

a. ATP is the universal catalyst.

b. energy released by ATP hydrolysis makes ΔG for coupled reactions more negative.

c. energy released by ATP hydrolysis makes ΔG for coupled reactions more positive.

d. the conversion of ATP to ADP is also endergonic.

34. Which of the following statements is NOT true about enzymes?

a. Enzymes use the three-dimensional shape of their active site to bind reactants.

b. Enzymes lower the activation energy for a reaction.

c. Enzymes make ΔG for a reaction more negative.

d. Enzymes can catalyze the forward and reverse directions of a reaction.

35. Where is the energy stored in a molecule of ATP?

a. Within the bonds between nitrogen and carbon

b. In the carbon-to-carbon bonds found in the ribose

c. In the phosphorus-to-oxygen double bond

d. In the bonds connecting the two terminal phosphate groups

36. Anaerobic respiration

a. occurs in humans in the absence of O_2. b. occurs in yeast and is how we make beer and wine.

c. yields less energy than aerobic respiration because other final electron acceptors have lower affinity for electrons than O_2.

d. yields more energy than aerobic respiration because other final electron acceptors have higher affinity for electrons than O_2.

Answer Key ------

1. c 2. a 3. c 4. c 5. b 6. b

7: Option b; 8: Option a; 9: Option d; 10: Option a; 11: Option b; 12: Option d;

13. b 14. a 15. d 16. c 17. b 18. b 19. c 20. B 21. c 22. d 23. b 24. d 25. b

26. b 27. d 28. c 29. b 30. d 31. c 32. d 33. b 34. C 35. d 36. c

Concept Application:

1. How do the four biological macromolecules differ from one another? How does the structure of each relate to its function?

Solution: The four biological macromolecules all have different structure and function. In comparing carbohydrates, nucleic acids, and proteins, we can think of these as being polymers with different monomers. In the case of carbohydrates, the polymers are all polymers of the simple sugar glucose. These are energy-storage molecules (with many C–H bonds) and structural molecules such as cellulose that make tough fibers. Nucleic acids are formed of nucleotide monomers, each of which consists of ribose, phosphate, and a nitrogenous base. These molecules are informational molecules that encode information in the sequence of bases. The bases interact in specific ways: A base-pairs with T, and G base-pairs with C. This is the basis for their informational storage. Proteins are formed of amino acid polymers. There are 20 different amino acids, and thus an incredible number of different proteins. These can have an almost unlimited number of functions. These functions arise from the amazing flexibility in structure of protein chains.

2. Hydrogen bonds and hydrophobic interactions each play an important role in stabilizing and organizing biological macromolecules. Consider the four macromolecules discussed in this chapter. Describe how these affect the form and function of each type of macromolecule. Would a disruption in the hydrogen bonds affect form and function? Would hydrophobic interactions do so?

Solution: Nucleic Acids—Hydrogen bonds are the basis for complementary base-pairing between the two strands of the double helix. Complementary base-pairing can also occur within the single nucleic acid strand of an RNA molecule. Hydrophobic interactions between stacked bases also stabilize the double helix.

Proteins—The α helices and β-pleated sheets of secondary structure are stabilized by hydrogen bond formation between the amino and carboxyl groups of the amino acid backbone. Hydrogen bond formation between R groups helps stabilize the three-dimensional folding of the protein at the tertiary level of structure. Hydrophobic interactions also stabilize tertiary structure.

Carbohydrates—Hydrogen bonds are less important for carbohydrates; however, these bonds are responsible for the formation of the fibers of cellulose that make up the cell walls of plants.

Lipids—Lipids do not form hydrogen bonds, but hydrophobic interactions are important. The hydrophobic nature of the fatty acids gives membranes structures.

3. Plants make both starch and cellulose. Would you predict that the enzymes involved in starch synthesis could also be used by the plant for cellulose synthesis? Construct an argument to explain this based on the structure and function of the enzymes and the polymers synthesized.

Solution: The enzymes that bind to starch in their active site would not be expected to bind to cellulose, as the shape of the bonds is different. Thus, these enzymes are unlikely to be involved in cellulose synthesis.

4. Prokaryotes are small cells that lack complex interior organization. The two domains of prokaryotes are archaea and bacteria. The cell wall of bacteria is composed of peptidoglycan, which is not found in archaea.

Archaea have cell walls made from a variety of polysaccharides and peptides, as well as membranes containing unusual lipids. Some bacteria move using a rotating flagellum. What features do bacteria and archaea share?

Solution: Bacteria and archaea both tend to be single cells that lack a membrane bounded nucleus, and lack extensive internal endomembrane systems. They both have a cell wall, although the composition is different. They do not undergo mitosis, although the proteins involved in DNA replication and cell division are not similar.

5. The endoplasmic reticulum (ER) is an extensive system of membranes that spatially organize the cell's biosynthetic activities. Lipid and membrane synthesis occurs on smooth ER, which also stores Ca2+. Rough ER (RER) is covered with ribosomes that synthesize proteins, which can be transported by vesicles to the Golgi apparatus, where they are modified, packaged, and distributed to their final location. Lysosomes contain digestive enzymes used to degrade materials such as invaders or worn-out organelles. Lipid droplets store neutral lipids and contain enzymes. Peroxisomes carry out oxidative metabolism that generates peroxides. Vacuoles are membrane-bounded structures with roles ranging from storage to cell growth in plants. They are also found in some fungi and protists. How do ribosomes on the RER differ from cytoplasmic ribosomes?

Solution: There will be no difference in the combination of subunits and mRNA as such combination depends upon the type of cell (such as prokaryotes and eukaryotes).

6.

21. Glycolysis splits the 6-carbon sugar glucose into two 3-carbon molecules of pyruvate. This uses two ATP molecules and produces four molecules of ATP per glucose, for a net yield of two ATP. Oxidation reactions in glycolysis transfer electrons to NAD^+, producing two NADH. When oxygen is abundant, NADH is oxidized by the electron transport chain, ultimately reducing O_2. When O2 is absent, NAD^+ is regenerated by a fermentation reaction that reduces an organic molecule. Does glycolysis taking place in the cytoplasm argue for or against the endosymbiotic origin of mitochondria?

Solution: Taken by itself, the location of glycolysis does not argue for or against the endosymbiotic origin of mitochondria. Glycolysis may have taken place in the mitochondria previously and moved to the cytoplasm over time, or it could have always taken place in the cytoplasm in eukaryotes.

22. The electron transport chain receives electrons from NADH and $FADH_2$ and passes them down the chain to oxygen, using the energy from electron transfer to pump protons across the membrane, creating an electrochemical gradient. The enzyme ATP synthase uses this gradient to drive the endergonic reaction of phosphorylating ADP to ATP. How would poking a small hole in the outer membrane affect ATP synthesis?

Solution: A hole in the outer membrane would allow protons in the intermembrane space to leak out, disturbing the proton gradient across the membrane. This would reduce or stop the phosphorylation of ADP by ATP synthase.

23. The number of ATP synthesized by chemiosmosis depends on the number of protons translocated by electron transport and the number used by ATP synthase. The maximum number of ATP per NADP is 2.5 (1.5 per $FADH_2$). This results in 32 ATP per glucose for prokaryotes and 30 for eukaryotes due to transport of cytoplasmic NADH into mitochondria. The amount of ATP per O_2 reduced is called the P/O ratio; this value has been contentious, but theoretical and measured values have converged. What factors affect the yield of ATP by chemiosmosis?

Solution: The number of ATP synthesized by chemiosmosis depends on the number of protons translocated by electron transport and the number used by ATP synthase.

24. Respiration is controlled by levels of ATP in the cell and levels of key intermediates in the process. The control point for glycolysis is the enzyme phosphofructokinase, which is inhibited by ATP or citrate (or both). The main control point in oxidation of pyruvate is the enzyme pyruvate dehydrogenase, inhibited by NADH. How does feedback inhibition ensure economic production of ATP?

Option: Feedback of NADH and ATP levels in the cells ensures that a cell does not invest too much of its existing ATP in the production of ATP that it does not necessarily need yet. This keeps cells from constantly producing ATP in situations that do not require the energy.

25. Nitrate, sulfur, and CO_2 are all used as terminal electron acceptors in anaerobic respiration of different organisms. Organic molecules can also accept electrons in fermentation reactions that regenerate NAD^+. Fermentation reactions produce a variety of compounds, including ethanol in yeast and lactic acid in humans. In what kinds of ecosystems would you expect to find anaerobic respiration?

Options: Anaerobic respiration is likely in ecosystems that have little or no free oxygen. This might include certain aquatic ecosystems and soil environments.

26. Proteins can be broken into their constituent amino acids, which are deaminated and can enter metabolism at glycolysis or the Krebs cycle. Fats are broken into units of acetyl-Co A by β oxidation and then fed into the Krebs cycle. Many metabolic processes are used reversibly for anabolic and catabolic pathways. Key intermediates, such as pyruvate and acetyl-Co A, connect these processes. Can fats be oxidized in the absence of O_2?

Options: No, for two reasons: (1) The oxidation of fatty acids feeds acetyl units into the Krebs cycle. The primary output of the Krebs cycle is electrons that feed into the electron transport chain to eventually produce ATP by chemiosmosis. (2) The process of β oxidation that produces the acetyl units is oxygen dependent as well (β oxidation uses FAD as a cofactor for oxidation, and the $FADH_2$ is oxidized by the electron transport chain).

27. What produces proton gradient during aerobic respiration?

Solution: The Electron Transport Chain Produces a Proton Gradient -- A proton gradient forms as electrons move through electron carriers. NADH is oxidized to NAD^+. The electrons move to cytochrome oxidase, where they join with H^+ and O_2 to form H_2O. This results in three protons being pumped into the intermembrane space.

28. "Central role of aerobic respiration to produce ATP." Is this statement true?

Solution: Yes; The ultimate goal of cellular respiration is synthesis of ATP, which is used to power most of the cell's activities. Cells make ATP by two fundamentally different mechanisms: substrate-level phosphorylation and oxidative phosphorylation.

29. Photosynthesis consists of light-dependent reactions that require sunlight, and others that convert CO_2 into organic molecules. The overall reaction is essentially the reverse of respiration and produces O_2 as a by-product. The thylakoid membrane is the site where photosynthetic pigments are clustered, allowing the passage of energy from one molecule to the next. How is the structure of the chloroplast similar to that of the mitochondria?

Solution: Both chloroplasts and mitochondria have an outer membrane and an inner membrane. The inner membrane in both forms an elaborate structure and contains an electron transport chain that moves protons across the membrane to allow for the synthesis of ATP via chemiosmosis. They also both have a soluble compartment in which a variety of enzymes carry out reactions.

30. Early experiments indicated that plants produce oxygen in the presence of sunlight. Further experiments showed that there are both light-dependent and light-independent reactions. The light-dependent reactions produce O_2 from H_2O and generate ATP and NADPH. The light- independent reactions synthesize organic compounds from CO_2. Where does the carbon in your body come from?

Solution: All of the carbon inside the human body comes from the organic compounds we ingest. Carbon and hydrogen are the basis of all organic compounds. The carbon in these compounds was once carbon dioxide in the atmosphere, which is fixed by autotrophs.

31. Pigment molecules absorb light energy. An absorption spectrum describes the wavelengths of light absorbed most efficiently by a pigment. The color of a pigment results from the wavelengths it does not absorb, which we see. The main photosynthetic pigment is chlorophyll, which exists in two forms with slightly different absorption spectra. Accessory pigments have absorption spectra different from that of chlorophyll. What is the difference between an action spectrum and an absorption spectrum?

Solution: The absorption spectrum for an individual pigment shows how much light is absorbed at different wavelengths. Action spectrum refers to the most effective wavelengths for a specific light-driven process—in the case of photosynthesis, wavelengths of light that promote photosynthesis are those absorbed by chlorophyll molecules.

32. Chlorophylls and accessory pigments are organized into photosystems in the thylakoid membrane. A photosystem consists of an antenna complex for light harvesting and a reaction center where photochemical reactions occur. An excited electron is passed to an acceptor, transferring energy away from the chlorophylls. This is key to converting light into chemical energy. Why were photosystems an unexpected finding?

Solution: Before photosystems were discovered, scientists had assumed that each chlorophyll molecule absorbed photons, resulting in excited electrons. This belief led scientists to predict that when photosynthetic rates were maxed out, all of a plant's pigment molecules were in use. Experimental evidence showed otherwise—that light is absorbed not by independent pigment molecules but instead by clusters of chlorophyll and accessory pigment molecules, collectively called photosystems. When photosynthetic rates are maxed out, the reaction centers of these photosystems are maxed out, not all the chlorophyll in a plant.

33. What are different steps restricted to the Thylacoid of Chloroplastids?

Solution: The thylakoid reactions can be broken into four steps:
1. Primary photo event. A photon of light is captured by a pigment. This primary photoevent excites an electron within the pigment.
2. Charge separation. This excitation energy is transferred to the reaction center, which transfers an energetic electron to an acceptor molecule, initiating electron transport.
3. Electron transport. The excited electrons are shuttled along a series of electron carrier molecules embedded within the photosynthetic membrane. This process is exergonic, with some of the energy released used to transport protons across the membrane, forming a proton gradient. The electrons are used to reduce the final acceptor, NADPH.

4. Chemiosmosis. The proton gradient is a form of potential energy that can be used by an ATP synthase enzyme that catalyzes the reaction of ADP and Pi to form ATP. This enzyme is evolutionarily related to the mitochondrial enzyme with the same function.

34. The chloroplast has two photosystems in the thylakoid membrane connected by an electron transport chain. Photosystem I passes an electron to NADPH. This electron is replaced by one from photosystem II. Photosystem II can oxidize water to replace the electron it has lost. A proton gradient is built up in the thylakoid space, then used to generate ATP by the ATP synthase enzyme. If the thylakoid membrane were leaky to protons, would ATP still be produced? Would NADPH?

Solution: If the thylakoid membrane were leaky to protons, the electrochemical gradient needed to produce ATP would not exist. So, ATP would not be produced; however, NADPH could still be synthesized because electron transport would continue to occur as long as photons were still being absorbed to begin the process.

35. Functional groups account for differences in chemical properties in organic molecules. Isomers are compounds with the same empirical formula but different structures. This difference may affect biological function. Macromolecules are polymers consisting of long chains of similar subunits that are joined by dehydration reactions and are broken down by hydrolysis reactions. What is the relationship between dehydration and hydrolysis?

Solution: Hydrolysis is the reverse reaction of dehydration. Dehydration is a synthetic reaction involving the loss of water and hydrolysis is cleavage by addition of water.

36. Monosaccharides have three to six or more carbon atoms typically arranged in a ring form. Disaccharides consist of two linked monosaccharides; polysaccharides are long chains of monosaccharides. Structural differences between sugar isomers can lead to functional differences. Starches are branched polymers of α-glucose used for energy storage. Cellulose in plants consists of unbranched chains of β-glucose that are not easily digested. How do the structures of starch, glycogen, and cellulose affect their function?

Solution: Starch and glycogen are both energy-storage molecules. Their highly branched nature allows the formation of droplets, and the similarity in the bonds holding adjacent glucose molecules together mean that the enzymes we have to break down glycogen allow us to break down starch. The same enzymes do not allow us to break down cellulose. The structure of cellulose leads to the formation of tough fibers.

37. "RNA has many roles in a cell." Justify this statement by furnishing at least five examples.

Solution: RNA is similar to DNA, but with two major chemical differences. First, RNA molecules contain ribose sugars, in which the C-2 is bonded to a hydroxyl group. (In DNA, a hydrogen atom replaces this hydroxyl group.) Second, RNA molecules use uracil in place of thymine. Uracil has a similar structure to thymine, except that one of its carbons lacks a methyl (—CH_3) group. RNA is produced by transcription (copying) from DNA, and is usually single-stranded. The role of RNA in cells is quite varied: it carries information in the form of mRNA, it is part of the ribosome, in the form of ribosomal RNA (rRNA), and it carries amino acids in the form of transfer RNA (tRNA). There has been a revolution of late in how we view RNA since it has been found to function as an enzyme, and other forms of RNA are involved in regulating gene expression.

38. A nucleic acid is a polymer composed of alternating phosphate and 5-carbon sugar groups with a nitrogenous base protruding from each sugar. In DNA, this sugar is deoxyribose. In RNA, the sugar is ribose. RNA also contains the base uracil instead of thymine. DNA is a double-stranded helix that stores hereditary information as a specific sequence of nucleotide bases. RNA has multiple roles in a cell, including carrying information from DNA and forming part of the ribosome. If an RNA molecule is copied from a DNA strand, what is the relationship between the sequence of bases in RNA and each DNA strand?

Solution: The sequence of bases in an RNA would be identical to one strand and complementary to the other strand of the DNA with the exception that U would be in place of T (complementary to A).

39. "Functional side group present in Amino Acid molecule often determines chemistry of the molecule." Justify this statement. Classify all the amino acids on the basis of the side group (R).

General formula of amino acid: H2N—CH (R) —COOH

Solution: The R group also determines the chemistry of amino acids. Serine, in which the R group is $—CH_2OH$, is a polar molecule. Alanine, which has $—CH_3$ as its R group, is nonpolar. The 20 common amino acids are grouped into five chemical classes, based on their R group:

a. Nonpolar amino acids, such as leucine, often have R groups that contain $—CH_2$ or $—CH_3$.
b. Polar uncharged amino acids, such as threonine, have R groups that contain oxygen (or —OH).
c. Charged amino acids, such as glutamic acid, have R groups that contain acids or bases that can ionize.
d. Aromatic amino acids, such as phenylalanine, have R groups that contain an organic (carbon) ring with alternating single and double bonds. These are also nonpolar.
e. Amino acids that have special functions have unique properties. Some examples are methionine, which is often the first amino acid in a chain of amino acids; proline, which causes kinks in chains; and cysteine, which links chains together.

40. What are domains of proteins?

Solution: Domains of proteins are functional units within a larger structure. They can be thought of as substructure within the tertiary structure of a protein). To continue the metaphor: Amino acids are letters in the protein language, motifs are words or phrases, and domains are paragraphs.

41. How do cells avoid having their proteins clump into a mass?

Solution: A vital clue came in studies of unusual mutations that prevent viruses from replicating in bacterial cells. It turns out that the virus proteins produced inside the cells could not fold properly. Further study revealed that normal cells contain chaperone proteins, which help other proteins to fold correctly. Molecular biologists have now identified many proteins that act as molecular chaperones. This large class of proteins can be divided into subclasses, and representatives have been found in essentially every organism that has been examined.

42. Proteins are molecules with diverse functions. They are constructed from 20 different kinds of amino acids. Protein structure can be viewed at four levels: (a) the amino acid sequence, or primary structure; (b) coils and sheets, called secondary structure; (c) the three-dimensional shape, called tertiary structure; and (d) individual polypeptide subunits associated in a quaternary structure. Different proteins often have similar substructures

called motifs and can be broken down into functional domains. Proteins have a narrow range of conditions in which they fold properly; outside that range, proteins tend to unfold (denaturation). Under some conditions, denatured proteins can refold and become functional again (renaturation). How does our knowledge of protein structure help us to predict the function of unknown proteins?

Solution: If an unknown protein has sequence similarity to a known protein, we can infer its function is also similar. If an unknown protein has known functional domains or motifs, we can also use these to help predict function.

43. Triglycerides are made of fatty acids linked to glycerol. Fats can contain twice as many C—H bonds as carbohydrates and thus they store energy efficiently. Because the C—H bonds in lipids are nonpolar, they are not water-soluble and aggregate together in water. Phospholipids replace one fatty acid with a hydrophilic phosphate group. This allows them to spontaneously form bilayers, which are the basis of biological membranes. Why do phospholipids form membranes while triglycerides form insoluble droplets?

Solution: Phospholipids have a charged group replacing one of the fatty acids in a triglyceride. This leads to an amphipathic molecule that has both hydrophobic and hydrophilic regions. This will spontaneously form bilayer membranes in water.

44. Glycolysis splits the 6-carbon molecule glucose into two 3-carbon molecules of pyruvate. This process uses two ATP molecules in "priming" reactions and eventually produces four molecules of ATP per glucose for a net yield of two ATP. The oxidation reactions of glycolysis require NAD^+ and produce NADH. When oxygen is abundant, NAD^+ is regenerated in the electron transport chain, using O_2 as an acceptor. When oxygen is absent, NAD^+ is regenerated in a fermentation reaction using an organic molecule as an electron receptor. Does glycolysis taking place in the cytoplasm argue for or against the endosymbiotic origin of mitochondria?

Solution: The location of glycolysis does not argue for or against the endosymbiotic origin of mitochondria. It could have been located in the mitochondria previously and moved to the cytoplasm or could have always been located in the cytoplasm in eukaryotes.

45. Pyruvate is oxidized in the mitochondria to produce acetyl-CoA and CO_2. Acetyl-CoA is the molecule that links glycolysis and the reactions of the citric acid cycle. What are the advantages and disadvantages of a multi-enzyme complex?

Solution: For an enzyme like pyruvate decarboxylase the complex reduces the distance for the diffusion of substrates for the different stages of the reaction. Any possible unwanted side reactions are prevented. Finally the reactions occur within a single unit and thus can be controlled in a coordinated fashion. The main disadvantage is that since the enzymes are all part of a complex their evolution is more constrained than if they were independent.

46. The citric acid cycle completes the oxidation of glucose begun with glycolysis. In the first segment, acetyl-CoA is added to oxaloacetate to produce citrate. In the next segment, five reactions produce succinate, two NADH from NAD^+, and one ATP. Finally, succinate undergoes three more reactions to regenerate oxaloacetate, producing one more NADH and one $FADH_2$ from FAD. What happens to the electrons removed from glucose at this point?

Solution: At the end of the Krebs cycle, the electrons removed from glucose are all carried by soluble electron carriers. Most of these are in NADH, and a few are in $FADH_2$. All of these are fed into the electron transport chain under aerobic conditions where they are used to produce a proton gradient.

47. The electron transport chain receives electrons from NADH and $FADH_2$ and passes them down the chain to oxygen. The protein complexes of the electron transport chain, in the inner membrane of mitochondria, use the energy from electron transfer to pump protons across the membrane, creating an electrochemical gradient. The enzyme ATP synthase uses this gradient to drive the endergonic reaction of phosphorylating ADP to ATP. How would poking a small hole in the outer membrane affect ATP synthesis?

Solution: A hole in the outer membrane would allow protons in the intermembrane space to leak out. This would destroy the proton gradient across the inner membrane, stopping the phosphorylation of ADP by ATP synthase.

48. Passage of electrons down the electron transport chain produces roughly 2.5 molecules of ATP per molecule of NADH (1.5 ATP per $FADH_2$). This process plus the ATP from substrate-level phosphorylation can yield a maximum of 32 ATP for the complete oxidation of glucose. NADH generated in the cytoplasm of eukaryotes yields only two ATP/NADH due to the cost of transport into the mitochondria, lowering the yield to 30 ATP. How does chemiosmosis allow for noninteger numbers of ATP/NADH?

Solution: Chemiosmosis means that the ATP/NADH ratio is not dependent on the number of "pumping" stations. Instead, it is dependent on the number of protons needed for one turn of the enzyme, and on the number of binding sites on the enzyme for ADP/ATP.

49: Energy is defined as the capacity to do work. Energy is either stored (potential) or energy of motion (kinetic). The Sun is the ultimate source of energy for living systems. Organisms derive energy from oxidation–reduction reactions. Oxidation is the loss of electrons; reduction is the gain of electrons. What energy source might ecosystems at the bottom of the ocean use?

Solution: Since light is not an option at the bottom of the ocean, energy in the form of reduced minerals, such as sulfur compounds, that can be oxidized is used. Hydrothermal vents, which are found at the junctions of tectonic plates, provide this energy source.

50: The First Law of Thermodynamics states that energy cannot be created or destroyed. The Second Law states that the loss of energy results in greater disorder, or entropy. Free-energy changes (ΔG) can predict whether chemical reactions take place. Reactions with a negative ΔG occur spontaneously, and those with a positive ΔG do not. If entropy in the world always increases, what has prevented the world from becoming totally disordered?

Solution: The loss of energy results in an increase in entropy, which occurs spontaneously. However, energy is not destroyed when it is lost; it is transferred. This energy can then be used for organization, which decreases entropy.

51: Enzymes are specific catalysts that accelerate chemical reactions in cells. Enzymes bind their substrates based on molecular shape, providing specificity. Enzyme activity is affected by temperature, pH, and the presence of inhibitors or activators. Some enzymes require an inorganic cofactor or an organic coenzyme. Can an enzyme make an endergonic reaction exergonic?

Solution: Enzymes can alter the rate of a reaction but not the thermodynamics of the reaction. The action of the enzyme does not change the ΔG for the reaction.

52: Metabolism is the sum of all chemical reactions in a cell. Anabolic reactions use energy to build molecules. Catabolic reactions release energy by breaking down molecules. In a metabolic pathway, the product of one reaction is the substrate for the next. Is a catabolic pathway likely to be subject to feedback inhibition?

Solution: Feedback inhibition is common in pathways that synthesize metabolites. In these anabolic pathways, when the end product builds up, it feeds back to inhibit its own production. Catabolic pathways are involved in the degradation of compounds. Feedback inhibition makes less biochemical sense in a pathway that degrades compounds, as these are usually involved in energy metabolism, or recycling or removal of compounds. Thus, the end product is destroyed or removed and cannot feedback. However, if the end product of a catabolic reaction is a compound that the cell requires, and is releasing through breakdown of larger biomolecules, it might feedback to slow or halt the biochemical pathway that produces it.

53. "Activation Energy Is the Energy Needed to Destabilize Chemical Bonds." Justify this statement.

Solution: Activation energy controls the rate of a chemical reaction. Reactions with high activation energy proceed slowly. A catalyst can lower the activation energy, allowing a reaction to proceed faster.

54. What would be the impact of enzyme on activation energy needed to initiate specific chemical reactions?

Solution : Enzymes Lower Activation Energy needed to start a reaction. An enzyme is a catalyst. Enzymes lower the activation energy needed to initiate specific chemical reactions in the cell.

55. Human babies and hibernating or cold-adapted animals are able to maintain body temperature (a process called thermogenesis) due to the presence of brown fat. Brown fat is characterized by a high concentration of mitochondria. These brown fat mitochondria have a special protein located within their inner membranes. Thermogenin is a protein that functions as a passive proton transporter. Propose a likely explanation for the role of brown fat in thermogenesis based on your knowledge of metabolism, transport, and the structure and function of mitochondria.

Solution: The electron transport chain of the inner membrane of the mitochondria functions to create a hydrogen ion concentration gradient by pumping protons into the intermembrane space. In a typical mitochondrion, the protons can only diffuse back down their concentration gradient by moving through the ATP synthase and generating ATP. If protons can move through another transport protein, then the potential energy of the hydrogen ion concentration gradient would be "lost" as heat.

56. Photosynthesis consists of light-dependent reactions that require sunlight, and others that convert CO2 into organic molecules. The overall reaction is essentially the reverse of respiration and produces O2 as a by-product. The chloroplast's inner membrane, the thylakoid, is the site in which photosynthetic pigments are clustered, allowing passage of energy from one molecule to the next. The thylakoid membrane is organized into flattened sacs stacked in columns called grana. How is the structure of the chloroplast similar to that of the mitochondria?

Solution: Both chloroplasts and mitochondria have an outer membrane and an elaborate inner membrane. These inner membrane systems have electron transport chains that move protons across the membrane to allow for the synthesis of ATP by chemiosmosis. They also both have a soluble compartment in which a variety of enzymes carry out reactions.

57. A pigment is a molecule that can absorb light energy; its absorption spectrum shows the wavelengths at which it absorbs energy most efficiently. A pigment's color results from the wavelengths it does not absorb, which we then see. The main photosynthetic pigment is chlorophyll, which exists in several forms with slightly different absorption spectra. Many photosynthetic organisms have accessory pigments with absorption spectra different from that of chlorophyll; these increase light capture. What is the difference between an action spectrum and an absorption spectrum?

Solution: The action spectrum for photosynthesis refers to the most effective wavelengths. The absorption spectrum for an individual pigment shows how much light is absorbed at different wavelengths.

58. Chlorophylls and accessory pigments are organized into photosystems found in the thylakoid membrane. The photosystem can be subdivided into an antenna complex, which is involved in light harvesting, and a reaction center, where the photochemical reactions occur. In the reaction center, an excited electron is passed to an acceptor; this transfers energy away from the chlorophylls and is key to the conversion of light into chemical energy. Why were photosystems an unexpected finding?

Solution: Before the discovery of photosystems, we assumed that each chlorophyll molecule absorbed photons resulting in excited electrons.

59. The chloroplast has two photosystems located in the thylakoid membrane that are connected by an electron transport chain. Photosystem I passes an electron to NADPH. This electron is replaced by one from photosystem II. Photosystem II can oxidize water to replace the electron it has lost. A proton gradient is built up in the thylakoid space, and this gradient is used to generate ATP as protons pass through the ATP synthase enzyme. If the thylakoid membrane were leaky to protons, would ATP still be produced? Would NADPH?

Solution: Without a proton gradient, synthesis of ATP by chemiosmosis would be impossible. However, NADPH could still be synthesized because electron transport would still occur as long as photons were still being absorbed to begin the process.

60. Carbon fixation takes place in the stroma of the chloroplast, where inorganic CO_2 is incorporated into an organic molecule. The key intermediate is the 5-carbon sugar RuBP that combines with CO_2 in a reaction catalyzed by the enzyme rubisco. The cycle can be broken down into three stages: carbon fixation, reduction, and regeneration of RuBP. ATP and NADPH from the light reactions provide energy and electrons for the reduction reactions, which produce G3P. Glucose is synthesized when two molecules of G3P are combined. How does the Calvin cycle compare with glycolysis?

Solution: A portion of the Calvin cycle is the reverse of glycolysis (the reduction of 3-phosphoglycerate to glyceraldehyde -3-phosphate).

61. Rubisco can also oxidize RuBP under conditions of high O_2 and low CO_2. In plants that use only C_3 metabolism (Calvin cycle), up to 20% of fixed carbon is lost to this photorespiration. Plants adapted to hot, dry environments are capable of storing CO_2 as a 4-carbon molecule and avoiding some of this loss; they are called C_4 plants. In

CAM plants, CO_2 is fixed at night into a C_4 organic compound; in the daytime, this compound is used as a source of CO_2 for C_3 metabolism when stomata are closed to prevent water loss. How do C_4 plants and CAM plants differ?

Solution: Both C_4 plants and CAM plants fix carbon by incorporating CO_2 into the 4-carbon malate and then use this to produce high local levels of CO_2 for the Calvin cycle. The main difference is that in C_4 plants, this occurs in different cells, and in CAM plants this occurs at different times.

62. Receptors may be internal (intracellular receptors) or external (membrane receptors). Membrane receptors include channel linked receptors, enzymatic receptors, and G protein–coupled receptors. Signal transduction through membrane receptors often involves the production of a second signaling molecule, or second messenger, inside the cell. Would a hydrophobic molecule be expected to have an internal or membrane receptor?

Solution: Hydrophobic molecules can cross the membrane and are thus more likely to have an internal receptor.

63. Large molecules and other bulky materials can enter a cell by endocytosis and leave the cell by exocytosis. These processes require energy. Endocytosis may be mediated by specific receptor proteins in the membrane that trigger the formation of vesicles. What feature unites transport by receptor-mediated endocytosis, transport by a carrier, and catalysis by an enzyme?

Solution: In all cases, there is recognition and specific binding of a molecule by a protein. In each case this binding is necessary for biological function.

64. Sister chromatid cohesion, combined with crossing over, connects homologous chromosomes during meiosis I. The centromere of each homologue shows monopolar attachment, leading to the alignment of homologous pairs at metaphase I. Loss of cohesion on the arms but not the centromere leads to homologues moving to opposite poles during anaphase I. During anaphase II, cohesin proteins holding sister chromatids together at the centromere are removed, allowing them to move to opposite poles. What would be the result of improper disjunction at anaphase I? At anaphase II?

Solution: An improper disjunction at anaphase I would result in 4 aneuploid gametes: 2 with an extra chromosome and 2 that are missing a chromosome.

Nondisjunction at anaphase II would result in 2 normal gametes and 2 aneuploid gametes: 1 with an extra chromosome and 1 missing a chromosome.

65. How meiosis cell division can be characterized?

Solution: Meiosis is characterized by four distinct features:

a. Homologous pairing and crossing over joins maternal and paternal homologues during meiosis I.

b. Sister chromatids remain connected at the centromere and segregate together during anaphase I.

c. Kinetochores of sister chromatids are attached to the same pole in meiosis I and to opposite poles in mitosis.

d. DNA replication is suppressed between the two meiotic divisions.

66. Hydrophobic signaling molecules can cross the membrane and bind to intracellular receptors. The steroid hormone receptors act by directly influencing gene expression. On binding hormone, the hormone–receptor complex moves into the nucleus to turn on (or sometimes turn off) gene expression. This may also require a coactivator that functions with the hormone–receptor complex. Thus, the cell's response to a hormone depends on the presence of a receptor and coactivators as well. Would these types of intracellular receptors be fast acting, or have effects of longer duration?

Solution: Channel proteins are aqueous pores that allow facilitated diffusion. They cannot actively transport ions. Carrier proteins bind to their substrates and can couple transport to some form of energy for active transport.

67. Meiosis is characterized by homologue pairing and crossing over; by loss of sister chromatid cohesion in the arms, but not at the centromere at the first division; by the suppression of DNA replication between the two meiotic divisions; and by sister kinetochores attachment to the same pole of the spindle. If replication were not suppressed between meiosis I and meiosis II, gametes would be diploid, and zygotes would be tetraploid. What features of meiosis lead to genetic variation in the products?

Solution: The independent alignment of homologous pairs at metaphase I and the process of crossing over. The first shuffles the genome at the level of entire chromosomes, and the second shuffles the genome at the level of individual chromosomes.

Review of Studies B

Q 1. What makes water molecule cohesive?

Solution: Hydrogen bonds between molecules of liquid water last for only a few trillionths of a second, yet at any instant, many molecules are hydrogen-bonded to others. This tendency of molecules of the same kind to stick together, called cohesion, is much stronger for water than for most other liquids. The cohesion of water is important in the living world. Trees, for example, depend on cohesion to help transport water and nutrients from their roots to their leaves. The evaporation of water from a leaf exerts a pulling force on water within the veins of the leaf. Because of cohesion, the force is relayed all the way down to the roots. Adhesion, the clinging of one substance to another, also plays a role.

Q 2. Why are blood and most other biological fluids classified as aqueous solutions?

Solution: The solvent in these fluids is water.

Q 3. Why is it important to keep the pH of our cellular environment relatively constant at a value not less than 7?

Solution: Most biological reactions require a pH around 7.

Q 3. Why is the presence of water important in the search for extraterrestrial life?

Solution: Water plays important roles in life as we know it, from moderating temperatures on the planet to functioning as the solvent of life.

Q 4. List of three functional group is provided:

A: An amino group has a nitrogen bonded to two hydrogens. It can act as a base by picking up an H+ from a solution and becoming ionized. Organic compounds with an amino group are called amines. The building blocks of proteins— amino acids—contain an amino and a carboxyl group.

B. A phosphate group consists of a phosphorus atom bonded to four oxygen atoms. It too is usually ionized, as you can see by the negatively charged oxygens in the figure. Compounds with phosphate groups are called organic phosphates and are often involved in energy transfers, as is the energy-rich compound ATP (adenosine triphosphate), shown in the table.

C. A methyl group consists of a carbon bonded to three hydrogen atoms. The methylated compound in the organic molecules (nitrogen bases)— a component of DNA—affects the expression of genes. You will meet these chemical groups again as you learn about the four major classes of organic molecules. But first, let's see how your cells make large molecules out of smaller ones.

D. A hydroxyl group consists of a hydrogen atom bonded to an oxygen atom. Ethanol, shown in the table, and other organic compounds containing hydroxyl groups are called alcohols. Identify the chemical groups that do not contain carbon.

Solution: The hydroxyl, amino, and phosphate groups.

Case Study: Structure of Fatty acids and lipid molecules.

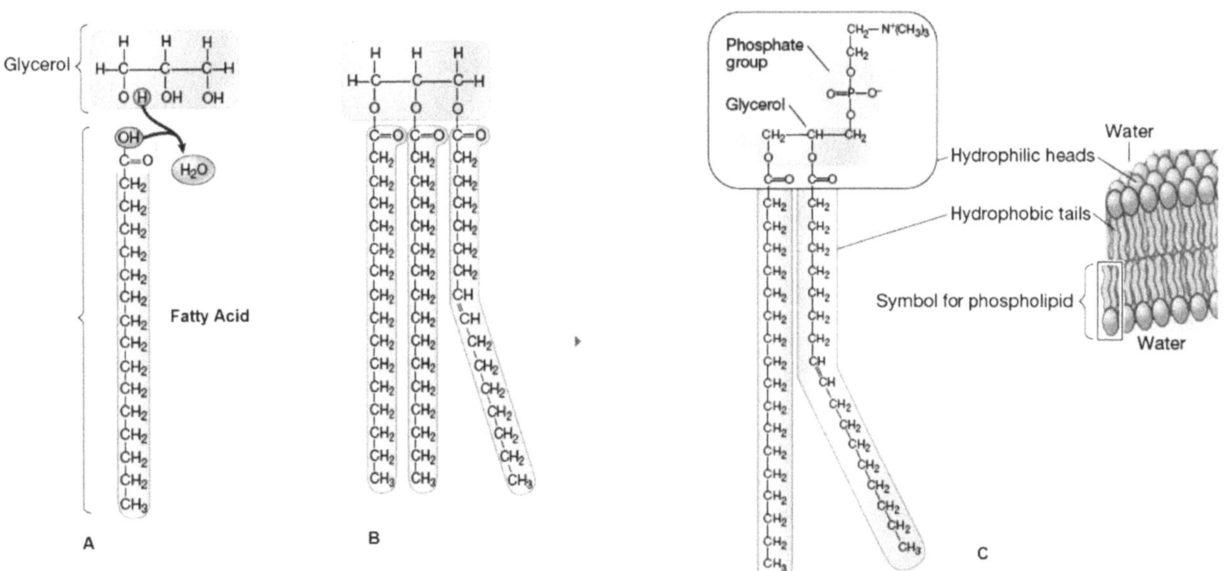

A: A dehydration reaction that will link a fatty acid to glycerol.

B. A fat molecule (triglyceride) consisting of three fatty acids linked to glycerol.

C. Section of a phospholipid membrane. Each gray-headed, yellow tailed structure is a phospholipid molecule; this visual representation is used throughout this book.

Steroids are lipids in which the carbon skeleton contains four fused rings, as shown in the structural formula of cholesterol in figure (The diagram omits the carbons and hydrogens making up the rings and the attached hydrocarbon chain.). Cholesterol is a common component in animal cell membranes and is also the precursor for making other steroids, including sex hormones.

Q. Compare the structure of a phospholipid with that of a fat.

Solution: A phospholipid has two fatty acids and a phosphate group attached to glycerol. Three fatty acids are attached to the glycerol of a fat molecule.

Q. Why anaerobic steroids are not good for health?

Solution: Anabolic steroids are synthetic variants of the male hormone testosterone. Testosterone causes a general buildup of muscle and bone mass in males during puberty and maintains masculine traits throughout life. Because anabolic steroids structurally resemble testosterone, they also mimic some of its effects. (The word anabolic comes from anabolism, the building of substances by the body.) Anabolic steroids are used to treat general anemia and diseases that destroy body muscle. Some athletes use these drugs to build up their muscles quickly and enhance their performance.

Q. Explain why fats and steroids, which are structurally very different, are both classed as lipids.

Solution: Fats and steroids are hydrophobic molecules, the key characteristic of lipids.

Q. Suppose you eat some cheese. What reactions must occur for the protein of the cheese to be broken down into its amino acid monomers and then for these monomers to be converted to proteins in your body?

Solution: In digestion, the proteins are broken down into amino acids by hydrolysis. New proteins are formed in your body cells from these monomers in dehydration reactions.

Q. Write the formula for a monosaccharide that has three carbons.

Solution: $C_3H_6O_3$

Q. Lactose, as you read in the chapter introduction, is the disaccharide sugar in milk. It is formed from glucose and galactose. The formula for both these monosaccharides is $C_6H_{12}O_6$. What is the formula for lactose?

Solution: $C_{12}H_{22}O_{11}$

Q. Sugars are often described as "empty calories." What do you think that means from a nutrition standpoint?

Solution: Added sugars provide energy but they do not provide other nutrients, such as protein, fats, vitamins, or minerals.

Q. Compare and contrast starch and cellulose, two plant polysaccharides.

Solution: Both are polymers of glucose, but the bonds between glucose monomers have different shapes. Starch functions mainly for sugar storage. Cellulose is a structural polysaccharide that is the main material of plant cell walls.

Q. ………………… is a structural polysaccharide used by insects and crustaceans to build their exoskeleton, the hard case enclosing the animal. ……………………… is also found in the cell walls of fungi.

Solution: Chitin.

Q. Why does a denatured protein no longer function normally?

Solution: The function of each protein is a consequence of its specific shape, which is lost when a protein denatures.

Q. How is it possible to make thousands of different kinds of proteins from just 20 amino acids?

Solution: Thousands of English words can be made by varying the sequence of letters and word length. Although the protein "alphabet" is slightly smaller (just 20 "letters," rather than 26), the "words" are much longer. Most polypeptides are at least 100 amino acids in length; some are 1,000 or more. Each different polypeptide has a unique sequence of amino acids.

Q. By what process do you digest the proteins you eat into their individual amino acids?

Solution: By hydrolysis, adding a molecule of water back to break each peptide bond.

Q: How does a peptide bond is formed?

Solution: Cells join amino acids together in a dehydration reaction that links the carboxyl group of one amino acid to the amino group of the next amino acid as a water molecule is removed. The resulting covalent linkage is called a peptide bond. The product of the reaction shown in the figure is called a dipeptide, because it was made from two amino acids.

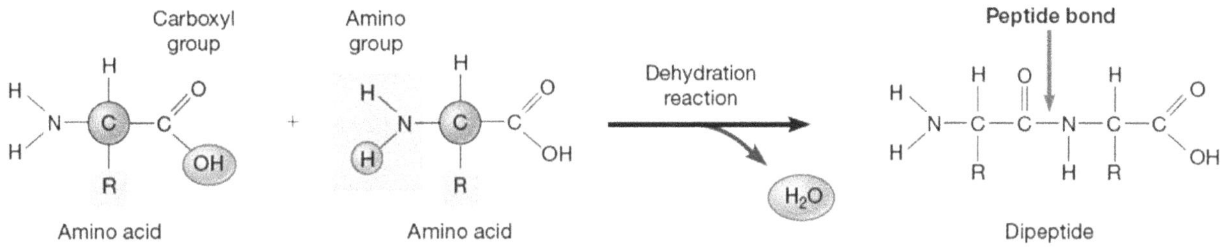

Q. If a genetic mutation changes the primary structure of a protein, how might this destroy the protein's function?

Solution: Primary structure determines the secondary and tertiary structure due to the chemical nature of the R groups of the amino acids in the chain. Even a slight change may affect a protein's shape and thus its function.

Q. the primary structure of a polypeptide determines the shape of a protein. But what determines this primary structure?

Solution: The amino acid sequence of a polypeptide is programmed by a discrete unit of inheritance known as a gene. Genes consist of DNA (deoxyribonucleic acid), one of the two types of polymers called nucleic acids. The name nucleic comes from DNA's location in the nuclei of cells. The other type of nucleic acid is RNA (ribonucleic acid). Its role is in assembling the polypeptides according to the instructions of DNA. Let's begin by examining the composition and structure of nucleic acids. Then we will explore how they function in the storage, transfer, and expression of hereditary information.

Q. What roles do complementary base pairing play in the functioning of DNA?

Solution: Complementary base pairing makes possible the precise replication of DNA, ensuring that genetic information is faithfully transmitted every time a cell divides. It also ensures that RNA molecules carry accurate instructions from DNA for the synthesis of proteins.

Q. Comprehension: Plasma membrane and Cell Wall

a) The cell membrane composed of lipids that arranged in bilayer.
b) Lipids are arranged within the membrane with the hydrophilic polar head towards the outer sides and the hydrophobic tails towards the inner part.
c) Non polar tail of saturated hydrocarbons is protected from the aqueous environment.
d) The lipid component of the membrane mainly consists of phophoglycerides.
e) Cell membrane also possesses protein and carbohydrates. Ratio of protein and lipids varies from cell to cell.
f) Human erythrocyte plasma membrane contains 52 % protein and 40 % lipids.
g) Membrane protein may be integral or peripheral. Peripheral protein lie on the surface and integral proteins are partially or totally buried in the membrane.
h) The improved model of the structure of plasma membrane was proposed by singer and Nicolson (1972) widely accepted as fluid mosaic model.
i) According to this the quasi fluid nature of lipid enables the lateral movement of proteins within the overall bilayer.
j) A non-living rigid structure called cell wall present outside the plasma membrane of plant and fungal cell. Algae have a cell wall made of cellulose, galactans, mannans and minerals like calcium carbonate. Plant cell wall consists of cellulose, hemicelluloses, pectins and proteins.
k) The cell wall of young plant is called primary cell wall.
l) On maturity secondary cell wall formed inner to it.
m) The middle lamella is a layer of calcium pectate which holds or glues the neighboring cells.
n) The cell wall and middle lamella may traversed by plasmodesmata; the cytoplasmic connection between two adjacent cell.

A: Compare structure and function of cell wall and cell membrane.
B: The organelles that are included in the endomembrane system are:
(a) Golgi complex, Mitochondria, Ribosomes and Lysosomes
(b) Golgi complex, Endoplasmic reticulus, Mitochondria and Lysosomes
(c) Endoplasmic reticulum, Mitochondria, Ribosomes and Lysosomes
(d) Endoplasmic reticulum, Golgi complex, Lysosomes and Vacuoles
Answer - (d)

C: The plasma membrane consists mainly of
(a) phospholipids embedded in a protein bilayer

(b) proteins embedded in a phospholipid bilayer
(c) proteins embedded in a polymer of glucose molecules
(d) proteins embedded in a carbohydrate bilayer
Answer - (b)

D. Choose incorrect match

(a) Chloroplast – Thylakoid   (b) Golgi bodies - Cristae

(c) Mitochondria – Oxysome   (d) Centriole - Microtubules

Answer - (b)

Assertion Reason

For Q 1 to 10: Directions: In the following questions, a statement of assertion is followed by a statement of reason. Mark the correct choice as:
(a) If both Assertion and Reason are true and Reason is the correct explanation of Assertion.
(b) If both Assertion and Reason are true but Reason is not the correct explanation of Assertion.
(c) If Assertion is true but Reason is false.
(d) If both Assertion and Reason are false.

1. Assertion: Rudolf Virchow modified the hypothesis of cell theory given by Schleiden and Schwann. Reason : Cell theory says that all cells arise from pre-existing cells.
Answer – (b)
2. Assertion: The Golgi apparatus mainly performs the function of packaging materials.

Reason: Materials to be packed in the form of vesicles from the ER fuse with trans face of the Golgi Apparatus
Answer – (c)
3. Assertion : Plasmids are double-stranded extra chromosomal DNA.

Reason : Plasmids are possessed by eukaryotic cells.
Answer – (c)
4. Assertion: Lysosomes are capable of digesting carbohydrates, proteins, lipids and nucleic acids. Reason: Lysosomes are rich in hydrolytic enzymes like lipases, proteases and carbohydrases

Answer – (a)

5.Assertion: The exoskeleton of arthropods is made up of a complex polysaccharide called chitin

Reason: Plant cell walls are made up of Cellulose

(A). If both assertion and reason are true and reason is the correct explanation of assertion (B). If both assertion and reason are true but reason is not the correct explanation of assertions

(C). If assertion is true but reason is false (D). If both assertion and reason or false

Answer: B

6. Assertion: All enzymes are proteins Reason: RNA molecules that possess catalytic activity are called ribozymes.

(A). If both assertion and reason are true and reason is the correct explanation of assertion (B). If both assertion and reason are true but reason is not the correct explanation of assertions

(C). If assertion is true but reason is false (D). If both assertion and reason or false

Answer: B

7. Assertion: Hydrolases are enzymes which catalyze the hydrolysis of ester, peptide, Glycosidic bonds. Reason: Lyases are enzymes catalyzing the linking together of two compounds like joining of C-O, C-N, P-O etc. bonds

(A). If both assertion and reason are true and reason is the correct explanation of assertion (B). If both assertion and reason are true but reason is not the correct explanation of assertions

(C). If assertion is true but reason is false (D). If both assertion and reason or false

Answer: C

8. Assertion: Each enzyme has a substrate binding site in its molecule which forms highly reactive enzymes substrate complex. Reason: The enzyme substrate complex is long lived and dissociates into its product and unchanged enzyme.

(A). If both assertion and reason are true and reason is the correct explanation of assertion (B). If both assertion and reason are true but reason is not the correct explanation of assertions

(C). If assertion is true but reason is false (D). If both assertion and reason or false

Answer: C

9. Assertion: The living state is an equilibrium steady state to be able to perform work.

Reason: Living process is a constant effort to prevent falling into non- equilibrium

(A).If both assertion and reason are true and reason is the correct explanation of assertion (B). If both assertion and reason are true but reason is not the correct explanation of assertions

(C). If assertion is true but reason is false (D). If both assertion and reason or false

Answer: D

10. Classify amino acids on the basis of chemical nature.

A: Acidic amino acids: e.g. Glutamic acid, Aspartic acid

B. Basic amino acids: e.g. Lysine, Arginine *Neutral amino acids: e.g. Valine

Some amino acids are aromatic. E.g. tyrosine, phenyl alanine and tryptophan. Amino acids are 2 types:

C. Essential amino acids: They cannot be synthesized by the body and should be supplied through diet. E.g. Lysine, leucine, isoleucine, tryptophan etc.

D. Non-essential amino acids: They can be synthesized by the body. E.g. Glycine, alanine, serine, arginine etc.

Short Answer Type

1. Explain how lactose tolerance involves three of the four major classes of biological macromolecules.
Solution: Lactose, milk sugar, is a carbohydrate that is hydrolyzed by the enzyme lactase, a protein. The ability to make this enzyme and the regulation of when it is made are coded for in DNA, a nucleic acid.

2. What ensures the fundamental structure of a protein?
Solution: A protein's functional shape results from four levels of structure. A protein's primary structure is the sequence of amino acids in its polypeptide chain. Its secondary structure is the coiling or folding of the chain, stabilized by hydrogen bonds. The tertiary structure is the overall three-dimensional shape of a polypeptide, resulting from interactions among R groups. Proteins made of more than one polypeptide have quaternary structure.

3. "The nucleic acids DNA and RNA are information-rich polymers of nucleotides." Justify this statement.
Solution: Nucleotides are composed of a sugar, a phosphate group, and a nitrogenous base. DNA is a double helix; RNA is a single polynucleotide chain. DNA and RNA serve as the blueprints for proteins and thus control the life of a cell. DNA is the molecule of inheritance.

4. One of the most common spontaneous lesions that occurs in DNA under physiological conditions is the hydrolysis of the amino group of cytosine, converting the cytosine to uracil. What would be the effect on DNA structure of a uracil group replacing cytosine?
Solution: Since cytosine pairs with guanine and uracil pairs with adenine, the result would be a base substitution of G:C to A:T after two rounds of replication.

5. You are provided with DNA samples from two newly discovered bacterial viruses. Based on the various analytical techniques discussed in this chapter, construct a research protocol that would be useful in characterizing and contrasting the DNA of both viruses. For each technique that you include in the protocol, indicate the type of information you hope to obtain.
Solution: (1) Heat application would yield a hyperchromic shift if the DNA is double stranded. One could also get a rough estimation of the GC content from the kinetics of denaturation and the degree of sequence complexity from comparative renaturation studies.
(2) Determination of base content by hydrolysis and chromatography could be used for comparative purposes and could also provide evidence as to the strandedness of the DNA.
(3) Antibodies for Z-DNA could be used to determine the degree of left-handed structures, if present.
(4) Sequencing the DNA from both viruses would indicate sequence homology.

6. How fatty acids are esterified?

Fatty acids are esterified with glycerol through ester bond forming monoglycerides, diglycerides& triglycerides.
1 glycerol + 1 fatty acid = Monoglyceride 1 glycerol + 2 fatty acid = Diglyceride 1 glycerol + 3 fatty acid = Triglyceride
*Based on melting point, lipids (triglycerides) are 2 types:

(i)Fats: Higher melting point. (ii)Oils: Lower melting point.

7. How many different tyes of fatty acids are there?
Solution: Fatty acids are 2 types: *Saturated fatty acids: They have no double or triple bonds between carbon atoms. E.g. Palmitic acid, Stearic acid ($C_{17}H_{35}COOH$) etc. *Unsaturated Fatty acids: They have one or more C=C bonds. E.g. Oleic acid ($C_{17}H_{33}COOH$), Arachidonic acid ($C_{19}H_{31}COOH$) etc.
8. What are compound lipids and derived lipids?
Compound lipids: These are the esters of fatty acids and alcohol with additional groups. E.g. Phospholipids (fatty acids+ glycerol + phosphate). They are found in cell membranes. E.g. Lecithin.
c. Derived lipids: These are the products of hydrolysis of simple lipids and compound lipids. E.g. Cholesterol.

9. Which one is the most abundant protein in the animal world?
(A) Collagen (B) Insulin (C) Trypsin (D) Haemoglobin
Answer:(A) Collagen

10. Example of a typical homopolysaccharide is
(A) Inulin (B) Suberin (C) Lignin (D) Starch
Answer: (D) Starch

11.The proteins associated with nucleic acids are
(A) albumins (B) globulins (C) histones (D) scleroproteins
Answer: (C) histones

12.The RNA contains a base uracil in place of
(A) adenine(B) guanine(C) cytosine (D) thymine
Answer: (D) thymine

13.One of the elements not found in living organisms either free or in form of compounds is
(A)Magnesium (B) Sodium (C) Iron (D) Silicon
Answer:(D) Silicon

14.Benedict test is conducted to confirm presence of
(A)Polysaccharide (B) Reducing sugar (C) Lipid (D) Protein
Answer:: (B) Reducing sugar

15.Quaternary structure of proteins have
(A) four subunits (B) either alpha or beta forms (C) No relation to protein function (D) Depends on primary structure of individual polypeptides
Answer: (A) four subunits

16. What does "S" stand for in the 70S and 80S ribosome?
"S" is the Svedberg's unit for sedimentation coefficient. It depicts the rate of sedimentation of a cell during ultracentrifugation. Heavier the cell structure, higher is the sedimentation coefficient.

17. Where is dynein present? In microtubules of flagella

18. Briefly describe the cell theory.

Solution: Schleiden and Schwann together formulated the cell theory (1838-39). This theory, however, did not explain as to how new cells were formed. Rudolf Virchow (1855) first explained that cells divided and new cells are formed from pre-existing cells (Omnis cellula-e cellula). He modified the hypothesis of Schleiden and Schwann to give the cell theory a final shape. Cell theory as understood today is (i) All living organisms are composed of cells and products of cells. (ii) All cells arise from pre-existing cells.
19. What are the cell inclusions in a prokaryotic cell? Cell inclusions in prokaryotic cells are granules or inclusion bodies. They lie freely in the cytoplasm. For example, phosphate granule; glycogen granules, sulphur granules, gas vacuole, poly-(ii) hydroxybutyrate. There may be metachromatic granules.

20. What is a mesosome in a prokaryotic cell? Mention the functions that it performs.

a. Mesosome is a membranous structure in prokaryotic cell, which is formed by the extensions of the plasma membrane into the cell in form of vesicles, tubules and lamellae.

b. Mesosomes are equal to mitochondria in eukaryotes, as they perform aerobic cellular respiration in prokaryotes.

c. It helps in DNA replication and distribution of genetic material to daughter cells. Mesosomes also help in respiration, increase the surface area of the plasma membrane and enzymatic content and cell wall formation.

21. What are the main functions of the cell wall? The main functions of the cell wall are:

a. It gives a definite shape to the cell and protects the internal organelles.

b. It provides a framework and lends support to the plasma membrane.

c. It prevents the cell from desiccation.

d. It counteracts physically the osmotic pressure produced by the cell contents.

e. It helps in the transport of materials and metabolites in and out of the cell.

22. Write the functions of the following: a. Centromere b. Smooth ER c. Centrioles
Solution; a. Centromere: Every chromosome essentially has a primary constriction or the centromere. Two sister chromatids are joined together at the centromere. b. Smooth ER: The smooth endoplasmic reticulum is the major site for synthesis of lipid. In animal cells lipid-like steroidal hormones are synthesised in SER. c. Centrioles: The centrioles form the basal body of cilia or flagella, and spindle fibres that give rise to spindle apparatus during cell division in animal cells.

23. Helical structure of protein is stabilized by
(A) Hydrogen bonds (B) Disulphide bonds (C) Peptide bonds (D) None of these
Answer: (A) Hydrogen bonds

24. Differentiate between Rough Endoplasmic Reticulum and Smooth Endoplasmic Reticulum.

Rough Endoplasmic Reticulum (RER)	Smooth Endoplasmic Reticulum (SER)
Ribosomes are attached to their surface.	Ribosomes are not attached to their surface.
Formed of cisternae and a few tubules.	Formed of vesicles and tubules.
It participates in the protein and enzyme synthesis.	Takes part in the synthesis of glycogen, lipids, and steroids.

25. Case Study: Primary, Secondary, Tertiary and Quaternary Proteins

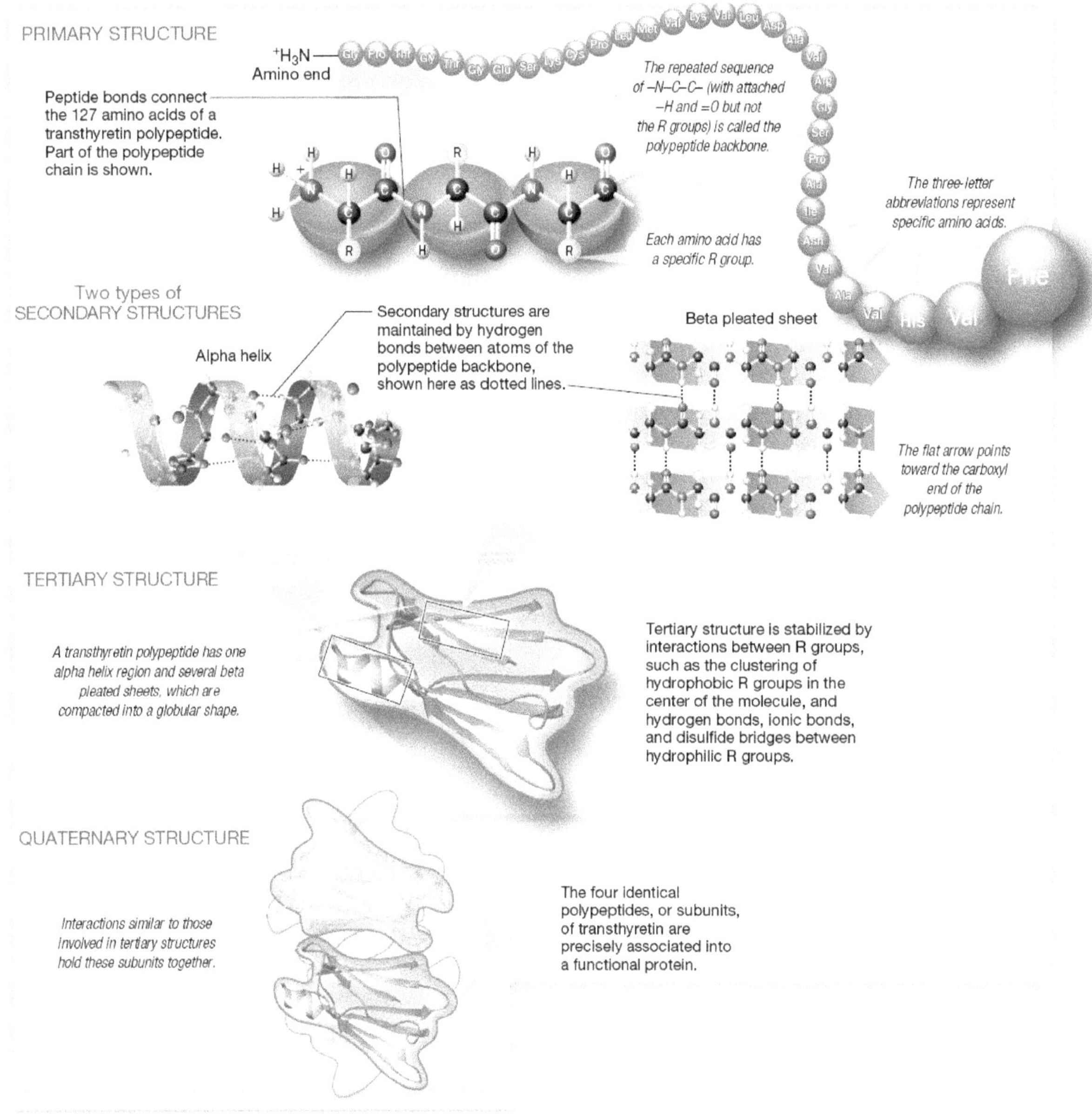

I: Write properties of four different types of proteins in outline.

Ans: Four different types of proteins are there.

Primary structure: It describes the sequence of amino acids, i.e. the positional information in a protein. Left end of the chain has first amino acid (N-terminal amino acid). Right end has last amino acid (C-terminal amino acid).

Secondary structure: Here, one or more polypeptide chains are folded in the form of a helix. It has only right handed helices. E.g. Keratin, Fibroin (silk fibre).

Tertiary structure: Here, helical polypeptide chain is further folded like a hollow woolen ball. It gives 3-D view. Tertiary structure is necessary for many biological activities of proteins. E.g. Myoglobin, enzymes.

Quaternary structure: Here, more than one polypeptide chains form tertiary structure and each chain functions as subunits of protein. E.g. Haemoglobin. It has 4 subunits (2 α subunits and 2 β subunits).

II. What are different factors that influence protein folding?

Solution: Following factors influence protein folding.

a. Little free space exists inside proteins, so the hydrophobic core resembles a hydrocarbon crystal more than an oil droplet.
b. Most charged and polar side chains are exposed on the surface, where they interact favorably with water.
c. The polar amide protons and carbonyl oxygens of the polypeptide backbone maximize their potential to form hydrogen bonds with other backbone atoms, side chain atoms, or water.
d. Most elements of secondary structure extend completely across compact domains. Consequently, most loops connecting α-helices and β-strands are on the stability. In other cases, mis-folding results in non-covalent polymerization of a protein into amyloid fibrils associated with serious diseases.

III. What determines property of an amino acid?

Solution: Each amino acid has a distinctive side chain, or R group, that determines its chemical and physical properties. Amino acids are conveniently grouped in small families according to their R groups. Side chains are distinguished by the presence of ionized groups, polar groups capable of forming hydrogen bonds and their apolar surface areas. Glycine and proline are special cases, owing to their unique effects on the polymer backbone.

Q. What are the building blocks of nucleic acids?

Solution: Nucleotides consist of three parts: (1) a base built of one or two cyclic rings of carbon and a few nitrogen atoms, (2) a five-carbon sugar, and (3) one or more phosphate groups. DNA uses four main bases: the purines adenine (A) and guanosine (G) and the pyrimidines cytosine (C) and thymine (T). In RNA, uracil (U) is found in place of thymine. Some RNA bases are chemically modified after synthesis of the polymer. The sugar of RNA is ribose, which has the aldehyde oxygen of carbon 4 cyclized to carbon 1. The DNA sugar is deoxyribose, which is similar to ribose but lacks the hydroxyl on carbon 2. In both RNA and DNA, carbon 1 of the sugar is conjugated with nitrogen 1 of a pyrimidine base or with nitrogen 9 of a purine base. The hydroxyl of sugar carbon 5 can be esterified to a chain of one or more phosphates, forming nucleotides such as adenosine monophosphate (AMP), adenosine diphosphate (ADP), and ATP.

Q. What roles do complementary base pairing play in the functioning of DNA?.

Solution: Complementary base pairing makes possible the precise replication of DNA, ensuring that genetic information is faithfully transmitted every time a cell divides. It also ensures that RNA molecules carry accurate instructions from DNA for the synthesis of proteins.

Test Paper I

1. All eukaryotic unicellular organisms belong to
(a) Monera (b) Protista (c) Fungi (d) Bacteria

2. The five kingdom classification was proposed by
(a) R.H. Whittaker (b) C. Linnaeus (c) A Roxberg (d) Virchow

3. Organisms living in salty areas are called as
(a) methanogens (b) halophiles (c) heliophytes (d) thermoacidophiles

4. Naked cytoplasm, multinucleated and saprophytic are the characteristics of
(a) Monera (b) Protista (c) Fungi (d) Slime molds

5. An association between roots of higher plants and fungi is called
(a) lichen (b) fern (c) mycorrhiza (d) BGA

6. A dikaryon is formed when
(a) meiosis is arrested (b) the two haploid cells do not fuse immediately
(c) cytoplasm does not fuse (d) None of the above

7. Contagium vivum fluidum was proposed by
(a) D.J. Ivanowsky (b) M.W. Beijernek
(c) Stanley (d) Robert Hook

8. Association between mycobiont and phycobiont are found in
(a) mycorrhiza (b) root
(c) lichens (d) BGA

9. Difference between virus and viroid is
(a) absence of protein coat in viroid, but present in virus.
(b) presence of low molecular weight RNA in virus, but absent in viroid
(c) Both (a) and (b) (d)None of the above

10. With respect to fungal sexual cycle, choose the correct sequence of events.
(a) Karyogamy, Plasmogamy and Meiosis
(b) Meiosis, Plasmogamy and Karyogamy
(c) Plasmogamy, Karyogamy and Meiosis
(d) Meiosis, Karyogamy and Plasmogamy

11. Viruses are non-cellular organisms, but replicate themselves once they infect the host cell. To which of the following kingdom do viruses belong to?
(a) Monera (b) Protista (c) Fungi (d) None of these

12. Members of phycomycetes are found in
(i) Aquatic habitats (ii) On decaying wood
(iii) Moist and damp places (iv) As obligate parasites on plants
Choose from the following options.
(a) (i) and (iv) (b) (ii) and (iii) (c) None of these (d) All of these

13. Which of the following are likely to be present in deep sea water ? [2013]
(a) Eubacteria (b) Blue-green algae (c) Saprophytic fungi (d) Archaebacteria

14. Which one of the following is true for fungi?
(a) They are phagotrophs (b) They lack a rigid cell wall
(c) They are heterotrophs (d) They lack nuclear membrane

15. Specialized cells for fixing atmospheric nitrogen in Nostoc are [NEET Kar. 2013]
(a) Akinetes (b) Heterocysts (c) Hormogonia (d) Nodules

16. Satellite RNAs are present in some [NEET Kar. 2013]
(a) Plant viruses (b) Viroids (c) Prions (d) Bacteriophages

17. Five kingdom system of classification suggested by R.H. Whittaker is not based on: [2014]
(a) Presence or absence of a well defined nucleus. (b) Mode of reproduction.
(c) Mode of nutrition. (d) Complexity of body organisation.

18. Which one of the following fungi contains hallucinogens?
(a) Morchella esculenta [2014]
(b) Amanita muscaria (c) Neurospora sp. (d) Ustilago sp.

19. Archaebacteria differ from eubacteria in: [2014]
(a) Cell membrane (b) Mode of nutrition
(c) Cell shape (d) Mode of reproduction

20. Which of the following shows coiled RNA strand and capsomeres? [2014]
(a) Polio virus (b) Tobacco mosaic virus
(c) Measles virus (d) Retrovirus

21. Viruses have: [2014]
(a) DNA enclosed in a protein coat (b) Prokaryotic nucleus
(c) Single chromosome (d) Both DNA and RNA

22. The motile bacteria are able to move by: [2014]
(a) Fimbriae (b) Flagella (c) Cilia (d) Pili

23. Which one one of the following matches is correct ? [2015 RS]
1. Alternaria Sexual Deuteromycetes reproduction absent
2. Mucor Reproduction Ascomycetes by Conjugation
3. Agaricus Parasitic fungus Basidiomycetes
4. Phytophthora Aseptate Basidiomycetes mycelium

24. True nucleus is absent in : [2015 RS]
(a) Mucor (b) Vaucheria (c) Volvox (d) Anabaena

25. Which of the following structures is not found in a prokaryotic cell? [2015 RS]
(a) Ribosome (b) Mesosome (c) Plasma membrane (d) Nuclear envelope

26. The imperfect fungi which are decomposers of litter and help in mineral cycling belong to: [2015 RS]

(a) Basidiomycetes (b) Phycomycetes (c) Ascomycetes (d) Deuteromycetes

27. The structures that help some bacteria to attach to rocks and / or host tissues are: [2015 RS]
(a) Fimbriae (b) Mesosomes (c) Holdfast (d) Rhizoids

28. Pick up the wrong statement [2015 RS]
(a) Prostista have photosynthetic and heterotrophic modes of nutrition
(b) Some fungi are edible
(c) Nuclear membrane is present Monera
(d) Cell wall is absent in Animalia

29. In which group of organisms the cell walls form two thin overlapping shells which fit together? [2015 RS]
(a) Euglenoids (b) Dinoflagellates
(c) Slime moulds (d) Chrysophytes

30. Choose the wrong statement: [2015 RS]
(a) Neurospora is used in the study of biochemical genetics
(b) Morels and truffles are poisonous mushrooms
(c) Yeast is unicellular and useful in fermentation
(d) Penicillium is multicellular and produces antibiotics

31. Which of the following are most suitable indicators of SO2 pollution in the environment? [2015 RS]
(a) Conifers (b) Algae (c) Fungi (d) Lichens

33. Which of the following statements is wrong for viroids?
(a) They lack a protein coat (b) They are smaller than viruses
(c) They cause infections (d) Their RNA is of high molecular weight

33. One of the major components of cell wall of most fungi is
(a) Chitin (b) Peptidoglycan [2016]
(c) Cellulose (d) Hemicellulose

34. Which one of the following statements is wrong? [2016]
(a) Cyanobacteria are also called blue-green algae (b) Golden algae are also called desmids
(c) Eubacteria are also called false bacteria (d) Phycomycetes are also called algal fungi

35. Chrysophytes, Euglenoids, Dinoflagellates and Slime moulds are included in the kingdom [2016]
(a) Monera (b) Protista
(c) Fungi (d) Animalia

36. Which of the following are found in extreme saline conditions ?
(a) Eubacteria (b) Cyanobacteria [2017]
(c) Mycobacteria (d) Archaebacteria

37. Which of the following components provides sticky character to the bacterial cell? [2017]
(a) Nuclear membrane (b) Plasma membrane
(c) Glycocalyx (d) Cell wall

38. Viroids differ from viruses in having; [2017]
(a) DNA molecules without protein coat (b) RNA molecules with protein coat
(c) RNA molecules without protein coat (d) DNA molecules with protein coat

39. Which among the following are the smallest living cells, known without a definite cell wall, pathogenic to plants as well as animals and can survive without oxygen? [2017]
(a) Pseudomonas (b) Mycoplasma
(c) Nostoc (d) Bacillus

Hints and Solution

1. (b) Protista is a group comprising of all unicellular eukaryotic plants and animals. The organisms included in this group are either photoautotrophs, heterotrophs or parasites.
Monera includes prokaryotic organisms like bacteria, unicellular organism.
Fungi are eukaryotic but are mostly multicellular (yeast is unicellular).

2. (a) R.H. Whittaker (1969), an American taxonomist divided organism into five kingdoms, in order to develop phylogenetic classification.
(i) Monera (ii) Protista (iii) Fungi (iv) Plantae (v) Animalia

C Linnaeus developed two kingdom classification. (i) Kingdom-Plantae (ii) Kingdom-Animalia.
and Virchow is associated with the discovery of cell theory.

3. (b) Halophiles are organisms inhabiting areas with high concentration of salts. The name halophiles means 'salt loving'.
Heliophytes are the plants that grow best in sunlight and can not survive in dark conditions.
Methanogens are the bacteria that produce methane as a metabolic byproduct under anaerobic conditions.
Thermoacidophiles are archaebacteria able to survive under strong acidic environments and high temperatures, but cannot tolerate high salt concentrations around them.

4. (d) Slime molds are saprophytic protists, that move along the dead leaves engulfing organic matter. These are multinucleated with no cell wall and have naked cytoplasm.
Monerans are prokaryotes, comprised of all bacteria.
Protists are a group of eukaryotic organisms, that bear a well defined membrane around cytoplasm, may be uninucleate or multinucleated. Their cell has well developed cell wall made of chitin.

5. (c) Mycorrhiza is a symbiotic association of fungus with the roots of a higher plants like gymnosperms and angiosperms.
The fungus is dependent on plants for food and shelter, while the plants are benefitted by the fungal hyphae as they help in absorption of water and dissolved minerals present in the soil debris and make it available to the plants.
Whereas lichens are the symbiotic association between algae and fungi. Ferns are a group of plants, belonging to pteridophytes like other vascular plants and BGA is blue-green algae with a prokaryotic cell.

6. (b) Dikaryon is a cell with two nucleus. This results when two somatic cells fuse but their nucleus do not fuse immediately. Meiosis does not result in such conditions.

7. (b) M.W. Beijerinck proposed contagium vivum fluidum which means contagious living fluid. This phrase was first used to describe virus, characteristic in escaping from the finest mesh available.

D.J. Ivanowsky was a Russian botanist who discovered the filterable nature of viruses and is one of the founders of virology.
Stanley Miller was a Jewish American chemist who experimented on origin of life on primitive earth.
Robert Hooke was the first to study and visualise cells using his primitive microscope.

8. (c) Lichens are organisms comprised of a permanent symbiotic association of a fungus and an alga.The fungal partner is called mycobiont an the algal partner is called phycobiont.
Mycorrhiza is an association of fungus with the roots of higher plants, but not with an algae, while BGA is blue green algae, a member of Monera with a prokaryotic cell structure.

9. (a) Viruses contain DNA or RNA as the genetic material and a protein coat, whereas viroids have no protein coat, but only RNA as their nucleic acid. This is the reason why viroids are carried inside viruses. e.g., hepatitis-D is a viroid carried inside the capsid of hepatitis-B virus.

10. (c) Plasmogamy mean s fusion of protoplasm while karyogamy means fusion of nucleus. These two events lead to the formation of zygote (2n) which is a diploid structure where meiosis occurs.

11. (d) In the five kingdom classification proposed by Whittaker, non-cellular organisms like viruses and viroids are not included. Viruses were not placed in the classification since they are not truly 'living' and hence, they are considered as non-cellular.

12. (d) Phycomycetes are fungi that can thrive on dead and decaying wood as saprophytes. These prefer to live in moist and damp places and need water for the movement of zoospore and sexual gametes.
Few members of phycomycetes are obligate parasites like Phytophthora infestans that causes late blight of potato and Peronospora viticola causing downy mildew of grapes.

13. (d) Archaebactera live in some of the most harsh habitats such as extreme salty areas (halophiles), hot springs (thermoacidophiles) and marshy areas (methanogens) and in deep sea water.

14. (c) Fungi lack chlorophyll, hence, they do not prepare their food by photosynthesis. They can grow where organic material is available. So, they are heterotrophs that acquire their nutrient by absorption and store in the form of glycogen.

15. (b) Heterocysts are large sized, thick-walled specialised cells which occur in terminal, intercalary or lateral position in filamentous cyanobacteria, e.g., Nostoc. They have enzyme nitrogenase and are specialised to perform biological nitrogen fixation.

16. (a) Plant viruses often contain parasites of their own, referred to as satellites. Satellite RNAs are dependent on their associated (helper) virus for both replication and encapsidation. Example—Tobacco Necrosis Virus (TNV). Viroids are infectious agents smaller than viruses.
Bacteriophages are viruses that infect the bacteria. A prion is an infectious agent that is composed primarily of protein.

17. (a) Five kingdom system of classification was proposed by R.H. Whittaker (1969). The five kin gdom classification is based on the following criteria :
• Complexity of cell structure – Prokaryotes or Eukaryotes
• Complexity of organisms body – Unicellular or Multicellular
• Mode of obtaining nutrition – Autotr oph ic or Heterotrophic
• Phylogenetic relationships

18. (b) Several mushrooms such as Amanita muscaria, Psilocybe mexicana and Panaeolus spp. secrete hallucinogenic substances like psilocybin and psilocin. These substances may destroy brain cells and power perception of in human beings.

19. (a) Archaebacteria differ from other bacteria in having a different cell wall structure. They lack peptidoglyan in cell wall and possess a monolayer of branched fatty acids attached to glycerol by ether bonds in their cell membranes.

20. (b) TMV (Tobacco Mosaic Virus) is a rod-shaped virus. The rod has a core which contains helically coiled single stranded RNA. There is a protective covering of protein called capsid around the infective part. Capsid consists of small subunits called capsomeres and has antigenic property.

21. (a) All viruses are nucleoproteins (Nucleic acid + Protein) in the structure. The nucleic acid (DNA and RNA) is the genetic material. In a particular virus either DNA or RNA is the genetic material. Both are never present in a virus. Single stranded RNA or ss RNA - Tobacco mosaic virus (TMV)

Virus envelope is known as capsid. The capsid is composed of protein subunits called capsomere.

22. (b) Motile bacteria have thin filamentous extensions on their cell wall called flagella.

23. (a) Alternaria belongs to class - Deuteromycetes, which lack sexual reproduction. Asexual reproduction takes place by conidia produced on conidiophores.

24. (d) Anabaena is a cyanobacteria which lack a true nucleus because of absence of nuclear membrane.

25. (d) Nuclear envelope is not found in a prokaryotic cell.

26. (d) Class- deuteromycetes comprises of imperfect fungi which play role in decomposition of organic wastes.

27. (a) Fimbriae assist some bacteria in attaching to rocks or host body for obtaining establishment and nutrition.

28. (c) The kingdom Monera possesses unicellular organisms (e.g - bacteria) having no nuclear membrane.

29. (d) In chrysophytes, the cell walls form two thin overlapping shells held together. The body of Diatoms appear like soap box due to overlapping shells.

30. (b) Morel and truffles are used as food and they are members of Ascomycetes fungi.

31. (d) Lichens cannot grow in places where sulphur dioxide is present in the environment.

32. (d) Viroids, the smallest known pathogens, are naked, circular, single-stranded RNA molecules that do not encode protein but autonomously replicate when introduced into host plants. Viroids only infect plants; some cause economically important diseases of crop plants, while others appear to be benign.

33. (a) A cell wall is a rigid structural layer, which provides protection and structural support to the cells. The composition of cell wall varies from one species to another. In fungi, the cell wall is composed of strong covalent linkages of chitin, glucans and glycoproteins.

Alternatively, in case of land plants, the cell wall is composed of cellulose and hemicellulose. Archean cell walls consists of peptidoglycans.

34. (c) Eubacteria are the true bacteria.

35. (b) All unicellular eukaryotic organism like diatoms, desmids (chrysophytes), euglenoids, dinoflagellates and slime mould are included in Protista.

36. (d) Archaebacteria are able to survive in harsh conditions due to the presence of branched lipid chain in cell membrane that reduces fluidity of cell membrane. It includes halophiles which are exclusively found in saline habitats.

37. (c) Sticky character of the bacterial wall is due to glycocalyx which is rich in glycoproteins.

38. (c) Viroids in nature are sub viral agents as infectious RNA particles, without protein coat.

39. (b) Mycoplasmas are smallest, prokaryotes lacking cell wall and are pleomorphic in nature. These are pathogenic to both plants and animals.

Test Paper II

1. Which statement is true for dinoflagellates flagella ?
(a) A single flagellum in the transverse groove between the cell plates.
(b) A single flagellum in the longitudinal groove between the cell plates.
(c) Two flagella, one lies longitudinally and one transversely in a furrow between the wall plates.
(d) No flagella.

2. Which is the correct option for the all given characteristics of fungi ?
I. It includes unicellular as well as multicellular fungi.
II. In multicellular forms hyphae are branched and septate.
III. Conidiophore produces conidia (spores) exogenously in chain.
IV. Sexual spores are ascopores produced endogenously in chain.
V. Fruiting body is called ascocarp.
(a) Phycomycetes (b) Sac fungi (c) Club fungi (d) Fungi imperfecti

3. Which one of the following option does not belong to Ascomycetes ?
(a) They are saprophytic, decomposer, coprophilous (growing on dung) and parasitic.
(b) They include unicellular (e.g. yeast) and multicellular forms.
(c) Their mycelium is coenocytic.
(d) Aspergillus, Claviceps, Neurospora are important members of Ascomycetes.

4. In Whittaker's five kingdom classification, eukaryotes were assigned to
(a) all the five kingdom
(b) only four of the five kingdoms
(c) only three kingdom
(d) only one kingdom

5. Mycorrhiza is
(a) a symbiotic association of plant roots and certain fungi.
(b) an association of algae with fungi.
(c) a fungus parasitie on root system of higher plants.
(d) an association of Rhizobium with the roots of leguminous plants.

6. Which one of the following statements is true about Archaea?
(a) Archaea resemble eukaryotes in all respects.
(b) Archaea have some novel features that are absent in other prokaryotes and eukaryotes.
(c) Archaea completely differ from both prokaryotes and eukaryotes.
(d) Archaea completely differ from prokaryotes.

7. Two species of Amoeba X and Y were kept in fresh water and got adapted. Species X developed contractile vacuole. When both were transferred to sea water and got adapted, both X and Y lost their contractile vacuole. From these observation we conclude that
(a) Both X and Y are marine species
(b) Species Y is marine species and X is fresh water species
(c) Species X is marine species and Y is fresh water species
(d) Both X and Y are fresh water species

8. Yeast is not included in protozoans but in fungi because
(a) it has no chlorophyll

(b) some fungal hyphae grow in such a way that they give the appearance of pseudomycelium
(c) it has eukaryotic organisation
(d) cell wall is made up of cellulose and reserve food material is starch

9. All of the following statements concerning the Actinomycetes filamentous soil bacterium Frankia are correct except that Frankia :
(a) Can induce root nodules on many plant species.
(b) Cannot fix nitrogen in the free-living state.
(c) Forms specialized vesicles in which the nitrogenase is protected from oxygen by a chemical barrier involving triterpene hopanoids.
(d) Like Rhizobium, it usually infects its host plant through root hair deformation and stimulates cell proliferation in the host's cortex.

10. Which one of the following statements about mycoplasma is wrong ?
(a) They are pleomorphic.
(b) They are sensitive to penicillin.
(c) They cause diseases in plants.
(d) They are also called PPLO.
11. In the light of recent classification of living organisms into three domains of life (bacteria, archaea and eukarya), which one of the following statements is true about archaea?
(a) Archaea resemble eukarya in all respects.
(b) Archaea have some novel features that are absent in other prokaryotes and eukaryotes.
(c) Archaea completely differ from both prokaryotes and eukaryotes.
(d) Archaea completely differ from prokaryotes.
12. Which one is the wrong pairing for the disease and its causal organism?
(a) Black rust of wheat - Puccinia graminis
(b) Loose smut of wheat - Ustilago nuda
(c) Root-knot of vegetables - Meloidogyne sp
(d) Late blight of potato - Alternaria solani
13. Virus envelope is known as:
(a) Capsid (b) Virion
(c) Nucleoprotein (d) Core

14. Which one single organism or the pair of organisms is correctly assigned to its taxonomic group?
(a) Paramoecium and Plasmodium belong to the same kingdom as that of Penicillium
(b) Lichen is a composite organism formed from the symbiotic association of an algae and a protozoan
(c) Yeast used in making bread and beer is a fungus
(d) Nostoc and Anabaena are examples of protista
15. Malignant tertian malaria is due to
(a) Plasmodium falciparum
(b) P. vivax
(c) P. ovale
(d) P. malariae

16. What is common about Trypanosoma, Noctiluca, Monocystis and Giardia ?
(a) They produced spores
(b) These are all parasites
(c) These are all unicellular protists
(d) They have flagella
17. Tobacco Mosaic Virus (TMV) has
(a) A single stranded RNA molecule
(b) A double stranded RNA molecule
(c) A single stranded DNA molecule
(d) A double stranded DNA molecule
18. Which one of the following pairs is correctly matched ?
(a) Rhizobium - Parasite in the roots of leguminous plants
(b) Mycorrhizae - Mineral uptake from soil
(c) Yeast - Production of biogas
(d) Myxomycetes - The disease ring worm
19. Which of the following are likely to be present in deep sea water ?
(a) Eubacteria (b) Blue-green algae
(c) Saprophytic fungi (d) Archaebacteria
20. Which one of the following is true for fungi?
(a) They are phagotrophs
(b) They lack a rigid cell wall
(c) They are heterotrophs
(d) They lack nuclear membrane
21. Specialized cells for fixing atmospheric nitrogen in Nostoc are
(a) Akinetes (b) Heterocysts
(c) Hormogonia (d) Nodules
22. Satellite RNAs are present in some
(a) Plant viruses (b) Viroids
(c) Prions (d) Bacteriophages
23. Aristotle used simple_______characters to classify plants into trees, shrubs and herbs.
(a) anatomical (b) biochemical
(c) morphological (d) physiological
24. Which of the following characteristic is not used by Whittaker for the classification organisms?
(a) Mode of nutrition
(b) Thallus organisation
(c) Phylogenetic relationships
(d) None of these
25. Which of the following processes are involved in the reproduction of protista?
(a) Binary fission and fragmentation
(b) Cell fusion and zygote formation
(c) Spore formation and fragmentation
(d) Budding and spore formation
26. Auxopores and hormocysts are formed, respectively, by:
(a) Some diatoms and several cyanobacteria

(b) Some cyanobacteria and diatoms
(c) Several cyanobacteria and several diatoms
(d) Several diatoms and a few cyanobacteria.
27. Which of the following statements is not true for retroviruses?
(a) DNA is not present at any stage in the life cycle of retroviruses
(b) Retroviruses carry gene for RNA-dependent DNA polymerase
(c) The genetic material in mature retroviruses is RNA
(d) Retroviruses are causative agents for certain kinds of cancer in man
28. The most thoroughly studied fact of the known bacteria-plant interactions is the
(a) cyanobacterial symbiosis with some aquatic ferns
(b) gall formation on certain angiosperms by Agrobacterium
(c) nodulation of Sesbania stems by nitrogen fixing bacteria
(d) plant growth stimulation by phosphate-solubilising bacteria
29. Viruses are no more “alive” than isolated chromosomes because
(a) both require the environment of a cell to replicate
(b) they require both RNA and DNA
(c) they both need food molecules
(d) they both require oxygen for respiration
30. The main role of bacteria in the carbon cycle involves
(a) photosynthesis
(b) chemosynthesis
(c) digestion or breakdown of organic compounds
(d) assimilation of nitrogenous compounds
31. Which of the following is not correctly matched?
(a) Root knot disease - Meloidogyne javanica
(b) Smut of bajra - Tolysporium penicillariae
(c) Covered smut of barley - Ustilago nuda
(d) Late blight of potato - Phytophthora infestans
32. Reverse transcriptase is
(a) RNA dependent RNA polymerase
(b) DNA dependent RNA polymerase
(c) DNA dependent DNA polymerase
(d) RNA dependent DNA polymerase
33. Organisms which are indicator of SO2 pollution of air
(a) Mosses (b) Lichens
(c) Mushrooms (d) Puffballs
34. Which of the following is an example of amoeboid protozoan?
(a) Trypanosoma (b) Paramoecium
(c) Gonyaulax (d) Entamoeba

35. Which of the following is a parasitic fungi on the mustard plant?
(a) Albugo (b) Puccinia
(c) Yeast (d) Ustilago

36. Which of the following is used extensively in biochemical and genetic work?
(a) Agaricus (b) Alternaria
(c) Neurospora (d) Mucor
37. Which of the following is/are example(s) of Deuteromycetes?
(a) Alternaria (b) Colletotrichum
(c) Trichoderma (d) All of these
38. Which of the following group of fungi is commonly known as imperfect fungi?
(a) Phycomycetes (b) Ascomycetes
(c) Basidiomycetes (d) Deuteromycetes
39. Bladderwort and Venus fly trap are examples of
(a) insectivorous plants (b) parasitic plants
(c) N2– rich plants (d) aquatic plants
40. The subunit of capsid is called
(a) Core (b) Nucleotide
(c) Amino acid (d) Capsomere
41. All are viral diseases except
(a) AIDS and mumps (b) Small pox and herpes
(c) Influenza (d) Cholera
42. Which option is true for A, B, C and D?
A B C D
(a) Tail fibres Head Sheath Collar
(b) Sheath Collar Head Tail fibres
(c) Head Sheath Collar Tail fibres
(d) Collar Tail fibres Head Sheath
43. Choose the correct names of the different bacteria according to their shapes.
(a) A – Cocci, B – Bacilli, C – Spirilla, D – Vibrio
(b) A – Bacilli, B – Cocci, C – Spirilla, D – Vibrio
(c) A – Spirilla, B – Bacilli, C – Cocci, D – Vibrio
(d) A – Spirilla, B – Vibrio, C – Cocci, D – Bacilli
44. Identify the following figures.
(a) A – Euglena, B – Paramecium, C – Agaricus
(b) A – Euglena, B – Planaria, C – Agaricus
(c) A – Planaria, B – Paramecium, C – Agaricus
(d) A – Euglena, B – Paramecium, C – Aspergillus
45. Match Column - I with Column - II
Column-I Column-II
A. Aerobic 1. Frankia
B. Cyanobacteria 2. Azospirillum
C. Casuarina 3. Clostridium
D. Tropical grasses 4. Aulosira
5. Azotobacter
(a) A 4; B 3; C 2; D 1
(b) A 3; B 5; C 4; D 2
(c) A 2; B 1; C 3; D 5
(d) A 5; B 4; C 1; D 2
46. Match Column - I with Column - II
Column-I Column-II

(Group Protista) (Example)
A. Chrysophytes 1. Paramecium
B. Dinoflagellates 2. Euglena
C. Euglenoids 3. Gonyaulax
D. Protozoans 4. Diatoms
(a) A 1; B 3; C 2; D 4
(b) A 2; B 4; C 3; D 1
(c) A 4; B 2; C 3; D 1
(d) A 4; B 3; C 2; D 1
47. Which of the following statement(s) is/are correct about mycoplasma ?
(1) Mycoplasma has no cell wall.
(2) Mycoplasma is the smallest living organism.
(3) Mycoplasma cannot survive without O2.
(4) Mycoplasma are pathogenic in animals and plants.
(5) True sexuality is not found in bacteria.
(6) A short of sexual reproduction by adopting a primitive DNA transfer from one bacterium to the other occurs.
Choose the answer from the following options
(a) All of these
(b) Only (3)
(c) (1), (2), (4), (5) and (6)
(d) (1), (3) and (6)

48. Which of the following is correct about the slime mould ?
(1) Its thalloid body, Plasmodium has pseudopodia for locomotion and engulfing organic matter.
(2) Duri ng un favour able con ditions Plasmodium differentiates and produces fruiting bodies, sporangium.
(3) Spores posses no true cell wall.
(4) They are dispersed by air current.
(5) Being extremely resistant, spores survive for many years.
(6) Plasmodium can grow upto several feet.
Choose the answer from the following options
(a) (1),(2), (4), (5) and (6) (b) (1),(2) and (3)
(c) (1),(2), (3) and (6) (d) (2),(3) and (6)
49. Fungi can be parasites on –
(1) Animals (2) Human being
(3) Plants
Choose the answer from the following options
(a) Only (1) (b) (2) and (3)
(c) (1) and (2) (d) All of these
50. Which of the following statments are true about virues ?
(1) Viruses are obligate parasites
(2) Viruses can multiply only when they are inside the living cells
(3) Viruses cannot pass through bacterial proof filters
(4) Viruses are made up of protein + DNA or RNA (never both DNA and RNA)
Choose the answer from the following options
(a) (1) and (2) (b) (1), (2) and (3)
(c) (1), (2) and (4) (d) All of these__

Answer Key and Hints

1. (c) 2. (b) 3. (c) 4. (b) 5. (a) 6. (b) 7. (c) 8. (b)

9. (b) Frankia, is a nitrogen fixing mycelial bacterium which is associated symbiotically (and not free living) with the root nodules of several non legume plants.

10. (b) While working at the Rockefeller Institute, Brown reported isolation of a PPLO from human arthritic joint tissue in 1938. In discussing the significance of this observation, Brown reported successful treatment of arthritic patients in 1949 with a new antibiotic called aureomycin (Clark, 1997).

11. (b) A domain of prokaryotic organisms containing the archaebacteria including the methanogens, which produce methane; the thermoacidophilic bacteria, which live in extremely hot and acidic environments, & the halophilic bacteria, which can only function at high salt concentrations are abundant in the world's oceans.

12. (d) Late blight is caused by the fungus Phytophthora infestans. Late blight appears on potato or tomato leaves as pale green, water-soaked spots, often beginning at leaftips or edges.

13. (a) Virus envelope is known as capsid. The capsid is composed of protein subunits called capsomere.

14. (c) Saccharomyces cervisiae is a yeast used in making bread (Baker's yeast) and commercial production of ethanol. Paramoecium & Plasmodium are of animal kingdom while Pencillium is a fungi. Lichen is composite organism formed from the symbiotic association of an algae and a fungus. Nostoc & Anabaena are examples of kingdom monera.

15. (a) 16. (c) 17. (a) 18. (b)

19. (d) Archaebactera live in some of the most harsh habitats such as extreme salty areas (halophiles), hot springs (thermoacidophiles) and marshy areas (methanogens) and in deep sea water.

20. (c) Fungi lack chlorophyll, hence, they do not prepare their food by photosynthesis. They can grow where organic material is available. So, they are heterotrophs that acquire their nutrient by absorption and store in the form of glycogen.

21. (b) Heterocysts are large sized, thick-walled specialised cells which occur in terminal, intercalary or lateral position in filamentous cyanobacteria, e.g., Nostoc. They have enzyme nitrogenase and specialised to perform biological nitrogen fixation.

22. (a) Plant viruses often contain parasites of their own, referred to as satellites. Satellite RNAs are dependent on their associated (helper) virus for both replication and encapsidation. Example—Tobacco Necrosis Virus (TNV).

23. (c) 24. (d) 25. (b)

26. (d) Binary fission in diatoms reduces the size of most daughters which is corrected through the development of auxospores.
In some filamentous cyanobacterial forms unisexual reproduction occurs by hormogonia (hormocysts). They are identified by presence of biconcave (one disk or separati on disc between two adjacent cells e.g. Oscillatoria).

27. (a) Retroviruses have RNA as the genetic material and hence they exhibit reverse transcription whereby DNA is synthesized on RNA template. They have reverse transcriptase as the enzyme.

28. (b) This phenomenon has been successfully used in genetic engineering to produce disease resistant varieties of plants.

29. (a) Viruses can live only inside the host cell, using their machinery for its own metabolism.

30. (a) These are archaebacteria which can tolerate high temperature.

31. (c) Phytoalexins are non-specific antibiotic substances produced by plants in response to infection by a fungus.

32. (b) All viruses are nucleoprotein (Nucleic acid + Protein) in their structure. The nucleic acid (DNA and RNA) is genetic material. In a particular virus either DNA or RNA is the genetic material. Both are never present in a virus.
Hence, viruses contains:
(i) Double stranded DNA (ds DNA) - Hepatitis B
(ii) Single stranded DNA (ss DNA) - Coliphage
(iii) Double stranded RNA (ds RNA) - Reo virus, wound Tumor virus
(iv) Single stranded RNA (ss RNA) - Tobacco mosaic virus (TMV)

33. (b) 34. (d) 35. (a) 36. (c) 37. (d) 38. (d) 39. (a) 40. (d) 41. (d) 42. (c) 43. (a) 44. (a)
45. (d) 46. (d) 47. (c) 48. (a) 49. (d) 50. (c)

Test Paper III

1. As we go from species to kingdom in a taxonomic hierarchy, the number of common characteristics
(a) will decrease (b) will increase (c) remain same (d) may increase or decrease
2. Which of the following 'suffixes' used for units of classification in plants indicates a taxonomic category of 'family'?
(a) – Ales (b) – Onae (c) –Aceae (d) – Ae
3. The term 'systematics' refers to
(a) identification and study of organ systems
(b) identification and preservation of plants and animals
(c) diversity of kinds of organisms and their relationship
(d) study of habitats of organisms and their classification
4. Genus represents
(a) an individual plant or animal (b) a collection of plants or animals
(c) group of closely related species of plants or animals (d) None of the above
5. The taxonomic unit 'Phylum' in the classification of animals is equivalent to which hierarchial level in classfication of plants.
(a) Class (b) Order (c) Division (d) Family
6. Botanical gardens and Zoological parks have
(a) collection of endemic living species only (b) collection of exotic living species only
(c) collection of endemic and exotic living species
(d) collection of only local plants and animals
7. Taxonomic key is one of the taxonomic tools in the identification and classification of plants and animals. It is used in the preparation of
(a) monographs (b) flora (c) Both (a) and (b) (d) None of these
8. All living organisms are linked to one another because
(a) they have common genetic material of the same type
(b) they share common genetic material but to varying degrees
(c) all have common cellular organisation (d) All of the above
9. Which of the following is a defining characteristic of living organisms?
(a) Growth (b) Ability to make sound
(c) Reproduction (d) Response to external stimuli
10. Match the following and choose the correct option.

Column I	Column II
A. Family	1. Tuberosum
B. Kingdom	2. Polymoniales
C. Order	3. Solanum
D. Species	4. Plantae
E. Genus	5. Solanaceae

Options

	A	B	C	D	E
(a)	4	3	5	2	1
(b)	5	4	2	1	3
(c)	4	5	2	1	3
(d)	5	3	2	1	4

11. Which one of the following is not a correct statement ? [2013]
(a) Botanical gardens have collection of living plants for reference.
(b) A museum has collection of photographs of plants and animals
(c) Key is taxonomic aid for identification of specimens.
(d) Herbarium houses dried, pressed and preserved plant specimens.
12. The common characteristics between tomato and potato will be maximum at the level of their [NEET Kar. 2013]
(a) Genus (b) Family (c) Order (d) Division
13. Nomenclature is governed by certain universal rules. Which one of the following is contrary to the rules of nomenclature? [2016]
(a) Biological names can be written in any language
(b) The first word in a biological name represents the genus name, and the second is a specific epithet
(c) The names are written in Latin and are italicised
(d) When written by hand, the names are to be underlined
14. It is much easier for a small animal to run uphill than for a large animal, because [2016]
(a) it is easier to carry a small body weight.
(b) smaller animals have a higher metabolic rate.
(c) small animals have a lower O2 requirement.
(d) the efficiency of muscles in large animals is less than in the small animals.

Answer Key/ Hints

1. (a) Lower the taxa, more are the number of shared characteristics within the members of the taxon. So, the lowest taxon shares the maximum number of morphological similarities. As we move towards the higher hierarchy, *i.e.*, class, kingdom, similarities decrease.

2. (c) The names of family, taxon in plants always end with suffix aceae, e.g., Solanaceae, Cannaceae and Poaceae. Suffix **ales** is used for taxon '**order**' while suffix **ae** is used for '**class**' and suffixes **onae** are not used in any of the taxons.

3. (c) The word systematics has been derived from the Latin word 'Systema' meaning systematic arrangement of organisms. Linnaeus used 'Systema Naturae' as a title of his publication. It describes the diversity of organisms and their relationship at every level of organisation.

4. (c) **Genus** comprises of a group of closely related species with more characters in common as compared to species of other genera.

5. (c) Division is inclusive of classes with few similar characters of a group of organism. It is equivalent to 'Phylum' used in case of animals.

6. (c) **Botanical gardens** and **Zoological parks** are used to restore depleted population, reintroduce species and restore degraded habitats of both exotic and endemic living species.

7. (c) **Taxonomic keys** are tools that help in identifying of an organism based on the characters. It includes both monograph and flora.

8. (b) All living organisms possess a common genetic material, DNA, but with variations, *e.g.*, DNA in bacteria is circular while in highly evolved eukaryotic cells as plants and animals, DNA is a long double stranded helix.

9. (d) Besides growth and reproduction response to an external stimuli or to the environment in which an organism dwells is the most important characteristic of any living organism. Howevers, virus (which is not included under living organisms) also show growth and reproduction. Thus,
these options are not true.

10. (b) The correct options matching with the columns represent the taxonomic classification of the plant potato :
Family - Solanaceae
Kingdom - Plantae
Order - Polymoniales
Genus - *Solanum*
Species - *tuberosum*

11. (b) **Museum** – Biological museums are generally set up in educational institutes such as schools and colleges. Museums have collections of preserved plant and animal specimens for study and reference. Specimens are preserved in the containers or jars in preservative solutions. Plant and animal specimens may also be preserved as dry specimens. Insects are preserved in insect boxes after collections, killing and pinning. Larger animals like birds and mammals are usually stuffed and preserved. Museums often have collections of skeletons of animals too.

12. (b) Families are characterised on the basis of both vegetative and reproductive features of plant species. Tomato *(Lycopersicon esculentum)* and potato *(Solanum tuberosum)* belong to the same family Solanaceae.

13. (a) Binomial nomenclature is a formal system of naming species of living things by giving each a name composed of two parts, both of which use Latin grammatical forms, although they can be based on words from other languages.

14. (b) Basal metabolic rate is inversely proportional to body size. So smaller animals have a higher metabolic rate. Hence production of energy is more.

***

Test Paper IV

Q 1. Consider the expression "central dogma," which refers to the flow of genetic information from DNA to RNA to protein. Is the word "dogma" appropriate in this context?

Q 2. In the electron micrograph, as displayed in the given figure, are the RNA polymerase molecules moving from right to left or from left to right? Why are the RNA transcripts so much shorter than the DNA segments (genes) that encode them?

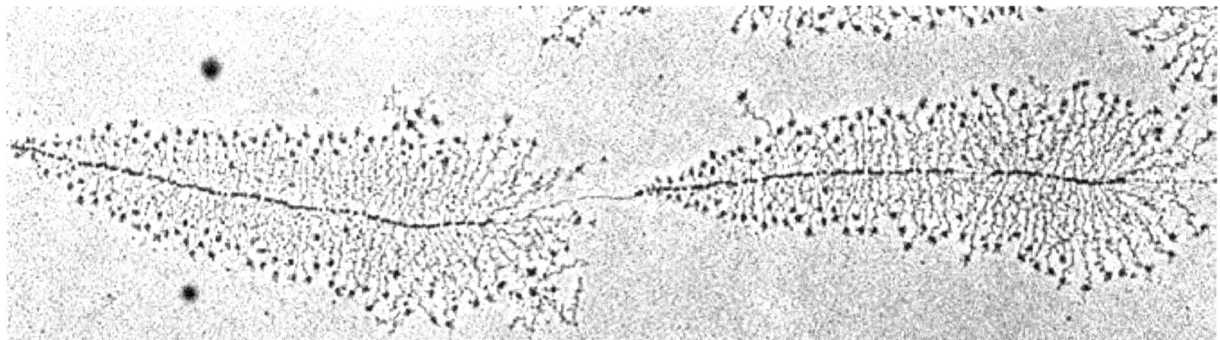

Fig: The micrograph shows many molecules of RNA polymerase simultaneously transcribing two adjacent ribosomal genes on a single DNA molecule. Molecules of RNA polymerase are barely visible as a series of tiny dots along the spine of the DNA molecule; each polymerase has an RNA transcript (a short, fine thread) radiating from it. The RNA molecules being transcribed from the two ribosomal genes—ribosomal RNAs (rRNAs)—are not translated into protein, but are instead used directly as components of ribosomes, macromolecular machines made of RNA and protein.]

Q 3. Could the RNA polymerase used for transcription be used as the polymerase that makes the RNA primer required for DNA replication?

Q 4. In a clever experiment performed in 1962, a cysteine already attached to its tRNA was chemically converted to an alanine. These "hybrid" tRNA molecules were then added to a cell free translation system from which the normal cysteine-tRNAs had been removed. When the resulting protein was analyzed, it was found that alanine had been inserted at every point in the polypeptide chain where cysteine was supposed to be. Discuss what this experiment tells you about the role of aminoacyl tRNA synthetases during the normal translation of the genetic code.

Q 5. A sequence of nucleotides in a DNA strand—5′-TT AACGG CTTTTTT C-3′— was used as a template to synthesize an mRNA that was then translated into protein. Predict the C-terminal amino acid and the N-terminal amino acid of the resulting polypeptide. Assume that the mRNA is translated without the need for a start codon.

Answer 1: Perhaps the best answer was given by Francis Crick himself, who coined the term in the mid-1950s: "I called this idea the central dogma for two reasons, I suspect. I had already used the obvious word hypothesis in the sequence hypothesis, which proposes that genetic information is encoded in the sequence of the DNA

bases, and in addition I wanted to suggest that this new assumption was more central and more powerful.... As it turned out, the use of the word dogma caused more trouble than it was worth. Many years later Jacques Monod pointed out to me that I did not appear to understand the correct use of the word dogma, which is a belief that cannot be doubted. I did appreciate this in a vague sort of way but since I thought that all religious beliefs were without serious
foundation, I used the word in the way I myself thought about it, not as the world does, and simply applied it to a grand hypothesis that, however plausible, had little direct experimental support at the time." (Francis Crick, What Mad Pursuit: A Personal View of Scientific Discovery. Basic Books, 1988.)

Answer 2: Actually, the RNA polymerases are not moving at all in the micrograph, because they have been fixed and coated with metal to prepare the sample for viewing in the electron microscope. However, before they were fixed, they were moving from left to right, as indicated by the gradual lengthening of the RNA transcripts. The RNA transcripts are shorter because they begin to fold up (i.e., to acquire a three-dimensional structure) as they are synthesized, whereas the DNA is an extended double helix.

Answer 3. At first glance, the catalytic activities of an RNA polymerase used for transcription could replace the DNA primase. Upon further reflection, however, there are some serious problems. (1) The RNA polymerase used to make primers would need to initiate every few hundred bases, which is much more often than promoters are spaced on the DNA. Initiation would therefore need to occur in a promoter-independent fashion or many more promoters would have to be present in the DNA, both of which would be problematic for the control of transcription. (2) Similarly, the RNA primers used in DNA replication are much shorter than mRNAs. The RNA polymerase would therefore need to terminate much more frequently than during transcription. Termination would need to occur spontaneously, i.e., without requiring a terminator sequence in the DNA, or many more terminators would need to be present. Again, both of these scenarios would be problematic for the control of transcription.
Although it might be possible to overcome this problem if special control proteins became attached to RNA polymerase during replication, the problem has been solved during evolution by using separate enzymes with specialized properties. Some small DNA viruses, however, do utilize the host RNA polymerase to make DNA primers for their replication.

Answer 4: This experiment demonstrates that the ribosome does not check the amino acid that is attached to a tRNA. Once an amino acid has been coupled to a tRNA, the ribosome will "blindly" incorporate that amino acid into the position according to the match between the codon and anticodon. We can therefore conclude that a significant part of the correct reading of the genetic code, i.e., the matching of a codon in an mRNA with the correct amino acid, is performed by the synthetase enzymes that correctly match tRNAs and amino acids.

Answer 5: The mRNA will have a 5′-to-3′ polarity, opposite to that of the DNA strand that serves as the template. Thus the mRNA sequence will read 5′-GAAAAAAGCCGUUAA-3′. The N-terminal amino acid coded for by GAA is glutamic acid. UAA specifies a stop codon, so the C-terminal amino acid is coded for by CGU and is an arginine. Note that the convention in describing the sequence of a gene is to give the sequence of the DNA strand that is not used as a template for RNA synthesis; this sequence is the same as that of the RNA transcript, with T written in place of U.

Test Paper V

Q 1. Discuss the following: "During the evolution of life on Earth, RNA lost its glorious position as the first self-replicating catalyst. Its role now is as a mere messenger in the information flow from DNA to protein."

Q 2. Which of the following statements are correct? Explain your answers.
A. An individual ribosome can make only one type of protein.
B. All mRNAs fold into particular three-dimensional structures that are required for their translation.
C. The large and small subunits of an individual ribosome always stay together and never exchange partners.
D. Ribosomes are cytoplasmic organelles that are encapsulated by a single membrane.
E. Because the two strands of DNA are complementary, the mRNA of a given gene can be synthesized using either strand as a template.
F. An mRNA may contain the sequence ATTGACCCCGGTCAA.
G. The amount of a protein present in a cell depends on its rate of synthesis, its catalytic activity, and its rate of degradation.

Q 3. The Lacheinmal protein is a hypothetical protein that causes people to smile more often. It is inactive in many chronically unhappy people. The mRNA isolated from a number of different unhappy individuals in the same family was found to lack an internal stretch of 173 nucleotides that is present in the Lacheinmal mRNA isolated from happy members of the same family. The DNA sequences of the Lacheinmal genes from the happy and unhappy family members were determined and compared. They differed by a single nucleotide substitution, which lay in an intron. What can you say about the molecular basis of unhappiness in this family?

Q 4. "The bonds that form between the anticodon of a tRNA molecule and the three nucleotides of a codon in mRNA are ______." Complete this sentence with each of the following options and explain why each of the resulting statements is correct or incorrect.
A. Covalent bonds formed by GTP hydrolysis
B. H ydrogen bonds that form when the tRNA is at the A site C. Broken by the translocation of the ribosome along the mRNA

Q 5. List the ordinary, dictionary definitions of the terms replication, transcription, and translation. By their side, list the special meaning each term has when applied to the living cell.

Answer 1: The first statement is probably correct: RNA is thought to have been the first self-replicating catalyst and, in modern cells, is no longer self-replicating. We can debate, however, whether this represents a "loss." RNA now serves many roles in the cell: as messengers, as adaptors for protein synthesis, as primers for DNA replication, and as catalysts for some of the most fundamental reactions, especially RNA splicing and protein synthesis.

Answer 2:
A. False. Ribosomes can make any protein that is specified by the particular mRNA that they are translating. After translation, ribosomes are released from the mRNA and can then start translating a different mRNA. It is true, however, that a ribosome can only make one type of protein at a time.

B. False. mRNAs are translated as linear polymers; there is no requirement that they have any particular folded structure. In fact, such structures that are formed by mRNA can inhibit its translation, because the ribosome has to unfold the mRNA in order to read the message it contains.
C. False. Ribosomal subunits exchange partners after each round of translation. After a ribosome is released from an mRNA, its two subunits dissociate and enter a pool of free small and large subunits from which new ribosomes assemble around a new mRNA.
D. False. Ribosomes are cytoplasmic organelles, but they are not individually enclosed in a membrane.
E. False. The position of the promoter determines the direction in which transcription proceeds and therefore which DNA strand is used as the template. Transcription in the opposite direction would produce an mRNA with a completely different (and probably meaningless) sequence.
F. False. RNA contains uracil but not thymine.
G. False. The level of a protein depends on its rate of synthesis and degradation but not on its catalytic activity.

Answer 3: Because the deletion in the Lacheinmal mRNA is internal, it is likely that the deletion arises from an mRNA splicing defect. The simplest interpretation is that the Lacheinmal gene contains a 173-nucleotide-long exon (labeled "E2" in Figure A7–8), and that this exon is lost during the processing of the mutant precursor mRNA (pre-mRNA). This could occur, for example, if the mutation changed the 3′ splice site in the preceding intron ("I1") so that it was no longer recognized by the splicing machinery. The snRNP would search for the next available 3′ splice site, which is found at the 3′ end of the next intron ("I2"), and the splicing reaction would therefore remove E2 together with I1 and I2, resulting in a shortened mRNA. The mRNA is then translated into a defective protein, resulting in the Lacheinmal deficiency. Because 173 nucleotides do not amount to an integral number of codons, the lack of this exon in the mRNA will shift the reading frame at the splice junction. Therefore, the Lacheinmal protein would be made correctly only through exon E1. As the ribosome begins translating sequences in exon E3, it will be in a different reading frame and therefore will produce a protein sequence that is unrelated to the Lacheinmal sequence normally encoded by exon E3. Most likely, the ribosome will soon encounter a stop codon, which in RNA sequences that do not code for protein would be expected to occur on average about once in every 21 codons (there are 3 stop codons in the 64 codons of the genetic code).

Answer 4: A. Incorrect. The bonds are not covalent, and their formation does not require input of energy.
B. Correct. The aminoacyl-tRNA enters the ribosome at the A site and forms hydrogen bonds with the codon in the mRNA.
C. Correct. As the ribosome moves along the mRNA, the tRNAs that have donated their amino acid to the growing polypeptide chain are ejected from the ribosome and the mRNA. The ejection takes place two cycles after the tRNA first enters the ribosome
Answer 5:
Replication. Dictionary definition: the creation of an exact copy; molecular biology definition: the act of duplicating DNA.
Transcription. Dictionary definition: the act of writing out a copy, especially from one physical form to another; molecular biology definition: the act of copying the information stored in DNA into RNA.
Translation. Dictionary definition: the act of putting words into a different language; molecular biology definition: the act of polymerizing amino acids into a defined linear sequence using the information provided by the linear sequence of nucleotides in mRNA. (Note that "translation" is also used in a quite different sense, both in ordinary language and in scientific contexts, to mean a movement from one place to another.)

Test Paper VI

Q 1. In an alien world, the genetic code is written in pairs of nucleotides. How many amino acids could such a code specify? In a different world, a triplet code is used, but the sequence of nucleotides is not important; it only matters which nucleotides are present. How many amino acids could this code specify? Would you expect to encounter any problems translating these codes?

Q 2. One remarkable feature of the genetic code is that amino acids with similar chemical properties often have similar codons. Thus codons with U or C as the second nucleotide tend to specify hydrophobic amino acids. Can you suggest a possible explanation for this phenomenon in terms of the early evolution of the protein-synthesis machinery?

Q 3. A mutation in DNA generates a UGA stop codon in the middle of the mRNA coding for a particular protein. A second mutation in the cell's DNA leads to a single nucleotide change in a tRNA that allows the correct translation of the protein; that is, the second mutation "suppresses" the defect caused by the first. The altered tRNA translates the UGA as tryptophan. What nucleotide change has probably occurred in the mutant tRNA molecule? What consequences would the presence of such a mutant tRNA have for the translation of the normal genes in this cell?

Q 4. The charging of a tRNA with an amino acid can be represented by the following equation:

amino acid + tRNA + ATP → aminoacyl-tRNA + AMP + PPi

where PPi is pyrophosphate. In the aminoacyl-tRNA, the amino acid and tRNA are linked with a high-energy covalent bond; a large portion of the energy derived from the hydrolysis of ATP is thus stored in this bond and is available to drive peptide bond formation at the later stages of protein synthesis. The free-energy change of the charging reaction shown in the equation is close to zero and therefore would not be expected to favor attachment of the amino acid to tRNA. Can you suggest a further step that could drive the reaction to completion?

Q 5. A. T he average molecular weight of a protein in the cell is about 30,000 daltons. A few proteins, however, are much larger. The largest known polypeptide chain made by any cell is a protein called titin (made by mammalian muscle cells), and it has a molecular weight of 3,000,000 daltons. Estimate how long it will take a muscle cell to translate an mRNA coding for titin (assume the average molecular weight of an amino acid to be 120, and a translation rate of two amino acids per second for eukaryotic cells).

B. Protein synthesis is very accurate: for every 10,000 amino acids joined together, only one mistake is made. What is the fraction of average-sized protein molecules and of titin molecules that are synthesized without any errors?

(Hint: the probability P of obtaining an error-free protein is given by $P = (1 - E)^n$, where E is the error frequency and n the number of amino acids.)

C. The molecular weight of all eukaryotic ribosomal proteins combined is about 2.5 × 106 daltons. Would it be advantageous to synthesize them as a single protein?

D. T ranscription occurs at a rate of about 30 nucleotides per second. Is it possible to calculate the time required to synthesize a titin mRNA from the information given here?

Answer 1. With four different nucleotides to choose from, a code of two nucleotides could specify 16 different amino acids (= 42), and a triplet code in which the position of the nucleotides is not important could specify 20 different amino acids (= 4 possibilities of 3 of the same bases + 12 possibilities of 2 bases the same and one different + 4 possibilities of 3 different bases). In both cases, these maximal amino acid numbers would need to be reduced by at least 1, because of the need to specify translation stop codons. It is relatively easy to envision how a doublet code could be translated by a mechanism similar to that used in our world by providing tRNAs with only two relevant bases in the anticodon loop. It is more difficult to envision how the nucleotide composition of a stretch of three nucleotides could be translated without regard to their order, because base-pairing can then no longer be used: AUG, for example, will not base-pair with the same anticodon as UGA.

Answer 2. It is likely that in early cells the matching between codons and amino acids was less accurate than it is in present-day cells. The feature of the genetic code described in the question may have allowed early cells to tolerate this inaccuracy by allowing a blurred relationship between sets of roughly similar codons and roughly similar amino acids. One can easily imagine how the matching between codons and amino acids could have become more accurate, step by step, as the translation machinery evolved into that found in modern cells.

Answer 3. The codon for Trp is 5′-UGG-3′. Thus a normal Trp-tRNA contains the sequence 5′-CCA-3′ as its anticodon. If this tRNA contains a mutation so that its anticodon is changed to UCA, it will recognize a UGA codon and lead to the incorporation of a tryptophan residue instead of causing translation to stop. Many other protein-encoding sequences, however, contain UGA codons as their natural stop sites, and these stops would also be affected by the mutant tRNA. Depending on the competition between the altered tRNA and the normal translation release factors, some of these proteins would be made with additional amino acids at their C-terminal end. The additional lengths would depend on the number of codons before the ribosomes encounter a non- UGA stop codon in the mRNA in the reading frame in which the protein is translated.

Answer 4. One effective way of driving a reaction to completion is to remove one of the products, so that the reverse reaction cannot occur. ATP contains two high-energy bonds that link the three phosphate groups. In the reaction shown, PPi is released, consisting of two phosphate groups linked by one of these high-energy bonds. Thus PPi can be hydrolyzed with a considerable gain of free energy, and thereby can be efficiently removed. This happens rapidly in cells, and reactions that produce and further hydrolyze PPi are therefore virtually irreversible

Answer 5. A. A titin molecule is made of 25,000 (3,000,000/120) amino acids. It therefore takes about 3.5 hours [(25,000/2)× (1/60) × (1/60)] to synthesize a single molecule of titin in muscle cells.

B. Because of its large size, the probability of making a titin molecule without any mistakes is only 0.08 [= (1 – 10–4)25,000]; i.e., only 8 in 100 titin moleculessynthesized are free of mistakes. In contrast, over 97% of newly synthesized proteins of average size are made correctly.

C. The error rate limits the sizes of proteins that can be synthesized accurately. Similarly, if a eukaryotic ribosomal protein were synthesized as a single molecule, a large portion (87%) of this hypothetical giant ribosomal protein would be expected to contain at least one mistake. It is therefore more advantageous to make ribosomal proteins individually, because in this way only a small proportion of each type of protein will be defective, and these few bad molecules can be individually eliminated by proteolysis to ensure that there are no defects in the ribosome as a whole.

D. To calculate the time it takes to transcribe a titin mRNA, you would need to know the size of its gene, which is likely to contain many introns. Transcription of the exons alone (25,000 × 3 = 75,000 nucleotides) requires about 42 minutes [(75,000/30) × (1/60)]. Because introns can be quite large, the time required to transcribe the entire gene is likely to be considerably longer.

Test Paper VII

Biological Membrane

Difference:

Semipermeable Membrane	Selectively Permeable Membrane
1: Solute cannot pass through; only solvent can pass through it.	1: Allows passage of solute and to solvent up to a considerable amount.
2: Helpful in dialysis, maintenance of turgidity and measurement of osmotic potential.	2: Helps in retaining ability of the cell to absorb solute.
3: Generally absent in biological system. Phospholipid bilayer without involvement of protein is the best example of this type of membrane.	3: Plasma membrane of a living cell is the best example.
Examples: egg membrane, parchment membrane, and tonoplast.	Example: Membrane of cell and other membrane bound organelles.

Technical Note A:[6]

Semipermeable membrane is a type of biological and polymeric membrane that will allow certain molecules to pass through it by reverse osmosis. The rate of passage depends on the pressure, and temperature of the molecules on both side, as well as the permeability of the membrane to each solute. Depending on the membrane and the solute, permeability may also depend on solubility, and properties. How the membrane is constructed to be selective in its permeability will determine the rate and the permeability.

Semipermeable membrane or Biological membranes are selectively permeable, with the passage of molecules controlled by facilitated diffusion, passive transport regulated through proteins embedded in the membrane.

An example of a semi-permeable membrane is the lipid bilayer, which is based on the plasma membrane that surrounds all biological cells. A group of phospholipids arranged into a double layer, the phospholipid bilayer is a semipermeable membrane that is very specific in its permeability. The hydrophilic phosphate heads are in the outside layer and exposed to the water content outside and within the cell. The main function of a biological semi-permeable membrane in cells is to separate the cell from the environment while allowing for the controlled transport of molecules in and out of the cell.

A biological semipermeable membrane allows some molecules. It is depending on the attributes of the molecules including size or quantity. An example of a semipermeable membrane is a cell membrane.

By keeping the inside of a cell at low concentration, it can keep absorbing the molecules it needs. This is used by most cells, which includes the roots of plants, which use osmosis to absorb the water.

[6] *Received: 01-Apr-2022, Manuscript No. JMST-22-16619; Editor assigned: 04-Apr-2022, Pre QC No. JMST-22-16619 (PQ); Reviewed: 19-Apr-2022,*
QC No. JMST-22-16619; Revised: 26-Apr-2022, Manuscript No. JMST-22-16619 (R); Published: 06-May-2022, DOI: 10.35248/2155-9589.22.12.273.
Citation:

The membrane is selectively permeable because materials do not cross it indiscriminately. Some molecules including hydrocarbons and oxygen can cross the membrane. The cell membrane is selectively permeable. It is made of a phospholipid bilayer, along with other various lipids, and carbohydrates. It is a barrier that will allow some molecules to pass through while blocking the passage of different molecules.

A semipermeable barrier is essentially acts as a filter. Different types of semipermeable membranes can block out different sized molecules and it can be made out of biological material.

A semipermeable membrane may also be known as a deferentially permeable membrane. Diffusion is generally occurs when molecules in a high concentration move to the other side of the membrane where there is a low concentration of those molecules. There are different types of biological semipermeable membranes, both organic and inorganic.

An example of a biological semipermeable membrane is kidney tissue. Kidneys allow for molecules to pass through them while blocking others which include human waste products. Synthetic versions of a semipermeable membrane are those used for water filtration.

Synthetic semipermeable membranes are usually polymers, but they can be made out of different materials. Artificial membranes have been used in the laboratory to show the effects of osmolality on cells. Much like cell membranes, a biological semipermeable membrane created artificially will only allow water pass, while restricting the solutes dissolved in the solution. If solution is connected through a semipermeable membrane, water will flow between them, but the solutes can be restricted to the side of the membrane they started on.

There are three types of permeability: effective permeability, absolute permeability, and relative permeability. Effective permeability is the ability of fluids to pass through pores of rocks in the presence of different fluids in the medium. When referring to membrane permeability there is found in living things: semipermeable and selectively permeable both allow molecules and water to move in and out of the cell, as needed to maintain homeostasis.

Technical Note B: Is biological membrane semipermeable?

Solution: The cell membrane is made of two layers of phospholipids (a phospholipid bilayer). Phospholipids are unique because they are amphipathic, meaning they have both hydrophobic parts and hydrophilic parts. The hydrophobic tails are fatty acid chains and are buried inside the membrane. The hydrophilic heads are made of a phosphate group and glycerol molecule, and they face the aqueous environment. The phospholipids are packed tightly together. This prevents the movement of molecules through the membrane unless they are extremely small, or hydrophobic. Molecules that fit this criterion can move through the membrane using diffusion, where molecules move from high concentration to low concentration directly through the membrane. Some examples of molecules that can move through the cell membrane using diffusion include: Oxygen, Carbon dioxide, Steroid hormones, such as estrogen Perspective.

Note C: What is membrane permeability? Briefly describe different types of membrane permeability.

Solution: Permeability of a membrane refers to that power of a membrane by virtue of which it allows materials to pass through it.

Depending on this property membrane can be categorise in to three types:

i) Impermeable- those who do not allow anything to pass through, like polythene.

ii) Semi-permeable – allow only the solvent to pass through. This type of membrane does not allow the solute part to pass through it. Recalled the osmosis process where a semipermeable membrane is getting involved. Plasma membrane of a cell is a semi-permeable membrane.

iii) Selectively permeable –this type of membrane allow the passage of only some selective materials through it, not all. Depending on the requirement it may allow both solvent and solute. So, plasma membrane is no doubt a semi-permeable membrane but more precisely it is a selectively permeable membrane. Phospholipid bilayer of this membrane is semipermeable. Involvement of different types of proteins in it makes it selectively permeable.

Integral Protein vs Trans-membrane proteins

Integral Protein	Trans-membrane Protein
1: All cannot be considered as trans—membrane proteins. Not all integral membrane proteins contain trans-membrane helices.	1: All are integral proteins. All proteins contain trans-membrane helices.
2: Permanently anchored to lipid bilayer. Some of these proteins may or may not traverse the lipid bilayer.	2: Stretches of nonpolar amino acids that span or traverse the membrane from one leaflet to the other.
3: May or may not take part in the formation of channel protein of plasma membrane. They can execute a variety of critical functions, sensors for receiving signals from outside the cell, or enzymes catalyzing activities within the membrane.	3: Most proteins can rotate or move laterally. Plays a vital role in transport of some specific types of large molecules. They can operate as channels for transferring chemicals across the membrane.
4:	4:

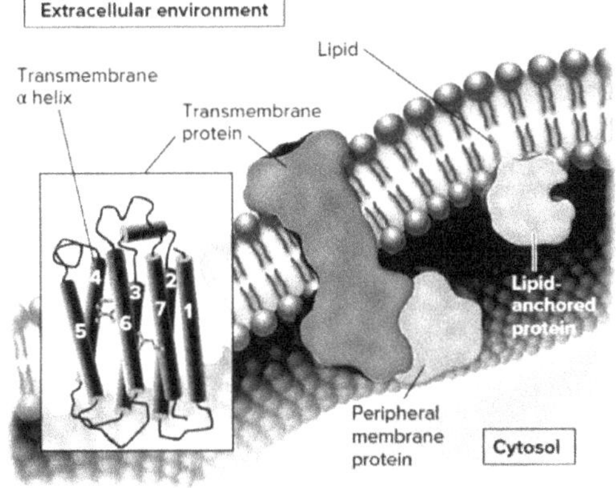

Technical Note:

A: A lipid-anchored protein associates with a membrane because it has a lipid molecule that is covalently attached to an amino acid side chain within the protein. The lipid tails are inserted into the hydrophobic portion of the membrane and thereby keep the protein firmly attached to the membrane. Both lipid-anchored proteins and transmembrane proteins are considered to be integral membrane proteins because they cannot be released from the membrane unless the membrane is dissolved with an organic solvent or detergent. In other words, they cannot be removed without disrupting the integrity of the membrane.

B: Peripheral Membrane Proteins Peripheral membrane proteins associate with membranes in a third way. They do not interact with the hydrophobic interior of the phospholipid bilayer. Instead, they are noncovalently bound to regions of integral membrane proteins that project out from the membrane (see Figure), or they are bound to the polar head groups of phospholipids. Peripheral membrane proteins are typically attached to the membrane by hydrogen and/or ionic bonds.

C: Transmembrane proteins have one or more regions that are physically inserted into the hydrophobic interior of the phospholipid bilayer. These regions, the transmembrane segments, are stretches of nonpolar amino acids that span or traverse the membrane from one leaflet to the other. In most transmembrane proteins, each transmembrane segment is folded into an α helix. Such a segment is stable in a membrane because the nonpolar amino acids interact favorably with the nonpolar lipid tails.

D. Flip-flop of transmembrane proteins does not occur, because the proteins also contain hydrophilic regions that project out from the phospholipid bilayer, and it would be energetically unfavorable for the hydrophilic regions of membrane proteins to pass through the hydrophobic portion of the phospholipid bilayer. Some transmembrane proteins have regions that extend into the cytosol and are anchored to large cytoskeletal filaments via linker proteins. Being bound to these large filaments restricts the movement of these proteins. Similarly, some transmembrane proteins are bound to large, immobile fibers in the extracellular matrix, which restricts their movement.

E. Peripheral proteins can usually be solubilized by extraction with high-concentration salt solutions that weaken the electrostatic bonds holding peripheral proteins to a membrane. In actual fact, the distinction between integral and peripheral proteins is blurred because many integral membrane proteins consist of several polypeptides, some that penetrate the lipid bilayer and others that remain on the periphery.

F. Proteins in the membrane confer the main differences between membranes of different cells. Their functions include transport, enzymatic action, reception of extracellular signals, cell-to-cell interactions, and cell identity markers. Peripheral proteins can be anchored in the membrane by modified lipids. Integral membrane proteins span the membrane and have one or more hydrophobic regions, called transmembrane domains, that anchor them. Why are transmembrane domains hydrophobic?

Solution: Transmembrane domains anchor protein in the membrane. They associate with the hydrophobic interior, thus they must be hydrophobic as well. If they slide out of the interior, they are repelled by water.

G. Cell membrane is said to be selectively permeable: Many important molecules required by cells cannot easily cross the plasma membrane. These molecules can still enter the cell by diffusion through specific channel proteins or carrier proteins embedded in the plasma membrane, provided there is a higher concentration of the molecule outside the cell than inside. We call this process of diffusion mediated by a membrane protein facilitated diffusion. Channel proteins have a hydrophilic interior that provides an aqueous channel through which polar molecules can pass when the channel is open. Carrier proteins, in contrast to channels, bind specifically to the molecule they assist, much like an enzyme binds to its substrate. These channels and carriers are usually selective for one type of molecule, and thus the cell membrane is said to be selectively permeable.

H. Active transport requires both a carrier protein and energy, usually in the form of ATP, to move molecules against a concentration gradient. The Na+/K+ pump uses ATP to moved Na+ in one direction and K+ in the other to create and maintain concentration differences of these ions. In coupled transport, a favorable concentration gradient of one molecule is used to move a different molecule against its gradient, such as in the transport of glucose by Na+. Can active transport involve a channel protein? Why or why not?

Solution: Channel proteins are aqueous pores that allow facilitated diffusion. They cannot actively transport ions. Carrier proteins bind to their substrates and can couple transport to some form of energy for active transport.

I. Channels and transporters allow the passage of solutes across membranes. However, at the molecular level, they work in fundamentally different ways. Explain how each type can transport solutes across a membrane.

Solution: When its gate is open, a channel provides a direct passageway for the movement of a solute across a membrane. A transporter does not provide a direct passageway for such movement. Instead, a solute must first enter a hydrophilic pocket on one side of the membrane. The transporter then undergoes a conformational change that exposes the pocket on the other side of the membrane, where the solute is released.

Test Paper

1. Which of the following statements best describes the chemical composition of biological membranes?

a. Biological membranes are bilayers of proteins with associated lipids and carbohydrates.

b. Biological membranes are composed of two layers—one layer of phospholipids and one layer of proteins.

c. Biological membranes are bilayers of phospholipids with associated proteins and carbohydrates.

d. Biological membranes are composed of equal numbers of phospholipids, proteins, and carbohydrates.

e. Biological membranes are composed of lipids with proteins attached to the outer surface.

2. Which of the following events can never be energetically favorable in a biological membrane and therefore will not occur spontaneously?

a. the rotation of phospholipids

b. the lateral movement of phospholipids

c. the flip-flop of phospholipids to the opposite leaflet

d. the rotation of membrane proteins

e. the lateral movement of membrane proteins

3. Let's suppose an insect, which doesn't maintain a constant body temperature, was exposed to a shift in temperature from 60°F to 80°F. Which of the following types of membrane changes would be the most beneficial in helping the insect cope with the temperature shift?

a. increase the number of double bonds in the lipid tails of phospholipids

b. increase the length of the lipid tails of phospholipids

c. decrease the amount of cholesterol in the membrane

d. decrease the amount of carbohydrate attached to membrane proteins

e. decrease the amount of carbohydrate attached to phospholipids

4. Carbohydrates of the plasma membrane

a. are bonded to a protein or lipid.

b. are located on the outer surface of the plasma membrane.

c. can function as cell markers for recognition by other cells.

d. All of the above are true of the carbohydrates.

e. Only a and c are true.

5. A transmembrane protein in the plasma membrane is glycosylated at two sites in the polypeptide sequence. Where in this protein would you expect these two sites to be?

a. in transmembrane segments

b. in hydrophilic regions that project into the extracellular environment

c. in hydrophilic regions that project into the cytosol

d. could be anywhere

e. b and c only

6. The tendency for Na+ to move into the cell can be due to

a. the higher numbers of Na+ outside the cell, resulting in a chemical concentration gradient.

b. the net negative charge inside the cell attracting the positively charged Na+.

c. the attractive force of K+ inside the cell pulling Na+ into the cell.

d. all of the above. e. a and b only.

7. Let's suppose the solute concentration inside the cells of a plant is 0.3 M and the concentration outside is 0.2 M. If we assume that the solute does not readily cross the membrane, which of the following statements best describes what will happen?

a. The plant cells will lose water, and the plasma membrane will push against the cell wall.

b. The plant cells will lose water, and the plasma membrane will pull away from the cell wall (plasmolysis).

c. The plant cells will take up a lot of water and undergo osmotic lysis.

d. The plant cells will take up a little water, and the plasma membrane will push against the cell wall.

e. both a and b.

8. What features of a biological membrane are major contributors to its selective permeability?

a. phospholipid bilayer b. transport proteins

c. glycolipids on the outer surface of the membrane

d. peripheral membrane proteins e. both a and b

9. What is the name given to the process in which solutes are moved across a membrane against their concentration gradient?

a. simple diffusion d. passive diffusion b. facilitated diffusion e. active transport

c. osmosis

10. Large particles or large volumes of fluid can be brought into the cell by

a. facilitated diffusion. d. exocytosis.

b. active transport. e. all of the above.

c. endocytosis.

11. Describe two different ways that integral membrane proteins associate with a membrane. How do peripheral membrane proteins associate with a membrane?

12. Energy and Matter Discuss how the lipid bilayer, channels, and transporters influence the ability of cells to control the amounts of solutes they contain.

Answer Key

1. c 2. c 3. b 4. d 5. b 6. e 7. d 8. e 9. e 10. C

11. Integral membrane proteins can contain transmembrane segments that cross the membrane, or they may contain lipid anchors. Peripheral membrane proteins are noncovalently bound to integral membrane proteins or to the polar heads of phospholipids.

12. The lipid bilayer, channels, and transporters cause the plasma membrane to be selectively permeable. This allows a cell to take up needed nutrients from its extracellular environment and to export waste products into the environment.

Q 13. Bacterial cells can take up the amino acid tryptophan (Trp) from their surroundings, or if there is an insufficient external supply they can synthesize tryptophan from other small molecules. The Trp repressor is a transcription regulator that shuts off the transcription of genes that code for the enzymes required for the synthesis of tryptophan.

A. W hat would happen to the regulation of the tryptophan operon in cells that express a mutant form of the tryptophan repressor that (1) cannot bind to DNA, (2) cannot bind tryptophan, or (3) binds to DNA even in the absence of tryptophan?

B. W hat would happen in scenarios (1), (2), and (3) if the cells, in addition, produced normal tryptophan repressor protein from a second, normal gene?

Q 14. In a particular kind of wildflower, the wild-type flower color is deep purple, and the plants are truebreeding.
In one true-breeding mutant stock, the flowers have a reduced pigmentation, resulting in a lavender color. In a different true-breeding mutant stock, the flowers have no pigmentation and are thus white. When a lavender-flowered plant from the first mutant stock was crossed to a white-flowered plant from the second mutant stock, all the F 1 plants had purple flowers. The F 1 plants were then allowed to self-fertilize to produce an F 2 generation. The 277 F 2 plants were 157 purple : 71 white : 49 lavender. Explain how flower color is inherited. Is this trait controlled by the alleles of a single gene? What kinds of progeny would be produced if lavender F 2 plants were allowed to self-fertilize?

Answer:

Are there any modes of single-gene inheritance compatible with the data? The observations that the F 1 plants look different from either of their parents and that the F 2 generation is composed of plants with three different phenotypes exclude complete dominance. The ratio of the three phenotypes in the F 2 plants has some resemblance to the 1:2:1 ratio expected from codominance or incomplete dominance, but the results would then imply that purple plants must be heterozygotes. This conflicts with the information provided that purple plants are true-breeding.
Consider now the possibility that two genes are involved. From a cross between plants heterozygous for two genes (*W* and *P*), the F 2 generation would contain a 9:3:3:1 ratio of the genotypes *W– P–, W– pp, ww P–,* and *ww pp* (where the dash indicates that the allele could be either a dominant or a recessive form). Are there any combinations of the 9:3:3:1 ratio that would be close to that seen in the F 2 generation in this example? The numbers seem close to a 9:4:3 ratio. What hypothesis would support combining two of the classes (3 1 1)? If *w* is epistatic to the *P* gene, then the *ww P–* and *ww pp* genotypic classes would have the same white phenotype. With this explanation, 1/3 of the F 2 lavender plants would be *WW pp,* and the remaining 2/3 would be *Ww pp.* Upon self-fertilization , *WW pp* plants would produce only lavender (*WW pp)* progeny, while *Ww pp* plants would produce a 3:1 ratio of lavender (*W– pp)* and white (*ww pp*) progeny.

***

2. Cell Cycle

A living cell always originates from pre-existing living cell.

- *Cell Theory*

Cell theory confers the fact that all living cells originate from pre existing living cells; it also encompasses the fact that cells can give birth to a new cell. To make all such activities ossible a cell must go through different stages of division, synthesis, development and resting phases. A division stage and growth stage must be searated by a distinct stage of gap; all such stages followd by a cell makes a complete cycle of cell cycle. This section is made interactive to reduce the burden of content areas and to ensure roper understanding of facts and figures along with their real life variations. This section will also point out some of the key points related to all the stages of cell cycle.

.

Worksheet 1

Q 1. Following images represent an equational cell division followed by somatic cells of some higher animals. Which stage(s) signify the equational division?

Phase	Events
Prophase	1. Chromosomal material condenses to form compact mitotic chromosomes. Chromosomes are seen to be composed of two chromatids attached together at the centromere. 2. Cytoskeleton is disassembled, and mitotic spindle is assembled. 3. Golgi complex and ER fragment. Nuclear envelope disperses.
Prometaphase	1. Chromosomal microtubules attach to kinetochores of chromosomes. 2. Chromosomes are moved to spindle equator.
Metaphase	1. Chromosomes are aligned along metaphase plate, attached by chromosomal microtubules to both poles.
Anaphase	1. Centromeres split, and chromatids separate. 2. Chromosomes move to opposite spindle poles. 3. Spindle poles move farther apart.
Telophase	1. Chromosomes cluster at opposite spindle poles. 2. Chromosomes become dispersed. 3. Nuclear envelope assembles around chromosome clusters. 4. Golgi complex and ER reforms. 5. Daughter cells formed by cytokinesis.

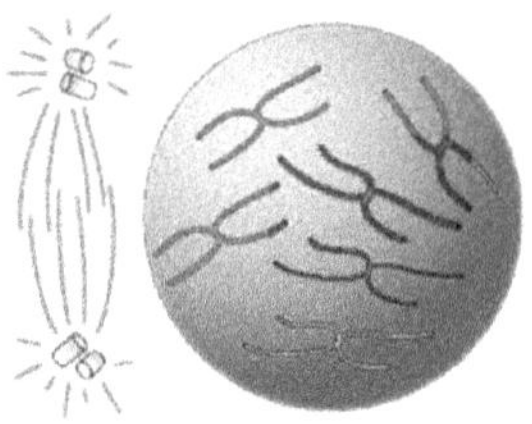

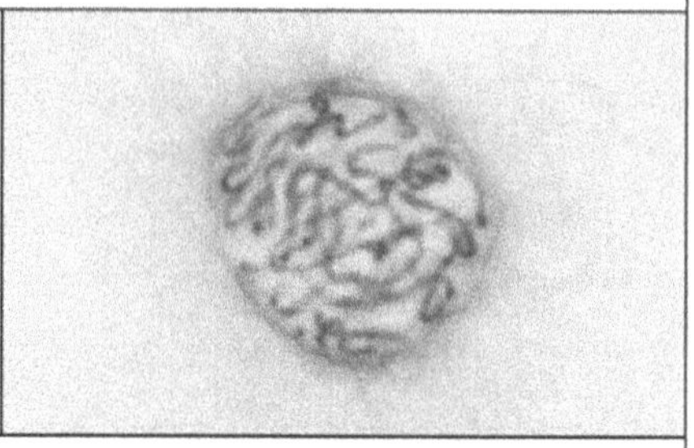

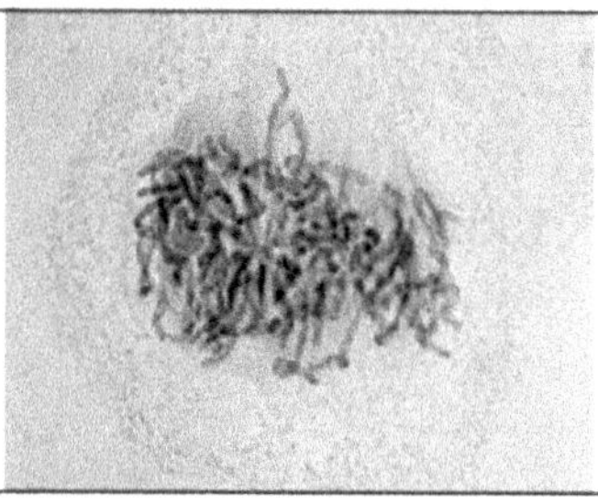

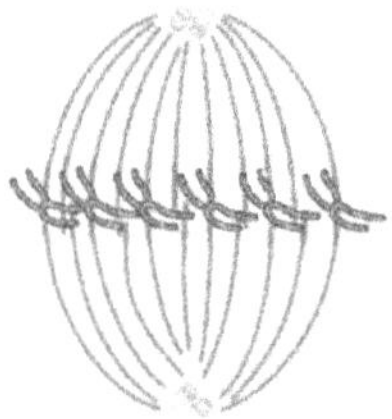

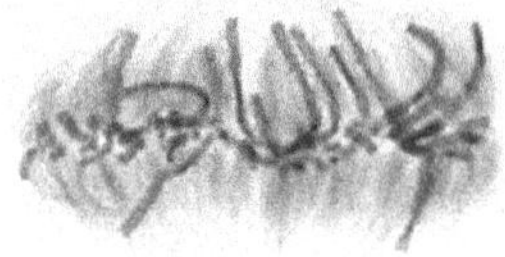

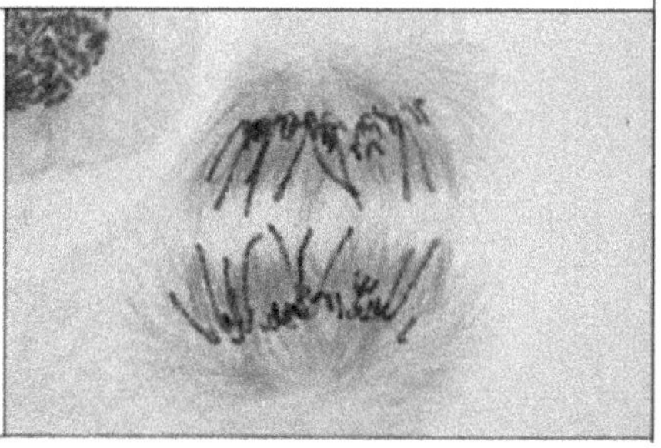

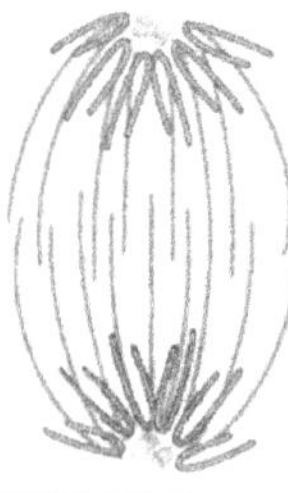

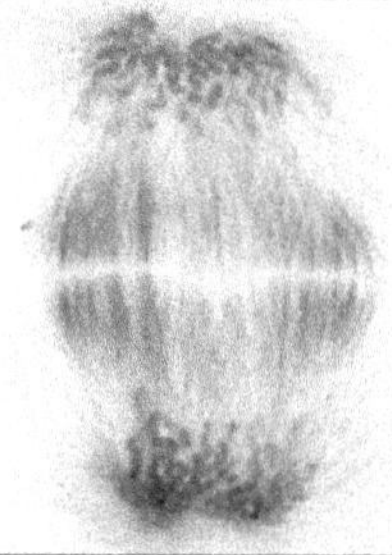

Q 2. What specific roles played by cohesion and condensine in formation of a chromosome?

Q 3. Elaborate the normal functioning of kinetochore on the basis of the following diagram.

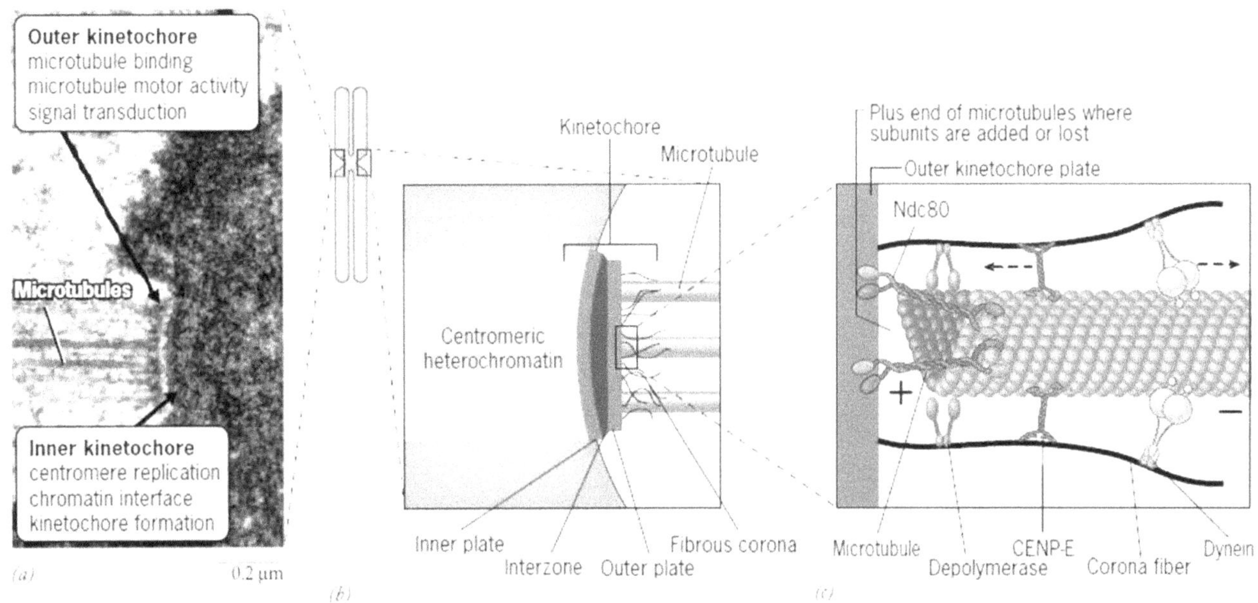

Q 4. Identify different stages of cell division as provided in the following diagram.

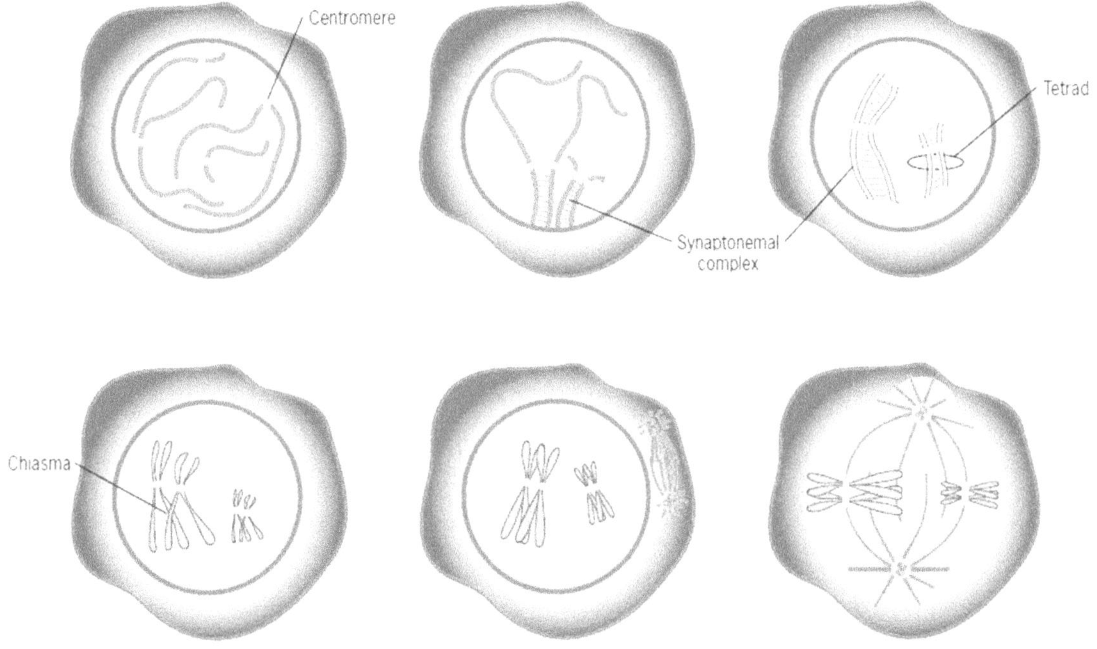

Q 5. Point out Evolutionary significance of recombination.

Q 6. What makes the separation of homologous chromosomes possible during Meiotic Anaphase I?

Q 7. Write three basic difference between Anaphase I and Anaphase II.

Q 8. Cells remain inactive during .... and .... phases of cell cycle.

Worksheet 2 [unsolved]

1. How do the events of mitotic prophase prepare the chromatids for later separation at anaphase?

2. What are some of the cellular level activities of the kinetochore during mitosis?

3. Describe the events that occur in a cell during prometaphase and during anaphase.

4. Describe the similarities and differences in microtubule dynamics between metaphase and anaphase. How are the differences, which can be observed, related to anaphase A and B movements?

5. What types of force-generating mechanisms might be responsible for ensuring ensured chromosome movement during anaphase?

6. Contrast the events that occur during cytokinesis in typical plant and animal cells.

7. Point out three differences between metaphase I and metaphase II which takes place during meiosis.

8. Provide names of different stages of cell division as displayed in the following diagram.

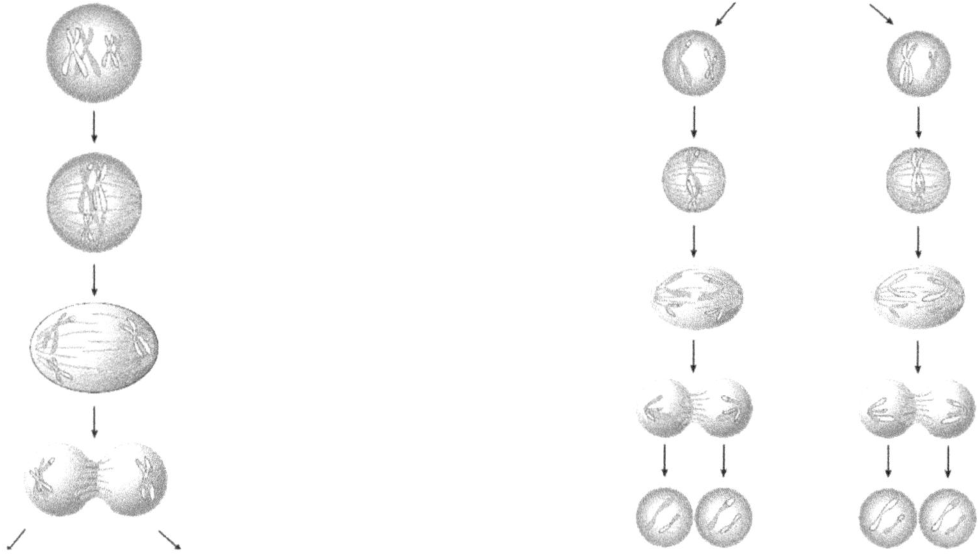

9. Which protein plays a vital role in formation of spindle fibres during cell division in animal cells?

10. Which cell organelle plays definite role in formation of spindle fibres in animal cells?

11. Distinguish cytokinesis of plant cells and animal cells.

12. Why matured nerve cells are not capable of performing cell division?

13. Centromere divides during .... Stage of meiotic cell division.

14. The usual result of meiosis is the production of four haploid .... cells· that are genetically variable. Genetic variation in meiosis is produced by crossing over and by the random distribution of .... and paternal ....

15. In eukaryotic cells, ... are typically found in homologous pairs.

Worksheet 3

Q 1. A cell in G1 of interphase has 8 chron1osomes. How many chromosomes and how many DNA molecules will be found per cell as this cell progresses through the following stages: G,. metaphase of mitosis, anaphase of mitosis, after cytokinesis in mitosis, metaphase 1 of meiosis. metaphase II of meiosis, and -after cytokinesis of meiosis II?

Q 2. What can be concluded from the following graph?

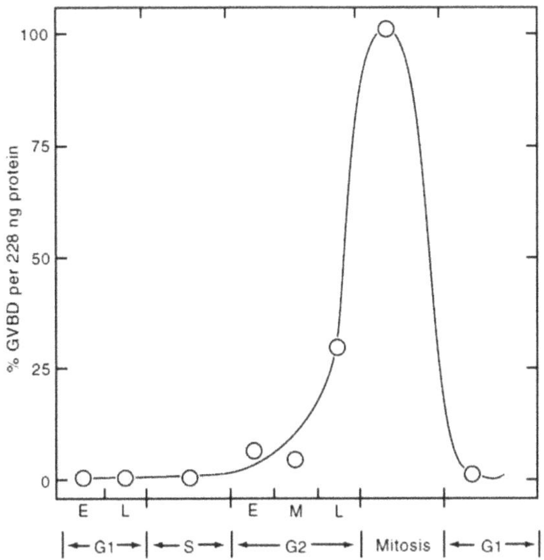

A Graph showing Maturation-promoting activity of HeLa cell extracts during different stages of the cell cycle. Because 228 ng of mitotic protein induced germinal vesicle breakdown (GVBD) in 100 percent of the cases, the percent activity for other phases of the cell cycle was normalized to that amount of protein.

E, early; M, mid-, and L, late.

(P. S. SUNKARA, D. A.WRIGHT AND P. N. RAO, PROC. NATL ACAD. SCIENCE USA 76:2801, 1979.)

Q 3. Answer the following.

A hematopoietic stem cell can give rise to two different progenitor cells: a myeloid progenitor cell that can differentiate into most of the various blood cells (e.g., erythrocytes, basophils, and neutrophils), macrophages, or dendritic cells; or a lymphoid progenitor cell that can differentiate into any of the various types of lymphocytes (NK cells, T cells, or B cells). T-cell precursors migrate to the thymus where they differentiate into T cells. In contrast, B cells undergo differentiation in the bone marrow. Cells in the various stages of B- and T-cell differentiation can be distinguished by the species of proteins at their cell surface and/or the transcription factors that determine the genes being expressed.

What type of regulatory mechanism is displayed through this inter-relationship of different cells and the Bone Marrow?

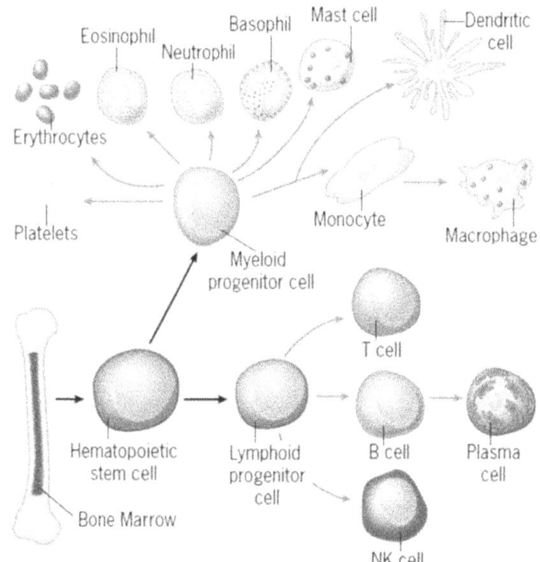

Q 4. How does meiosis plays a role in keeping the number of chromosome in an individual constant?

Q 5. What happens to one of the X-Chromosomes in females (especially of placental mammals) during phases of development? [Extract answer from previous studies]

Worksheet 4

Q 1. Find out the basic principle which is proposed by Mendel after conducting the following test.

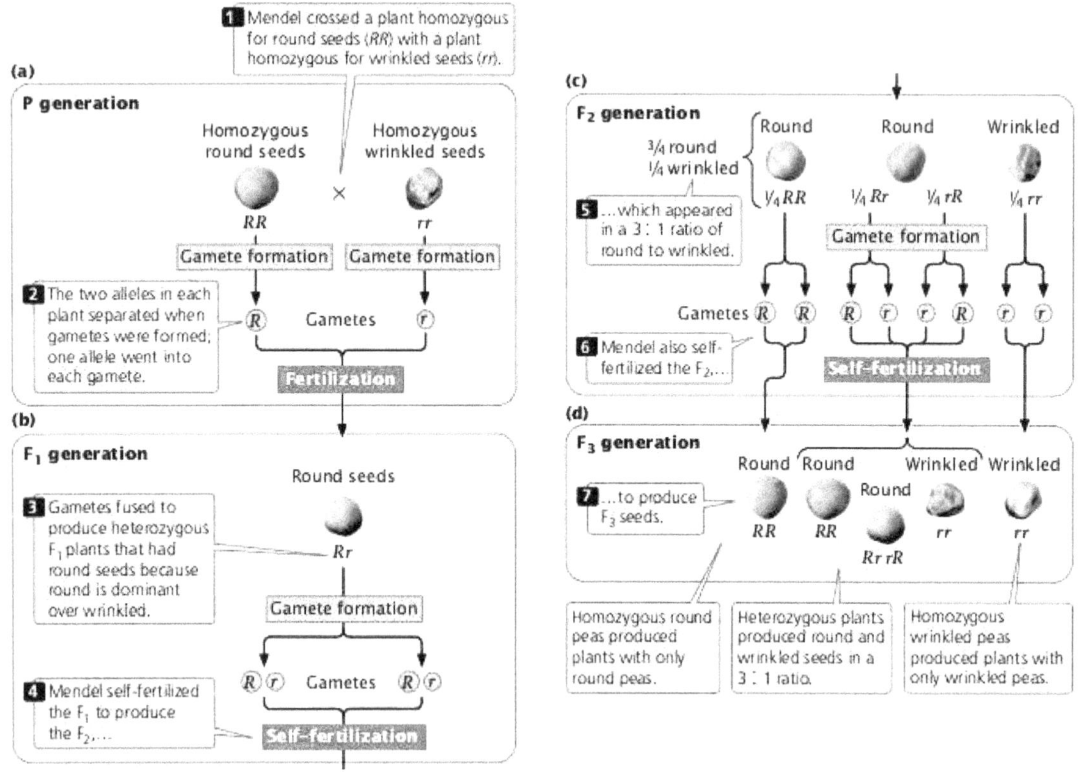

Q 2. Is there any cytological evidence which confers that crossing over has occurred? When and where would you trace it out?

Q 3. A geneticist has estimated the number of exchanges that occurred during meiosis on each of 100 chromatids that were recovered in gametes. The data sheet duly provided is as follows:

Number of Exchanges	Frequency
0	18
1	20
2	40
3	16
4	6

Find out what is the genetic length in centi-Morgans of the chromosome analyzed in this study?

Q 4. Mendel did not know of the existence of chromosomes. During that time chromosome was yet to be discovered. Had he known, what change might he have made in his Principle of Independent Assortment?

Q 5. What is linked gene? What are the probable impacts which can be expected in the process of inheritance due to linked genes?

Worksheet 5

Q 1. A phenotypically wild-type female fruit fly (heterozygous for genes controlling body colour and wing length) was crossed to a homozygous mutant male with black body (specified by allele b) and vestigial wings (specified by allele vg). The cross produced the following progeny:

grey body, normal wings 126; grey body, vestigial wings 24; black body, normal wings 26;

black body, vestigial wings 124.

Do these data indicate linkage between the genes for body colour and wing length? What is the frequency of recombination?

Q 2. An organism has 38 autosomes in their genome, each about the same size. If two autosomal genes are chosen randomly, what is the chance that they will be located on the same chromosome?

Q 3. A phenotypically wild-type female fruit fly heterozygous for the two genes (heterozygous for genes controlling body colour and wing length) was crossed to a homozygous black, vestigial male. The cross produced the following progeny:

grey body, normal wings 23; grey body, vestigial wings 127; black body, normal wings 124;

black body, vestigial wings 26.

On the basis of the above mentioned combination do we say that it indicates linkage? What is the frequency of recombination?

Q 4. Complete the following statements:

a. The genotypic function, ... : The genetic material must store genetic information and accurately transmit that information from parents to offspring, generation after generation.

b. The phenotypic function, ... : The genetic material must control the development of the phenotype of the organism. The genetic material must dictate the growth of the organism from the single-celled zygote to the mature adult as per the template of development and maturation duly provided in the set of genome.

c. The evolutionary function, ...: The genetic material must undergo changes in the gene sequence or gene types along with various possible combinations to produce variations that allow organisms to adapt to modifications in the environment so that evolution can be advanced.

Q 5. What is folded genome?

Q 6. What is Nucleosome Core? Write its constituents.

Q 7. What is the substructure of the 30-nm fiber seen in chromosomes?

Q 8. What is Telomere? Write its importance.

Q 9. Write at least three differences between centromere and telomere.

Q 10. Is there any instance in the living world when RNA instead of DNA acts as a genetic material? If yes How?

Q 11. Elaborate basic difference between gene and genome.

Q 12. Define : Satellite bands of Chromosome and Satellite DNA.

Worksheet 6

Q 1. What differences in the chemical structures of DNA and protein allow scholars and scientists to label one or the other of these macromolecules with a radioactive isotope?

Q 2. If the sequence of one strand of a DNA double helix is ATCG, what is the sequence of the other strand?

Q 3. How are the single-stranded regions of DNA molecules at the ends of human chromosomes remain protected from degradation by nucleases and other enzymes?

Q 4. The mixture of DNA and protein is shown to contain genetic information by some assay such as transformation in bacteria, how can a person determine whether that genetic information is present in the DNA or in the protein component?

Q 5. The red alga *Polyides rotundus* stores its genetic information in double-stranded DNA. When DNA was extracted from *P. rotundus* cells and analyzed, 32 percent of the bases were found to be guanine residues. From this information, can you determine what percentage of the bases in this DNA were thymine residues? If so, calculate what percentage? If not, why this situation differ?

Q 6. The centriole of a chromosome undergoes duplication during .... phase of a cell cycle.

Ans 6. Synthetic phase.

Q 7. Indicate whether following statements about structure of DNA are true of false.

Indicate whether each of the following statements about

the structure of DNA is true or false. (Each letter is used to

refer to the concentration of that base in DNA.)

(a) A + T = G + C

(b) A = G; C = T

(c) A/T = C/G

(d) T/A = C/G

(e) A + G = C + T

(f) G/C =1

(g) A = T within each single strand of double stranded DNA molecule.

(h) Hydrogen bonding provides stability to the double helix in aqueous cytoplasm.

(i) Hydrophobic bonding provides stability to the double helix in aqueous cytoplasm.

(j) When separated, the two strands of a DNA double helix are considered to be identical.

(k) Once the base sequence of one strand of a DNA double helix is known, the base sequence of the second strand can be deduced easily by utilising the mechanism of complementary base pairing.

(l) The structure of a DNA double helix is invariant.

(m) Each nucleotide pair contains two phosphate groups, two

Deoxyribose molecules and two bases.

Q 8. (a) If a virus particle contained double-stranded DNA with 200,000 base pairs, how many nucleotides would be present? (b) How many complete spirals would occur on each strand? (c) How many atoms of phosphorus would be present?(d) What would be the length of the DNA configuration in the virus?

Q 9. DNA was extracted from cells of *Staphylococcus afermentans* and analyzed for base composition. It was found that 37 percent of the bases are cytosine. With this information, is it possible to predict what percentage of the bases are adenine? If so, what percentage? If not, why not?

Q 10. The spaces between adjacent turns of the helix form two grooves of different width—a wider major groove and a more narrow minor groove—that spiral around the outer surface of the double helix. Proteins that bind to DNA often contain domains that fit into these grooves. In many cases, a protein bound in a groove is able to read the sequence of nucleotides along the DNA without having to separate the strands.

Q 11. What is meant by saying that a DNA strand has polarity? That the two strands are antiparallel? That the molecule has a major groove and a minor groove? That the strands are complementary to one another?

Q 12. What is a genome? How does the complexity of bacterial genomes differ from that of eukaryotic genomes?

Q 13. What is meant by the term DNA denaturation? How does denaturation depend on the GC content of the DNA? How does this variable affect the Tm?

Q 14. What is a microsatellite DNA sequence? What role do these sequences play in human disease?

Q 15. Which fraction of the genome contains the most information? Why is this true?

***.

Solution to Worksheet 1

Ans 1: Anaphase and Telophase;

Ans 2: Role of cohesion and condensine...

As the cell entered mitosis, the compaction process would begin, aided by condensin molecules. In this model, condensin brings about chromosome compaction by forming a ring around supercoiled loops of DNA within chromatin. Cohesin molecules would continue to hold the DNA of sister chromatids together. It is proposed, that cooperative interactions between condensin molecules would then organize the supercoiled loops into larger coils, which are then folded into a mitotic chromosome fiber. The subunit structure of an individual cohesin and condensin complex are built around a pair of SMC subunits.

Each of the SMC polypeptides folds back on itself to form a highly elongated antiparallel, coiled coil with an ATP-binding globular domain where the N- and C-termini come together. Cohesin and condensin also have two or three non-SMC subunits that complete the ring-like structure of these proteins.

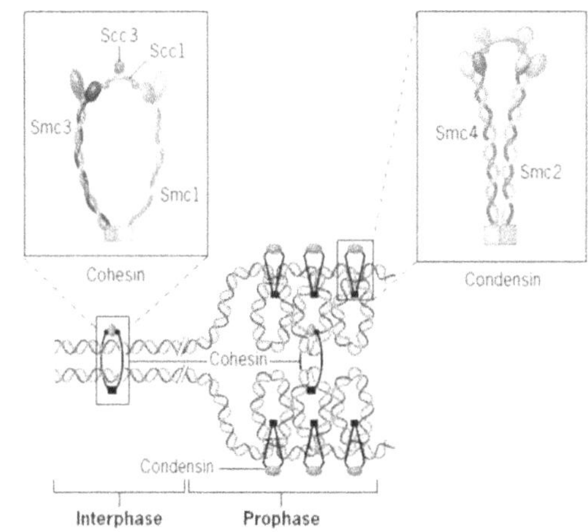

Ans 3: kinetochore, which contains an electron-dense inner and outer plate separated by a lightly staining interzone, provides attachment site for microtubules of the spindle fibres. The inner plate contains a variety of proteins attached to the centromeric heterochromatin of the chromosome. Associated with the outer plate is the fibrous corona, which binds motor proteins remaining involved in chromosome movement. This model is also showing a proposed disposition of several of the proteins found at the outer surface of the kinetochore. Among the motor proteins associated with the kinetochore, cytoplasmic dynein moves toward the minus end of a microtubule, whereas CENP-E moves toward the plus end. It is also

becoming evident that these motors may also play a role in tethering the microtubule to the kinetochore. The protein labelled "depolymerase" is a member of the kinesin superfamily that functions in depolymerisation of microtubules rather than motility.

Ans 4: Leptotene, Zygotene, Pachytene, Diplotene, Diakinesis and Metaphase I;

Ans 5: We can appreciate the evolutionary advantage of recombination by comparing two species, one capable of reproducing sexually and the other is not capable of doing so. Let's suppose that a beneficial mutation has arisen in each species. In due course of time, we would expect these mutations to spread widely. While they are spreading, as per our general expectations, another beneficial mutation occurs in a nonmutant individual within each species. In the asexual organism, there is no possibility that this second mutation will be recombined with the first one due to lack of any exchange of genetic materials, but in the sexual organism, the two mutations can be recombined to produce a strain that is better than either of the single mutants by itself. This recombinant strain will be able to spread through the whole population of the species. Better to speak In evolutionary terms, recombination can permit favorable alleles of different genes to come together in the same organism.

Solution to Workksheet 3

Ans 1: Tabulated solution is provided.

Stage	Number of chromosomes per cell	Number of DNA molecules per cell
G_1	8	8
G_2	8	16
Metaphase of mitosis	8	16
Anaphase of mitosis	16	16
After cytokinesis of mitosis	8	8
Metaphase I of meiosis	8	16
Metaphase II of meiosis	4	8
After cytokinesis of meiosis II	4	4

Ans 2: Extracts from cultured HeLa cells prepared from early G1-, late G1-, or S-phase cells lack MPF[7] activity. MPF appears in early G2, rises dramatically in late G2, and reaches a peak in mitosis.

Ans 3: Pathways of differentiation of a hematopoietic stem cell of the bone marrow. It shows the linkage of stem cells manufactured by Bone Marrow with the activities related to Immune Response.

Solution to Worksheet 4:

1: Principle of Segregation and the concept of Dominance and Recessive alleles were proposed by Mendel.

Ans 2: Crossing over probably occurs in the interval of early to mid-prophase of meiosis I. The chromosomes may not be easily analyzed in these stages, and mechanism of exchanges is difficult to trace out, if not impossible, to identify by cytological methods. The best cytological evidence which can confer that crossing over has occurred is obtained from cells near the end of the prophase of meiosis I. During this specific stage, paired homologues repel each other slightly, and the exchanges between them are seen in the form of chiasmata.

Ans 3: The genetic length of a chromosome is the average number of exchanges on a chromatid at the end of meiosis. For the data as being provided, the average is

$= 0 \times (18/100) + 1 \times (20/100) + 2 \times (40/100) + 3 \times (16/100) + 4 \times (6/100)$

= 1.72 Morgans or 172 centi-Morgans.

---

[7] *MPF stands for Maturation Promoting Factor; Because it was assumed primarily that MPF was involved specifically in triggering oocyte maturation, relatively little interest was paid at first to the substance or its possible mechanism of action.*

Solution to Worksheet 5

Ans 4: replication; gene expression ; mutation;

Ans 5: When E. coli chromosomes are isolated by gentle procedures in the absence of ionic detergents (commonly used to lyse cells) and are kept in the presence of a high concentration of cations such as polyamines (small basic or positively charged proteins) or 1M salt to neutralize the negatively charged phosphate groups of DNA, the chromosomes remain in a highly condensed state comparable in size to the nucleoid which can be recognised in vivo. This structure (the folded genome), is the functional state of a bacterial chromosome.

Ans 6: Nucleosome Core: After process of partial digestion of the DNA in chromatin with an endonuclease (an enzyme that can cleave DNA internally), DNA approximately 200 nucleotide pairs in length is found associated with each nucleosome (produced by a cleavage in each linker region of the prolonged chain). After extensive nuclease digestion, a 146-nucleotide-pair-long segment of DNA remains linked in each nucleosome. This nuclease-resistant structure of the prolonged segment is called the nucleosome core. Its structure (Considered as essentially invariant in eukaryotes) consists of a 146-nucleotide-pair length of DNA and two molecules comprising each of histones H2a, H2b, H3, and H4.

Ans 7: In vivo, the nucleosomes clearly interact with one another to condense the 11-nm nucleosomes into 30-nm chromatin fibers. Chromatin structure is not static at any instance of the Cell Cycle; chromatin can expand and contract in response to chemical modifications of histone H1 (another major participant of the chromatin sub unit) and the histone tails that protrude from the nucleosomes.

Ans 8: Some of the postulates elaborated the fact that telomeres have unique structures, which can be ascribed on the basis of fact that the known mechanisms of replication of linear DNA molecules do not permit duplication of both strands of DNA at the ends of the molecules. Those unique structures must be facilitating their replication, or there must be some special replication enzyme that resolves this issue. Telomeres, instead of having any special structure, must provide at least three important functions. They must (a) prevent deoxyribonucleases from degrading the terminal parts of the linear DNA molecules, (b) prevent fusion of the ends with other adjacent segments of DNA molecules, and (c) facilitate replication of the ends of the linear DNA molecules without losing the segment and configuration of the material.

Ans 12: Small bands of DNA present in chromosome are called satellite bands (from the Latin word satelles, meaning “an attendant” or “subordinate”) and the DNAs in these bands are often called satellite DNAs. These are small bands of the molecule accommodated in a chromosome. The genome of Drosophila virilise (a distant relative of Drosophila melanogaster) contains three distinct satellite DNAs, each composed of a repeating sequence of seven base pairs. Some of the satellite DNAs in eukaryotes have long repetitive sequences.

Solution to Worksheet 6

Ans 1: DNA contains phosphorus (the common isotope is ^{31}P) but sulphur is absent; DNA can be labelled by growing cells on medium containing the radioactive isotope of phosphorus, ^{32}P. Proteins contain sulphur (the common isotope is ^{32}S) but devoid of any higher percentage of phosphorus; proteins can be labelled by growing cells on medium containing the radioactive isotope of sulphur, ^{35}S.

Ans 2: Because the two strands of a double helix are complementary (adenine always paired with thymine and guanine always paired with cytosine) the sequence of the second strand can be deduced from the sequence of the first strand by working out the complementary pairing. For ATCG, the double helix will have the following structure: TAGC.

Ans 4: The biological specificity of enzymes is the key which provides a powerful tool for use in many investigations. The enzyme deoxyribonuclease (DNase) degrades DNA to mononucleotides, and proteases degrade proteins to smaller components. If the mixture of DNA and protein is treated with DNase and the genetic information is allowed to be destroyed, then we can confirm that it is stored in DNA. If the mixture is treated with protease and the genetic information is lost, then we can conclude the fact that genetic information was residing in the protein component of the mixture which was provided for testing.

Ans 5: It is confirmed from the structure of a DNA strand that the concentrations of G and C are always equal, as are the concentrations of A and T. If 32 percent of the bases in double-stranded DNA are G residues, then another 32 percent are C residues. Together, G and C comprise 64 percent of the bases in *P. rotundus* DNA; thus, 36 percent of the bases are A's and T's. Since the concentration of A must equal the concentration of T, 18 percent (36% 1/2) of the bases must be T residues.

3. Chemical Basis of Genes

At the time of Mendel, the nature of the inheritance patterns and the genetic basis of such patterns and associated 'factors' regulating the pattern of inheritance was not clear. Over the next hundred years, the nature of the putative genetic material was investigated culminating in the realisation that DNA – deoxyribonucleic acid – is the genetic material, at least for the majority of organisms; with some exceptions of some monerans maintaining RNA as their basis of genetic infoormation.

We all know that nucleic acids (both DNA and RNA) are polymers of nucleotides. Deoxyribonucleic acid (DNA) and ribonucleic acid (RNA) are the two types of nucleic acids found in living systems. DNA acts as the genetic material in most of the organisms. RNA, being the genetic material in some viruses, mostly functions as a simple messenger. RNA also functions as adapter, structural, and in some cases as a catalytic molecule. The structures of nucleotides and the way these monomer units are linked to form nucleic acid polymers.

DNA[8], a long polymer of deoxyribonucleotides (the length is usually defined as number of nucleotides present in it; number of nucleotides[9] differ considerably.[10]); accommodate nitrogen bases[11] along with deoxyribose sugar. . A nitrogenous base is linked to the OH of 1' C pentose sugar through a N-glycosidic linkage to form a nucleoside[12]. When a phosphate group is linked to OH of 5' C of a nucleoside through phosphoester linkage, a corresponding nucleotide (or deoxynucleotide depending upon the type of sugar present) is formed. Two nucleotides are linked through 3'-5' phosphodiester linkage to form a dinucleotide; in gradual succession, polynucleotide[13] chain is formed. Similarly, at the other end of the polymer the sugar has a free OH of 3'C group which is referred to as 3' -end of the polynucleotide chain. The backbone of a polynucleotide chain is formed due to sugar and phosphates. The nitrogenous bases linked to sugar moiety project from the backbone. In RNA, every nucleotide residue has an additional –OH group present at 2' -position in the ribose; the uracil is found at the place of thymine (5-methyl uracil, another chemical name for thymine). Double helical model of DNA is proposed by Watson and Crick in 1953.[14] Observation of Chargaff was another reason which confirmed the model.[15]

Nitrogen bases are said to be complementary to each other, and therefore if the sequence of bases in one strand is known then the sequence in other strand can be predicted. Also, if each strand from a DNA acts as a template for synthesis of a new strand, the two double stranded DNA thus, produced would be identical to the parental (or source) DNA molecule.

---

[8] *DNA as an acidic substance present in nucleus was first identified by Friedrich Meischer in 1869. He named it as 'Nuclein'.*

[9] *A nucleotide has three components – a nitrogenous base, a pentose sugar (ribose in case of RNA, and deoxyribose for DNA), and a phosphate group;*

[10] *a bacteriophage known as φ ×174 has 5386 nucleotides, Bacteriophage lambda has 48502 base pairs (bp), Escherichia coli has 4.6 × 106 bp, and haploid content of human DNA is 3.3 × 109 bp.*

[11] *There are two types of nitrogenous bases – Purines (Adenine and Guanine), and Pyrimidines (Cytosine, Uracil and Thymine). Cytosine is common for both DNA and RNA and Thymine is present in DNA. Uracil is present in RNA at the place of Thymine.*

[12] *Soome common nucleosides: adenosine or deoxyadenosine, guanosine or deoxyguanosine, cytidine or deoxycytidine and uridine or deoxythymidine.*

[13] *A polymer thus formed has at one end a free phosphate moiety at 5' -end of sugar, which is referred to as 5'-end of polynucleotide chain.*

[14] *James Watson and Francis Crick (1953), based on the X-ray diffraction data produced by Maurice Wilkins and Rosalind Franklin, proposed a very simple but famous Double Helix model for the structure of DNA.*

[15] *observation of Erwin Chargaff that for a double stranded DNA, the ratios between Adenine and Thymine and Guanine and Cytosine are constant and equals one.*

The salient features of the Double-helix structure of DNA are as follows:

(i) It is made of two polynucleotide chains, where the backbone is constituted by sugar-phosphate, and the bases project inside.

(ii) The two chains have anti-parallel polarity. It means, if one chain has the polarity 5'à3', the other has 3'à5'.

(iii) The bases in two strands are paired through hydrogen bond (H-bonds) forming base pairs (bp). Adenine forms two hydrogen bonds with Thymine from opposite strand and vice-versa. Similarly, Guanine is bonded with Cytosine with three H-bonds. As a result, always a purine comes opposite to a pyrimidine. This generates approximately uniform distance between the two strands of the helix.

(iv) The two chains are coiled in a right-handed fashion. The pitch of the helix is 3.4 nm (a nanometre is one billionth of a metre, that is 10-9 m) and there are roughly 10 bp in each Rationalised Double stranded polynucleotide chain ; the distance between a bp in a helix is approximately 0.34 nm.

(v) The plane of one base pair stacks over the other in double helix. This, in addition to H-bonds, confers stability of the helical structure.

Compare the structure of purines and pyrimidines. Can you find out why the distance between two polynucleotide chains in DNA remains almost constant?

The proposition of a double helix structure for DNA and its simplicity in explaining the genetic implication became revolutionary. Very soon, Francis Crick proposed the Central dogma in molecular biology, which states that the genetic information flows from DNAàRNAàProtein. Central dogma Nucleosome - 'Beads-on-String' In some viruses the flow of information is in reverse direction, that is, from RNA to DNA. Can you suggest a simple name to the process?

Packaging of DNA Helix Taken the distance between two consecutive base pairs as 0.34 nm (0.34×10–9 m), if the length of DNA double helix in a typical mammalian cell is calculated (simply by multiplying the total number of bp with distance between two consecutive bp, that is, 6.6 × 109 bp × 0.34 × 10-9m/bp), it comes out to be approximately 2.2 metres. A length that is far greater than the dimension of a typical nucleus (approximately 10–6 m).

How is such a long polymer packaged in a cell?

If the length of E. coli DNA is 1.36 mm, can you calculate the number of base pairs in E.coli?

In prokaryotes, such as, E. coli, though they do not have a defined nucleus, the DNA is not scattered throughout the cell; it is held with some proteins (that have positive charges) in a region termed as 'nucleoid'. The DNA in nucleoid is organised in large loops held by proteins.

In eukaryotes, there is a set of positively charged, basic proteins called histones. A protein acquires charge depending upon the abundance of amino acids residues with charged side chains. Histones are rich in the basic amino acid residues lysine and arginine. Both the amino acid residues carry positive charges in their side chains. Histones are organised to form a unit of eight molecules called histone octamer. The negatively charged DNA is wrapped around the positively charged histone octamer to form a structure called nucleosome (it constitute the repeating unit of a structure in nucleus called chromatin; these are seen as 'beads-on-string' structure when viewed under electron microscope). A typical nucleosome contains 200 bp of DNA helix.

Theoretically, how many such beads (nucleosomes) do you imagine are present in a mammalian cell?

The beads-on-string structure in chromatin is packaged to form chromatin fibers that are further coiled and condensed at metaphase stage of cell division to form chromosomes. The packaging of chromatin at higher level requires additional set of proteins that collectively are referred to as Non-histone Chromosomal (NHC) proteins. In a typical nucleus, some region of chromatin are loosely packed (and stains light) and are referred to as euchromatin; and some are more densely packed (heterochromatin). Euchromatin is said to be transcriptionally active chromatin, whereas heterochromatin is inactive.

An Experiment

Observation: When Streptococcus pneumoniae (pneumococcus) bacteria are grown on a culture plate, some produce smooth shiny colonies (S) while others produce rough colonies (R).

Reason: The S strain bacteria have a mucous (polysaccharide) coat, while R strain does not. Mice infected with the S strain (virulent) die from pneumonia infection but mice infected with the R strain do not develop pneumonia. After injecting a mixture of heat-killed S and live R bacteria, the mice died.

Conclusion: the R strain bacteria had somehow been transformed by the heat-killed S strain bacteria; this must be accomplished due to transfer of some genetic material to R strain and made it virulent.

Before further studies the biochemical regulator (Transforming Principle , as the name coined by Griffith) was considered as protein.

Further studies: Oswald Avery, Colin MacLeod and Maclyn McCarty (1933-44) purified biochemical (proteins, DNA, RNA, etc.) from the heat-killed S cells to see which ones could transform live R cells into S cells. DNA alone from S bacteria caused R bacteria to become transformed; protein-digesting enzymes (proteases) and RNA-digesting enzymes (RNases) did not affect transformation; DNA caused the transformation.

Trancription Regulators

Transcription regulators work together as a "union" to establish a definite regulation upon the expression of a eukaryotic gene. The general transcription factors that assemble at the promoter are the same for all genes transcribed by RNA polymerase, the transcription regulators and the locations of their DNA binding sites relative to the promoters are different for different genes. These regulators, along with chromatin modifying proteins, are assembled at the promoter by the Mediator. The effects of multiple transcription regulators combine to determine the final rate with which transcription can be initiated and accelerated.

Q. Can you think of any difference between DNAs and DNase?

Revision Exercise (Solved)

Q 1. Compare statements I and II as provided below:

Statement I: Proteins are not considerably stable. It changes with different stages of life cycle, age or with change in physiology of the organism.

Statement II: Stability as one of the properties of genetic material was very evident in Griffith's 'transforming principle' itself that heat, which killed the bacteria, at least did not destroy some of the properties of genetic material.

Solution 1: Both the statements support each other. On the basis of both the statements it can be concluded that proteins have no capabilities of playing the role of genetic materials.

Q 2. Consider all the statements.

Statement I: "DNA is the genetic material came from the experiments of Alfred Hershey and Martha Chase (1952). They worked with viruses that infect bacteria called bacteriophages."

Statement II: The bacteriophage attaches to the bacteria and its genetic material then enters the bacterial cell. Alfred Hershey and Martha Chase (1952) grew some viruses on a medium that contained radioactive phosphorus and some others on medium that contained radioactive sulfur. Viruses grown in the presence of radioactive phosphorus contained radioactive DNA but not radioactive protein because DNA contains phosphorus but protein does not. Similarly, viruses grown on radioactive sulfur contained radioactive protein but not radioactive DNA because DNA does not contain sulfur.

Statement III: Radioactive phages were allowed to attach to E. coli bacteria. Bacteria which was infected with viruses that had radioactive DNA were radioactive, indicating that DNA was the material that passed from the virus to the bacteria. Bacteria that were infected with viruses that had radioactive proteins were not radioactive. This indicates that proteins did not enter the bacteria from the viruses.

What can be concluded on the basis of all the three statements?

Solution 2: DNA is the genetic material that is passed from virus to bacteria. DNA as the genetic material was unequivocally resolved from Hershey-Chase experiment.

Q 3. What are the criteria to be fulfilled by a chemical (molecule complex) to become a genetic material?

Solution 3: A molecule that can act as a genetic material must fulfill the following criteria: (i) It should be able to generate its replica (Replication). (ii) Such molecule should be chemically and structurally stable enough. (iii) It should provide the scope for slow changes in the genetic information and sequences off genes (mutation) that are required for initiating evolution. (iv) Such molecule should be able to express itself in the form of 'Mendelian Characters'.

Q 4. What regulates expression of genes?

Solution 4. The genes in a cell are expressed to perform a particular function or a set of functions. For example, if an enzyme called beta-galactosidase is synthesised by E. coli, it is used to catalyse the hydrolysis of a disaccharide, lactose is converted into galactose and glucose; the bacteria such molecules as a source of energy. If the bacteria do not have lactose around them to be utilised for energy source, they would no longer require the synthesis of the enzyme beta-galactosidase. Therefore, it is the metabolic, physiological or environmental conditions that regulate the expression of genes. The development and differentiation of embryo into adult organisms are also a result of the coordinated regulation of expression of several sets of genes. In prokaryotes, control of the rate of transcriptional initiation is the predominant site for control of gene expression. In a transcription unit, the activity of RNA polymerase at a given promoter is in turn regulated by interaction with accessory proteins, which affect its ability to recognise start sites. These regulatory proteins can act both positively (activators) and negatively (repressors).

Q 5. What is replication fork?

Solution 5. For long DNA molecules, since the two strands of DNA cannot be separated in its entire length (due to very high energy requirement), the replication occur within a small opening of the DNA helix, referred to as replication fork.

Q 6. What complications often develop at replication fork due to DNA dependent DNA Polymerase?

Solution 6: The DNA-dependent DNA polymerases catalyse polymerisation only in one direction, that is 5'→3'. This creates some additional complications at the replicating fork. Consequently, on one strand (the template with polarity 3'→5'), the replication is continuous, while on the other (the template with polarity 5'à3'), it is discontinuous.

Q 7. Why both strands of DNA double helix are not copied during transcription?

Solution 7: First, if both strands act as a template, they would code for RNA molecule with different sequences (Remember complementarity does not mean identical), and in turn, if they code for proteins, the sequence of amino acids in the proteins would be different. Hence, one segment of the DNA would be coding for two different proteins, and this would complicate the genetic information transfer machinery. Second, the two RNA molecules if produced simultaneously would be complementary to each other, hence would form a double stranded RNA. This would prevent RNA from being translated into protein and the exercise of transcription would become a futile one.

Q 8. Define Temlate Strand and Coding Strand of DNA.

Solution 8: Since the two strands of double stranded DNA have opposite polarity and the DNA-dependent RNA polymerase also catalyse the polymerisation in only one direction, that is, 5'→3', the strand that has the polarity 3'→5' acts as a template, and is also referred to as template strand. The other strand which has the polarity (5'→3') and the sequence same as RNA (except thymine at the place of uracil), is displaced during transcription. Strangely, this strand (which does not code for anything) is referred to as coding strand.

Q 9. How do promoter and terminator works along with structural gene in a transcription unit?

Solution 9: The promoter and terminator flank the structural gene in a transcription unit. The promoter is said to be located towards 5' -end (upstream) of the structural gene[16]. It is a DNA sequence that provides binding site for RNA polymerase, and it is the presence of a promoter in a transcription unit that also defines the template and coding strands. It is evident from studies that by switching its position with terminator, the definition of coding and template strands could be reversed. The terminator is located towards 3' -end (downstream) of the coding strand and it usually defines the end of the process of transcription.

Q 10. What can be concluded if an inheritable mutation is observed in a population at high frequency?

Solution 10: if an inheritable mutation is observed in a population at high frequency, it is referred to as DNA polymorphism. The probability of such variation to be observed in noncoding DNA sequence would be higher as mutations in these sequences may not have any immediate effect/impact in an individual's reproductive ability. These mutations keep on accumulating generation after generation, and form one of the basis of variability/polymorphism.

Q 11. Define repetitive DNA and Satellite DNA.

Solution 11. DNA fingerprinting involves identifying differences in some specific regions in DNA sequence called as repetitive DNA, because in these sequences, a small stretch of DNA is repeated many times. These repetitive DNA are separated from bulk genomic DNA as different peaks during density gradient centrifugation. The bulk DNA forms a major peak and the other small peaks are referred to as satellite DNA. Depending on base composition (A : T rich or G:C rich), length of segment, and number of repetitive units, the satellite DNA is classified into many categories, such as micro-satellites, mini-satellites etc. These sequences normally do not code for any proteins, but they form a large portion of human genome.

Q 12. Justify this statement: "DNA is very useful identification tool in forensic applications."

Solution 12: Since DNA from every tissue (such as blood, hair-follicle, skin, bone, saliva, sperm etc.), from an individual show the same degree of polymorphism, they become very useful identification tool in forensic applications. Further, as the polymorphisms are inheritable from parents to children, DNA fingerprinting is the basis of paternity testing, in case of disputes.

Q 13. Beta galactosidase is termed as inducer. Discuss.

Solution 13: Lactose is the substrate for the enzyme beta-galactosidase and it regulates switching on and off of the operon. Hence, it is termed as inducer. In the absence of a preferred carbon source such as glucose, if lactose is provided in the growth medium of the bacteria, the lactose is transported into the cells through the action of permease (Remember, a very low level of expression of lac operon has to be present in the cell all the time, otherwise lactose cannot enter the cells).

Q 14. What is *lac operon*?

Solution 14: In lac operon (here lac refers to lactose), a polycistronic structural gene is regulated by a common promoter and regulatory genes. Such arrangement is very common in bacteria and is referred to as operon. To name few such examples, lac operon, trp operon, ara operon, his operon, val operon, etc. The lac operon consists of one regulatory gene (the i gene – here the term i does not refer to inducer, rather it is derived from

[16] *the reference is made with respect to the polarity of coding strand*

the word inhibitor) and three structural genes (z, y, and a). The i gene codes for the repressor of the lac operon. The z gene codes for beta-galactosidase (β-gal), which is primarily responsible for the hydrolysis of the disaccharide, lactose into its monomeric units, galactose and glucose. The y gene codes for permease, which increases permeability of the cell to β-galactosides. The a gene encodes a transacetylase. Hence, all the three gene products in lac operon are required for metabolism of lactose.

Q 15. How and at what different levels genes can be regulated?

Ans 15. Considering that gene expression results in the formation of a polypeptide, it can be regulated at several levels. In eukaryotes, the regulation could be exerted at (i) transcriptional level (formation of primary transcript), (ii) processing level (regulation of splicing), (iii) transport of mRNA from nucleus to the cytoplasm, (iv) translational level.

Q 16. Elaborate functions of RNA Polymerase I, II and III.

Solution 16. There are at least three RNA polymerases in the nucleus (in addition to the RNA polymerase found in the organelles). There is a clear cut division of labour. The RNA polymerase I transcribes rRNAs (28S, 18S, and 5.8S), whereas the RNA polymerase III is responsible for transcription of tRNA, 5srRNA, and snRNAs (small nuclear RNAs). The RNA polymerase II transcribes precursor of mRNA, the heterogeneous nuclear RNA (hnRNA).

Q 17. What makes primary transcript a functional mRNA?

Solution 17. The primary transcripts, the segment of RNA which is transcribed directly from genetic sequence seated on DNA, contain both the exons and the introns and are non-functional. It is subjected to a process called splicing where the introns are removed and exons are joined in a defined order. hnRNA undergoes additional processing called as capping and tailing. In capping an unusual nucleotide (methyl guanosine triphosphate) is added to the 5'-end of hnRNA. In tailing, adenylate residues (200-300) are added at 3'-end in a template independent manner. It is the fully processed hnRNA, now called mRNA, that is transported out of the nucleus for translation.

Q 18. Point out salient features of Genetic Code.

Solution 18: (i) The codon is triplet. 61 codons code for amino acids and 3 codons do not code for any amino acids, hence they function as stop codons. (ii) Some amino acids are coded by more than one codon, hence the code is degenerate. (iii) The codon is read in mRNA in a contiguous fashion. There are no punctuations. (iv) The code is nearly universal: for example, from bacteria to human UUU would code for Phenylalanine (phe). Some exceptions to this rule have been found in mitochondrial codons, and in some protozoans. (v) AUG has dual functions. It codes for Methionine (met) , and it also act as initiator codon. (vi) UAA, UAG, UGA are stop terminator codons.

Q 19. Given that a eukaryotic cell uses a group of transcription regulators to control each of its genes, how can it rapidly and decisively switch whole groups of genes on or off?

Solution 19: Even though control of gene expression is combinatorial, the effect of a single transcription regulator can still be decisive in switching any particular gene on or off, simply by completing the combination needed to activate or repress that gene; just like dialing in the final number of a combination lock: the lock will spring open if the other numbers have been previously registered. Just as the definite set of numbers can complete the combination for different locks, the same protein can complete the combination for several different genes. As long as different genes contain regulatory DNA sequences that are recognized by the same transcription regulator, being the part of the same functional unit they can be switched on or off together, as a coordinated unit.

Q 20. What is Untranslated region of mRNA?

Solution 20. A translational unit in mRNA is the sequence of RNA that is flanked by the start codon (AUG) and the stop codon and codes for a polypeptide. An mRNA also has some additional sequences that are not translated and are referred as untranslated regions (UTR). The UTRs are present at both 5' -end (before start codon) and at 3' -end (after stop codon). They are required for efficient translation process.

Q 21. "From studies it is proposed that the transcript can be considered the basic unit of inheritance, rather than the DNA from which it is transcribed. " Justify this statement.

Solution 21. Following reasons can be advanced:

a. RNA splicing occurs during transcription. Introns were seen to be spliced in primary transcripts that were still in the process of being transcribed.
b. Genes express many splicing variants simultaneously. Approximately two-thirds of protein-coding genes express at least two different splicing variants, with an average of four alternative transcripts per locus. Splicing variants expressed by each gene are expressed at different levels, with one variant being the predominant one.
c. Substantial regulation of gene expression must occur at posttranscriptional levels in eukaryotic cells. As regulatory roles are being discovered for many of the small noncoding RNAs as well as some long noncoding RNAs.
d. Functions will be discovered for more of these RNAs. It is also proposed that the term gene would encompass a higher-order concept that includes all of the sequences encoding RNAs that contribute to a specific phenotype.

Revision Works (Unsolved)

Q 1. a hypothetical sequence from a transcription unit is represented below:

3' -ATGCATGCATGCATGCATGCATGC-5' Template Strand

5' -TACGTACGTACGTACGTACGTACG-3' Coding Strand

Can you now write the sequence of RNA transcribed from the above DNA?

Q 2. A. If following is the sequence of nucleotides in mRNA, predict the sequence of amino acid coded by it (take help of the checkerboard):

-AUG UUU UUC UUC UUU UUU UUC

B. Following is the sequence of amino acids coded by an mRNA. Predict the nucleotide sequence in the RNA:

Met-Phe-Phe-Phe-Phe-Phe-Phe

Do you face any difficulty in predicting the opposite?

Q. 3: Observe the following activities. Consider a statement that is made up of the following words each having three letters like genetic code.

RAM HAS RED CAP

If we insert a letter B in between HAS and RED and rearrange the statement, it would read as follows:

RAM HAS BRE DCA P

If we now insert two letters at the same place, say BI'. Now it would read, RAM HAS BIR EDC AP

If we insert three letters together, say BIG, the statement would read RAM HAS BIG RED CAP

The same exercise can be repeated, by deleting the letters R, E and D, one by one and rearranging the statement to make a triplet word.

RAM HAS EDC AP

RAM HAS DCA P

RAM HAS CAP

Remarks: Insertion or deletion of one or two bases changes the reading frame from the point of insertion or deletion. Such mutations are referred to as frameshift insertion or deletion mutations. Insertion or deletion of three or its multiple bases insert or delete in one or multiple codon hence one or multiple amino acids, and reading frame remains unaltered from that point onwards.

Is it appropriate to say that point mutation and Frameshift Mutation rightly confers the character of genetic code as a trilet?

Q 4. If the sequence of one strand of DNA is written as follows:

5' -ATGCATGCATGCATGCATGCATGCATGC-3'

Write down the sequence of complementary strand in 5'→3' direction.

Q 5. If the sequence of the coding strand in a transcription unit is written as follows:

5' -ATGCATGCATGCATGCATGCATGCATGC-3'

Write down the sequence of mRNA.

Q 6. Can you think for how long the lac operon would be expressed in the presence of lactose?

Q 7. Regulation of lac operon by repressor is referred to as negative regulation. Lac operon is under control of positive regulation as well. Elaborate the fact.

Q 8. The hormone estrogen converts the estrogen receptor (ER) protein from an inactive molecule to an active transcription factor. The ER binds to cis-acting sites that act as enhancers, located near the promoters of a number of genes. In some tissues, the presence of estrogen appears to activate transcription of ER-target genes, whereas in other tissues, it appears to repress transcription of those same genes. Offer an explanation as to how this may occur.

[Hint: This problem involves an understanding of how transcription enhancers and silencers work. The key to its solution is to consider the many ways that trans-acting factors can interact at enhancers to bring about changes in transcription initiation.]

Q 9. Is it true that the number of proteins in a eukaryotic cell is higher than the number of genes? Explain.

Q 10. Compare the control of gene regulation in eukaryotes and prokaryotes at the level of initiation of transcription. How do the regulatory mechanisms work? What are the similarities and differences in these two types of organisms in terms of the specific components of the regulatory mechanisms?

Q 11. A number of experiments have demonstrated that areas of the genome that are relatively inert transcriptionally are resistant to DNase I digestion; however, those areas that are transcriptionally active are DNase I sensitive. Describe how DNase I resistance or sensitivity might indicate transcriptional activity.

Q 12. Compare following pair of statements:

Statement I: The genes encoding several muscle-specific proteins are all switched on coordinately as the muscle cell differentiates. Studies of developing muscle cells in culture have identified a small number of key transcription regulators, expressed only in potential muscle cells, that coordinate muscle-specific gene expression and are thus crucial for muscle- cell differentiation. This set of regulators activates the transcription of the genes that code for muscle-specific proteins by binding to specific DNA sequences present in their regulatory regions.

Statement II: Combinational control of gene expression can generate possibility of development of different cell types.

Options:

A. Both the statements are true, but statement II cannot be accepted as a concluding remark on the basis of statement I.

B. None of the statements are true.

C. Statement are paprtially true.

D. Both the statements are true, and statement II can be accepted as a concluding remark on the basis of statement I.

Q 13. Which of the following is not a feature of the nucleus?

a. bounded by a double membrane

b. nuclear envelope contains nuclear pores

c. contains a nucleolus

d. contains microtubules

e. has chromosomes located in chromosome territories.

4. Regulations of Genes

Some feature of Human Genoome

Some of the salient observations drawn from human genome project are as follows: (i) The human genome contains 3164.7 million bp. (ii) The average gene consists of 3000 bases, but sizes vary greatly, with the largest known human gene being dystrophin at 2.4 million bases. (iii) The total number of genes is estimated at 30,000–much lower than previous estimates of 80,000 to 1,40,000 genes. Almost all (99.9 per cent) nucleotide bases are exactly the same in all people. (iv) The functions are unknown for over 50 per cent of the discovered genes. (v) Less than 2 per cent of the genome codes for proteins. (vi) Repeated sequences make up very large portion of the human genome. (vii) Repetitive sequences are stretches of DNA sequences that are repeated many times, sometimes hundred to thousand times. They are thought to have no direct coding functions, but they shed light on chromosome structure, dynamics and evolution. (viii) Chromosome 1 has most genes (2968), and the Y has the fewest (231). (ix) Scientists have identified about 1.4 million locations where singlebase DNA differences (SNPs – single nucleotide polymorphism, pronounced as 'snips') occur in humans. This information promises to revolutionise the processes of finding chromosomal locations for disease-associated sequences and tracing human history.

BAC and YAC

For sequencing, the total DNA from a cell is isolated and converted into random fragments of relatively smaller sizes (recall DNA is a very long polymer, and there are technical limitations in sequencing very long pieces of DNA) and cloned in suitable host using specialised vectors. The cloning resulted into amplification of each piece of DNA fragment so that it subsequently could be sequenced with ease. The commonly used hosts were bacteria and yeast, and the vectors were called as BAC (bacterial artificial chromosomes), and YAC (yeast artificial chromosomes).

VNTR

The technique of DNA Fingerprinting was initially developed by Alec Jeffreys. He used a satellite DNA as probe that shows very high degree of polymorphism. It was called as Variable Number of Tandem Repeats (VNTR). The technique, as used earlier, involved Southern blot hybridisation using radiolabelled VNTR as a probe. It included (i) isolation of DNA, (ii) digestion of DNA by restriction endonucleases, (iii) separation of DNA fragments by electrophoresis, (iv) transferring (blotting) of separated DNA fragments to synthetic membranes, such as nitrocellulose or nylon, (v) hybridisation using labelled VNTR probe, and (vi) detection of hybridised DNA fragments by autoradiography. A schematic representation of DNA fingerprinting is shown in Figure 5.16. The VNTR belongs to a class of satellite DNA referred to as mini-satellite. A small DNA sequence is arranged tandemly in many copy numbers. The copy number varies from chromosome to chromosome in an individual. The numbers of repeat show very high degree of polymorphism. As a result the size of VNTR varies in size from 0.1 to 20 kb. Consequently, after hybridisation with VNTR probe, the autoradiogram gives many bands of differing sizes. These bands give a characteristic pattern for an individual DNA. It differs from individual to individual in a population except in the case of monozygotic (identical) twins..

Review 1

1. Explain how Griffith's experiment and Avery, MacLeod, and McCarty's experiment determined that DNA in bacteria transmits a trait that kills mice.

2. Explain Chargaff's observation that a DNA molecule contains equal amounts of A and T and equal amounts of G and C.

3. Write the complementary DNA sequence of each of the following base sequences:

a. A G G C A T A C C T G A G T C

b. G T T T A A T G C C C T A C A

c. A A C A C T A C C G A T T C A

4. Put the following in order from smallest to largest: nucleotide, genome, nitrogenous base, gene, nucleus, cell, codon, chromosome.

5. What is the function of DNA?

6. List the three major types of RNA and their functions.

7. Some people compare DNA to a blueprint stored in the office of a construction company. Explain how this analogy would extend to transcription and translation.

8. List the sequences of the mRNA molecules transcribed from the following template DNA sequences:

a. T G A A C T A C G G T A C C A T A C

b. G C A C T A A A G A T C

9. How many codons are in each of the mRNA molecules that you wrote for question 8?

10. If a protein is 1259 amino acids long, what is the minimum size of the gene that encodes the protein? Why might the gene be longer than the minimum?

11. The amount of melanin in the skin is controlled by genes, yet melanin is not a protein. How can this be?

12. The roundworm C. elegans has 556 cells when it hatches. Each cell contains the entire genome but expresses only a subset of the genes. Therefore, the cells "specialize" in particular functions. List all of the ways that a roundworm cell might silence the unneeded genes. 144 UNIT TWO DNA, Inheritance, and Biotechnology

13: Duchenne muscular dystrophy (DMD) is caused by a relatively rare X-linked recessive allele. It results in progressive muscular wasting and usually leads to death before age 20.

a. What is the probability that the first son of a woman whose brother is affected will be affected?

b. What is the probability that the second son of a woman whose brother is affected will be affected, if her first son was affected?

c. What is the probability that a child of an unaffected man whose brother is affected will be affected?

d. An affected man mates with his unaffected first cousin; there is otherwise no history of DMD in this family. If the mothers of this man and his mate were sisters, what is the probability that the couple's first child will be an affected boy? An affected girl? An unaffected child?

e. If two of the parents of the couple in part (d) were brother and sister, what is the probability that the couple's first child will be an affected boy? An affected girl? An unaffected child?

14. What is the job of the tRNA during translation?

a. It carries amino acids to the mRNA.

b. It triggers the formation of a covalent bond between amino acids.

c. It binds to the small ribosomal subunit.

d. It triggers the termination of the protein.

7. How does the lac operon regulate lactose digestion in bacteria?

a. The repressor protein becomes a lactose-digesting enzyme only when lactose is present.

b. The repressor protein binds to the lac operon when lactose is present, blocking transcription.

c. When lactose is present, it binds to the operator region of the lac operon, activating transcription of the repressor protein gene.

d. The repressor protein falls off the lac operon when lactose is present, and lactose-digesting genes are expressed.

8. Certain portions of the mRNA transcribed from the tropomyosin gene can act as either introns or exons. As a result,

a. one gene may encode many different possible proteins.

b. each codon may encode many different amino acids.

c. an amino acid may correspond to many different codons.

d. a single protein may determine many different traits.

15. A protein-encoding region of a gene has the following DNA sequence:

T T T C A T C A G G A T G C A A C A

Determine how each of the following mutations alters the amino acid sequence:

a. Substitution of an A for the T in the first position

b. Substitution of a G for the C in the 17th position

c. Insertion of a T between the fourth and fifth DNA bases

d. Insertion of a GTA between the 12th and 13th DNA bases

e. Deletion of the first DNA nucleotide.

16. A protein-encoding region of a gene has the following DNA sequence:

T T T C A T C A G G A T G C A A C A

Determine how each of the following mutations alters the amino acid sequence:

a. Substitution of an A for the T in the first position

b. Substitution of a G for the C in the 17th position

c. Insertion of a T between the fourth and fifth DNA bases

d. Insertion of a GTA between the 12th and 13th DNA bases

e. Deletion of the first DNA nucleotide

17. Explain how a mutation in a protein-encoding gene, an enhancer, or a gene encoding a transcription factor can have the same effect on an organism.

18. 1. Why does DNA replicate?

19. What is semiconservative replication?

20. What are the steps of DNA replication?

21. Could DNA replication occur if primase were not present in a cell?

22. Why do enzymes work at multiple origins of replication?

23. What are the three main events of the cell cycle?

24. What happens during interphase?

25. Suppose a centromere does not split during anaphase. Describe the chromosomes in the daughter cells.

26. Distinguish between mitosis and cytokinesis.

27.

***

5. Mendelism and Inheritence

Experimentations and intensive studies related to onset and development of variations among organisms are on the study table of scholars since pre-historic ages. "Thread of Qualities" (GUNA SUTRA) was the key word often used by Vedic saints to elaborate transmission of qualities from parents to offsprings. It was the time when Darwin and Mendel started experimenting on the principle of inheritance from two distinctly varied angles. Charles Darwin was puzzling over natural selection and evolution at the same time that Mendel was tending his plants. No one knew it at the time, but each scientist was exploring genetic variation from a different point of view. Mendel focused on the fate of specific traits from generation to generation; Darwin studied larger-scale shifts in variation within populations. Thanks to another century of biological research, we now know that all variation traces to mutations in DNA. That insight ties together the ideas of Mendel, Darwin, and many other scientists. The so-called modern evolutionary synthesis integrates genetic variation, inheritance, and natural selection to explain evolutionary changes in populations. Biology has made great strides since Mendel and Darwin's time. Today, genetics and DNA are familiar to nearly everyone, and the entire set of genetic instructions to build a person—the human genome—has been deciphered. Even so, every family encounters the same principles of heredity that Mendel derived in his experiments with peas. Our look at genetics begins the traditional way, with Gregor Mendel, but we can now appreciate his genius in light of what we know about DNA.

Inheritence

***

Test Papers

Review 1

Q 1. Complete the following:

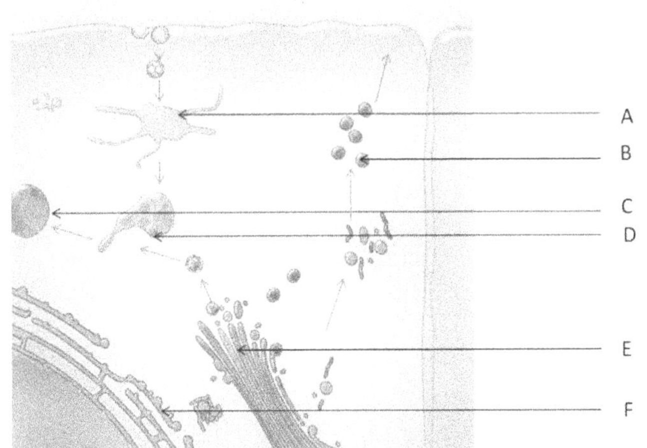

Diagram showing secretory cycle which is followed by organelles of a living cell. Identify different structures. Both Endo-cytic pathway and Exo-cytic pathway are displayed in this diagram.

I: ....:Late Endosome;
II: ....: Early Endosome;
III: ....: Receives secretory vesicles from Endoplasmic Reticulum and takes part in maturation of proteins;
IV: ....: Possesses Hydrolytic Enzymes;
V: ....: These vesicles directly involve in cellular secretion;
VI: ....: It is formed after accumulation of different endocytic vesicles;
VII: ....: The site of Protein Synthesis and formation of secretory vesicles ;

Q 2. Identify different groups of molecules displayed in the following diagram.

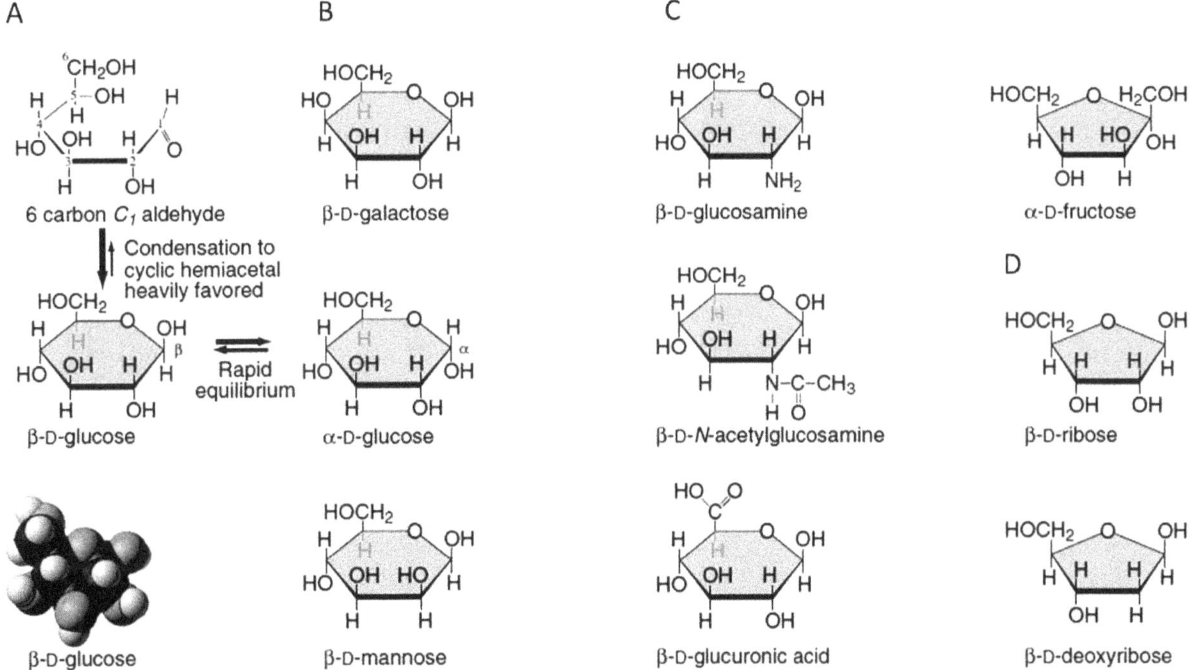

Q 3. Organism A manufactures 2 molecules of ATP by utilising 1 molecule of glucose. Organism B manufactures 38 molecules of ATP by consuming 1 molecule of glucose. During first case ethanol is manufactured and during second case CO_2 and water molecules are formed. Identify types of respiration performed by organism A and B. In which of the cases of metabolism mitochondria gets involved?

Q 4. During the process of aerobic respiration partial breakdown of carbohydrate takes place in site P and complete breakdown of the biproduct of reaction took place at site P is performed at site Q. A kind of enzyme R embedded in the membrane of site Q plays a vital role in liberating ATP. Identify P, Q and R.

Review 2

Q 1. Complete the following.

The complex of DNA with its packaging proteins is called .... Nuclei contain two broad classes of .... : .... , which is highly condensed throughout the cell cycle and is generally inactive in transcription, and .... , which is less condensed and contains actively .... Different types of these molecule molecular groups are defined by complex patterns of posttranslational modifications of the .... proteins. These modifications direct the binding of protein readers that establish .... states to promote or repress .... or serve other structural roles.

Q 2. Characteristics of a densely packed zone present in eukaryotic nucleus can be visualised by observing following features:

a) The nucleus contains a number of substructures specialised for taking u different functions. The most prominent of these is the densely packed structure, a versatile factory for transcription of ribosomal RNA (rRNA) from a tandem array of genes and processing of the same and other noncoding RNAs, as well as ribosome assembly.

b) Small RNA molecule housed in this site is serving as assembly site for certain transcriptional co-repressor complexes (PML and Polycomb group bodies).

c) This unit gets disintegrated during mitotic and meiotic process of cell division.

d) This unit remains membrane less.

Q 3. What is telomere? What specific role do these structures perform?

Q 4. Net result of Glycolysis is displayed in the form of a schematic diagram. .... molecules of ATP can be obtained through this process by consuming 12 molecules of Carbohydrate.

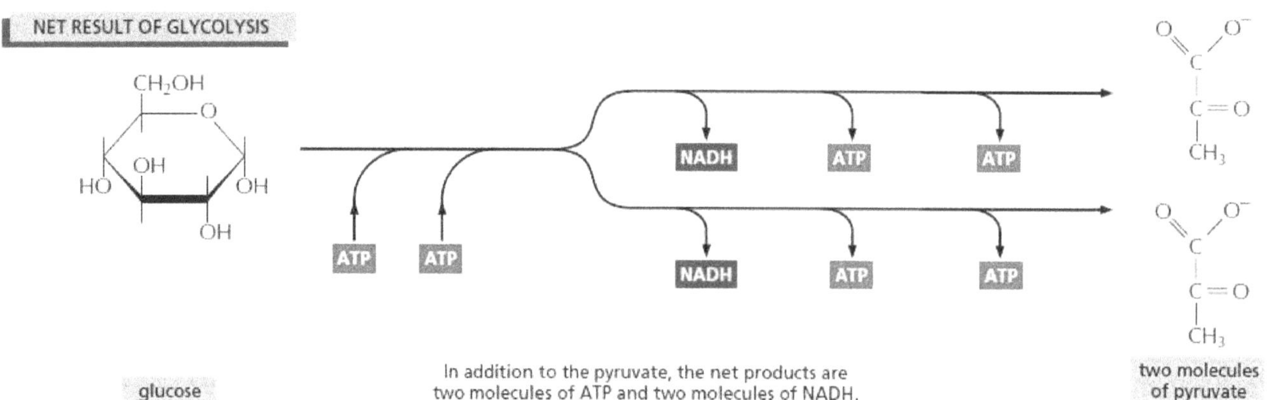

Q 5. In aerobic metabolism in eukaryotic cells, the .... produced by glycolysis is actively pumped into the mitochondrial matrix. At that site, it is rapidly decarboxylated by a giant complex of three enzymes, called the ....

Q 6. Fat is also a major source of energy giving nutrient in case of non-green plants and other heterotrophs. How do fat molecules enter the TCA Cycle?

Review 3

Q 1. Following biochemical cycle displays .... metabolism in mitochondrial matrix.

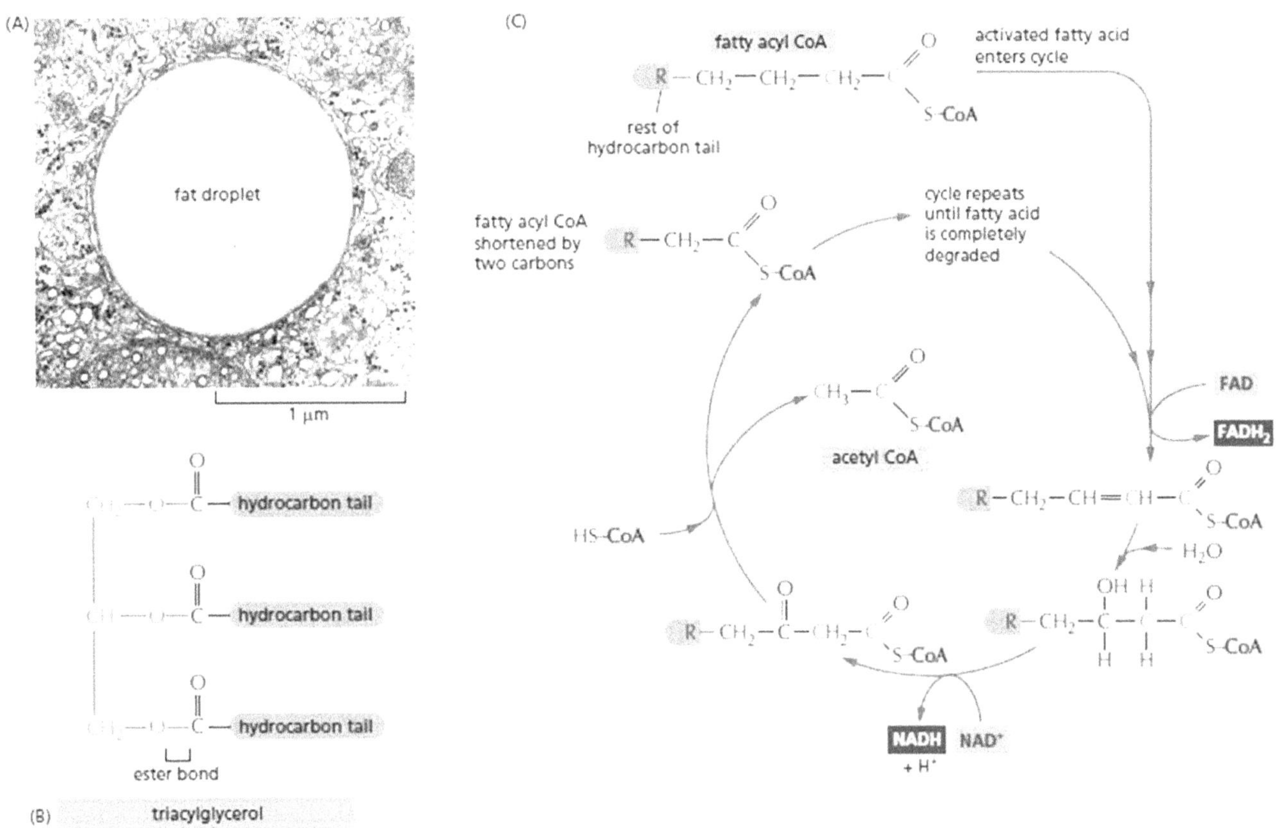

Q 2. What is the source of oxygen in TCA Cycle? How many molecules of O2 will be liberated if 32 molecules of Carbohydrate is consumed during aerobic respiration?

Fact Sheet related to source of Oxygen during Aerobic Respiration:

A common misconception about the citric acid cycle is that the atmospheric O_2 required for the process to proceed is converted into the CO_2 that is released as a waste product. In fact, the oxygen atoms required to make CO_2 from the acetyl groups entering the citric acid cycle are supplied not by O_2 but by water. Three molecules of water are split in each cycle, and the oxygen atoms of some of them are ultimately used to make CO_2. As we see shortly, the O_2 that we breathe is actually reduced to water by the electron-transport chain; it is not incorporated directly into the CO_2 we exhale.

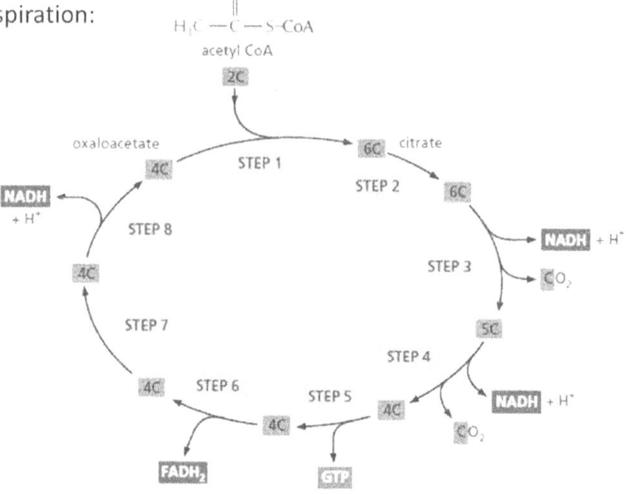

Q 3. Complete the following statement.

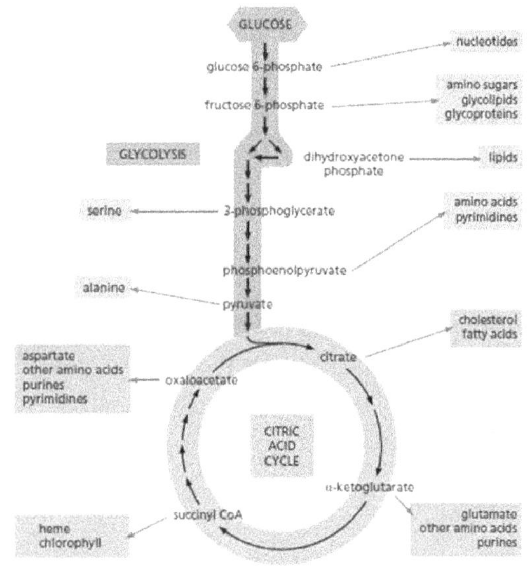

molecules—shown here as products—in turn serve as the precursors for many of the cell's macromolecules. Each black arrow in this diagram denotes a single enzyme catalyzed reaction; some of the selected molecules of the pathway generally represent pathways with many steps that are required to produce the indicated products. many of the intermediates formed in glycolysis and the citric acid cycle are siphoned off by such ...., in which they are converted by series of .... into amino acids, nucleotides, lipids, and other small organic molecules that the cell needs. Oxaloacetate and α-ketoglutarate from the citric acid cycle, for example, are transferred from the mitochondrial matrix back to the cytosol, where they serve as precursors for the production of many essential molecules, such as the amino acids aspartate and glutamate, respectively

Q 4. Identify steps of reaction as displayed in the following chart.

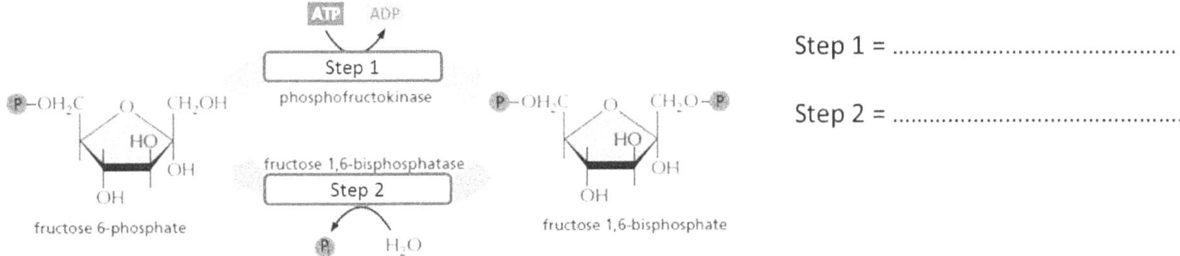

Step 1 = ...

Step 2 = ...

The enzyme phosphofructokinase catalyzes the phosphorylation of fructose 6-phosphate to form fructose 1, 6-bisphosphate in step 3 of glycolysis. This reaction is so energetically favorable that the enzyme will not work in reverse. To produce fructose 6-phosphate in gluconeogenesis, the enzyme fructose 1,6-bisphosphatase removes the phosphate from fructose 1,6-bisphosphate. Coordinated feedback regulation of these two enzymes helps control the flow of metabolites toward glucose synthesis or glucose breakdown.

Q 5. Complete the following ....

Human body (specially hepatic cells store glucose in the form of Glycogen and provide energy to other parts of the organ system whenever needed.
A specific enzyme involved in this reaction is .... which converts glycogen to glucose. helps to prevent glycogen breakdown when ATP glycogen phosphorylase, which breaks down glycogen , is inhibited by glucose 6-phosphate, as well as by ATP. This regulation is plentiful and to favor glycogen synthesis when glucose 6-phosphate concentration is high. The balance between glycogen synthesis and breakdown is further regulated by intracellular signaling pathways that are controlled by the hormones .... , ... and ....

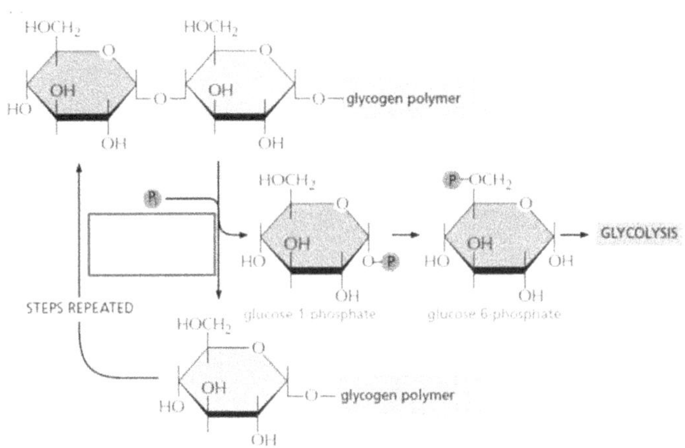

Review 4

Q 1. Compare the following pair of statements regarding cellular respiration:

Statement P: Both Prokaryotic and eukaryotic cells of different types obtain Most of Their Energy by a Membrane-based Mechanism.

Statement Q: Most of their ATP is produced by oxidative phosphorylation. The generation of ATP by the process of oxidative phosphorylation differs from the way ATP is produced during glycolysis, in that it requires a membrane linked system of specialised proteins. Oxidative phosphorylation (especially in eukaryotic cells) takes place in mitochondria, and it depends on an electron- transport process that drives the transport of protons (H^+) across the inner mitochondrial membrane. A related membrane-based process of transport system produces ATP during photosynthesis in plants, algae, and photosynthetic bacteria.

Options:

A: Statement P and Q are true and support each other by all means.

B: Statement P and Q are not true and cannot support each other by all means.

C: Statement P and Q are true but cannot support each other by all means.

D: Statement P is true but Statement Q is not true and cannot support each other.

Q 2. There are cell organelles in eukaryotes having some sort of similarity and partial autonomy. Provide missing information to complete the following fact sheet given below on the basis of homology and function.

A: Both organelles contain their own DNA-based genome and the machinery to copy this DNA and to make RNA and protein.
B: The inner compartments of these organelles contain the DNA and a special set of ribosomes.
C: Parts of Inner Membranes in both organelles the contain the protein complexes which remain involved in ATP production.
D: Both the organelles can divide to give birth to new organelles by the process of fission.
E: Both the organelles remain involved in the biochemical processes related to Carbohydrate molecules.

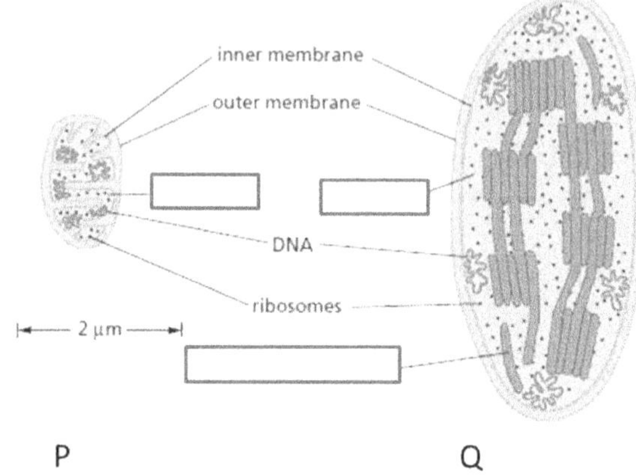

F: Name of the sap filled in inner chamber of P = ... and in Q that sap is called ....
G: Folded inner membrane of P is .... And that of Q makes ....

Q 3. It is observed that patients with an inherited disorder called myoclonic epilepsy and ragged red fiber disease (MERRF) are deficient in multiple proteins duly required for accomplishing .... They typically experience different symptoms: like muscle weakness, heart problems, epilepsy, and often dementia. Muscle and nerve cells are especially sensitive to the type of defects of different parts of the specific cell organelle, because they need so much derived energy to function normally.

Identify the cell organelle and also the part thereof which becomes badly affected in this regard.

Q 4. Compare the following statements.

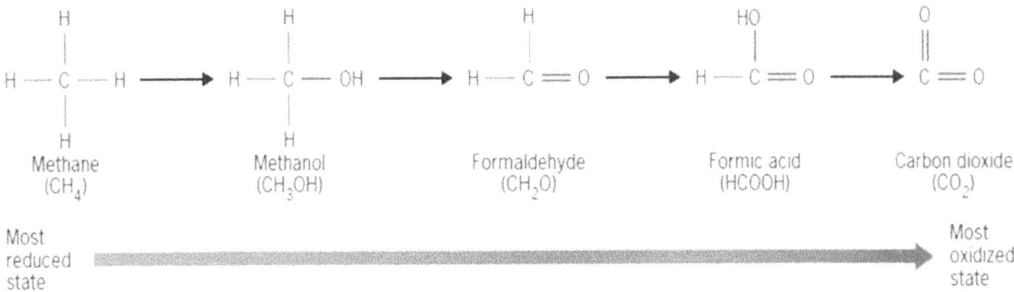

Assertion: Oxidation of Carbohydrate molecule and Fat molecules take place during respiration.
Reason: The oxidation state of a carbon atom depends on the other atoms to which it is bonded. Each carbon atom can form a maximum of four bonds with other atoms. This series of simple, one-carbon molecules illustrates the various oxidation states in which the carbon atom can exist. In its most reduced state, the carbon is bonded to four hydrogen atoms (forming methane); in its most oxidized state, the carbon atom is bonded to two oxygens (forming carbon dioxide).

A: Both the statements are false.

B: Both the statements are true but they cannot support each other.

C: Both the statements are true and they can support each other.

Q 5. Assertion and Reason ...

Assertion: Mitochondria can change their shape, location, and number to suit a cell's needs. Isolated mitochondria are generally similar in size and shape to their bacterial ancestors. They may exhibit partial autonomy but they are no longer capable of living independently and are remarkably adaptable and can adjust their location, shape, and number to suit the needs of the cell. In some cells, these organelles remain fixed in one location, where they supply ATP directly to a site of unusually high energy consumption. In a heart muscle cell, for an example to elaborate the fact, mitochondria are located close to the contractile apparatus, whereas in a sperm they are wrapped tightly around the motile flagellum.

Reason: Mitochondria ceaselessly remain involved in manufacturing ATP by operating different activities related to aerobic respiration. Majority of these activities are membrane led activities having involvement of Electron Transport Chain and ATPase. This organelle also holds its own DNA molecule and ribosomes for operating self-regulated synthesis of protein. For another set of molecules this organelle depends on the Nucleus of living cell.

Options:

A: Both the statements are false.

B: Both the statements of Assertions and reasons are true and they can support each other.

C: Both the statements are true but they cannot support each other.

D: Assertion is correct but reasons are not supporting it.

Review 5

I: Statements regarding nucleus are listed below. Complete all the statements...

1. Like the cell membrane, the nuclear envelope consists of .... that form a lipid bilayer. The nucleus provides a site for genetic .... that is segregated from the location of .... in the cytoplasm, allowing levels of .... that are not available to .... The main function of the cell nucleus is to control .... and mediate the .... of DNA during the cell cycle. It controls the .... characteristics of an organism. The organelle is also responsible for .... , cell division, growth, and .... Storage of ...., the genes in the form of long and thin DNA (deoxyribonucleic acid) strands, referred to as .... Storage of proteins and RNA (ribonucleic acid) in the .... The nucleus is a site for .... in which messenger RNA (mRNA) are produced for .... During the cell division, ... are arranged into chromosomes in the nucleus. Production of .... (protein factories) in the nucleolus.
2. Selective .... of regulatory factors and energy molecules through nuclear pores. The .... helps to maintain the shape of the nucleus and assists in regulating the flow of .... into and out of the nucleus through .... The nucleus communicates with the remaining of the cell or the cytoplasm through several openings called .... Such structures are the sites for the exchange of .... between the nucleus and cytoplasm. A fluid-filled space or .... is present between the two layers of a nuclear membrane.
3. .... is the gelatinous substance within the nuclear envelope. Also called ...., this semi-aqueous material is similar to the cytoplasm and is composed mainly of water with dissolved salts, enzymes, and organic molecules suspended within. The nucleolus .... and .... are surrounded by nucleoplasm, which functions to .... and protect the contents of the nucleus. .... also supports the nucleus by helping to maintain its shape. Additionally, nucleoplasm provides a medium by which materials, such as enzymes and ...., can be transported throughout the nucleus. Substances are exchanged between the .... and .... through nuclear pores.
4. .... , also known as .... and ...., is a pentose sugar (monosaccharide containing five carbon atoms) that is a key component of the nucleic acid deoxyribonucleic acid (DNA). It is derived from the .... Deoxyribose has the chemical formula $C_5H_{10}O_4$. .... is the sugar component of DNA, just as .... serves that role in RNA (ribonucleic acid). Alternating with .... , deoxyribose forms the backbone of the DNA, binding to the nitrogenous bases .... , thymine, guanine, and cytosine. As a component of DNA, which represents the genetic information in all living cells, ... is critical to life. This ubiquitous sugar reflects a .... among all living organisms.
5. The .... forms the structural framework of nucleic acids, including DNA. This backbone is composed of .... and phosphate groups and defines the .... of the molecule. DNA are composed of .... that

are linked to one another in a chain by chemical bonds, called ...., between the sugar base of one nucleotide and the phosphate group of the adjacent nucleotide. The sugar is the 3′ end, and the .... is the 5′ end of each nucleotide .... The .... attached to the 5′ carbon of the sugar on one nucleotide forms an ester bond with the free hydroxyl on the 3′ carbon of the next .... These bonds are called ...., and the .... is described as extending, or growing, in the 5′ to 3′ direction when the molecule is synthesized.

6. In ...., the molecular double-helix shape is formed by two linear .... that run opposite each other and twist together in a helical shape. The .... is negatively charged and hydrophilic, which allows the DNA backbone to form bonds with water. DNA .... is the process by which an organism .... its DNA into another copy that is passed on to daughter cells. .... occurs before a cell divides to ensure that both cells receive an exact copy of the parent's ....

7. Chromatin becomes highly .... during .... to form the compact .... that are distributed to daughter nuclei . During .... , some of the .... remains highly condensed and is transcriptionally............................ inactive; the remainder of the chromatin (euchromatin) is .... and distributed throughout the nucleus. Cells contain two types of .... contains DNA sequences that are never ...., such as the .... present at centromeres. .... contains sequences that are not .... in the cell being examined, but are transcribed in other cell types. Consequently, the amount of .... varies depending on the .... activity of the cell. Much of the .... is localized to the .... of the nucleus, possibly because one of the .... associated with .... binds to a protein of the inner nuclear membrane.

8. The phenomenon of .... inactivation provides an example of the role of .... in gene expression. In many animals, including humans, females have two X chromosomes, and males have one X and one Y chromosome. The X chromosome contains thousands of .... that are not present on the much smaller .... Thus, females have twice as many X chromosome genes as males have. Despite this difference, female and male cells contain equal amounts of the proteins .... by X chromosome genes. This results from a dosage .... mechanism in which one of the two X chromosomes in female cells is .... by being converted to .... early in development. Consequently, only one copy of the .... is available for .... in either female or male cells. The mechanism of .... inactivation is fascinating though not yet fully understood; it appears to involve the action of a .... that coats the inactive X chromosome and induces its conversion to ....

9. Although interphase chromatin appears to be uniformly distributed, the .... are actually arranged in an organized fashion and divided into discrete functional domains that play an important role in regulating .... The non-random distribution of

…………………… within the interphase nucleus was first suggested in 1885 by C. Rabl, who proposed that each chromosome occupies a distinct territory, with ………………………. and ……………………… attached to opposite sides of the ……………. ……………… This basic model of chromosome organization was confirmed nearly a hundred years later (in 1984) by detailed studies of ……………… …………………………. in Drosophila salivary glands………………… ………………. Rather than randomly winding around one another, each …………………………. was found to occupy a ……………. ……………… of the nucleus. The ……………………… are closely associated with the nuclear envelope at many sites, with their ………………………….. and ……………………………. clustered at opposite poles………………………………………….

10. Like the DNA in metaphase chromosomes, the chromatin in interphase nuclei appears to be organized into ………… …………………… containing approximately 50 to 100 kb of DNA. A good example of this ………………… ………………… ………………. is provided by the highly …………………… ……………………… of amphibian oocytes, in which ………… …………………… regions of DNA can be visualized as extended loops of …………………… …………………….. These chromatin domains appear to ……………. ……………… functional units, which independently regulate ……………………… ………………………

11. The effects of ……………………… ……………………… on gene expression have been demonstrated by a variety of experiments during different instances showing that the position of a ……………. in chromosomal DNA affects the level at which the ………………. is expressed. For example, the transcriptional activity ………………. ……………………. of genes introduced into ………………….. mice depends on their sites of …………………… in the mouse genome ………………………. This effect of …………………… ……………………… on gene expression can be alleviated by sequences known as ……………… …………………….. ……………………….., which result in a high level of expression of the ……………… ………………………. irrespective of their site of integration. In contrast to ……………………… ……………………………., locus control regions stimulate only ……………………… …………………… that are integrated into …………………………. ………….; they do not affect the expression of ……………………… ……………………… DNAs in transient assays. In addition, rather than affecting individual promoters, …………………… …………………… …………………. appear to activate large …………………… ……………………….., presumably by inducing long-range alterations in chromatin structure.

12. ………………………….. are concentrations of components involved in RNA processing. They often correspond to clusters of …………………… ……………………………… seen by electron microscopy. They may serve as storage depots of ………………. ………………. , or they may play a more active role in ……………. …………………… …………………. and/or assembly.

13. Formerly known as ………………… ………………… . Approximately 0.2 to 1.0 μm in diameter, ……………………. …………………… have a coiled fibrous substructure. First identified by electron microscopy, up to 10 of these structures are seen in transformed cells. They are usually absent from ……………………………………. normal cells. They contain the ……………………… ………………………… ……………… and survival of …………………… ………………… ……………………, which is encoded by the gene mutated in ………………….. ………………… ……………………., a severe, inherited, human, muscular wasting disease. They are involved in …………… …………………….. ……………………………… and ……………………… ……………………… …………………………. assembly and in maturation of telomerase (which also contains an RNA component).

14. The separation between .... is maintained by boundary sequences or ...., which prevent the chromatin structure of one domain from spreading to its neighbours. .... act as barriers that prevent enhancers in one domain from acting on .... located in an adjacent domain. Like .... , insulators function only in the context of ...., suggesting that they regulate higher-order .... Although the mechanisms of action of .... and insulators remain to be elucidated, their functions clearly indicate the importance of .... organization in the control of eukaryotic gene expression.

15. Mammalian nuclei also contain approximately 10 to 30 bodies, varying in size from 0.3 to 1.0 µm, known as .... bodies. PML bodies were initially defined by the presence of a protein called .... , an important regulator of cell growth and .... PML has a .... motif and is therefore probably an E3 ligase for ubiquitin or ubiquitin-like proteins. PML bodies apparently have a role in assembling .... that modify chromatin to repress transcription.

16. .... with nuclear pores can have both positive and negative effects on .... In mammalian cells, the chromatin near pores appears .... than most chromatin adjacent to .... The significance of these interactions is still under study. .... of the nuclear envelope during .... releases the chromosomes so that they can be segregated to the .... by the cytoplasmic mitotic spindle .... Mitotic segregation of .... to daughter cells takes place within the nucleus in many other eukaryotes, including yeasts.

17. Nuclear pore complexes have a .... consisting of three stacked rings each with .... symmetry. .... and ....rings flank a prominent ....that is intimately associated with the .... membrane linking the inner and outer nuclear membranes. The .... is anchored to the nuclear lamina. A less-prominent fourth .... surrounds the .... in the NE lumen. The minimum diameter of the .... through the pore is approximately 40 nm, and the channel is approximately 50- to 70-nm long.

18. The protein composition of nuclear .... is remarkably conserved. Approximately 30 core proteins, called .... , are present in multiples of .... Mass differences between electron .... and mass .... measurements may be accounted for by .... and other auxiliary subunits that do not have a key ....

19. Nucleoside derivatives may be grouped differently in accord to their structure and function.

    a. .... nucleotides: ATP, ADP, AMP, Cyclic AMP

    b. .... nucleotides: GTP, GDP, GMP, Cyclic GMP

    c. .... nucleotides: CTP, CDP, CMP and certain deoxy CDP derivatives of glucose, choline and ethanolamine

    d. .... nucleotides: UDP

e. .... : PAPS (active sulphate), SAM (active methionine), certain coenzymes like NAD+, FAD, FMN, Cobamide coenzyme, CoA

20. .... often involves disruption or displacement of .... located on specific regulatory regions. Before the discussion of specific ...., it is useful to consider some aspects of .... structure. The nucleosome consists of .... wrapped in a left-handed helix around an .... of histone subunits. The histone core .... makes numerous contacts with the DNA .... and phosphate backbone, leading to tight but relatively .... This aspect of the .... allows for a .... with DNA, because binding of the .... to DNA is nearly as .... for all sequences. However, ... are not positioned uniformly along the DNA. First, some .... sequences do not bend in a manner that can form a stable .... Such sequences are often found in .... Second, nucleosomes are less stable if the .... are modified, for example by .... or the inclusion of variant .... The presence of unstable .... enables the .... to access key regulatory sequences. .... remodelling complexes can either expose or shield .... by altering the location of nucleosomes on the .... These .... remodelling complexes use energy from .... to destabilize interactions between .... and DNA thus altering the position of the .... and "remodelling" the .... One example is the ....that is recruited to a specific subset of .... through interactions with transcription activators.

21. Observe the following statements and strike out the wrong one out:

a. This special type of structure, popularly called Enhancers, is clusters of regulatory DNA sequences that resemble promoter proximal elements.

b. These enhancers are considerably more complicated and have several distinguishing features.

c. An enhancer can increase the rate of initiation of the biochemical process from a basal promoter even if it is located up to 100 kb away along the chromosome.

d. The enhancer element will work in either orientation relative to the promoter.

e. Enhancers can function in coordination with a heterologous promoter.

f. A sequence in an intron of the immunoglobulin heavy-chain gene enhances transcription in case of lymphocyte and monocytes. That sequence works with same efficiency in case of other cell types.

g. Many genes are associated with multiple enhancers. In a general status each enhancer usually works in a cell type–specific fashion.

22. How do coprocessors and co-activators work during transcription?

23. What is combinational control of transcription?

24. Write important features of pentose sugar.

25. Discuss role of nucleotides as neurotransmitters, as activator of reactions and role played as intermediates of some biochemical reactions.

.

Key : Review 5

1: phospholipids; transcription; translation; gene regulation; prokaryotes; gene expression ; replication; hereditary; protein synthesis; differentiation; hereditary material; chromatin; nucleolus; transcription; protein synthesis; chromatins; ribosomes;

2: transportation; envelope; molecules; nuclear pores ; nuclear pores ; large molecules (proteins and RNA); perinuclear space ;

3: Nucleoplasm; karyoplasm; chromosomes; cushion; Nucleoplasm; nucleotides (DNA and RNA subunits); cytoplasm; nucleoplasm;

4: Deoxyribose; D-Deoxyribose and 2-deoxyribose; pentose sugar ribose; Deoxyribose; ribose; phosphate bases; adenine; deoxyribose; commonality;

5: sugar-phosphate backbone ; alternating sugar ; directionality; nucleotides ; ester bonds; phosphate; phosphate group ; nucleotide; phosphodiester bonds; sugar-phosphate backbone;

6: double-stranded DNA ; sugar-phosphate backbones ; sugar-phosphate backbone ; replication; duplicates; Replication; genetic material;

7: condensed; mitosis or meiosis; metaphase chromosomes; interphase; chromatin (heterochromatin) ; decondensed ; heterochromatin; Constitutive heterochromatin ; transcribed; satellite sequences ; Facultative heterochromatin; transcribed; facultative heterochromatin; transcriptional ; heterochromatin; periphery; principal proteins ; heterochromatin;

8: X chromosome; heterochromatin; genes; Y chromosome; encoded; compensation; inactivated; heterochromatin ; X chromosome; transcription; X chromosome; regulatory RNA; heterochromatin;

9: chromosomes ; gene expression; chromatin; centromeres and telomeres; nuclear envelope; polytene; chromosomes; chromosome; discrete region ; chromosomes; centromeres and telomeres ;

10: looped domains ; looped-domain organization; transcribed chromosomes; actively transcribed ; decondensed chromatin; represent discrete; gene expression

11: chromosome organization ; gene; gene; transgenic; integration; chromosomal position; locus control regions ; introduced genes; transcriptional enhancers; transfected genes; chromosomal DNA; unintegrated plasmid; locus control regions ; chromosome domains;

12: Speckles; interchromatin granules ; splicing factors ; splicing factor modification ;

13: coiled bodies ; Cajal bodies ; nontransformed; human autoantigen p80-coilin ; motor neurons (SMN) protein; spinal muscular atrophy; small nuclear ribonucleoprotein (snRNP); small nucleolar ribonucleoprotein (snoRNP);

14: chromosomal domains ; insulator elements ; Insulators ; promoters; locus control regions ; chromosomal DNA ; chromatin structure ; locus control regions; higher-order chromatin;

15: promyelocytic leukemia (PML); PML; genome stability; RING-finger amino acid sequence; corepressor complexes;

16: Chromatin interactions ; gene expression ; less condensed (less heterochromatic) ; the lamina ; Disassembly; mitosis in metazoan ; daughter cells ; chromosomes ;

17: scaffold; eightfold; Cytoplasmic and nuclear ; spoke ring ; pore; nuclear ring ; luminal ring; pore membrane ; central channel ;

19: Adenosine; Guanosine; Cytidine; Uridine; Miscellaneous;

20: Gene activation; nucleosomes; mechanisms; nucleosome ; DNA; octamer; minor groove; nonspecific binding; nucleosome; dynamic association; histone core; energetically favourable; nucleosomes; AT-rich; nucleosome; promoter regions; histones; acetylation; histone proteins; nucleosomes; transcription machinery; Nucleosome; regulatory elements; DNA template; multiprotein; ATP hydrolysis; histones; nucleosome; chromatin; SWI/SNF (yeast mating type switching defective/sucrose nonfermenting) complex ; genes;

21: Statement f is not properly represented.

22: Corepressors act in opposition to coactivators by repressing the biochemical process of transcription. The most common form of repression, as evident from different studies, involves chromatin modifications that block TF access. Histone deacetylase complexes like Sir2 and NuRD remove acetyl modifications. This activity is finally advances leading to chromatin compaction and repression of the biochemical process of transcription.

23: The complicated system of eukaryotic regulatory systems allows for the integration of multiple regulatory signals at individual site of genes. Such combinatorial control is seen acting in a limited way in prokaryotes. The E. coli lac genes are regulated by both lactose and glucose. Only when glucose is low and lactose is provided in the medium do the activator (CAP) and repressor (lac repressor) function to maximize the phenomenon of lac expression. Regulation of transcription initiation (especially in case of eukaryotes) is based on similar principles involving DNA-binding activators and repressors controlling individual genes.

24: Features of Pentose Sugar…

a) This sugar molecule is a monosaccharide with five carbon atoms.
b) Ribose (the most common pentose) is lashed with one oxygen atom attached to each carbon atom.
c) Deoxyribose sugar is derived by loss of an oxygen atom from the ribose sugar.
d) The aldehyde functional group (as present in the carbohydrates) react with neighbouring hydroxyl functional groups present in the same molecule to form intramolecular hemiacetals.
e) The resulting ring structure is related to furan (also termed a furanose).
f) The ring spontaneously opens and closes (allowing rotation to occur about the bond between the carbonyl group and the neighbouring carbon atom). This specific type of rotation (mutarotation) ensures yielding of two distinct configurations (α and β). This process is termed.

25: Serving as neurotransmitters and as signal receptor ligands. Adenosine can function as an inhibitory neurotransmitter, while ATP also affects synaptic neurotransmission throughout the central and peripheral nervous systems. ADP is an important activator of platelet functions resulting in control of blood coagulation; controlling numerous enzymatic reactions facilitated through allosteric effects on enzyme activity; serving as activated intermediates in different types of biosynthetic reactions. Some of the activated intermediates: S-adenosylmethionine (S-AdoMet or SAM) involved in methyl transfer reactions, many sugar coupled nucleotides involved in glycogen and glycoprotein synthesis.

Review 6

Q 1. Complete the following chart.

P Generation Yellow Round Green Wrinkled

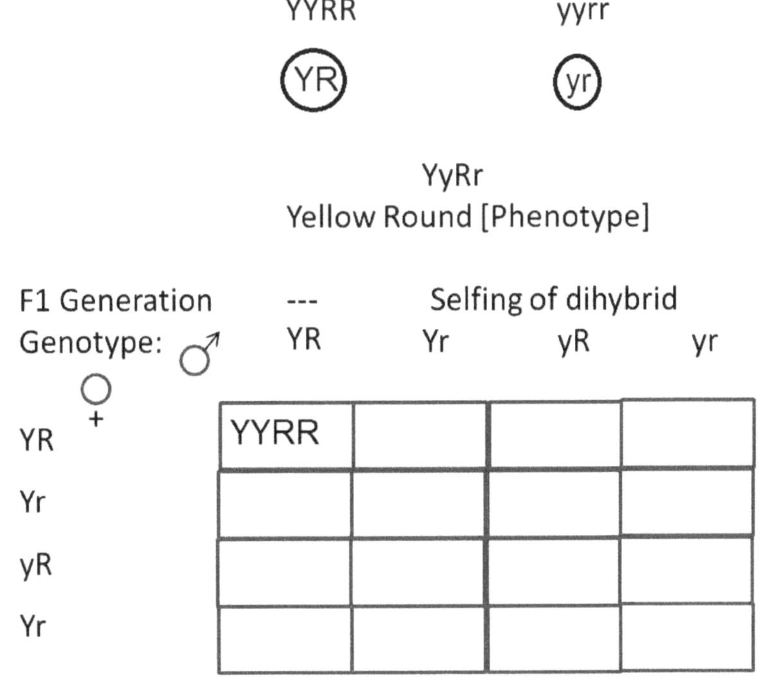

Phenotype Ration:

Yellow	Yellow	Green	Green
Round	Wrinkled	Round	Wrinkled

Based on the above test cross one can prepare different types of chart to study the principle of genetics for rest of the other contrasting characters of pea plant duly proposed by Mendel[17].

---

[17] *Mendel studied the inheritance of seven different traits in garden peas, each trait being controlled by a different gene having contrasting alleles. Mendel's research led him to formulate three principles of inheritance: (1) the alleles of a gene are either dominant or recessive, (2) different alleles of a gene segregate from each other during the formation of gametes, and (3) the alleles of different genes assort independently.*

According to Mendel it is proposed that when the two alleles of a pair segregate or separate during gamete formation such that a gamete receives only one of the two factors. In homozygous parents, all gametes produced are similar; while in heterozygous parents, two kinds of gametes are produced in equal proportions. Homozygous recessive parents always give birth to offsprings having homozygous recessive genotype and recessive phenotype.

Mendel also proposed the nature of genes as they were found to be transmitting from one generation to the other without remaining linked to any other gene or set of genes.

Q 2. Human gene HBB coding and execution is displayed through a schematic diagram. Identify and describe all the three steps displayed in this diagram.

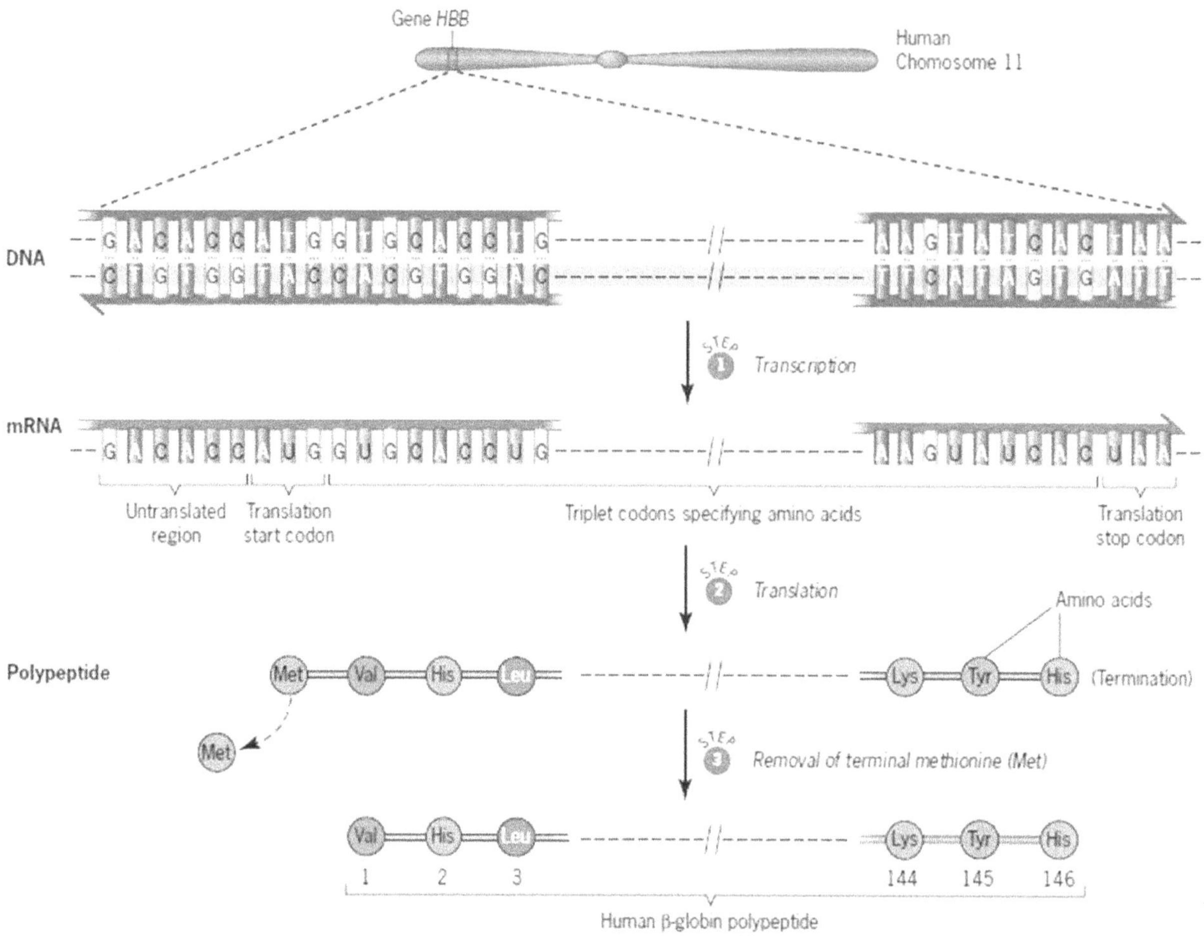

Q 3. What is the evolutionary significance of mutation?

Q 4. Provide Keywords:

I: .... : Pattern of inheritance that follows the principles proposed by botanist Gregor Mendel. Mechanistically, this pattern of inheritance follows two distinct laws: the law of segregation and the law of independent assortment.

II: .... : Alleles get separated from each other when gametes (sperm and egg) are formed during meiosis (division of cells to form specialized reproductive cells). Each gamete thus carries only one version of the paired set a specific gene (one allele).

III: .... : The alleles of any one gene will segregate independently from the paired set of the specific genes located closed to each other (with the exception of genes located close together on a chromosome).

IV: Single locus autosomal dominant, autosomal recessive, and X-linked inheritance patterns follow Mendel's laws and are said to be .... inheritance patterns can be caused by .... and other complex genetic phenomena including multiple genes and environmental components.

V: .... : A specialized cell that produces melanin. Found in the skin, some structures of the eye, the inner ear, and several other tissues.

VI: ....: A type of cancer, typically in the skin, that arises from changes in an individual's melanocytes.

VII: ....: Regions of repeated DNA found abundantly throughout the genome, often in non-coding areas, and which are highly variable and prone to mutation (see short tandem repeats). The various forms of a given structure of such type (identified by differences in the number of repeats) are referred to as alleles, and these are inherited in a Mendelian fashion of inheritance. Genetic variation at the specific site of such level can be used to identify individuals. These can be classified as markers too.

VIII: .... : Specific type of sequences (short tandem repeats) found at a particular location on a chromosome that are often used in various kinds of genetic analyses. These specific markers can be used to identify individuals and have applications in forensics, parentage analysis, and studies of populations.

IX: .... : A specific type of change in the nucleotide sequence of an organism's DNA in which a single change in the DNA sequence causes alteration in the building block (peptide chain of amino acids) of the gene product (a polypeptide chain or protein).

X: These cell organelles are membrane bound organelles, or specialized parts of cells which play a key role in generating cellular energy known as adenosine triphosphate (ATP). This organelle possess their own .... separate from the DNA found in the nucleus. This DNA is a single, circular chromosome of primitive type. In mammals, this DNA sequence is transmitted primarily from mother to offspring via maternal egg cells.

XI: ....: Mitochondrial haplotype; a set of variants (alleles) that are inherited together on the mitochondrial DNA.

Q 5. We all know that Mendel used Pea plants for accomplishing his gene related studies. One or many of the following facts may not explain the real facts for which Mendel might have selected Pea plants for his gene related experimentations:

a) The garden pea, Pisum sativum, is easily grown in experimental gardens or in pots in a greenhouse.
b) Pea flowers contain both male and female organs (bi-sexual in nature). The male organs, called anthers, produce sperm-containing pollen, and the female organ (ovary), produces eggs.
c) The petals of the flower close down tightly, preventing pollen grains from entering or leaving. This enforces a system of self-fertilization, in which male and female gametes from the same flower unite with each other to produce seeds. Individual pea strains are highly inbred, displaying little if any genetic variation from one generation to the next. It helped to confer the fact that such strains are true-breeding.
d) Mendel obtained many different true-breeding varieties of peas, each distinguished by a particular characteristic; tallness, dwarf-ness, seed texture, seed colour petal colour etc. Advantage of these contrasting traits is applied by Mendel to determine how the characteristics of pea plants are inherited.
e) Mendel's focus on these singular differences between pea strains allowed him to study the inheritance of one trait at a time.
f) Other biologists had attempted to follow the inheritance of many traits simultaneously, but because the results of such experiments were complex, they were unable to discover any fundamental principles about heredity.

g) Pea plant resembles recombination and free flow of genes from generation to generation without implying any impact upon the variations and linked genes.

Q 6. Let's consider a couple who are each heterozygous for a recessive allele that, when get transmitted to offsprings in homozygous condition, causes cystic fibrosis (a serious disease in which breathing is impaired by an accumulation of mucus in the lungs and respiratory tract). If the couple were to have four children, would we expect exactly three to be unaffected and one to be affected by cystic fibrosis?

Q 7. Solve the following.

A couple, denoted R and S in Figure , is concerned about the possibility that they will have a child (T) with albinism, a recessive condition characterized by a complete absence of melanin pigment in the skin, eyes, and hair. S, the prospective mother, has albinism, and R, the prospective father, has two siblings with albinism. It would therefore seem that the child has some risk of being born with albinism.

Is there any risk factors? What are the probable conditions regulate this risk factor?

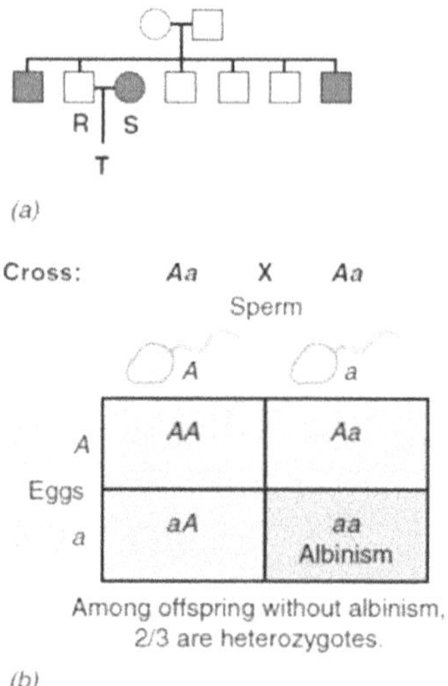

Q 8. Observe the pedigree and answer the question as follows.

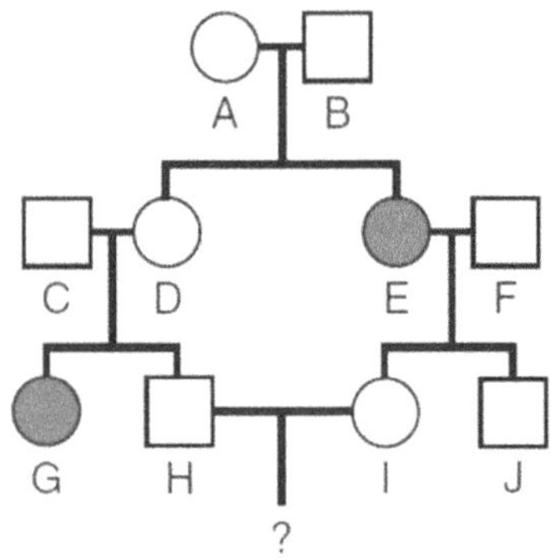

This pedigree shows the inheritance of a recessive trait in humans. Individuals that have the trait are homozygous for a recessive allele

If H and I, who happen to be first cousins, marry and have a child, what is the chance that this child will have the recessive trait?

Concept (Hints) The child can show a recessive trait only if both of its parents carry the recessive allele. One parent (H) has a sister (G) with the trait. The other parent (I) has a mother (E) with the trait.

Q 9. Two highly inbred strains of mice, one with black fur and the other with gray fur, were crossed, and all of the offspring duly obtained had black fur. Predict the outcome of intercrossing the offspring.

Q 10. A plant, which is heterozygous for three independently assorting genes, Aa Bb Cc, is self-fertilized. Among the offspring, predict the frequency of (a) AA BB CC individuals, (b) aa bb cc individuals, (c) individuals that are either AA BB CC or aa bb cc, (d) Aa Bb Cc individuals, (e) individuals that are not heterozygous for all three genes.

Q 11. Identify different possibilities when genotype and phenotype of an organism will become identical.

Q 12. Answer the following.

Offspring P is segregating a definite character from both the parents showing no effect for presence of the trait. Is the offspring "P" displayed in the pedigree has dominant or recessive trait?

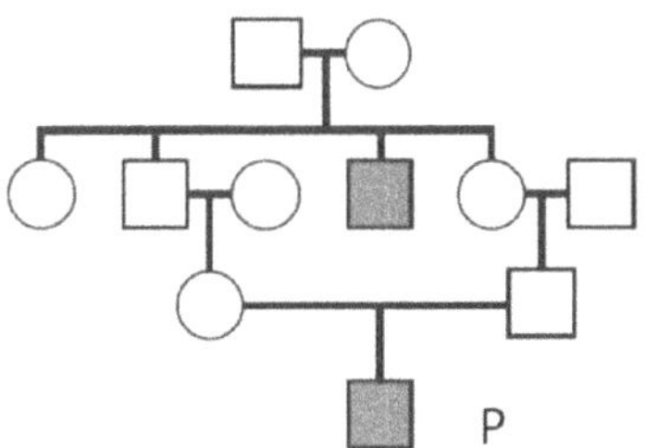

Q 13. Complete the following statement.

Genetic basis of flower color in snapdragons. The allele W is incompletely dominant over w. Differences among the phenotypes could be due to differences in the amount of the product specified by the W allele. If the W allele specifies this product and the w allele does not, WW homozygotes will have twice as much of the product as Ww heterozygotes do and will therefore show deeper color.

This is an example of .... Or .... Dominance of the specific allele which is responsible for the color of flower.

Phenotype	Genotype	Amount of gene product
Red	WW	2x
Pink	Ww	x
White	ww	0

Q 14. The ability to produce the M and N antigens is determined by a gene with two alleles. One allele allows the M antigen to be produced; the other allows the N antigen to be produced. Homozygotes for the M allele produce only the M antigen, and homozygotes for the N allele will exclusively produce only the N antigen. Heterozygotes for these two alleles produce both kinds of antigens (an exception which is some sort of intermediate in between dominance and recessive character of contrasting alleles). Because the two alleles appear to contribute independently to the phenotype of the heterozygotes, they are said to be............................ This type of dominance implies that there is an independence of allele function which is followed by contrasting alleles responsible for finalizing character of antigens. Neither allele is dominant, or even .... dominant, over the other.

Q 15. A classic example of a gene with .... alleles is the one that controls coat color in rabbits.

Rabbits	Genotype	Phenotype
Albino	cc	White hairs over the entire body
Himalayan	c^hc^h	Black hairs on the extremities; white hairs everywhere else
Chinchilla	$c^{ch}c^{ch}$	White hair with black tips on the body
Wild Type	c^+c^+	Colored hairs over the entire body

The color-determining gene, denoted by the lowercase letter c, has four alleles, three of which are distinguished by a superscript: c (albino), c^h (Himalayan), c^{ch} (chinchilla), and c^+ (wild-type). In homozygous condition, each allele has a characteristic effect on the coat color. Because most rabbits in wild populations are homozygous for the c^+ allele, this allele is called the ....type.

Q 16. How many alleles specify ABO – Blood Typing system in human beings?

Q 17. Answer the following.

A popular study of epistasis was performed by George Shull using a weedy plant called the Shepherd's purse, Bursa bursa-pastoris. The seed capsules of this plant are either phenotypically triangular or ovoid in shape. Ovoid capsules are produced only if a plant is homozygous for the recessive alleles of two genes (if it has the genotype aa bb). If the dominant allele of either gene is present, the plant produces triangular capsules. The cross between doubly heterozygous plants produce progeny in a ratio of 15 triangular:1 ovoid, indicating that the dominant allele of one gene is epistatic over the recessive allele of the other.

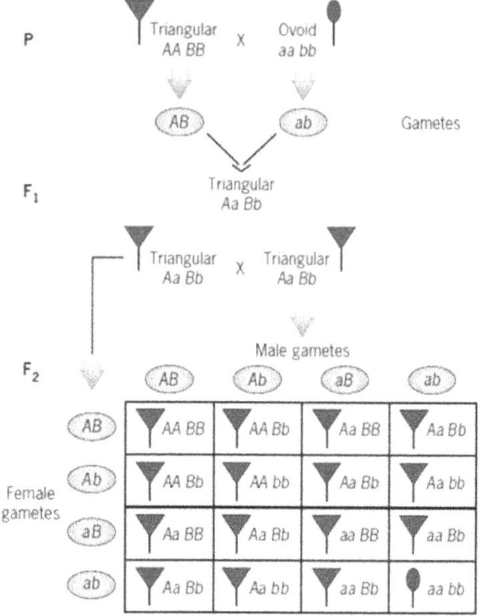

What feature of the precursors specify this type of epistatic results?

Q 18: Complete the following...

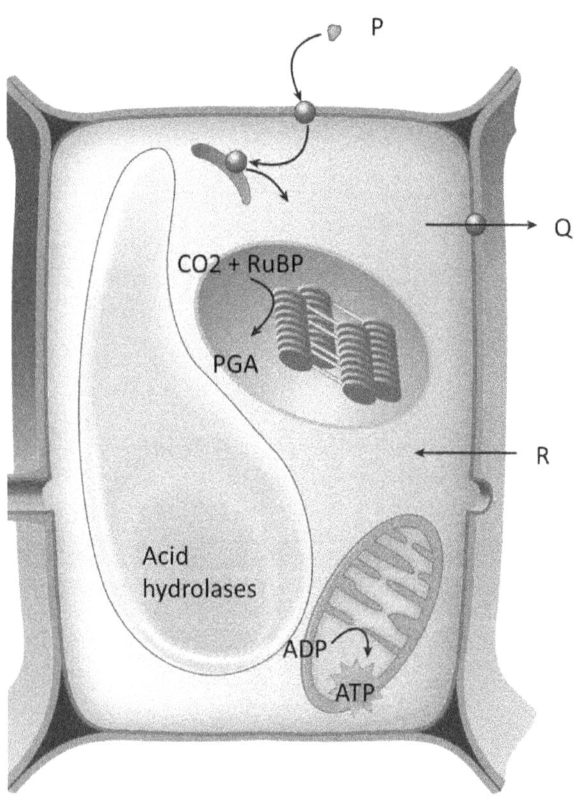

Identify types of Transport.

A: .... --- An example of the role of membranes as a selectively permeable barrier. Water molecules are able to penetrate rapidly through the plasma membrane, causing the plant cell to fill out the available space and exert pressure against its cell wall.

B : .... -- An example of solute transport. Hydrogen ions, which are produced by various metabolic processes in the cytoplasm, are pumped out of plant cells into the extracellular space by a transport protein located in the plasma membrane.

C :............ --An example of the involvement of a membrane in the transfer of information from one side to another (signal transduction). In this case, a hormone (e.g., abscisic acid) binds to the outer surface of the plasma membrane and triggers the release of a chemical message (such as IP 3) into the cytoplasm. In this case, IP 3 causes release of Ca 2+ ions from a cytoplasmic warehouse.

.... -

Q 19: What types of reactions are displayed in the following diagram? What type of role is played by Acetyl Co-A in the following reactions?

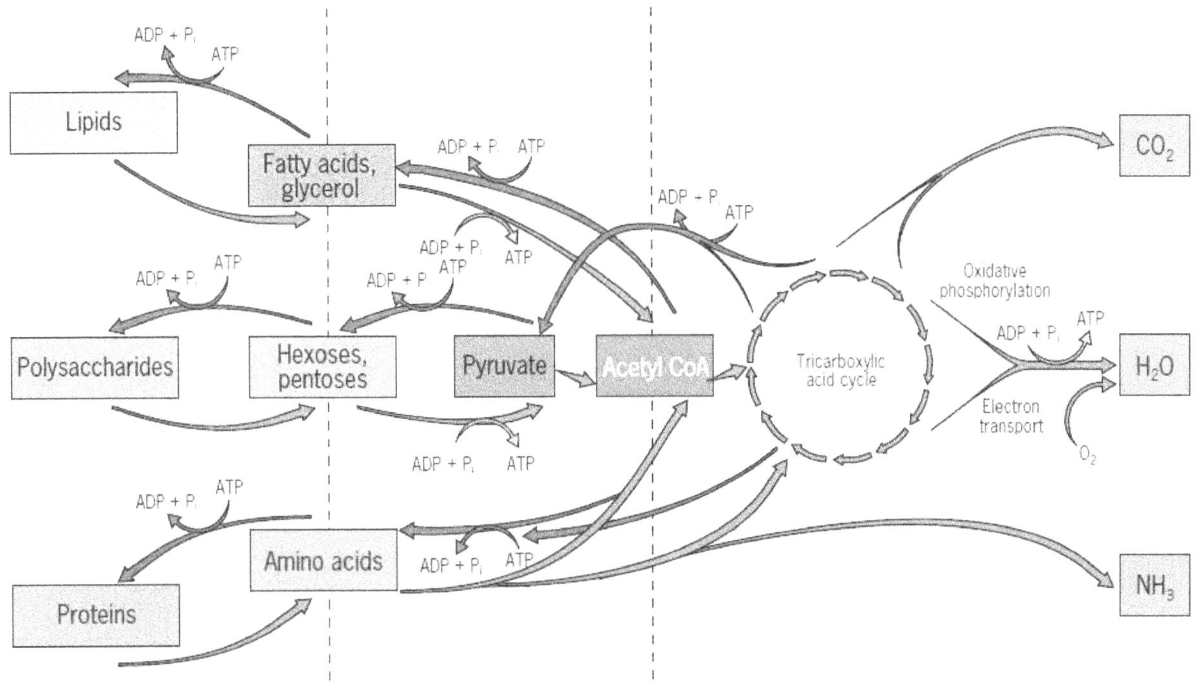

Q 20. Complete the following figure by providing suitable keywords.

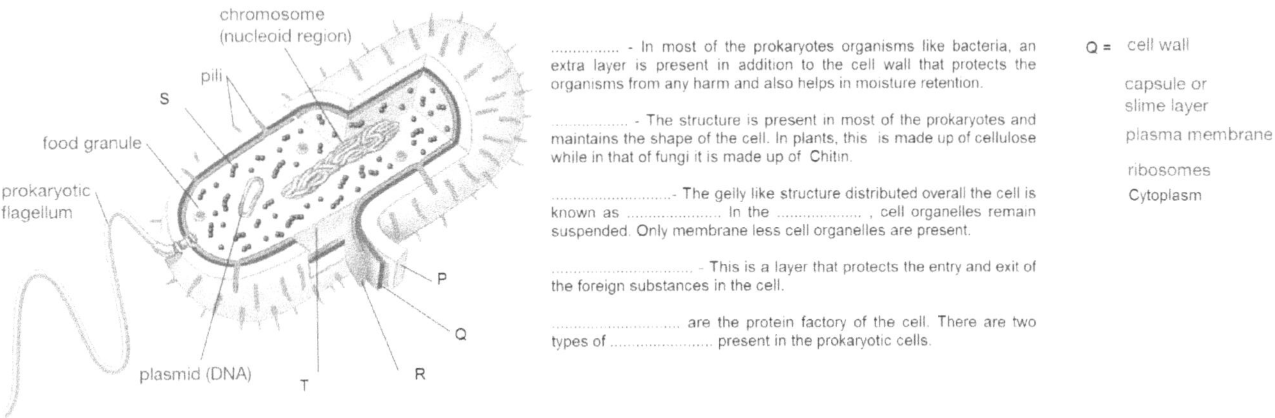

chromosome (nucleoid region)
pili
S
food granule
prokaryotic flagellum
plasmid (DNA)
T
R
P
Q
.... - In most of the prokaryotes organisms like bacteria, an extra layer is present in addition to the cell wall that protects the organisms from any harm and also helps in moisture retention.
.... - The structure is present in most of the prokaryotes and maintains the shape of the cell. In plants, this is made up of cellulose while in that of fungi it is made up of Chitin.
.........................- The gelly like structure distributed overall the cell is known as .... In the .... , cell organelles remain suspended. Only membrane less cell organelles are present.
.... - This is a layer that protects the entry and exit of the foreign substances in the cell.
.... are the protein factory of the cell. There are two types of .... present in the prokaryotic cells.
Q = cell wall
capsule or slime layer
plasma membrane
ribosomes
Cytoplasm

Q 21. Identify the type of cell on the basis of the properties mentioned in the following set of characters.

- These cells are microscopic, relatively simple and single celled organisms.
- They do not have any membrane bound true nucleus present in them.
- Pilli, flagella, and capsule are some unique features of these types of cells.
- The extra-chromosomal DNA, (plasmids) are remain suspended in the cytoplasm.
- They have different types of shapes (like -rod shape, cocci, vibrio, spirilla, and bacillus) and get their names accordingly.
- Generally, these cells are 0.2 to 0.5 in diameter but some of the single celled organisms are so large in sizes that are visible to the unaided eye. Example - Thiomargarita namibiensis.
- They can be aerobic, anaerobic, facultative, and obligatory type of nutrient seeker.

Q 22. Involvement of different types of RNAs in Cellular metabolic process is listed below. Identify them on the basis of roles played in cellular biochemical processes.

a) .... – It is the RNA that carries information from DNA to the ribosomes (site of protein synthesis) in the cell. The mRNA code sequences determine the amino acid sequence in the protein that is produced.
b) – It incorporates into the ribosomes.
c) – It is used to transfer specific amino acids to growing polypeptide chains at the ribosomal site of protein synthesis during translation.
d) – Small sized RNA present in nucleus.
e) – They are used to regulate gene activity; they are tiny (~22 nucleotides) RNA molecules that regulate the expression of messenger RNA (mRNA) molecules.
f) – Small sized RNA present in nucleolus.
g) – Long chain RNA which cannot take part in coding.
h) – These RNA functions as an enzymatically active RNA molecule.

Q 23. What types of RNA are present (in higher percentage) in nucleolus of the nucleus of a eukaryotic cell?

Q 24. Which cell organelle takes part in the formation of specialised cellular projections of a nerve cell?

Q 25. A special type of RNA is responsible for selecting and binding definite types of Amino Acid during the process of Translation of a Polypeptide chain of protein. Identify that RNA.

Q 26. What type of molecule ensures binding of two sub units of ribosomes to ensure beginning of the growth of polypeptide chain during synthesis of protein?

Q 27: Following set of property indicates discussion about a special type of RNA. Identify that RNA.

a) It is synthesized in the cell nucleus and then transported out of the cell to facilitate protein synthesis and code sequencing on proteins through an organised biochemical process with the help of ribosomes.
b) The sequence encoded in this molecule is finally translated into polypeptide chain.
c) It comes in a wide range of sizes which reflects the length of the polypeptide that it encodes.
d) Most cells produce thousands of different types of this type of molecules in small amounts, which are used by ribosomes for materialising gene signalling system at molecular level.
e) Many of these types of molecules are common to most cells which encode for proteins that ensure cellular level metabolisms (by providing basic format of enzymes and hormones).
f) Some types of these molecules are specific for certain types of cells, which encode for the proteins that are needed for the function of that particular cell such as coding for haemoglobin is found exclusively in Red Blood Cells (RBCs).

Q 28. On the basis of the following figure identify the type of molecules which played a vital role in bringing diversification in the living world.

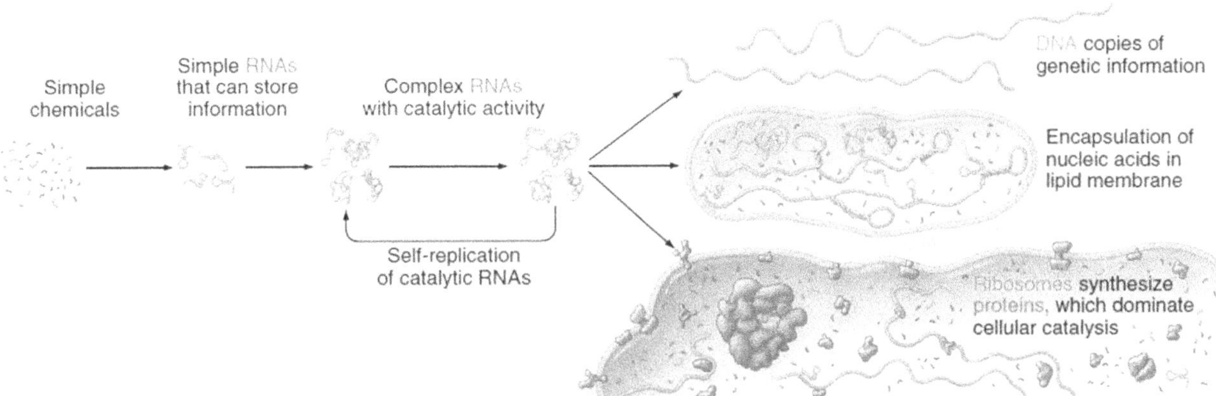

This diagram indicates the probable path of organic evolution through which cellular life forms came into existence in our surrounding. Involvement of different types of organic molecules in this process is also advanced.

Simple chemical reactions are postulated to have given rise to ever more complicated RNA molecules to store genetic information and catalyze chemical reactions, including self-replication, in a prebiotic "RNA world." Polymorphism of RNA molecules in due course of time is also advanced in this regard to ppropose evolution of some higher order intermediates before advent of modern forms. Eventually, genetic information was stored in more stable combinations of DNA molecules and proteins and replaced RNAs as the primary catalysts in primitive cells bounded by a lipid membrane.

Solutions: 21: Prokaryotic (Bacteria);
22: messenger RNA (mRNA) ; ribosomal RNA (rRNA); transfer RNA (tRNA); small nuclear RNA (snRNA); microRNA (miRNA); small nucleolar RNA (snoRNA); long non-coding RNA (lncRNA); catalytic RNA (ribozymes) ;
23: Ribosomal RNA; 24: Centrosome; 25: tRNA(Transfer RNA); 26: mRNA.

27 : mRNA; 28: DNA and RNA.

Solution: Review 6

Ans 2:

Step 1: One strand of the HBB DNA (here the bottom strand shown highlighted) serves as a template for the synthesis of a complementary strand of RNA. After undergoing modifications, the resulting mRNA (messenger RNA) is used as a template to synthesize the β-globin polypeptide. (Translation)

Step 2: During translation each triplet codon embedded in the mRNA strand specifies the incorporation of an amino acid in the polypeptide chain. Translation is initiated by an initiation codon, which specifies the incorporation of the amino acid methionine (met), and it is terminated by a termination codon, which does not specify the incorporation of any of the 20 different types of amino acids.

Step 3: After translation is completed, the initially incorporated methionine is removed from the polypeptide chain to produce the mature molecule of β -globin polypeptide.

Answer 3: Mutation creates variation in the DNA sequences of genes (and in the nongenic components of genomes as well). This variation accumulates in group of organisms over time and may eventually produce observable differences among the newly introduced group of organisms. One population may come to differ from another according to the kinds of mutations that have accumulated in the genome over time. Thus, mutation provides the input for different evolutionary outcomes at the different strata of population levels.

Ans 4: Keywords..

I : Mendelian (Mendelian inheritance) ; II: Law of segregation ; III: Law of independent assortment ;
IV: Mendelian; Non-Mendelian; epistasis; V: Melanocyte; VI: Melanoma; VII: Microsatellite;
VIII: Microsatellite marker ; IX: Missense mutation; X: independent genome ; XI: Mitotype;

Ans 5: Statement g is not correct;

Ans 6: Although this is a possible outcome if considered on the basis of the recommendations made by Mendel, it is not the only one. There are, in real life situation, five distinct possibilities can be advanced:

a. Four unaffected, none affected. b. Three unaffected, one affected.
c. Two unaffected, two affected. d. One unaffected, three affected.
e. None unaffected, four affected.

Intuitively, the second outcome seems to be the most likely, since it conforms to Mendel's 3:1 ratio. We can calculate the probability of this outcome, and of each of the others, by using Mendel's principles and by treating each birth as an independent event.

Ans 7: There are two distinct factors: (a) the probability that R is a heterozygous carrier of the albinism allele (a), and (b) the probability that he will transmit this allele to T if he actually is a carrier. S, who is obviously homozygous for the albinism allele, must transmit this allele to her offspring.

Ans 8:

Condition: I must be a heterozygous carrier of the recessive allele because her mother E is homozygous for it (but not showing the trait) I therefore has a 1/2 chance of transmitting the recessive allele to her child. Because H's sister has the trait, both of her parents must be heterozygotes. H has a 2/3 chance of being a heterozygote, and if he is, there is a 1/2 chance that he will transmit the recessive allele to his child.

Chance that the child of H and I will show the trait =1/2 X 2/3 X ½ = 1/6 ; 1/6, [a fairly substantial risk].

Ans 9: By considering allele G for dominant character black and g for recessive allele grey we can explain this process. G and g alleles will segregate from each other to produce an F_2 population consisting of three genotypes, GG, Gg, and gg, in the ratio 1:2:1. Because of the dominance of the G allele, the GG and Gg genotypes will have the same phenotype (black fur); thus, the phenotypic ratio in the F_2 will be 3 black: 1 gray.

Ans 10: (a) Possibility of AA BB CC offspring as (1/4) X (1/4) X (1/4) = 1/64.

(b) Possibility of aa bb cc offspring as (1/4) X (1/4) X (1/4) = 1/64.

(c) Offspring that are either triple dominant homozygotes or triple recessive homozygotes—these are mutually exclusive events—we sum the results of (a) and (b): 1/64 + 1/64 = 2/64 = 1/32.

(d) The frequency of triple heterozygotes should be (1/2) X (1/2) X (1/2) = 1/8.

Ans 11: pure dominant and pure recessive organisms exhibit similarity of genotype and phenotype.

Ans 12: Recessive; as both the parents exhibited the trait as hidden recessive type.

Ans 13: Partial or incomplete dominance; 14: codominant; partially; 15: multiple; wild;

Ans 16: The gene responsible for producing the A and B antigens is denoted by the letter I. It has three contrasting alleles: I^A, I^B, and I. The allele I^A specifies the production of the A antigen, and the I^B allele specifies the production of the B antigen in the living body. The third type i allele does not specify any of the antigen. Among the six possible genotypes, there are four distinguishable phenotypes. Because of that reason we have four different blood types: Type A, B, AB, and O.

Ans 17: A precursor substance can be converted into a product that leads to a triangular seed capsule through either of these pathways having involvement of gene A or B. Only when both pathways are blocked by homozygous recessive alleles is the situation when triangular phenotype gets suppressed and an ovoid capsule produced.

Review 7

1. Which level of organisation enables a group of cells to perform jointly in a perfect coordination?

2. What will happen if differentiated cells lose their coordination and start dividing ceaselessly?

3. A cell is considered as a fundamental structural and functional unit of life. Why is a cell, and not an atom or a molecule, considered such kind of basic unit of life?

4. Think of an analogy that will help you remember the differences between populations, communities, and ecosystems.

5. There are several examples of instances during which organisms develop emergent properties. Name an example of emergent properties from everyday life.

6. There exist different types of organisms on the basis of their food habits and modes of nutrition. Draw and explain the relationship between producers and consumers (including decomposers).

7. Define homeostasis. How does a home's air conditioning system illustrate homeostasis?

8. What is adaptation? Explain why populations of organisms are typically well adapted to their environment. What is basic difference between primary and secondary adaptation? What types of adaptations can be observed in case of Xerophytes and whales?

9. What are three distinct domains of life? How are the members of the three domains similar? How are they different?

10. What makes an organism unfit to the surrounding? Why birds migrate?

11. Provide two examples of questions that you cannot answer using the scientific method. Explain your reason for choosing each example.

12. There are different types of organisations through which molecules combine to form bio-molecules. Ne such combination is displayed below. Identify the type of organisation and write name of the unit.

Phosphate group

Nitrogenous base

Sugar (Deoxyribose)

Adenine (A) | Cytosine (C) | Guanine (G) | Thymine (T) | Uracil (U)

DNA and RNA | DNA only | RNA only

13. .... consists of three long hydrocarbon chains called .... bonded to glycerol, a three-carbon molecule that forms the .... backbone. Although these molecules do not consist of long strings of similar monomers, cells nevertheless use dehydration synthesis to produce them. Enzymes link three .... to one .... molecule, yielding three water molecules per unit of molecule.

14. Answer the following.

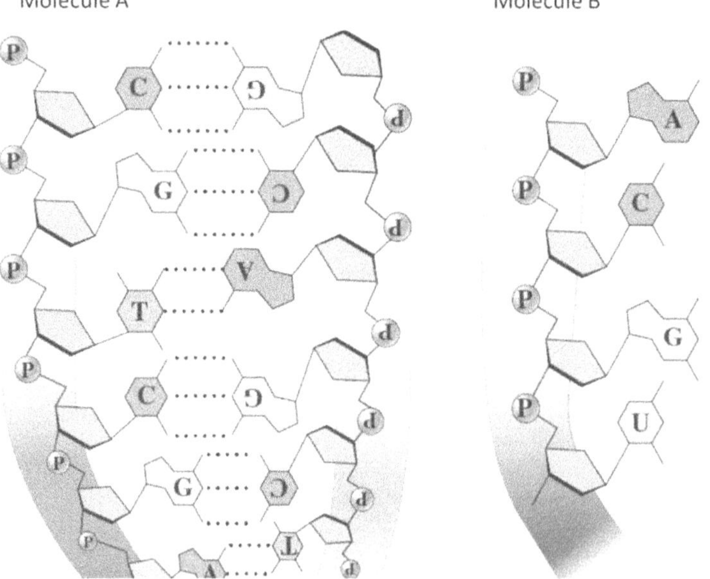

Two different types of molecules are displayed in the given structures. Both the molecules take part in the manifestation of genetic information differently by taking part in the entire process at different levels of transcription and translation.
Try to point out three basic differences in between these two molecules.

Which molecule is responsible for holding and propagating genetic information in Eukaryotes?

15. What is a saturated fatty acid?

16. What are unsaturated fatty acids? What is the advantage of this fat over the saturated counterpart?

17. Who proposed Cell Theory? What were the basic postulates?

18. Complete the following statement:

Every .... is subject to random .... that are inherited by succeeding generations. Some .... change single base pairs. Other .... add or delete larger blocks of DNA such as sequences coding a ...., an independently folded part of a .... These events inevitably produce .... through divergence of .... or creation of novel combinations of ....

19. Which of the following units require electron microscope?

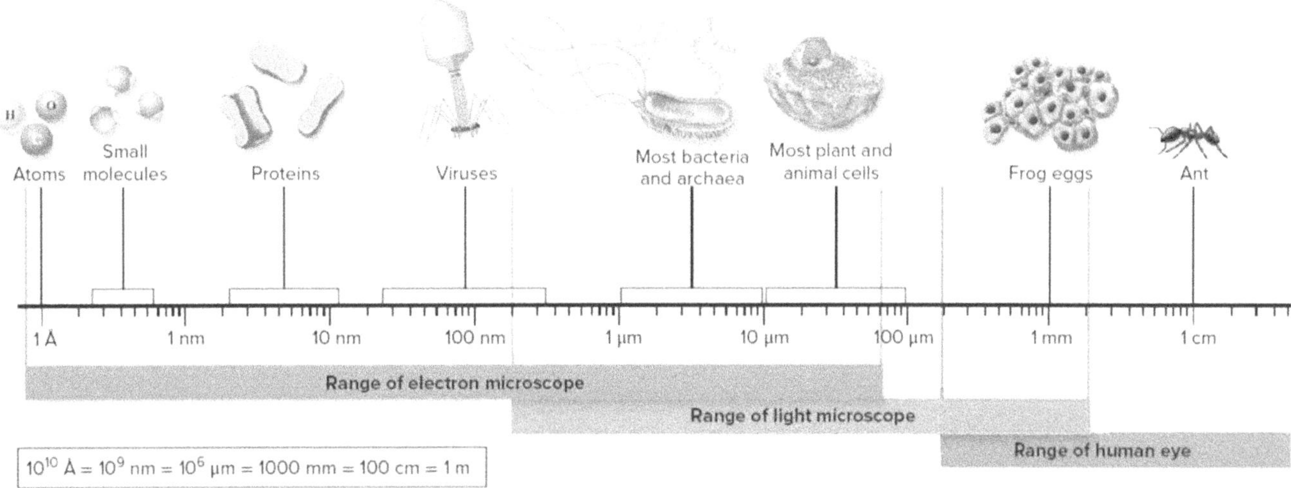

Solution: 12: Nucleotide;

13: A triglyceride (more commonly known as a fat); fatty acids; triglyceride's; fatty acids; glycerol;

14: DNA is the molecule which holds the genetic information in eukaryotes.

15: A saturated fatty acid contains all the hydrogen it possibly can accommodate in the prolonged carbon chain. Single bonds connect all the carbons, and each carbon has two hydrogen. Animal fats are saturated and remains in solid form at room temperature; (Examples: bacon fat and butter) Experts recommend a diet low in saturated fats, which, on entering the circulatory system, tend to clog arteries and cause heart disease.

16: An unsaturated fatty acid has at least one double bond between carbon atoms in the carbon skeleton of the molecule. These fats have an oily (liquid) consistency at room temperature and rarely take the solid or crystal state at 30^0 C or above. (Examples: Olive oil, is an unsaturated fat, as are most plant-derived lipids). These fats are healthier than compared to their saturated counterparts.

17: In 1839, German biologists Mathias J. Schleiden and Theodor Schwann proposed a new theory related to structure and function of cells. Their theory was prepared based on many observations made with microscopes. Schleiden first noted that cells are the basic structural and functional units of plants, and then Schwann compared animal cells to plant cells and coined their similarities as well as differences. After observing similarities in many different types of plant and animal cells, Schleiden and Schwann formulated the most popular "cell theory", which originally had two main components:

Part I: All organisms, whatever types may be, are made of one or more cells.

Part II: The cell is the fundamental structural and functional unit of all life forms starting from bacteria to mammals.

Part III: all cells, at all instances of development and propagation, come from pre-existing cells

(German physiologist Rudolf Virchow added a third component to the cell theory in 1855)

The French chemist and microbiologist Louis Pasteur finally disproved spontaneous generation in 1859 and provided additional evidence in support of the "cell theory".

18: gene; mutations; mutations; mutations; protein domain; protein; genetic diversity; sequences; domains .

Solution : Review 1.

Ans 1: A = Early Endosome; B = Regulatory Secretory Vesicles; C = Lysosome; D = Late Endosome; E = Golgi body; F = Rough E.R.

2: (A), three modifications of glucose; (B), a 6-carbon keto sugar condensed into a 5-membered ring (C), and two 5-carbon riboses (D).

3: A performs fermentation and B performs aerobic respiration; mitochondria is involved in case of B.

4: P = cytoplasm; Q = mitochondria and R = F0-F1 Complex (Oxysome or ATPase)

Solution Review 2:

1: chromatin; chromatin; heterochromatin; euchromatin; transcribed genes; histone; chromatin; gene expression;

2: Nucleolus;

3: Most prokaryotic and mitochondrial chromosomes are composed of circular DNA molecules that lack telomeres, but naturally occurring eukaryotic nuclear chromosomes are generally accumulator of one linear DNA molecule that stretches between the telomeres at either end. Evidence of presence of such a single DNA molecule in chromosome was obtained for budding and fission yeasts, where intact chromosomal DNA molecules may be visualized by pulsed-field gel electrophoresis as a characteristic series of bands.

4: 24 molecules of ATP; 5: pyruvate; pyruvate dehydrogenase complex ;

6: Being Energy giving nutrient, fat is a major source of energy for most non-photosynthetic organisms, including mammals and humans. Like the pyruvate, which is derived from carbohydrate during glycolysis, the fatty acids derived from fat are also converted into acetyl CoA in the mitochondrial matrix. Fatty acids are first activated by covalent linkage to CoA and are then broken down completely by a cycle of reactions that trims two carbons at a time from their carboxyl end, generating one molecule of acetyl CoA for each turn of the cycle.

Solution: Review 3 ...

Ans 1: Fat Metabolism; 2: Total O_2 = 32 X 6 = ... ; 3: anabolic pathways; enzyme-catalysed reactions;

4: Step 1 = Glycolysis Step 3; Step 2 = Gluconeogenesis; 5: Glycogen phosphorylase and insulin, adrenaline, and glucagon;

Solution Review 4:

1: Option A is correct;

2: P = Mitochondria; Q = Plastid; F = mitochondrial matrix and the chloroplast stroma; G = Mitochondrial crest and Thylacoid; 3: Electron Transport Chain and Mitochondria; 4: Option C; 5: Option B;

Selected Worksheets

Worksheet 1

1: Complete the following.

A: Glycolysis, the process that breaks down glucose, occurs in the cytoplasm (fluid portion) of every cell. Pyruvic acid, the product of glycolysis, moves from the cytoplasm into the cellular organelle called the mitochondrion, the cell's "powerhouse." The Krebs cycle, also called the ……………………. ………… ………… or the citric acid cycle, takes place in the mitochondrion.

B: At the completion of the Krebs cycle, the high-energy molecules that are created during the cycle move into the membrane of the………………………., where they're passed down the electron transport chain. At the end of that chain, the molecules are used to form ATP from adenosine diphosphate (ADP) and ………………………………………… , and water is released.

C: ATP is the cell's "…………………. ……………………..." Just as you can't keep spending money without earning some money to replenish your supply, your body can't keep expending energy without taking in more fuel. When the cell needs energy to fuel its metabolism, it "pays" with ATP molecules.

D: Glycolytic pathway (glycolysis) glucose — the smallest molecule that a carbohydrate can be broken into during digestion — goes through the process of glycolysis, which starts cellular respiration and uses some energy (ATP) itself. Glycolysis occurs in the …………………..and doesn't require oxygen.

E; Two molecules of ATP are required to start each molecule of glucose rolling down the glycolytic pathway; although four molecules of ATP are generated during glycolysis, the net production of ATP is two molecules.

F: In addition to the two ATPs, two molecules of pyruvic acid (also called pyruvate) are generated. They move into a mitochondrion and enter the Krebs cycle.

G: Krebs cycle ---The Krebs cycle is a major biological pathway in the metabolism of every multicellular organism. It's an aerobic pathway, requiring oxygen. As the pyruvate enters the mitochondrion, a molecule of a compound called ……………………………………….. joins it. NAD+ is an electron carrier (that is, it carries energy), and it gets the process moving by bringing some energy into the pathway. The NAD+ provides enough energy that when it joins with pyruvate, carbon dioxide is released, and the high-energy molecule NADH is formed. The product of the overall reaction is acetyl coenzyme A (acetyl CoA), which is a carbohydrate molecule that puts the Krebs cycle in motion.

2. A diagram of ADP and ATP molecule is displayed below.

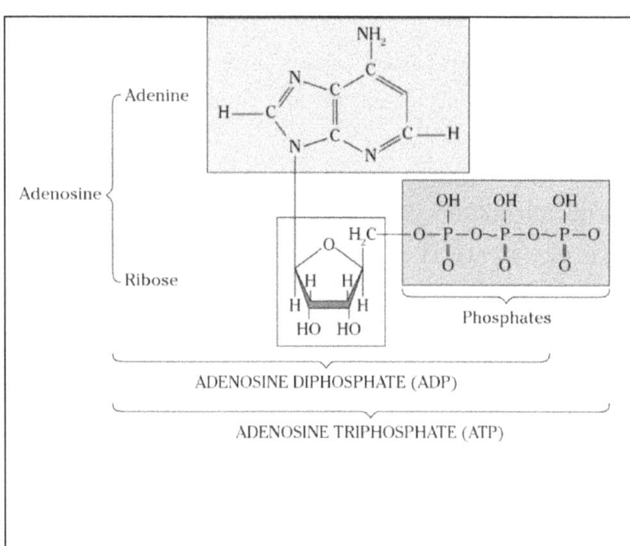

As NADH and FADH2 pass down the respiratory (or electron transport) chain, they lose energy as they become oxidized and reduced repeatedly. Their energy supplies become exhausted for a good cause. The energy that these electron carriers lose is used to add a molecule of phosphorus to adenosine diphosphate (ADP) to make it adenosine triphosphate — the coveted ATP. And ATP is the goal for converting the chemical energy trapped in food to energy that the cells in the body can use. For each NADH molecule that's produced in the Krebs cycle, ... molecules of ATP can be generated. For each molecule of FADH2 that's produced in the Krebs cycle, ...molecules of ATP are made.

3. During the entire process of aerobic cellular respiration (including glycolysis, Krebs cycle, and oxidative phosphorylation) it is observed that combustion of one molecule of glucose generates a total of .... molecules from the energy in trapped in one molecule of glucose: 2 from glycolysis, 2 from the Krebs cycle, and .... from oxidative phosphorylation. However, this theoretical yield is never quite reached because processes, especially biological processes, are never ....efficient. In the real world, usually around ....ATP molecules are obtained after aerobic combustion of one molecule of glucose.

4. The complicated chemistry of life and metabolic activity of living forms are extremely sensitive to the external and internal environmental conditions; the .... environment is the body itself. .... is the term physiologists use to mean the subset of metabolic reactions that keep the internal environment of the body in a state conducive to the chemical reactions that maintain the living body.

5. The word .... describes all the chemical reactions that happen in the living body. These reactions are of two kinds — anabolic reactions make things (molecules) by using energy, and catabolic reactions break things down to release chemical energy which remained trapped in nutrients. Chemosynthesis is an example of ....

6. The amount of glucose in the blood is controlled mainly by the intestines and by the hormone .... It is a hormone released from the pancreas, an endocrine part of the gland, into the blood in response to increased blood glucose levels above the admissible range specified for a healthy and matured human being. Most cells have .... that bind the hormone ...., which increases the activity of glucose transporters through the cell membrane by means of active transport. Glucose is removed from the blood and into storage, mostly within the cells of the liver, the muscles, and to the fat cells of the adipose tissue. At times when our intestines are not releasing much glucose, such as some hours after a meal, or during a tenure of prolonged fast, the production of .... is suppressed and the stored glucose is released into the blood again for ensuring continuation of the process of metabolism.

7. Observe the following set of clips and compare with descriptions.

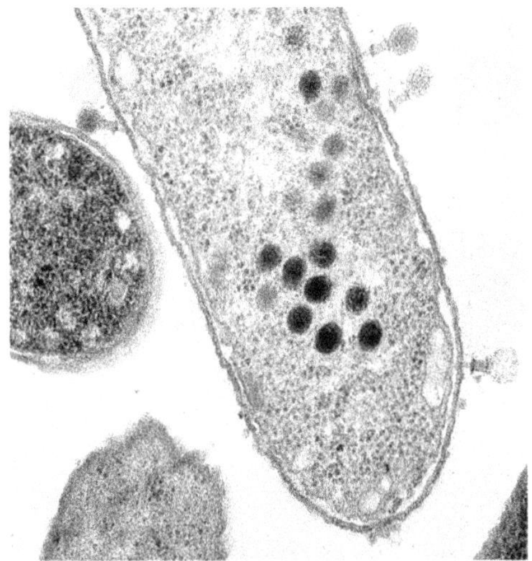

Clip A: Infection of Virus.

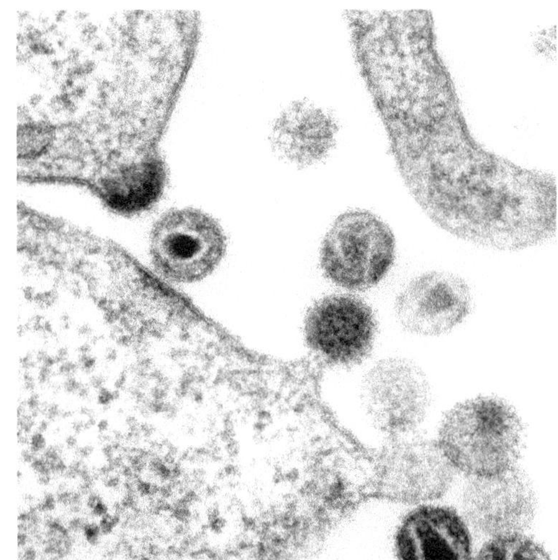

Clip B: Budding of Virus

Identify statement(s) which is/are not confirming the character of a virus

I: Bacterial cells containing a provirus behave normally until and unless exposed to a stimulus (such as ultraviolet radiation, adverse chemical environment etc.), that activates the dormant viral DNA, leading ultimately to the lysis of the cell and release of viral progeny.

II: Some animal cells (may be a somatic cell or germe cell) containing a provirus produce new viral progeny that bud at the cell surface without lysing the infected cell. Human immunodeficiency virus (HIV), as displayed in Clip B, acts in this way without lysing the infected cell. After getting infected by virus cell may remain alive for a period, acting as a factory for the production of new virions.

III: Some animal cells, like those of prokaryotic bacterial cells, containing a provirus lose control over their own process of growth and division and become malignant. This phenomenon is readily studied in the laboratory by infecting cultured cells with the appropriate variant of tumor virus. [Clip A shows the mechanism of such type of infection.]

IV: Only viral genome is actively play a role during continuation of the infection cycle.

V: Viruses are not active at any instance without their virtues. The activities of viral genes mimic those of host genes. This process enabled investigators to use viruses for decades as a research tool to study the mechanism of DNA replication and gene expression in their specified hosts. Viruses are now being successfully used as a means to introduce foreign genes into human cells and cells of other animals. This is a technique, with some sort of an ease of applicability and convenience that will positively serve as the basis for the treatment of human diseases by gene therapy.

VI: Insect and bacteria-killing viruses may play an increasing role in the control drive against insect pests and bacterial pathogens. Bacteriophages have been used for decades to treat bacterial infections in different places, while physicians in the West have relied on antlblotlcs.

VII: Given the rise in antibiotic-resistant bacteria, it is expected that bacteriophages may be making a comeback on the heels of promising studies on infected organism.

8. Observe the following sequence of a biochemical cellular process and select the statement which requires modification. Also provide the modified statement.

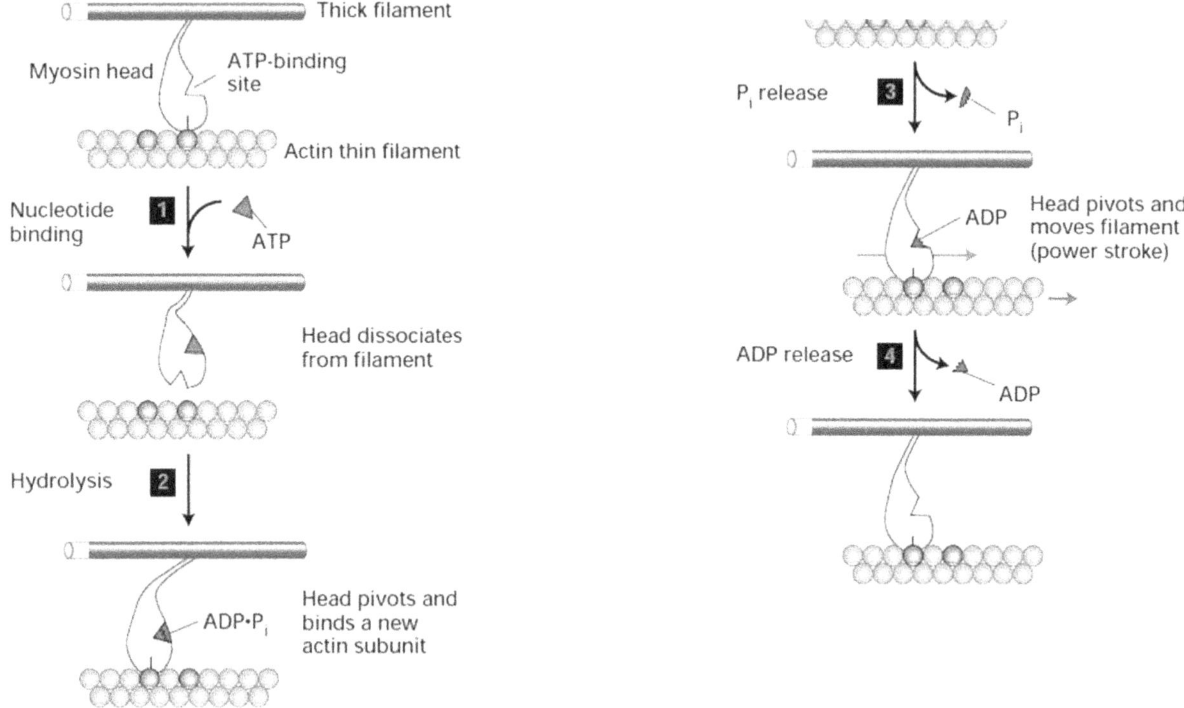

Statements:

I: The cycle for a myosin II head that is part of a thick filament accommodated in cells of muscle bands, but other myosins that attach to other cargo (e.g., the membrane of a vesicle) are thought to operate according different cyclical mechanism. In the absence of independent nucleotide, a myosin head binds actin tightly in a "rigor" state.

II: Step 1 exhibits the binding of ATP opens the cleft in the myosin head, disrupting the actin-binding site and weakening the interaction with actin.

III: Step 2 indicates freed of actin, the myosin head hydrolyzes ATP, causing a conformational change in the head that moves it to a new position, closer to the (+) end of the actin filament. At that position it rebinds to the filament.

IV: Step 3 indicates that phosphate (Pi) dissociates from the ATP-binding pocket, the myosin head undergoes a second conformational change (namely the power stroke) which restores myosin to its rigor conformation. As myosin is bound to actin, this conformational change exerts a force that causes finally myosin to move the actin filament.

V: Step 4 shows the release of ADP. This step confers the completion of the cycle.

9. Observe the following diagram and complete the statements as follows.

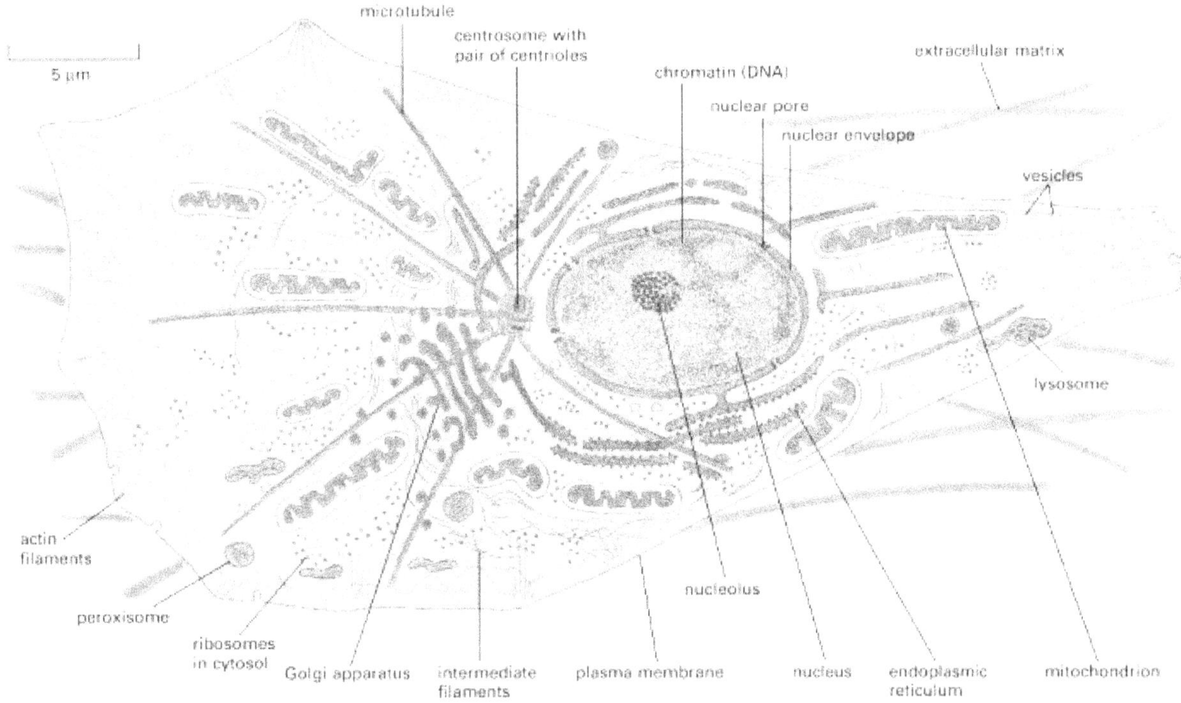

I: The critical function of the nuclear membranes is to act as a barrier that separates the contents of the nucleus from the cytoplasm and also prevents the nuclear components from getting disintegrated under the influence of ....enzymes which is there remaining packed in lysosomes.

II: Like other cell membranes, the nuclear membranes are .... bilayers, which are permeable only to small nonpolar molecules. Other complex molecules are unable to diffuse through the phospholipid bilayer.

III: The inner and outer nuclear membranes are joined at nuclear pore complexes, the sole channels through which small polar molecules and macromolecules are able to travel through the nuclear envelope. This nuclear pore complex is a complicated structure that is responsible for the .... of proteins and RNAs between the nucleus and the cytoplasm.

IV: Underlying the inner nuclear membrane is the nuclear lamina ...., a fibrous meshwork that provides structural and mechanical support to various components of nucleus. It is composed of one or more related proteins called .... Most mammalian cells, for an example to understand the process better, contain four different ...., designated A, B1, B2, and C. All these layers are 60- to 80-kilodalton (kd) fibrous proteins that are related to the intermediate filament proteins of the cytoskeleton. Like other intermediate filament proteins, these associate with each other to form ....

V: The first stage of this association is the interaction of two .... to form a dimer in which the α-helical regions of two .... chains are wound around each other in a structure called a coiled coil. These specialised dimers then associate with each other to form the filaments that make up the nuclear .... The association of these structures with the inner nuclear membrane is facilitated by the post-translational addition of lipid—in particular, prenylation of C-terminal cysteine residues.

10. Statements related to the Nuclear ore Complex. Complete all the statements by providing keywords.

I: These are the only channels through which small .... molecules, ions, and macromolecules (proteins and RNAs) are able to travel between the nucleus and the cytoplasm.

II: It is an extremely large structure, compared to other .... present in plasma membrane and other unit membranes, with a diameter of about 120 nm and an estimated molecular mass of approximately 125 million daltons (about 30 times the size of a ribosome).

III: In nuclear membrane of vertebrates, this structure is composed of 50 to 100 different types of proteins. By controlling the traffic of molecules between the nucleus and cytoplasm, it plays a vital role in the physiology and related cellular regulations of all .... cells.

IV: RNAs that are synthesized in the nucleus must be efficiently exported to the cytoplasm without getting distorted during the process of transportation, where they ensure the initiation of the protein synthesis by switching on the process of .... Conversely, proteins required for nuclear functions (e.g., transcription factors, recharging of Nucleolus, and packing of Chromatin fibres) must be transported into the nucleus from their sites of .... (which are located in the cytoplasm). Many proteins shuttle continuously between the nucleus and the .... for ensuring various cellular activities.

V: The regulated traffic of proteins and RNAs through the nuclear pore complex thus determines the composition of the nucleus and plays a key role in gene expression.

VI: Depending on their size, molecules can travel through the nuclear pore complex by one of two different mechanisms. Small molecules and some proteins with molecular mass less than approximately 50 kd pass freely across the nuclear envelope in either direction: cytoplasm to nucleus or nucleus to cytoplasm. These molecules diffuse passively through open .... channels, estimated to have diameters of approximately 9 nm, located in the nuclear pore complex. Macromolecules pass through the nuclear pore complex by an active process .... in which appropriate proteins and RNAs are recognized and .... in only one direction (nucleus to cytoplasm or cytoplasm to nucleus). It is also confirmed through experimentations that the traffic of large molecules occurs through .... in the nuclear pore complex that, in response to appropriate signals, can open to a diameter of more than 25 nm (It is a size sufficient to accommodate large ribonucleoprotein complexes, such as ribosomal subunits). It is through these regulated channels that nuclear proteins are .... from the cytoplasm to the nucleus while RNAs are .... from the nucleus to the cytoplasm.

11. RNAs are transported across the nuclear envelope as .... (P) RNA-protein complexes, which in some cases are large enough to visualize by .... The substrates for transport are these macromolecule (P) rather than naked RNAs, and RNAs are targeted for transport from the nucleus by .... on the proteins bound to them. These proteins are recognized by exportins and transported from the nucleus to the .... as described earlier. Pre-mRNAs and mRNAs are associated with a set of at least 20 proteins (forming heterogeneous nuclear ribonucleoproteins, or hnRNPs) throughout their processing in the nucleus .... and eventual transport to the .... At least two of these hnRNP proteins contain.................... .... and are thought to function as carriers of mRNAs during their export to the cytoplasm. As discussed in a later section of this chapter, ribosomal RNAs are assembled with ribosomal proteins in the nucleolus, and intact .... are then .... to the cytoplasm. Their export from the .... to be mediated by nuclear

export signals present on ribosomal proteins. For tRNAs, the specific proteins that mediate .... to be identified.

12. Observe the following diagram and answer the question as follows.[18]

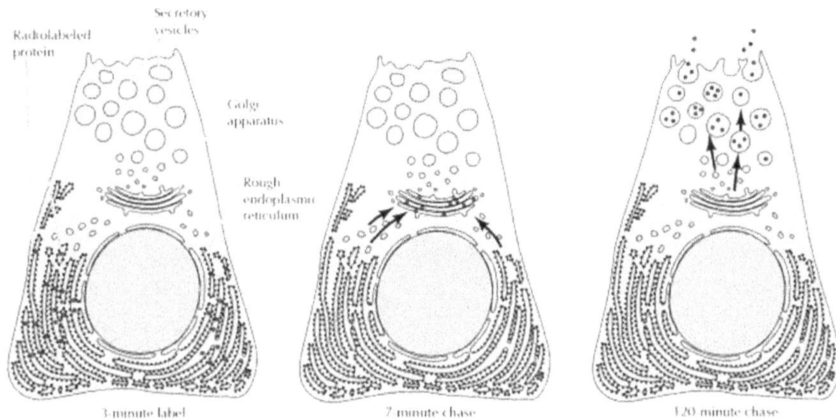

The secretory pathway. Pancreatic acinar cells, which secrete most of their newly synthesized proteins into the digestive tract, were labeled with radioactive amino acids to study the intracellular pathway taken by secreted proteins

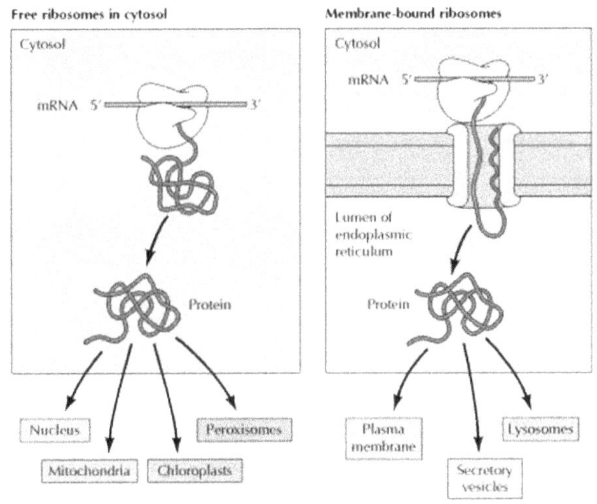

In mammalian cells, the initial sorting of proteins to the ER takes place while translation is in progress. Proteins synthesized on free ribosomes either remain in the cytosol or are transported to the nucleus, mitochondria, chloroplasts, or peroxisomes. In contrast, proteins synthesized on membrane-bound ribosomes are translocated into the ER while their translation is in progress. They may be either retained within the ER or transported to the Golgi apparatus and, from there, to lysosomes, the plasma membrane, or the cell exterior via secretory vesicles.

Statements:

I: These experiments defined a pathway taken by secreted proteins to move through site of synthesis to site of action , the secretory pathway:.. (provide the pathway).

II: This pathway is not restricted to .... destined for secretion from the cell. .... and .... also travel from the rough ER to the Golgi .... and then to their final destinations. Still other proteins travel through the initial steps of the secretory pathway but are then retained and function within either the ER or the Golgi apparatus.

---

[18] *Source: Cooper GM. Sunderland (MA , The Cell: A Molecular Approach. 2nd edition.*
):

III: The entrance of proteins into the Endomembrane System thus represents a major branch point for the traffic of proteins within ....

IV: Proteins destined for secretion or incorporation into the ...., ... and .... (list of organelles and structure) are initially targeted to the ER.

V: In mammalian cells, most proteins are transferred into the ER while they are being translated on .... Protein molecules destined to remain in the cytosol or to be incorporated into the organelles or cellular components (..................... , ..., ... etc.) are synthesized on .... and released into the ....when their translation gets completed.

13. Some of the statements related to functions of Endoplasmic Reticulum are listed below. Provide suitable phrases to complete the statements.

I: Proteins destined for incorporation into the plasma membrane or the membranes of the ER, Golgi, or lysosomes are initially (A) .... instead of being released into the lumen. From the definite site of the ER membrane, they proceed to their final destination along the same pathway as that of the pathway followed by secretory proteins: (B) .... These proteins are transported along this pathway as membrane components, however, rather than as soluble proteins.

II: Integral membrane proteins are embedded in the membrane by (C) .... regions that span the phospholipid bilayer. The membrane-spanning portions of these proteins are usually α-helical regions consisting of (D) .... acids. The formation of an α helix maximizes (E) .... between the (F) .... , and the hydrophobic amino acid side chains interact with the (G) .... of the phospholipids.

III: Different integral membrane proteins differ considerably on the basis of how they are inserted. Some integral membrane proteins, for an example, span the membrane only once, others have multiple membrane-spanning regions. Some proteins are oriented in the membrane with their (H) .... terminus on the cytosolic side; some other proteins have their (I) .... exposed to the cytosol. These orientations of proteins inserted into the (J) .... are established at different instances as the growing polypeptide chains as translocated into the ER.

14: The folding of polypeptide chains into their (A) .... , the assembly of polypeptides into (B) .... , and the covalent modifications involved in protein processing requires involvement of ER and Ribosomes. For proteins that enter the secretory pathway, many of these events occur either during (C) .... or within the ER lumen. One such processing event is the (D) .... of the signal peptide as the polypeptide chain is (F) .... The ER is also the site of protein folding, assembly of multisubunit proteins, disulfide bond formation, the initial (G) .... , and the addition of (H) .... to some plasma membrane proteins. Indeed, the primary role of lumenal ER proteins is to catalyze the folding and assembly of newly translocated polypeptides.

15. The .... is synthesized on a lipid (dolichol) carrier which remains anchored in the ER membrane. It is then transferred as a unit to acceptor asparagine residues in the specific consensus sequence by a membrane-bound enzyme called oligosaccharyl transferase.

Worksheet 2

1: Observe the following biochemical process and select the statement(s) which cannot support the process.

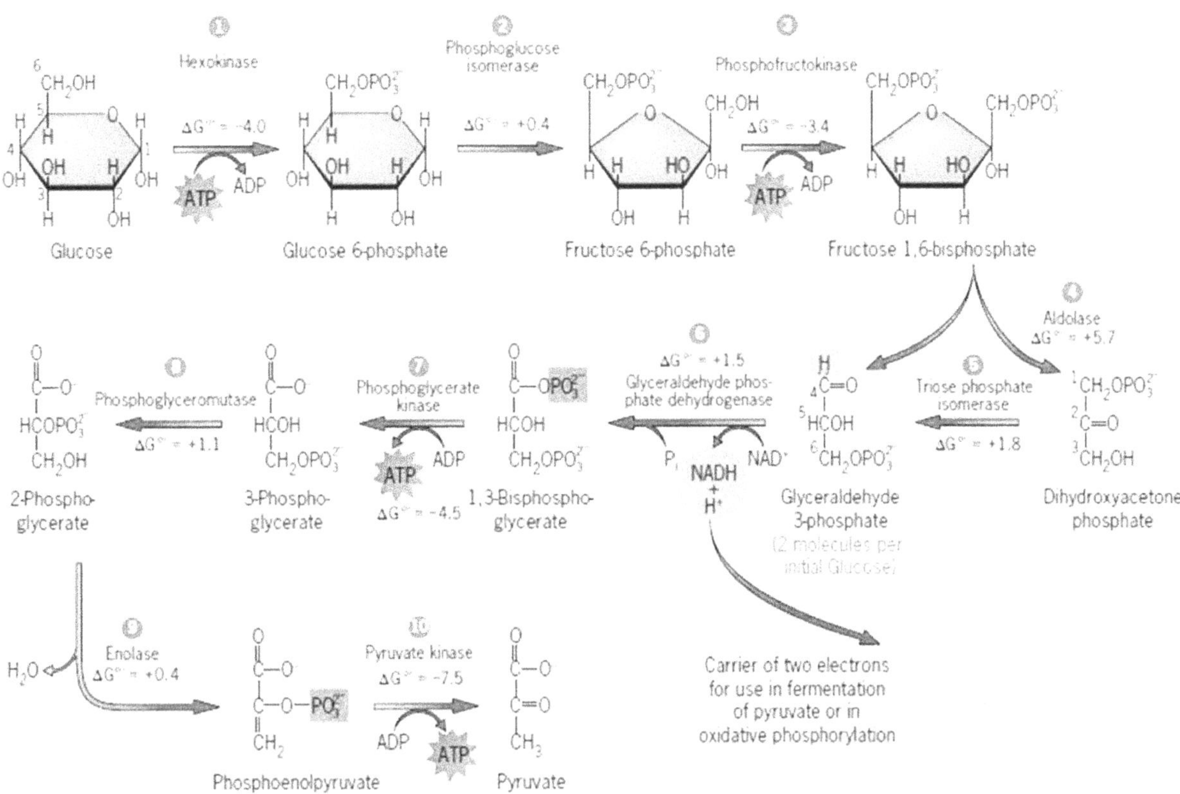

I: This process involves a partial breakdown of glucose molecule.

II: The process continues without getting adequate involvement of any enzymes.

III: Two electrons move out and gets involved in the formation of pyruvate or may move to conduct oxidative phosphorylation.

IV: Fructose 6-phosphate and Fructose 1-6-biphosphate are intermediates of this biochemical cycle.

V: This biochemical cycle takes place completely in the cytoplasm.

2. There are three different transport agents which intermediate the inter-cellular exchange of nutrients, gases and excretory products. The .... transports substances around the body through a large network of blood vessels. In adults

the body contains 5 to 6 litres of blood. It consists of two parts – a fluid called plasma and blood cells suspended in the plasma. .... is mainly water with a wide range of substances dissolved or suspended in it. These include: nutrients absorbed from the alimentary canal; oxygen absorbed from the lungs; chemical substances synthesised by body cells, e.g. hormones, waste materials produced by all cells to be eliminated from the body by excretion. ....There are three distinct groups, classified according to their functions. One of such unit is responsible for transport of oxygen, another group of these units are responsible for generating response to germs and foreign particles.

3. Identify the marked parts of the following figure.

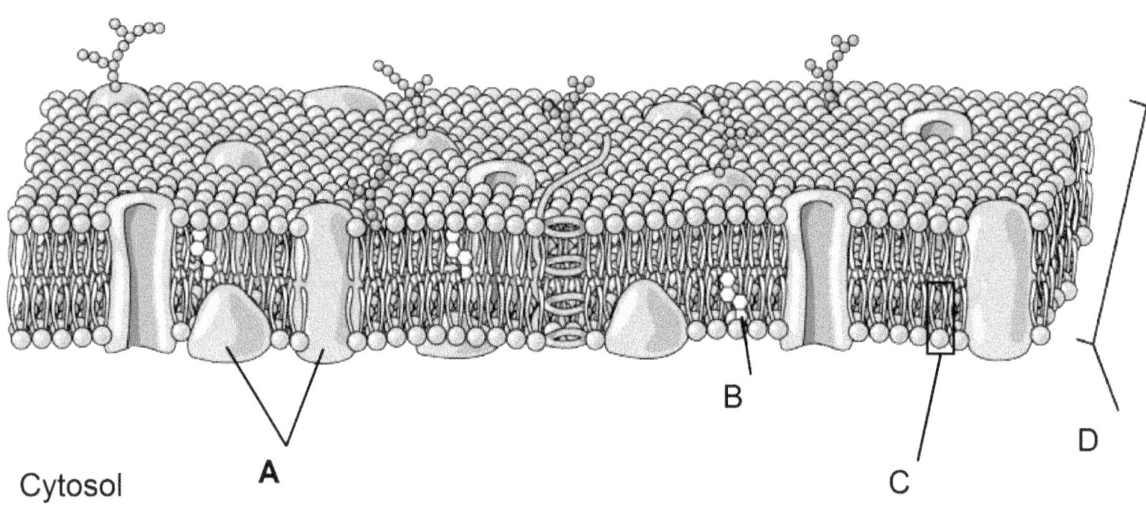

4. Complete the following:

Red cell numbers remain fairly constant, because the ………………… ………………… produces erythrocytes at the rate at which they are destroyed. This is due to a homeostatic negative feedback mechanism …………………………… …………………………… …………………………… . The hormone that regulates red blood cell production is …………………………… , produced mainly by the kidney. The primary stimulus to increased ………………………… is ………………………………… . This occurs when: the oxygen-carrying power of blood is reduced by, e.g., ………………………… or …………………… due to disease the oxygen tension in the air is reduced, as at high altitudes. …………………… increases erythrocyte formation by stimulating ……………………………… production. This hormone stimulates an increase in the production of ………………………………………… and the release of increased numbers of reticulocytes into the blood. It also speeds up ……………………………… maturation. These changes increase the …………………… ……………………….. …………………… of the blood and ………………………………, the original stimulus. When the tissue hypoxia is overcome, erythropoietin production declines. When …………………………… levels are low, red cell formation does not take place even in the presence of ……………………………, and ……………………………… develops.

5. Provide names of organelles on the basis of their specific functions.

A: It binds amino acids together to form a polypeptide chain on the basis of encoded sequence obtained from the DNA segments (genetic materials) housed inside the nucleus of a living cell.

B: It traps solar radiation and utilises that energy for breaking down water molecule.

C: It ensures complete break down of energy giving food materials for liberating chemical energy trapped in nutrients and store energy in the form of ATP.

D: It packages cellular products in sacs and ensures cellular secretion through liberating secretory vesicles.

6. Statement about lipids present in Plasma Membrane listed below. Strike the odd one out.

I: All the glycolipids of the plasma membrane, as become evident from different studies, are in the outer leaflet where they often serve as receptors for extracellular ligands and for other foreign chemicals.

II: Phosphatidylethanolamine (often remains concentrated in the inner leaflet) tends to promote the curvature of the membrane, which is important in ensuring regularised membrane budding and fusion activities. Phosphatidylserine or PS (as often remains concentrated in the inner leaflet) has a net negative charge at physiologic pH. It makes it a candidate for binding positively charged lysine and arginine residues, such as those adjacent to the membrane spanning α helix of glycophorin A.

III: The appearance of PS on the outer surface of matured lymphocytes marks the cells ready for undergoing destruction by macrophages, whereas its appearance on the outer surface of platelets leads to facilitation of blood coagulation.

IV: Phosphatidylinositol or PI (often remains concentrated in the inner leaflet of Plasma Membrane) can be phosphorylated at different sites on the inositol ring, which switches on the convertion of the lipid into a phosphoinositide.

V: Phosphoinositides play a defining role in the transfer of stimuli from the plasma membrane to the cytoplasm and the recruitment of proteins to the cytosolic face of the plasma membrane for different purposes.

VI: Protein accumulation on either side of Plasma Membrane is principally regulated by the lipid bilayer to ensure functional diversification of the membrane at different instances.

VII: The lipid bilayer can be thought of as composed of two more-or-less stable, independent monolayers having different physical and chemical properties.

7. Compare the statements....

Assertion: Diagram of a hemoglobin molecule, which consists of two α -globin chains and two β-globin chains (a hetero-tetramer) joined by non-covalent bonds. When the four globin polypeptides are assembled into a complete hemoglobin molecule, the kinetics of O_2 binding and release appears quite different from those exhibited by isolated units of individual polypeptides.

Reason:
The binding of O_2 to one polypeptide causes a conformational change in the other polypeptides that alters their affinity for O_2 molecules. the binding of oxygen was accompanied by the movement of the bound iron atom closer to the plane of the heme group. This type of seemingly inconsequential shift in position of a single atom pulled on an α helix to which the iron is connected, which in turn led to a series of increasingly larger movements within and between the subunits of the hemoglobin complex. It indicates the significance of conformational change in protein molecules. The complex functions of proteins may be carried out by means of small changes in their conformation.

Options: A: Both the statements are true and they support each other.

B: Both the statements are not true and they are not supporting each other perfectly.

C: Statements are true but they are not supporting each other.

8. A fact sheet related to function of haemoglobin molecule is displayed below. Complete the statements.

I: Each of the four subunits in haemoglobin contains one .... molecule, which consists of an iron atom held within a .... The heme groups are the .... of haemoglobin. The binding of oxygen to the heme molecule in one of the four hemoglobin subunits induces a local .... change whose effect spreads to the other subunits, lowering the Km for the binding of .... molecules and yielding a .... Consequently, the sequential binding of oxygen is facilitated, permitting hemoglobin to load more oxygen in .... than it otherwise could at normal ....

9. Compare the following statements;

Statement I: Deoxyribonucleic acid (DNA), often considered as a chemical basis of genetic information system and inheritance, contains all the information required to build the cells and tissues of an organism. The exact replication of this information system as encoded in the DNA molecules in any species assures its genetic continuity from generation to generation and is critical to the normal development of an individual. The information stored in DNA is arranged in hereditary units (popularly titled as genes) that control identifiable traits of an organism. During continuation of the process of transcription, the information stored in DNA is copied and transferred into ribonucleic acid (RNA) of specific type namely messenger RNA (mRNA). This mRNA has three distinct roles in protein synthesis.

Statement II: Messenger RNA (mRNA), as duly manufactured during the process of transcription, carries the encoded instructions from DNA that specify the correct order of amino acids to be incorporated in the polypeptide chains during protein synthesis. The remarkably accurate, stepwise assembly of amino acids into proteins occurs by translation of codes provided by mRNA. In this process, the information in mRNA is interpreted by a second type of RNA called transfer RNA (tRNA) with the aid of a third type of RNA and its associated proteins, ribosomal RNA. tRNA are specific for selecting, binding and transporting specific types of amino acids.

Statement III: the simplified representation of the central dogma as DNA-n-RNA-n-protein does not reflect the role of proteins in the synthesis of nucleic acids.

Options:

A: All the three statements provide a perfect idea of the manifestation of genes at cellular and molecular level to confer the regulation of cellular functions by genes.

B: Role of DNA and RNA are perfectly represented in all the three statements. All these statements provide information related to the principle of Central Dogma and also elaborates the functioning of DNA.

C: Statements require more elaboration to support the principle of Central Dogma.

D: None of the statements are perfectly represented. All statements require modifications.

10. In addition to its activities related to the processing of .... and .... proteins of different types, the ER is the major site at which ....are synthesized in eukaryotic cells. Because they are extremely .... , lipids are synthesized in association with pre-existing segment of cellular membranes rather than in the aqueous environment of the .... Although some lipids are synthesized in association with other membranes, majority of such units are synthesized in the ....ER. They are then transported from the .... to their ultimate destinations either in .... or by carrier .... Proteins.

11: Golgi bodies perform some unique functions which are often considered as an inter-mediate between the external and internal environment of a cell.

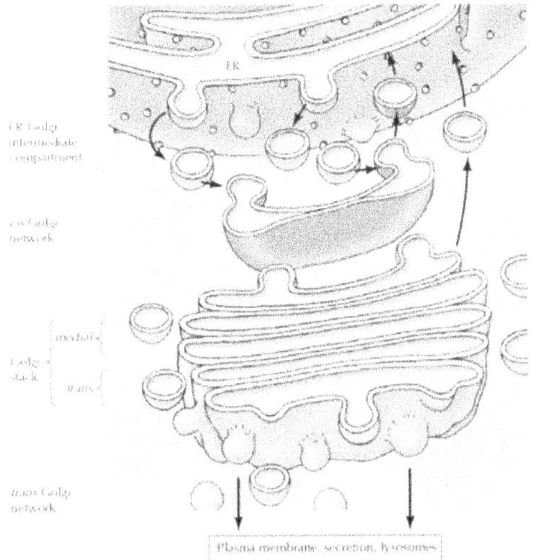

Distinct processing and sorting events appear to take place in an ordered sequence within different regions of the Golgi complex, so the Golgi is usually considered to consist of multiple discrete compartments. Although the number of such compartments has not been established by any of the experimentations, the Golgi is most commonly viewed as consisting of four functionally distinct regions: the cis-Golgi network, the Golgi stack (which is divided into the medial and trans sub-compartments), and the trans-Golgi network Proteins from the ER are transported to the ER-Golgi intermediate compartment and then enter the Golgi apparatus at the cis – Golgi network. They then progress to the medial and trans compartments of the Golgi stack, within which most metabolic activities of the Golgi apparatus are performed. The modified proteins, lipids, and polysaccharides then move to the trans Golgi network, which acts as a sorting and distribution center, directing molecular traffic to lysosomes, the plasma membrane, or the cell exterior.

Statements related to function of Golgi complex are listed below. Strike odd ones out.

I: The phosphorylation of mannose residues appears to be a critical step in sorting lysosomal proteins to their correct intracellular destination. The specificity of this process resides in the enzyme that catalyses the first step in the reaction sequence (the selective addition of N-acetylglucosamine phosphates to lysosomal proteins.

II: This enzyme (N-acetylglucosamine) recognizes a specific structural determinant accommodated on lysosomal proteins but not on proteins destined for the plasma membrane or merely for fulfilling secretory purposes.

III: Simple proteins move through different types of folding and coiling in this site. This recognition determinant is not a simple sequence of amino acids. This mechanism is formed in the folded protein by the juxtaposition of amino acid sequences collectively obtained from different regions of the polypeptide chain under processing.

IV: , the recognition determinant that leads to <u>mannose phosphorylation</u>, and by doing so ultimately targets proteins to lysosomes.

V: In contrast to the usual signal sequences that normally direct protein translocation to the ER depends on the three-dimensional conformation of the folded protein (determinants are popularly called signal patches).

VI: Some proteins can also be modified, as duly performed inside the Golgi complex at different instances, by the addition of carbohydrates to the side chains of acceptor serine and threonine residues within specific sequences of amino acids (O-linked glycosylation). This activity is performed in this organelle by the process of sequential addition of single –sugar residues. Serine or threonine, for an example, is usually linked directly to N-acetylgalactosamine, to which other sugars can then be added. These sugar molecules, at different instances, are further modified by the addition of sulphate groups in the specific sites.

VII: The glycerol phospholipids, cholesterol, and ceramide are synthesized in the Endoplasmic Reticulum. Sphingomyelin and glycol-lipids are then synthesized specifically from ceramide present in the Smooth E.R.

VIII: It is becoming evident that sphingomyelin is synthesized on the lumenal surface of the Golgi complex, but glucose is added to ceramide molecule at places located on cytosolic side .

12. Observe the diagram and provide the sequence of activity as listed in it.

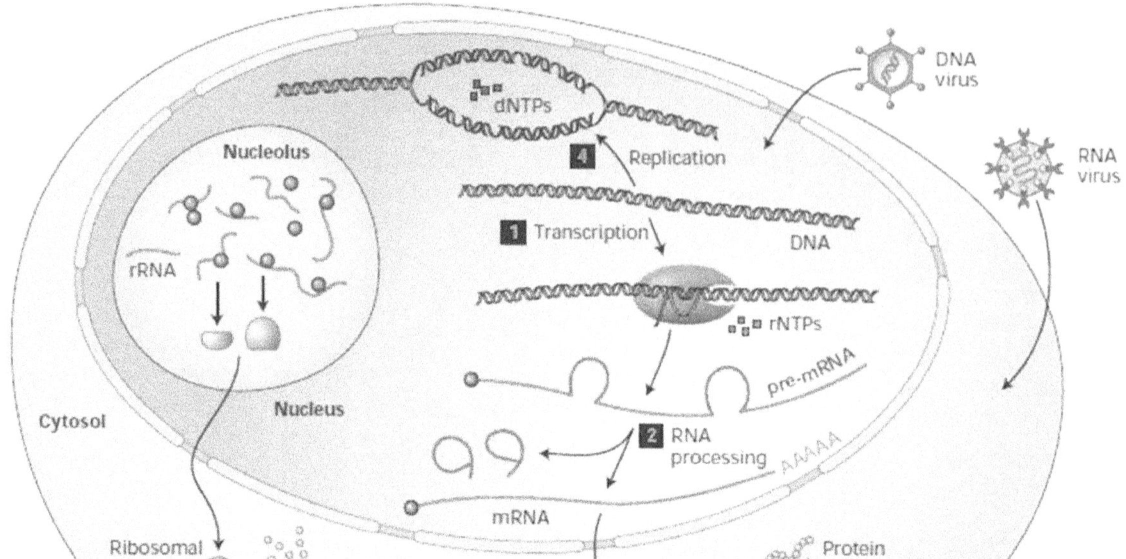

P: During DNA replication, which occurs only in particular cells preparing to divide mitotically or meiotically, deoxyribonucleoside triphosphate monomers (dNTPs) are polymerized to yield two identical copies of each chromosomal DNA molecule. Each daughter cell receives one of the identical copies of that chromosomal DNA molecule.

Q: During transcription of a protein-coding gene by RNA polymerase, the four-base DNA code having triplet of codons specifying the particular amino acid to be incorporated in sequence of a protein is copied into a precursor messenger RNA (prem-RNA) by the polymerization of ribonucleoside triphosphate monomers (rNTPs).

R: Removal of extraneous sequences and other modifications to the pre-mRNA, collectively known as to elaborate the entire mechanism in a specific way of RNA processing, produce a functional mRNA, which is transported to the cytoplasm actively through nuclear pore complex.

S: During translation , the four-base code of the mRNA, as duly provided in the form of specific triplet of codons meant for accommodating a specific amino acid in the peptide chain, is decoded into the sequence of polypeptide chain comprising differently arranged 20–amino acid "language" of proteins. Ribosomes, the macromolecular machines that translate the mRNA code with the help of tRNA, are composed of two subunits duly assembled in the nucleolus previously by utilising ribosomal RNAs (rRNAs) and multiple proteins of various types. After transport to the cytoplasm, ribosomal subunits intend to associate with an mRNA and carry out protein synthesis with the help of transfer RNAs (tRNAs) and various translation factors as per need. mRNA, rRNA and tRNA work jointly in a perfect coordination to ensure scheduled progression of the polypeptide chains during the process of translation.

Arrange above mentioned descriptions in accord to their sequence depicted in the image.

13. An information clip depicting structural features of DNA is provided. On the basis of this clip answer the questions as follows.

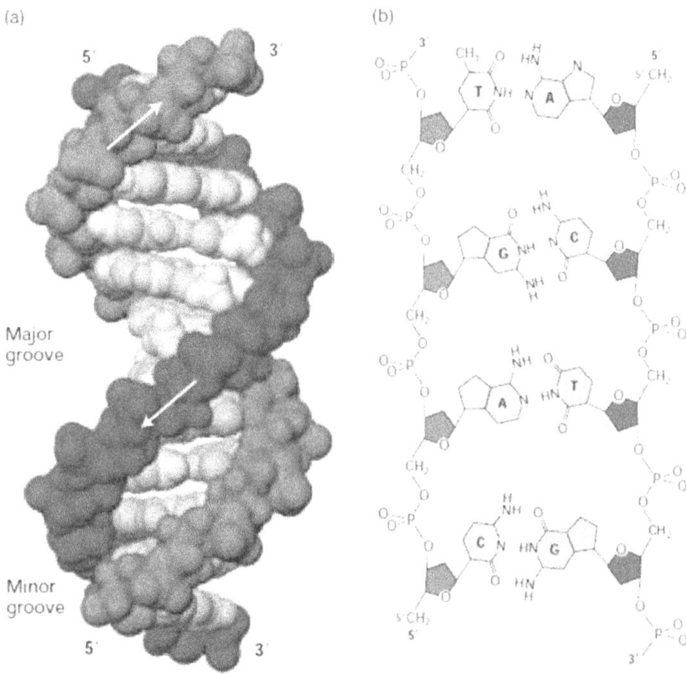

(a) Space-filling model of B DNA, the most common form of DNA in cells. The bases (light shades) project inward from the sugar-phosphate backbones (dark red and blue) of each strand, but their edges are accessible through major and minor grooves. Arrows indicate the 5'n3' direction of each strand. Hydrogen bonds between the bases are in the center of the structure. The major and minor grooves are lined by potential hydrogen bond donors and acceptors (highlighted in yellow). (b) Chemical structure of DNA double helix. This extended schematic shows the two sugar-phosphate backbones and hydrogen bonding between the Watson-Crick base pairs, AT and GC.

In natural DNA, A always hydrogen bonds with T and G with C, forming A·T and G·C base pairs as shown in Figure. These associations between a larger purine and smaller pyrimidine are often called Watson-Crick base pairs. Two polynucleotide strands, or regions thereof, in which all the nucleotides form such base pairs are said to be complementary. However, in theory and in synthetic DNAs other base pairs can form. For example, a guanine (a purine) could theoretically form hydrogen bonds with a thymine (a pyrimidine), causing only a minor distortion in the helix. The space available in the helix also would allow pairing between the two pyrimidine: cytosine and thymine. Although the nonstandard G·T and C·T base pairs are normally not found in DNA, G·U base pairs are quite common in double-helical regions that form within otherwise single-stranded RNA. Most DNA in cells is a right-handed helix. The x-ray diffraction pattern of DNA indicates that the stacked bases are regularly spaced 0.36 nm apart along the helix axis. The helix makes a complete turn every 3.6 nm; thus there are about 10.5 pairs per turn. This is referred to as the B form of DNA, the normal form present in most DNA stretches in cells. On the outside of B-form DNA, the spaces between the intertwined strands form two helical grooves of different widths described as the major groove and the minor groove (see Figure a). As a consequence, the atoms on the edges of each base within these grooves are accessible from outside the helix, forming two types of binding surfaces. DNA binding proteins can "read" the sequence of bases in duplex DNA by contacting atoms in either the major or the minor grooves.

Source: Part (a) from R. Wing et al., 1980, *Nature* 287:755; part (b) from R. E. Dickerson, 1983, *Sci. Am.* 249:94.

A: Which type of association of nitrogen bases will form a

B: Which are Watson – Crick Base pairs?

14. Complete the following statements related to different types of RNA:

The folded domains of .... not only are structurally analogous to the α helices and β strands found in proteins, but in some cases also have catalytic capacities. Such catalytic RNAs are called ribozymes. Although .... usually are associated with proteins that stabilize the ...., it is the RNA that acts as a catalyst. Some .... can catalyze splicing, a remarkable process in which an .... sequence is cut and removed, and the two resulting chains then .... This process occurs during formation of the majority of .... molecules in eukaryotic cells, and also occurs in ....and .... Some RNAs carry out ...., with the .... residing in the sequence that is removed.

15. Following statement specifies a definite structural component of a particular type of membrane bound cell organelle. Identify the organelle structure for replacing coded letters.

I: It is the simplest unit of the membrane bound cell organelle present in most of eukaryotic cells and remain associated to the cellular secretory pathway. It is often termed as the........................ (P).

II: .... (P) (about 1 μm in diameter) are central, flattened, plate-like or saucer-shaped closed compartment like structure that are held in parallel bundles or arranged in the form of stacks by placing each units one above the other.

III: In each stack, ... (P) are separated by a space of 20 to 30 nm which may contain rod-like elements or fibers (meant primarily for providing mechanical strength to the entire arrangement).

IV: Each stack of .... (P) forms a .... (Q) which may contain 5 to 6 .... (P) in animal cells or 20 or more of such units in plant cells.

V: Each .... (P) is bounded by a smooth unit membrane (7.5 nm thick), having a lumen varying in width from about 500 to 1000 nm depending upon the strength of the functional specifications.

VI: The margins of each unit structure of .... (P) are gently curved so that the entire .... (Q) of the .... (R) Golgi apparatus takes on a definite as well a unique appearance which can be recognised easily as an essential part of the endomembrane system.

VII: The cisternae at the convex end of the dictyosome comprise proximal, forming or cis-face and cisternae at the concave end of the dictyosome comprise the distal, maturing or trans-face.

16. The Golgi complex in animal cells is involved in the packaging and exocytosis of different types of cellular components and chemicals of different types. Provide a comprehensive list of such types of chemicals (at least six different types of cellular, extra cellular and organic compounds).

17. Point out four major functions of a cell organelle which is responsible for the sulfation process of certain molecules and phosphorylation of certain molecules by utilising ATP.

18. What is the specific function performed by the single membrane bound cell organelle in plant cells, which also remains responsible for manufacturing phopholipids and glycolipids?

19. How does a single membrane bound cell organelle regulate cellular secretion? Identify the organelle.

Worksheet 3

1. Provide the suitable names of the molecule (different RNAs) which are playing a definite role in the biochemical process displayed in the following diagram.

1. .... carries the genetic information transcribed from DNA in the form of a series of three nucleotide sequences, called codons, each of which specifies a particular amino acid.
2 .... is the key to deciphering the codons in this molecule. Each type of amino acid has its own subset of this molecules, which bind the amino acid and carry it to the growing end of a polypeptide chain if the next codon in the sequence of this RNA calls for it. The correct type of this RNA with its attached amino acid is selected at each step because each specific type of this RNA molecule contains a three-nucleotide sequence, an anticodon, that can base-pair with its complementary codon in the RNA molecule provided by the nucleus.
3. .... associates with a set of proteins to form ribosomes. These complex structures, which physically move along a coded RNA molecule duly obtained during transcription, catalyze the assembly of amino acids into polypeptide chains. They also bind special type of RNAs and various accessory proteins necessary for protein synthesis. Ribosomes are composed of a large and a small subunit, each of which contains its own specified molecule of this type of RNA.

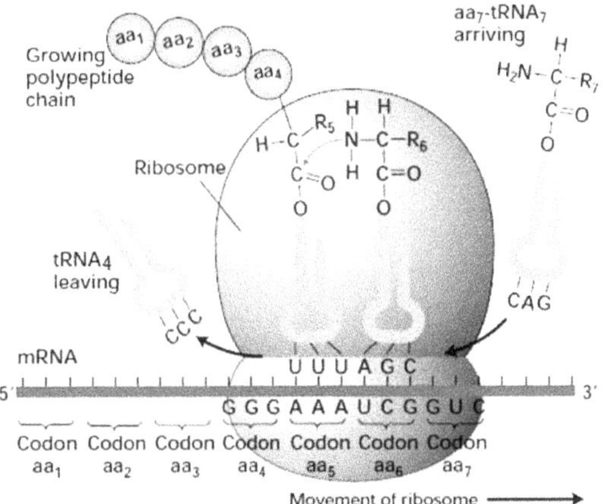

These three types of RNA participate in translation in all cells. Indeed, development of three functionally distinct RNAs was probably the molecular key to understanding the organic process of the origin of life.

2. (a) Which class of chromosomal proteins, histones or non-histones, is the more highly conserved in different eukaryotic species? Why might this difference be expected? (b) If one compares the histone and nonhistone chromosomal proteins of chromatin isolated from different tissues or cell types of a given eukaryotic organism, which class of proteins will exhibit the greater heterogeneity? Why are both classes of proteins not expected to be equally homogeneous in chromosomes from different tissues or cell types?

Q 3. When two unlike unit factors responsible for a single character are present in a single individual, one unit factor is ....(P). to the other, which is said to be ....(Q) In each monohybrid cross, the trait expressed in the F1 generation is controlled by the ....(P). unit factor. The trait not expressed in the same generation is controlled by the ....(Q) unit factor. The terms ....(P) and ....(Q) are also used to designate traits. In this case, tall stems are said to be .... (P) over .... (Q) dwarf stems.

Q 4. What is Test Cross? Provide suitable example to elaborate significance of this mechanism.

Q 5. What ratio of all the organisms at F2 Generation will be pure dominant individual in terms of the genotype if we conduct experimentation by considering a dihybrid cross?

Q 6. What is Pedigree analysis? Elaborate your understanding with one example.

Q 7. Which type of cell division can be observed during following cases?

a) Spermatogenesis b) Budding c) Oogenesis d) Sore formation by Amoeba

e) Binary fission performed by Amoeba f) Conjugation by Spirogyra

Worksheet 4

Q 1. What types of features and recommendation can be made by observing the following chart?

Character	Contrasting traits	F_1 results	F_2 results	F_2 ratio
Seed shape	round/wrinkled	all round	5474 round 1850 wrinkled	2.96:1
Seed color	yellow/green	all yellow	6022 yellow 2001 green	3.01:1
Pod shape	full/constricted	all full	882 full 299 constricted	2.95:1
Pod color	green/yellow	all green	428 green 152 yellow	2.82:1
Flower color	violet/white	all violet	705 violet 224 white	3.15:1
Flower position	axial/terminal	all axial	651 axial 207 terminal	3.14:1
Stem height	tall/dwarf	all tall	787 tall 277 dwarf	2.84:1

Statements:

I: Seven pairs of contrasting traits and the results of Mendel's seven monohybrid crosses of the garden pea (Pisum sativum).

II: In each case, pollen derived from plants exhibiting one trait was used to fertilize the ova of plants exhibiting the other trait.

III: In the F1 generation, one of the two traits was exhibited by all plants.

IV: The contrasting trait reappeared in approximately 1/4 of the F2 plants.

V: In addition to his choice of a suitable organism, he preferably restricted his examination to one or very few pairs of contrasting traits in each experiment.

VI: Mendel also kept accurate quantitative records, a necessity initiative in conducting any genetic experiments.

VII: From the analysis of his data, Mendel derived certain postulates that have become the principles of transmission genetics.

VIII: This result also displays the average phenotype of monohybrid cross as Dominant: Recessive = 3:1. This ratio will be obtained regarding all types of monohybrid cross involving all the organisms.

Find out whether any of the following statements are not perfectly describes the correlation of experiments and postulates proposed by Mendel.

Q 2. On the basis of the pedigree chart identify types of pedigree displayed in the following charts.

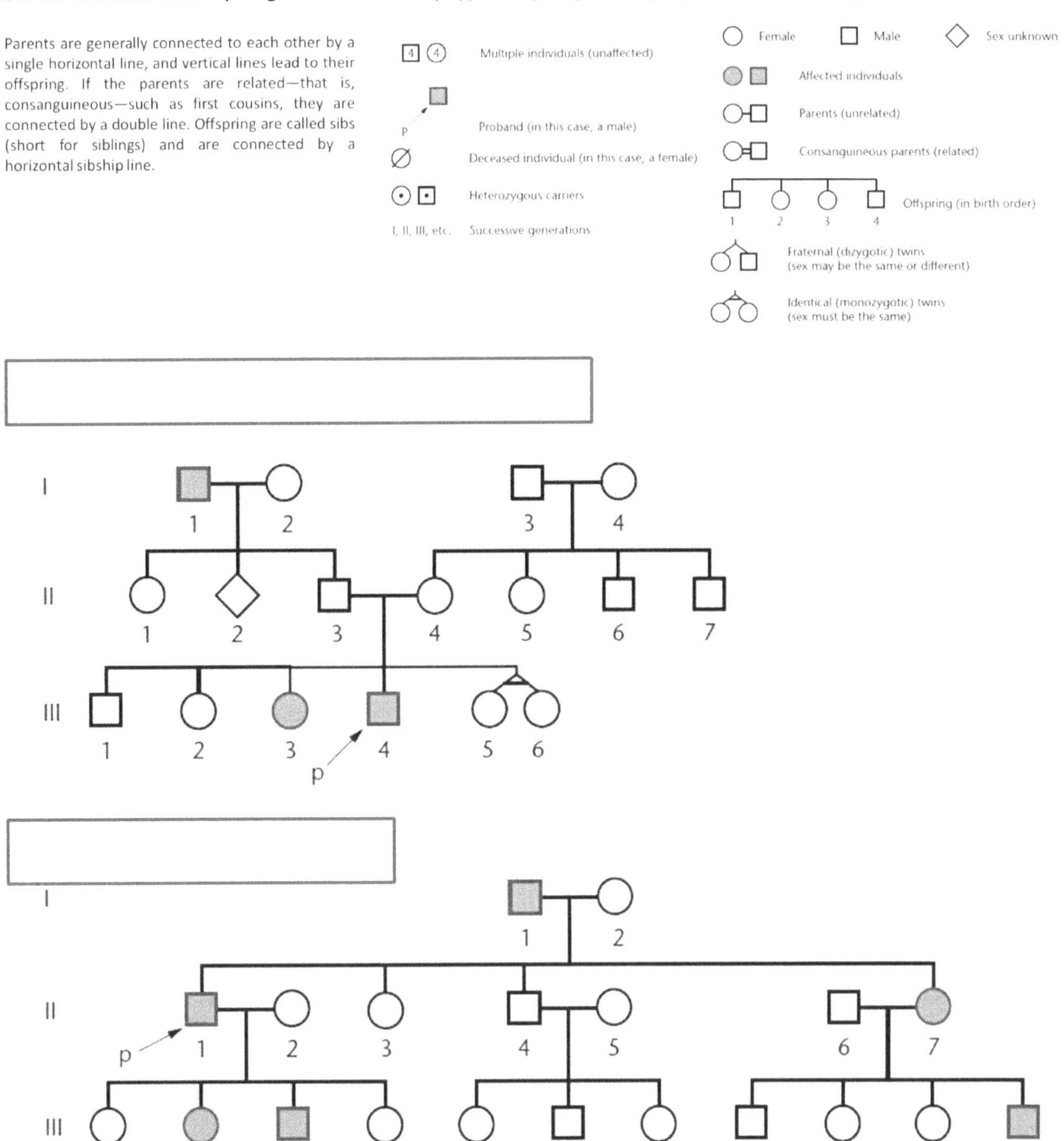

Q 3. Albinism, related to lack of pigmentation in humans, results from an autosomal recessive gene (a). Two parents with normal pigmentation have an albino child.

(a) What is the probability that their next child will be albino?

(b) What is the probability that their next child will be an albino girl?

(c) What is the probability that their next three children will be albino?

Worksheet 5

Q 1. Provide missing data in the following chart of dihybrid cross.

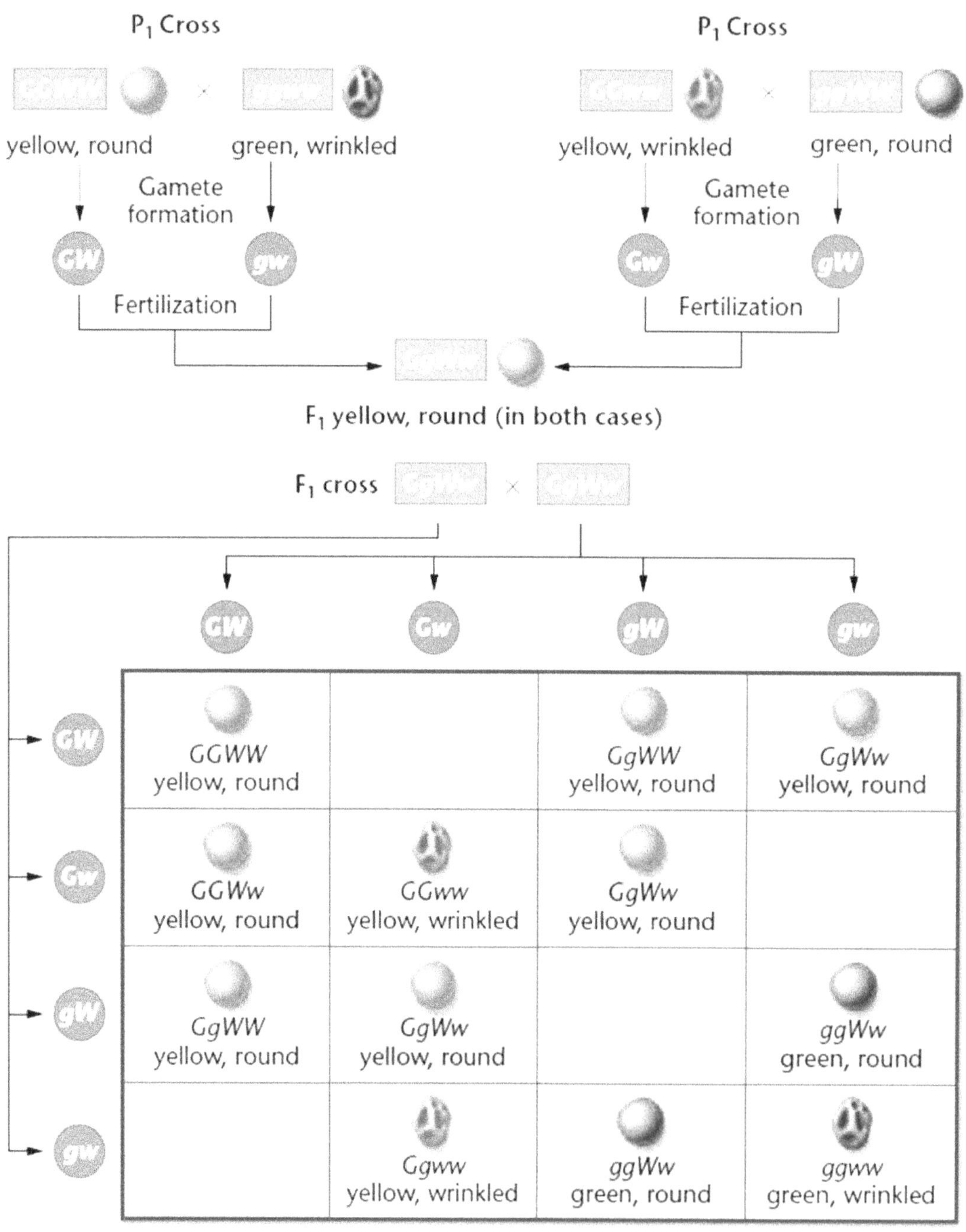

Q 2. In a study of black guinea pigs and white guinea pigs, 100 black animals were crossed with 100 white animals, and each cross was carried to an F2 generation. In 94 of the crosses, all the F1 offspring were black and an F2 ratio of 3 black:1 white was obtained. In the other 6 cases, half of the F1 animals were black and the other half were white. Why? Predict the results of crossing the black and white F1 guinea pigs from the 6 exceptional cases.

Q 3. Thalassemia is an inherited anaemic disorder in humans. Affected individuals exhibit either a minor anaemia or a major anaemia. Assuming that only a single gene pair and two alleles related to such genes are involved in the inheritance of these conditions, is thalassemia a dominant or recessive disorder?

Q 4. What is recessive lethal allele?

Q 5. Which of the following may not be considered as elements of a microbial structure?

a) All cells active and living have a permeability barrier called the cytoplasmic membrane that separates the inside of the cell, the cytoplasm, from the outside world. The cytoplasm is an aqueous mixture of macromolecules (for example proteins, lipids, nucleic acids, and polysaccharides), small organic molecules (mostly imparting in the structure as the precursors of macromolecules), various inorganic ions, and ribosomes.

b) Ribosomes, basically made up of two distinct sub units along with mRNA molecule, are the structures responsible for protein synthesis and are found in all active cells.

c) Some cells have a well-defined cell wall that lends mechanical structural strength to a cell and also provides a definite shape.

d) The cell wall is a relatively permeable structure located outside the cell membrane and is a much stronger, non-flexible and rigid layer than compared to the membrane bilayer of the same cell.

e) Different types of orientations of microfilaments, as evident from the endoskeleton of a cell, provide a definite shape to a living cell and also takes part in the formation of spindle fibres (especially in eukaryotes) for smooth accomplishment of cell divisions.

f) Cells having identical roles to play unite and start acting jointly in the form of tissue; group of tissues unite to form an organ.

g) Nuclear membranes are composed of two unit membranes having specialised pores at different places to ensure transport of macro-molecules in between nucleoplasm and cytoplasm.

Q 6. Some of the features as recognisable from the following pair of diagram signifies that these cells are of organisms belonging to Eukarya. Identify five such features.

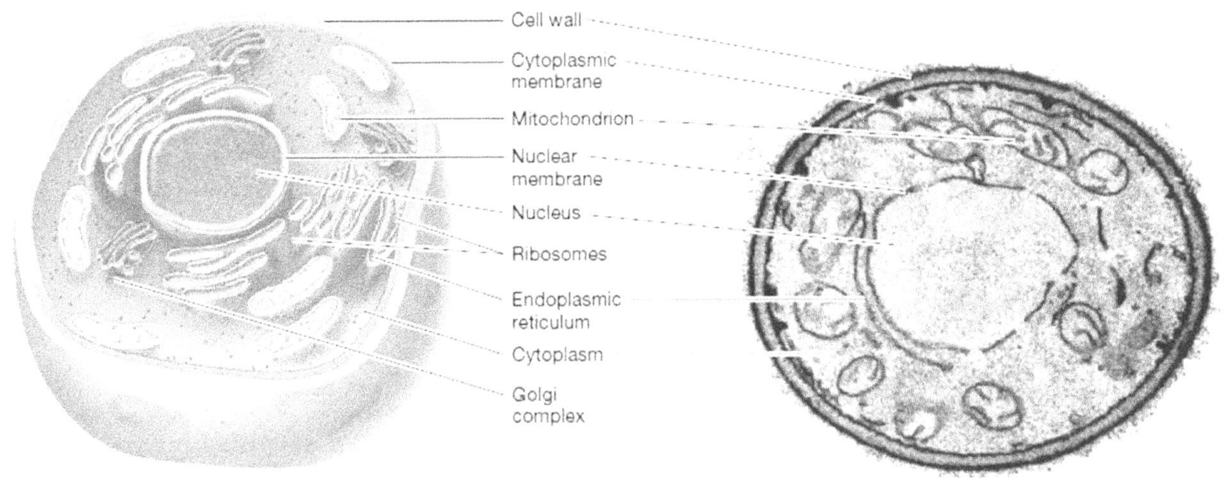

Q 7. What cellular and molecular structures distinguish prokaryotic and eukaryotic cells? What are some differences between a cell wall and a cell membrane? In what types of organisms would you expect to find these structures?

Q 8. What is the difference between magnification and resolution? Can either increase without the other?

Q 9. Describe the experiments that proved DNA to be the molecule at the basis of heredity.

Q 10. Provide suitable keyword for the following:

a) ……………………. ……………………… :the manipulation of sterile instruments or culture media in such a way as to maintain sterility.
b) …………… ………………. :a rigid layer present outside the cytoplasmic membrane; it confers structural strength on the cell.
c) ………………………… . : a form of metabolism in which energy is generated from the oxidation of inorganic compounds.
d) ………………………… . : a macroscopically visible population of cells growing on solid medium, arising from a single cell Contrast the ability to resolve a cell or structure from its surroundings.
e) ………………………… . : a collection of microbial cells grown using a nutrient medium
f) ………………………… . : the fluid portion of a cell, enclosed by the cytoplasmic membrane
g) ………………………… . : membrane a semipermeable barrier that separates the cell interior (cytoplasm) from the environment.
h) ………………………… . : modification of cellular components to form a new structure, such as a spore
i) ………………………… . : one of the three main evolutionary lineages of cells: the Bacteria, the Archaea, and the Eukarya.
j) ………………………… . : the process by which information from DNA is copied into a new strand of DNA.
k) ………………………… . : a protein (or in some cases an RNA) catalyst that functions to speed up chemical reactions.
l) ………………………… . : having a membrane-enclosed nucleus and various other membrane-enclosed organelles; cells of Eukarya.
m) ………………………… . : a change over time in gene sequence and frequency within a population of organisms, resulting in descent with modification.
n) ………………………… . : microorganisms that inhabit environments characterized by extremes of temperature, pH, pressure, or salinity.

Q 11. Complete the following statement:

The cellular walls of Bacteria contain a structure made up of rigid polysaccharide called peptidoglycan ……………………………… (A) that confers increase of structural strength on the cell. It is found in all Bacteria that contain a cell wall, but it is not present in the cell walls of organisms belonging to Archaea or Eukarya. …………………………………… (A) is composed of alternating repeats of two modified glucose residues called N-acetylglucosamine and N-acetylmuramic acid along with the amino acids l-alanine, d-alanine, d-glutamic acid, and either l-lysine or diaminopimelic acid (DAP).

Q 12. Distinguish Gram Positive and Gram Negative Bacteria. What factor determines the response of bacteria to gram stainer?

Q 13. Why viral genome is not considered as fully functional part of any living entity?

Worksheet 6

Q 1. What conclusion can be worked out after observing following facts (duly obtained by observing participant chromosomes during the process of reductional division, or meiosis).

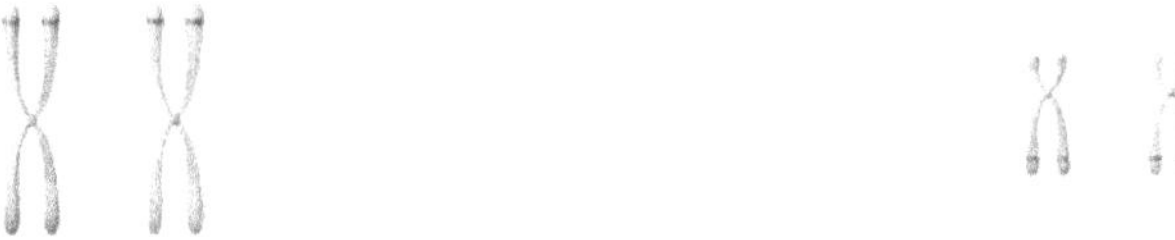

Genes located on chromosomes and homologous chromosomes indulged in pairing

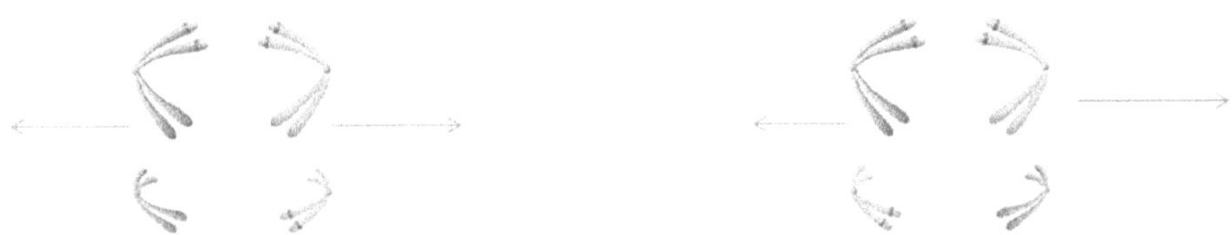

Independent assortment of segregating unit factors (following many meiotic events)

Nonhomologous chromosomes assort independently

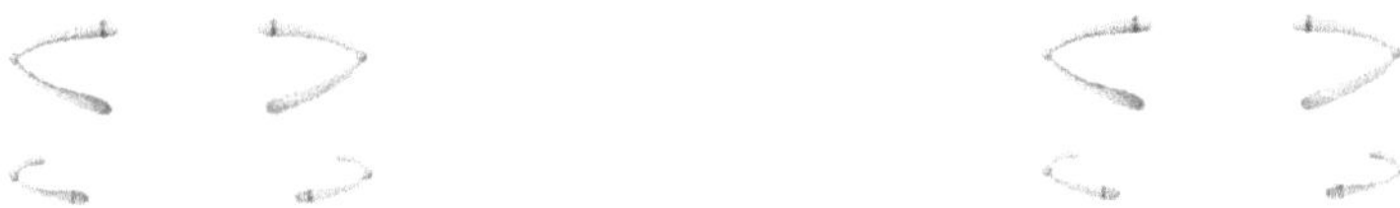

Q 2. Complete the following:

a) .... an organism's full complement of genes
b) .... a bacterial cell with a cell wall containing small amounts of peptidoglycan and an outer membrane.
c) .... a bacterial cell whose cell wall consists chiefly of peptidoglycan; it lacks the outer membrane of gram-negative cells.
d) .... a differential staining procedure that stains cells either purple (gram-positive cells) or pink (gram-negative cells).
e) .... in microbiology, an increase in cell number with time
f) .... :the microbial communities present in the animal gastrointestinal tract
g) .... : transfer the transfer of genes between cells through a process uncoupled from reproduction.

Q 3. What types of chemicals constitute the cell wall in bacteria? What are the basic differences between cell wall of bacteria and plants?

Q 4. Is there any similarity between membrane architecture of mitochondria and plastids? Give explanations.

Q 5. What types of chemicals constitute microtubules in a eukaryotic cell?

Q 6. At what stage of mitotic cell division nuclear membranes get disintegrated?

Q 7. .... and .... are double membrane structure present in a plant cell of mesophyll tissue.

Worksheet 7

Q 1. Identify the following:

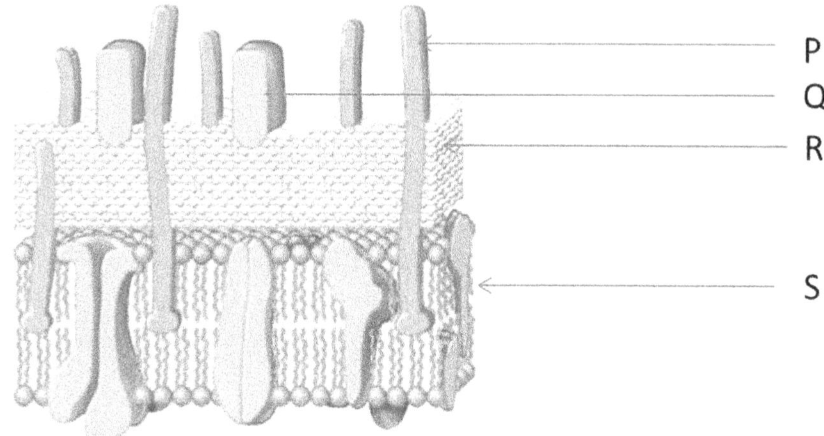

.......: Lipoteichoic acid ; ......: Plasma membrane;

.......: Wall-associated protein; ....Peptidoglycan

Q 2. Identify the following statement related to genetic code which is not true regarding genetic code.

a) The genetic code is written in linear form, using as "letters" the ribonucleotide bases that compose strand of mRNA molecules.

b) The ribonucleotide sequence which is transcribed on the strand of mRNA is derived primarily from the complementary nucleotide bases present in DNA.

c) Each "word" within the mRNA consists of three ribonucleotide letters, thus referred to as a triplet code (or triplet).

d) With several exceptions, each group of three ribonucleotides (codons or triplet), specifies one amino acid from the collection of 20 different amino acids.

e) The code is unambiguous (each triplet specifies only a single amino acid). There exists more than one codon which can specify a definite type of amino acid.

f) The code is degenerate, meaning that a given amino acid can be specified by more than one triplet codon. This is evident for 18 of the 20 amino acids.

g) The code contains one "start" and three "stop" signals, triplets that initiate and terminate translation, respectively during execution of the coded signals provided by mRNA to Ribosomes.

h) No internal punctuation (analogous, for example, to a comma) is used for representing the code. Thus, the code is said to be commaless while representing in any kind of explanations. Once translation of mRNA begins, the codons are read one after the other with no breaks between them (until and unless a stop signal is reached and is readily executed).

i) The code, as embedded in the molecule of mRNA , is non-overlapping. After translation commences, any single ribonucleotide within the mRNA is part of only one triplet.

j) The sequence of codons in a gene is collinear, with the sequence of amino acids making up the encoded protein with the help of mRNA.

k) Poly A tail of mRNA is also capable of executing the elongation of polypeptide chain during translation process with support of ribosomal subunits and tRNA.

l) The code is nearly universal. With only minor exceptions, a single coding dictionary is used by almost all the organisms: viruses, prokaryotes, Archaea, and eukaryotes.

Q 3. Complete the following:

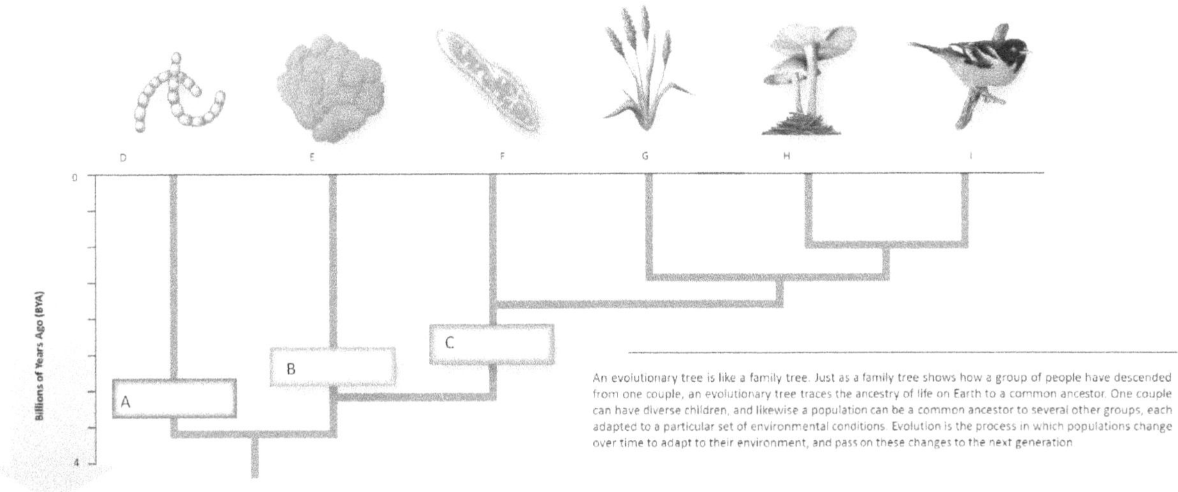

Q 4. Like carbon, silicon has four electrons in its outer shell, yet life evolved to be carbon-based since the early days of organic evolution. What is there about silicon's structure that might have prevented it from sharing with four other elements and prevented it from forming the many varied shapes of carbon containing molecules?

Q 5. Elaborate uses of cholesterol and anabolic steroids in daily life with suitable examples.

Q 6. .... are hydrophobic molecules that often serve as long-term energy storage molecules. Fats and oils, which are composed of .... and .... , are called .... These compounds made of saturated fatty acids (having no double bonds) are solids and are called fats. Some other similar compounds composed of unsaturated fatty acids (having double bonds) attain liquid state at room temperature and are called oils. .... are unsaturated fats with a unique form of chemical bond in the .... chain.

Q 7: Which of the following comparison requires modification?

	DNA	RNA
Sugar	Deoxyribose	Ribose
Bases	Adenine, guanine, thymine, Cytosine	Adenine, guanine, uracll, cytosine
Strands	Double-stranded with base pairing	Single-stranded
Helix	Yes	No

Worksheet 8

Q 1. Identify different parts of the plasma membrane as displayed in the following diagram.

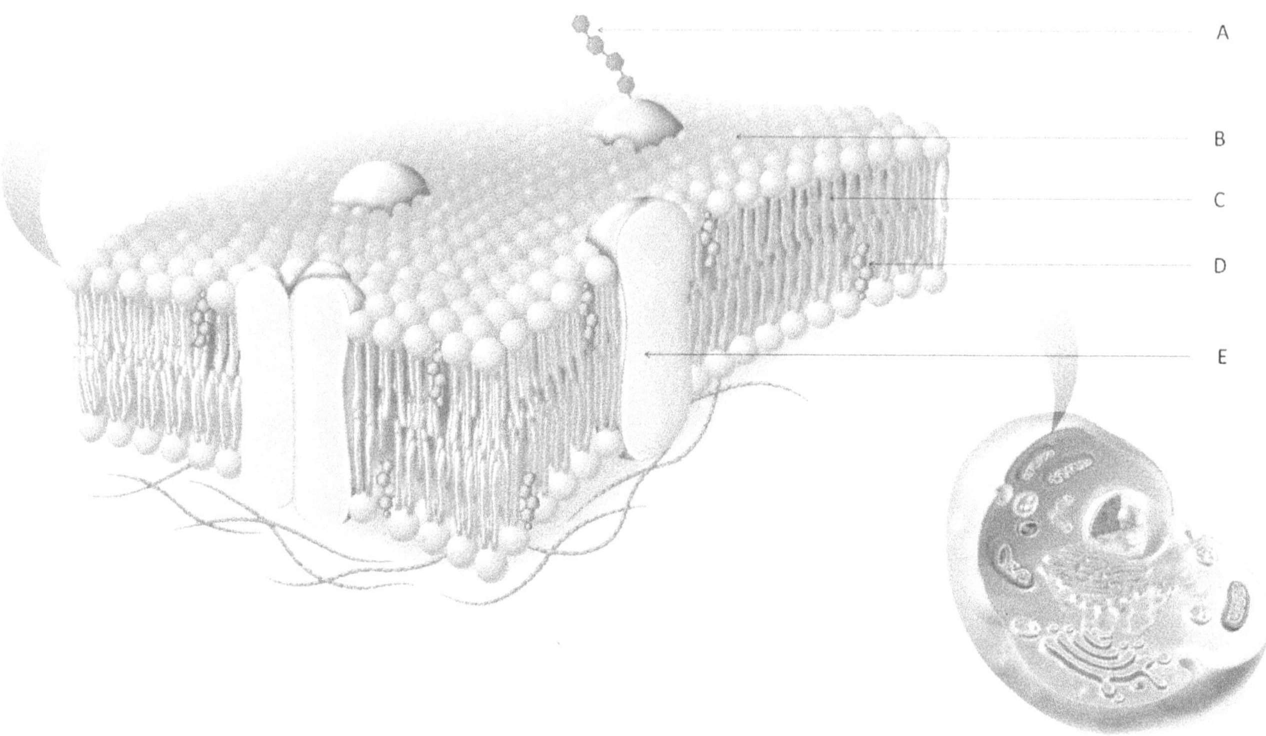

Q 2. A schematic diagram of nucleus is provided as follows. Identify different parts of this diagram.

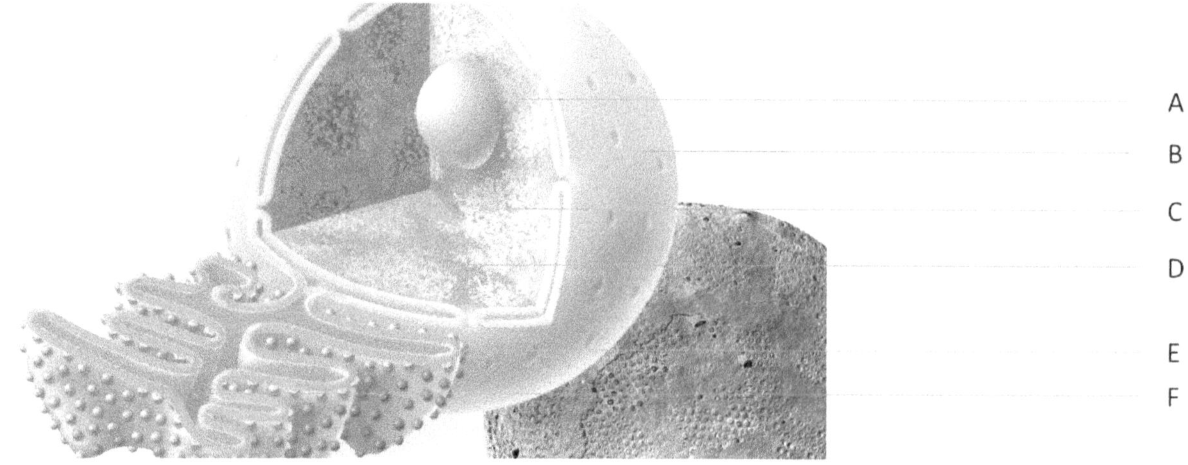

Q 3. Which cell organelles take part in forming the Endo-Membrane System of a Eukaryotic Cell?

Q 4. What will happen if volume of cytoplasm is doubled in a cell?

Q 5. What factors induce a cell to divide?.

Worksheet 9

Q 1: Observe the following structure of a combination of cell membrane and cell wall. Identify the type of organism having combination of this structure.

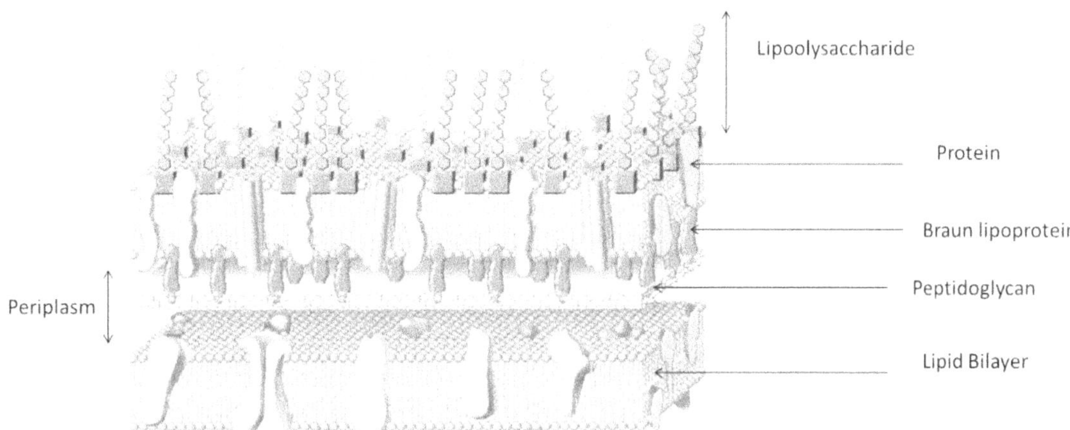

Q 2. Three different structures displayed in the following diagram are associated with making inter-cellular linkages in eukaryotes. Identify them.

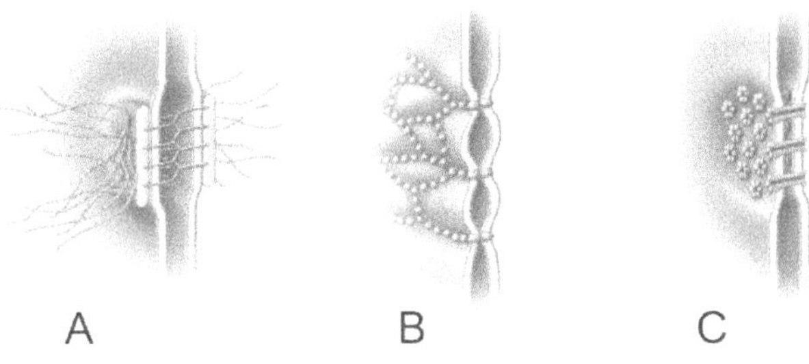

I: ...... : In this type of junctions, internal cytoplasmic plaques, firmly remain attached to the cytoskeleton present within each cell and are joined by intercellular filaments. A sturdy but flexible sheet of cells remain linked together. Example: In some organs, such as the heart, stomach, and bladder, where tissues experience must stretching, this junctions hold the cells together.

II: .....: Adjoining cells are more closely joined by this type of junctions, in which plasma membrane proteins actually attach to each other, producing a zipperlike fastening effect to hold the cells firmly. The cells of tissues that serve as barriers are held together by this type of junctions; (example: urine stays within kidney tubules because the cells of the tubules are joined by this type of junctions which provide the organ a considerable amount of flexibility.

III: .....: This type of junction is formed when two identical plasma membrane channels join. The channel of each cell is lined by six plasma membrane proteins that allow the junction to open and close. This type of junction lends strength to the cells, but it also allows small molecules and ions to pass and get exchanged between them.

Q 3. By which structure adjacent plant cells communicate each other?

Term End Assignment

Q 1: Identify following molecules.

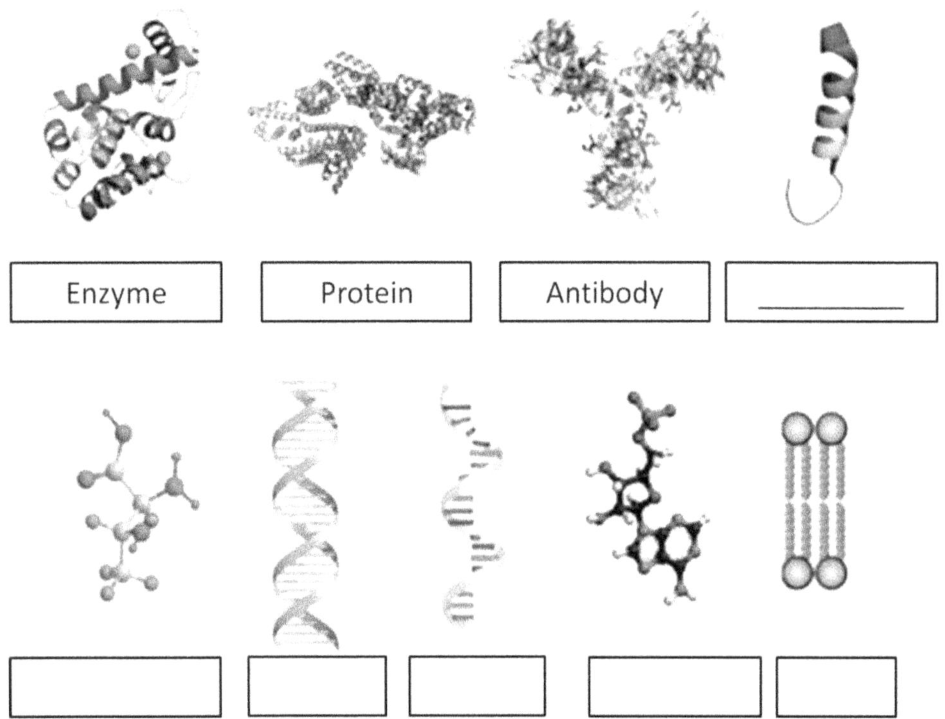

Q 2: Mark different parts..

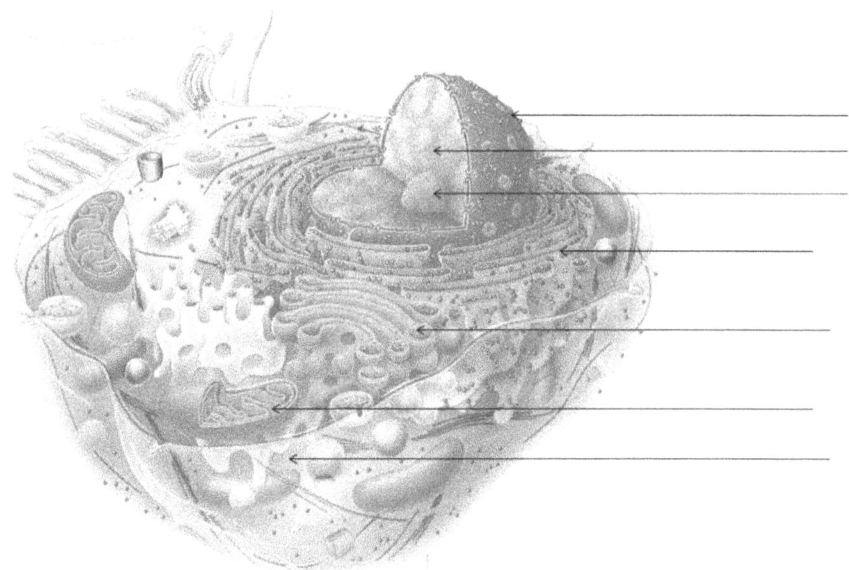

Q 3. Diagram of a nerve cell is provided. Mark all the parts.

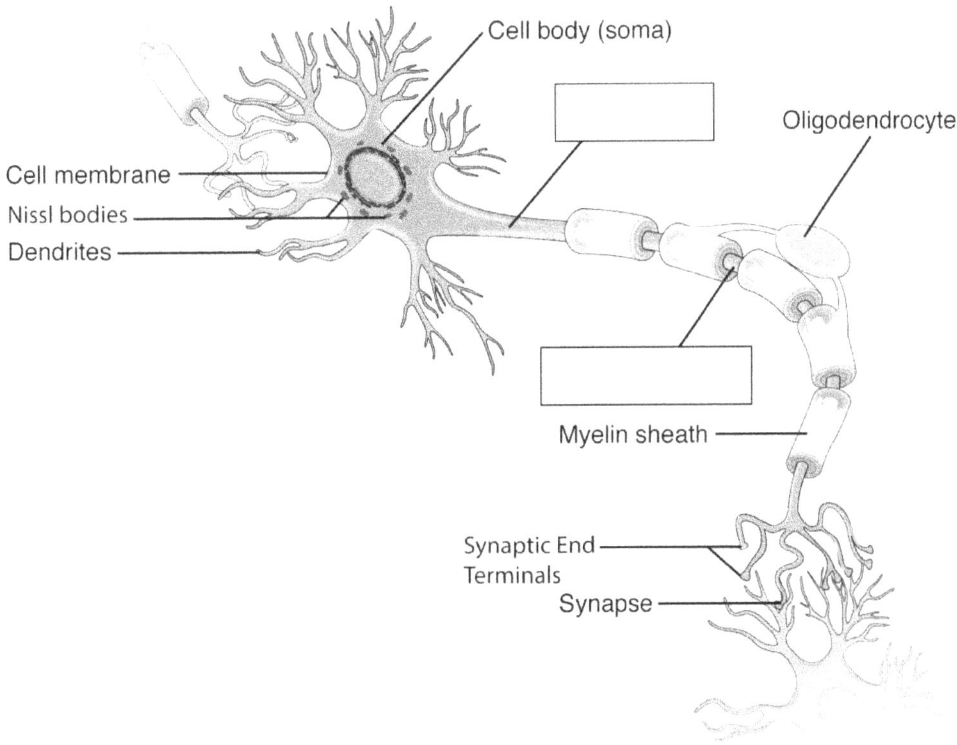

Q 4. Complete the following:

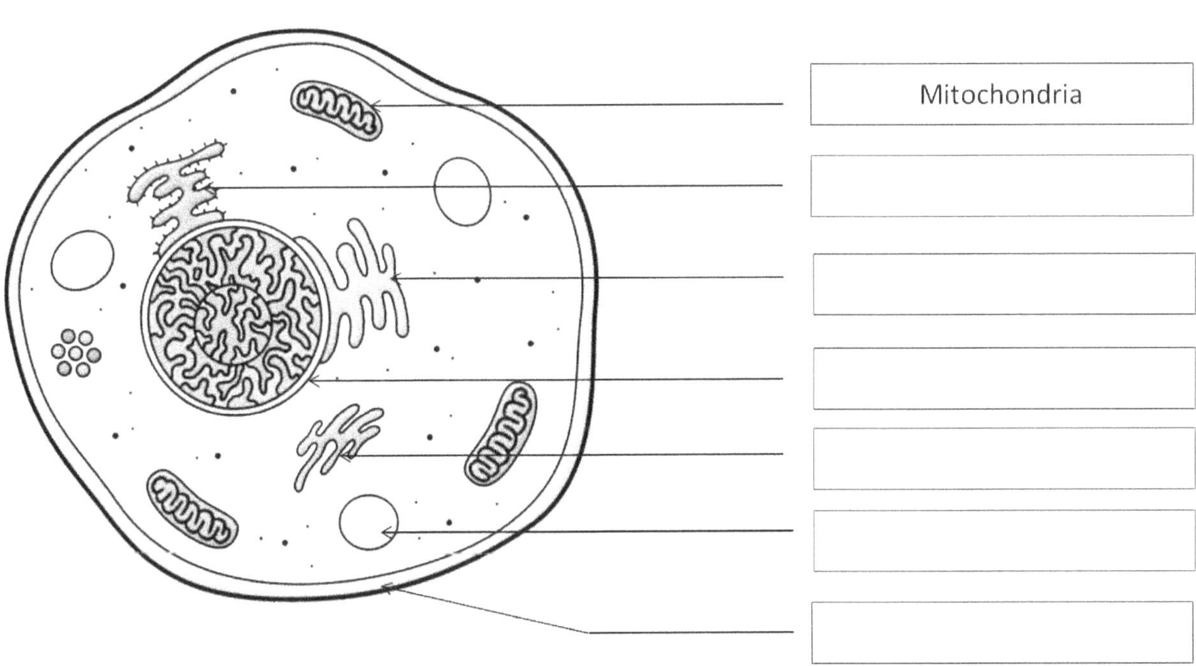

Q 4. The plasma membrane is considered as a fluid-mosaic model because it contains

a. waxes suspended within a mosaic of phospholipids.

b. a mosaic of proteins suspended within a phospholipid bilayer.

c. a polysaccharide mosaic suspended within a protein bilayer.

d. a mosaic of phospholipids suspended within a protein bilayer.

Q 5. What type of cellular transport is displayed in the following diagram?

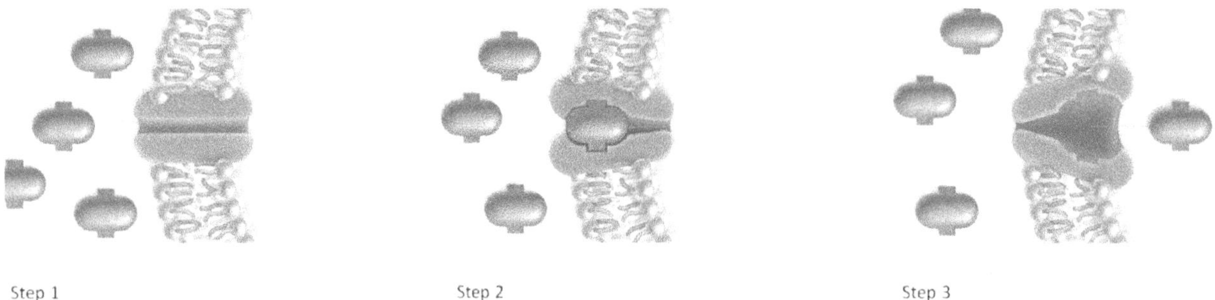

Q 6. Identify three types of solution by observing the ways cells are responding. Also provide suitable reasons in support of your answer.

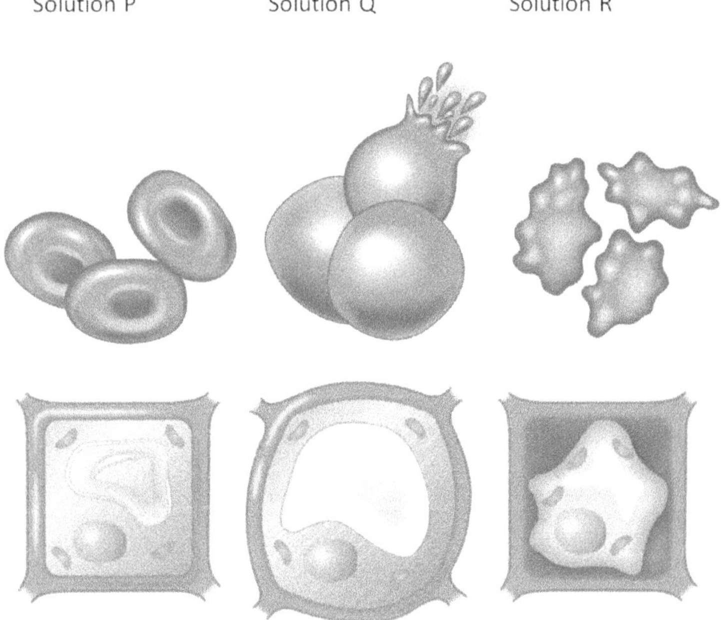

Q 7. Active transport requires metabolic ………………………………. ……………………………… and moves substances across a membrane from an area of lower concentration to an area of higher concentration. In many cases, a ……………………… …………………………. acts as a pump that causes a substance to move against its concentration gradient. For example, the …………………………. …………………………. pump allows Na^+ to move out and K^+ to move in a cell.

Q 8. Which part of mitochondria is responsible for conducting Oxidative Phosphorylation?

Q 9. What type of molecules are allowed by plasma membrane to pass through the lipid bilayer directly?

Q 10. The movement of water across the plasma membrane of a living cell is facilitated by

a. aquaporins.
b. substrate-mediated endocytosis.
c. receptor-mediated diffusion.
d. channel proteins.
e. Both a and d are correct.

Q 11. A fact sheet of Chloroplast is provided. On the basis of this fact sheet identify various parts of chloroplastid and answer questions as follows.

Fact Sheet of Chloroplast

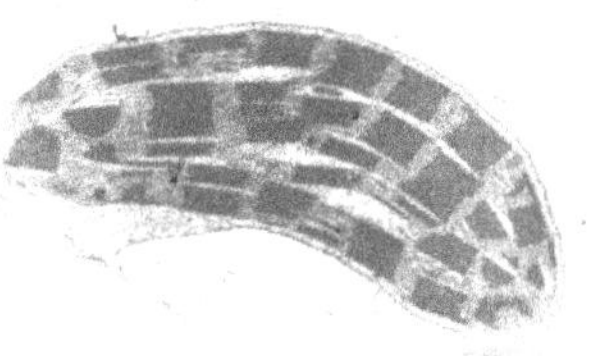

The green portions of plants, particularly the leaves, carry on photosynthesis. Carbon dioxide (CO_2), the raw material for photosynthesis, enters the leaf through small openings called *stomata* (sing., stoma). Spaces within the leaf temporarily store CO_2 until it is needed for photosynthesis.

Special cells, called mesophyll cells, conduct photosynthesis. CO2 and water diffuse into these cells, and then into the chloroplasts, the organelles that carry out photosynthesis.

In a chloroplast, a double membrane structure surrounds a fluid-filled area called the stroma. A separate membrane system other than the double membrane outer covering located within the stroma forms flattened sacs called thylakoids, which in some places are stacked to form grana (collection of granum), so named because early observers of biological studies thought they looked like piles of seeds.

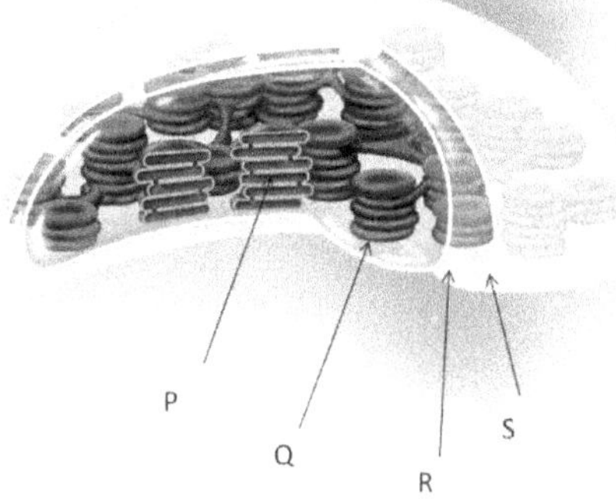

Chlorophyll and other pigments reside within the membranes of the thylakoids. These pigments are capable of absorbing solar energy, the energy that drives photosynthesis. A thylakoid membrane also contains protein complexes that convert solar energy into a chemical form. This energy is used in the stroma, where enzymes reduce CO_2 to carbohydrate.

The space within each thylakoid is connected to the space within every other thylakoid, thereby forming an inner compartment within chloroplasts called the *thylakoid space*. It is also observed that grana is the site of light facilitated reaction and stroma is the site of dark reaction involving Calvin Cycle.

Q a) Which part of chloroplast is the site of photo-phosphorylation?

Q b) Which part of the chloroplast is filled with enzymes required for conducting C3 pathway of dark reaction?

Q c) Which part of this organelle is responsible for absorbing solar radiation?

Q 12. The following fact sheet displays two distinct sets of reaction through which photosynthesis is performed by green plants. Identify sets of reactions and answer the questions as follows.

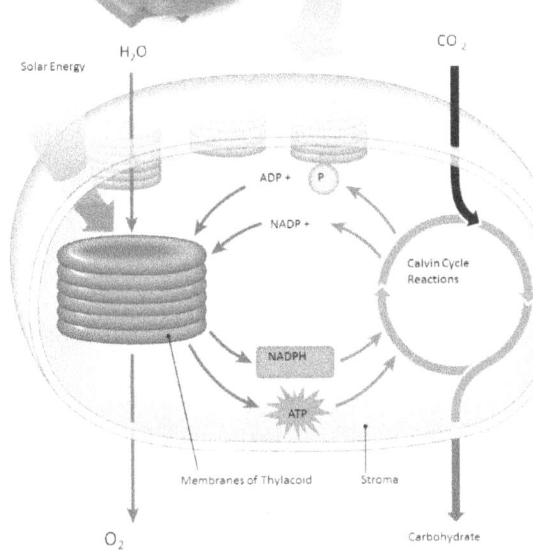

During photosynthesis, electrons are removed from H_2O and energized by solar energy. An enzyme helper called NADP+ then transfers these high-energy electrons to CO_2, thus forming carbohydrate. These electrons are accompanied by hydrogen ions (H+), and that's why it is possible to track the movement of electrons during photosynthesis by following the movement of the hydrogen ions. Reduction occurs when a molecule gains electrons (e–) and hydrogen ions (H+), and the molecule is said to be reduced. In the equation above, CO_2 is reduced when it becomes CH_2O. Oxidation occurs when a molecule gives up (e–) and hydrogen ions, and the molecule is said to be oxidized. In our equation, water is oxidized to form O_2. In a cell, reduction reactions are often coupled with oxidation reactions. Collectively, these coupled reactions are commonly called redox reactions.

Reaction Set I

- Chlorophyll within the thylakoid membranes absorbs solar energy and energizes electrons.
- Water is oxidized, releasing electrons, hydrogen ions (H^+), and oxygen.
- ATP is produced from ADP + P with the help of an electron transport chain.
- $NADP^+$, an enzyme helper, accepts electrons (is reduced) and becomes NADPH.

Reaction Set II

CO_2 is taken up by one of the molecules in the cycle.

- ATP and NADPH from the light reactions reduce CO_2 to a carbohydrate (G3P).

Q 13. Role of visible spectrum in activating chlorophyll pigments is elaborated in the following chart. Study the chart and answer questions as follows.

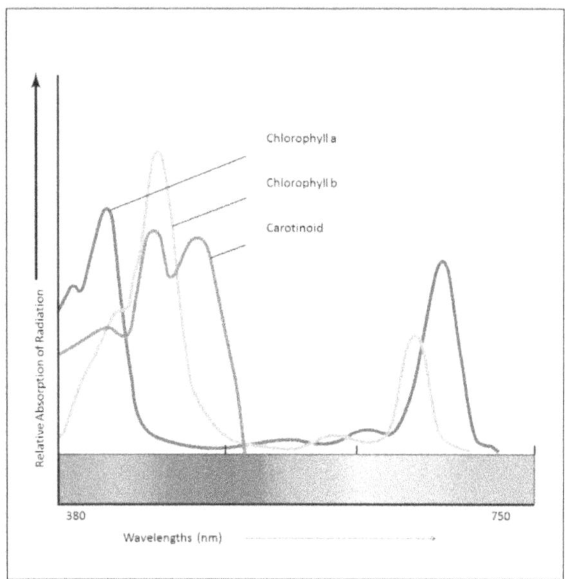

The pigments found within majority of photosynthesizing cells are primarily chlorophylls and carotenoids. These pigments are capable of absorbing definite portions of visible spectrum of white light. Both chlorophyll *a* and chlorophyll *b* absorb violet, blue, and red wavelengths better than those of other radiations of visible spectrum.

Because green light is reflected and only minimally absorbed by chlorophylls, leaves appear green to us. Accessory pigments, such as the carotenoids, appear yellow or orange because they are capable of absorbing light in the violet-blue-green range, but not the yellow-orange range. These pigments and others become noticeable in the fall when chlorophyll breaks down and the other pigments are uncovered.

Leaves of plants growing in hot climate appear green and leaves of plants growing in winter climate appear mostly yellow to brown.
Daylight induces synthesis of Chlorophyll in a plant.

a) What regulates the absorption of visible spectrum of white light by plants?
b) Do all types of plants are capable of absorbing all the wavelengths of visible spectrum?
c) Why leaves of plants growing in tropical climate appear green?
d) Which wavelengths of solar radiation are suitable for autotrophic plants?

Q 14. Two distinct types of arrangement of mesophyll tissues in plants are displayed as follows. Identify them on the basis of explanations of structure and function.

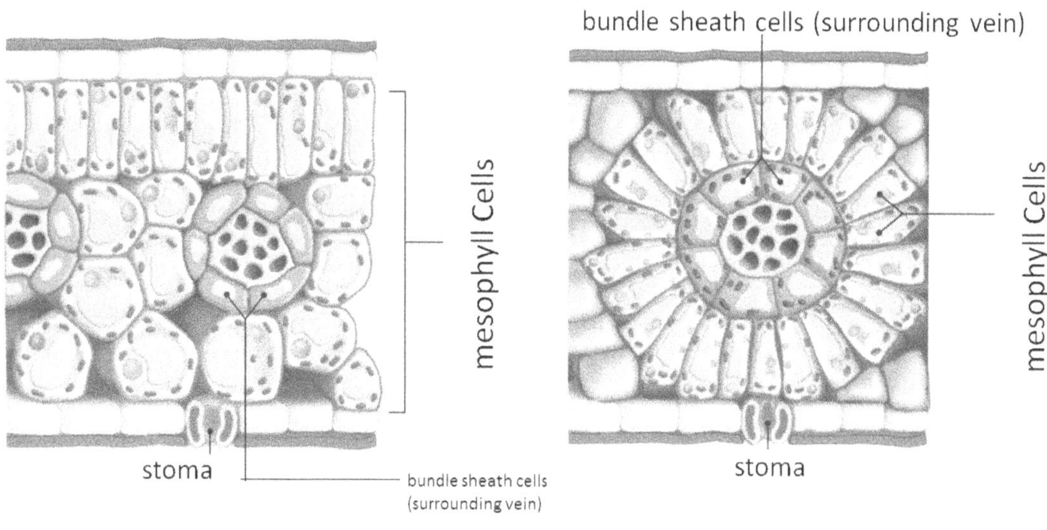

Plant Type A

Plant Type B

I: .... : mesophyll cells are arranged in rings around bundle sheath cells, and both contain chloroplasts. CO_2 fixation occurs within mesophyll cells, and the Calvin cycle occurs in the bundle sheath cells.

II: .... : In leaves of these plants mesophyll cells are arranged in rows and contain chloroplasts. The Calvin cycle, including CO_2 fixation, occurs in mesophyll cells.

III: Some plants have evolved an adaptation that allows them to be successful in hot and dry conditions, like that of xerophytes growing in deserts. These plants carry out .... photosynthesis instead of ...... photosynthesis. In a type .... plant, the first detectable molecule following CO_2 fixation is a molecule composed of four carbon atoms. These plants are able to avoid the uptake of O_2 by rubisco.

Q 15. On the basis of fact sheet of Calvin Cycle answer the questions as follows.

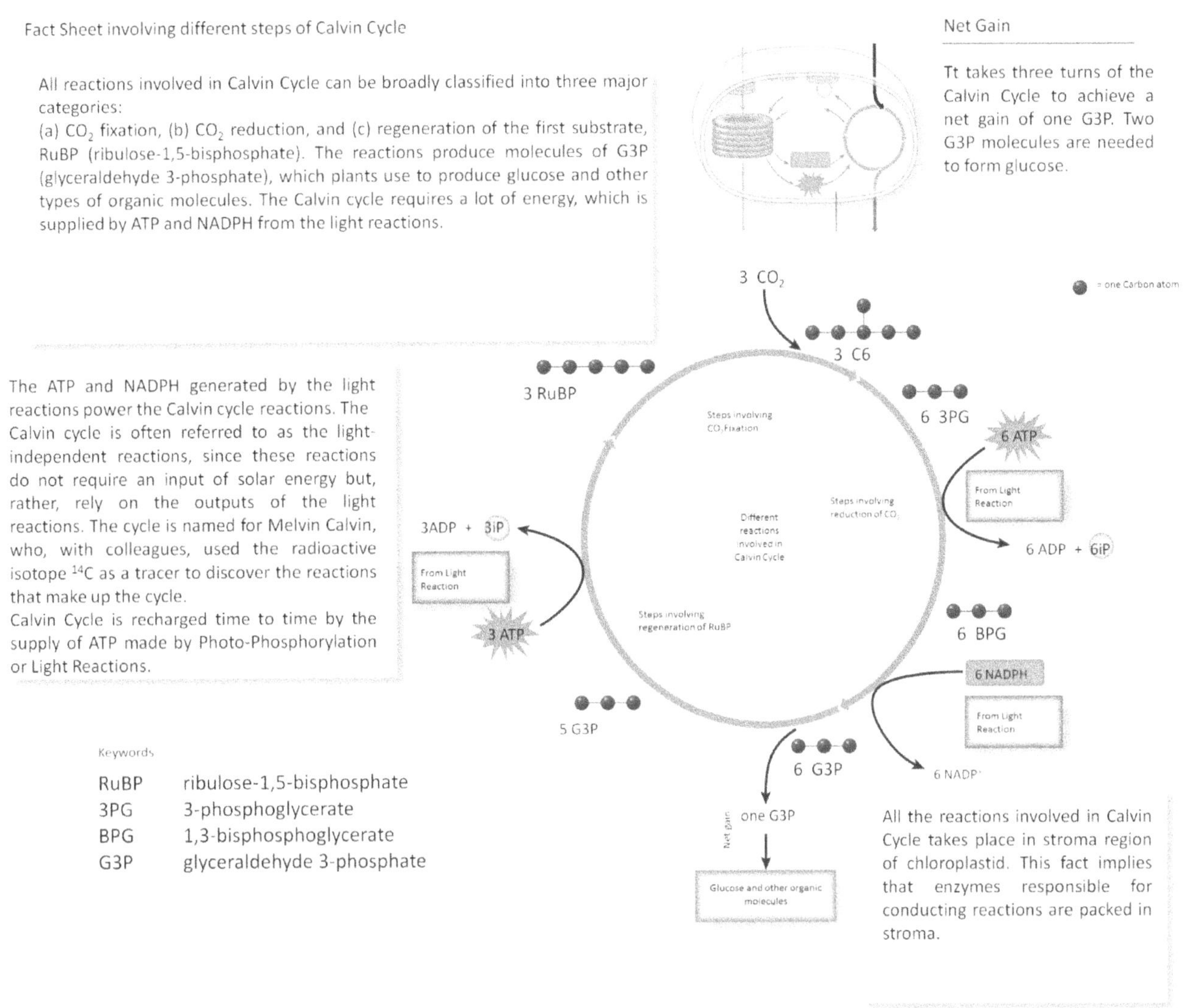

Q a) How many turns of Calvin Cycle required to manufacture 20 molecules of Carbohydrate?

Q b) Is there any functional linkage between Calvin Cycle and Photo-Phosphorylation?

Q c) Which product can be considered as the first product of Calvin Cycle?

Q 16. What is CAM Photosynthesis?

Q 17. Which of the following phase of reactions (biological activity) can be considered as more beneficial in terms of the number of ATP molecules duly manufactured during that step?

A: Glycolysis B: Citric Acid Cycle C: Electron Transport Chain

Q 18. What is fermentation? Why fermentation often occur in muscle bands of human beings? What factors regulate fermentation which often takes place in skeletal muscles of human beings?

Q 19. Elaborate chain reaction which takes place inside Mitochondria during aerobic respiration.

Q 20. Describe the process by which mitochondria takes part in the ATP synthesis mechanism performed by Electron Transport Chain.

Q 21. Different levels of organisations of DNA molecule is displayed in the following diagram. Identify them along with their specific features.

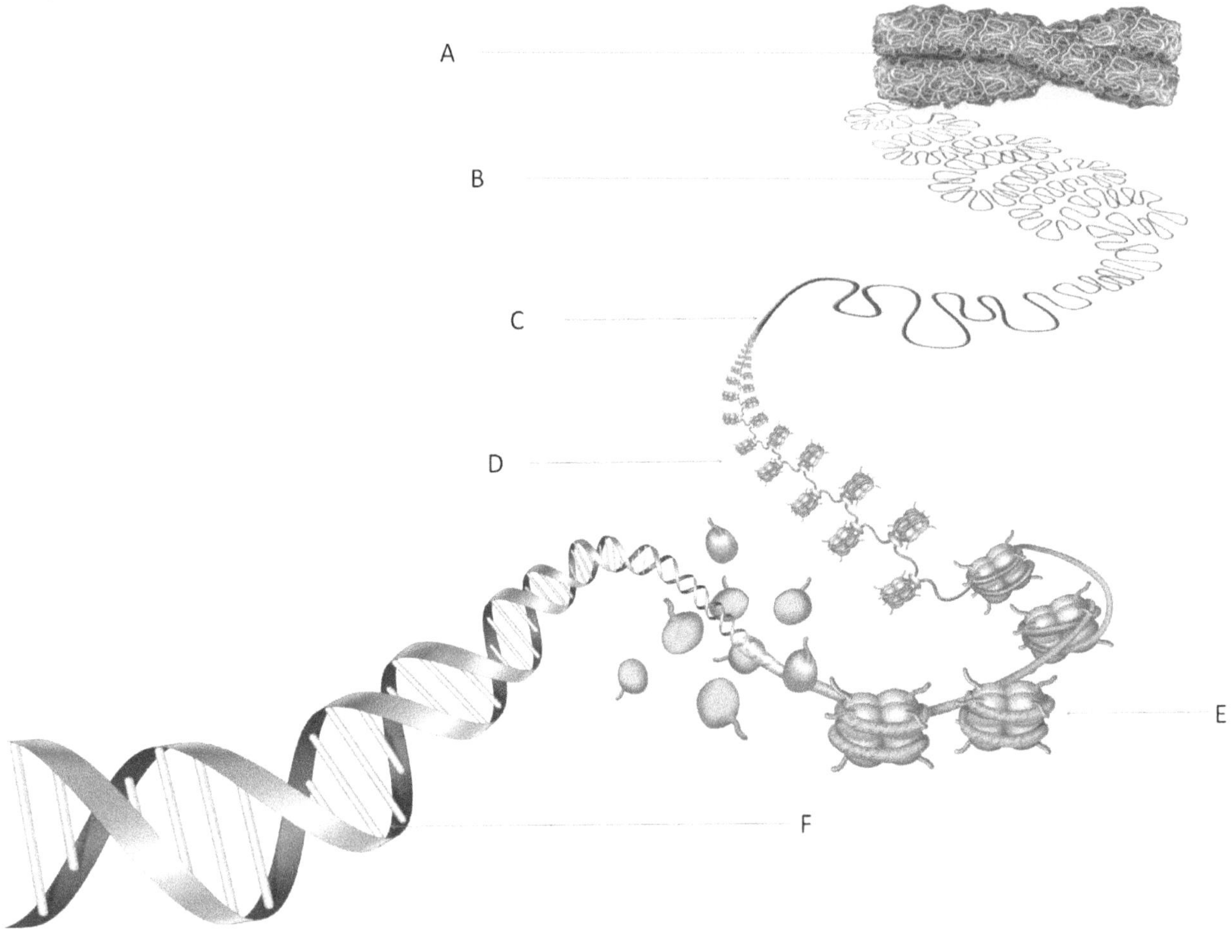

A

B

C

D

E

F

I : .... : Looped Chromatin segment which takes part in the formation of chromatid.
II: ....: Zigzag fashion of the orientation of chromatin involving binding of histone proteins.
III: ....: More compact structure of looped chromatin before getting involved into zigzag fashion of binding;
IV: ....: Double helical twisted coil of DNA molecule made up of complementary base pairing of nitrogen bases.
V: ....: One of the paired segment of a chromosome which accommodates coiled structure of DNA molecule.
VI: ....: Binding of DNA molecule facilitated by histone octamer gives this unit structure (a unit of chromatin)

Q 22. Identify different stages of Karyokinetic Cell Division as displayed in the following diagram.

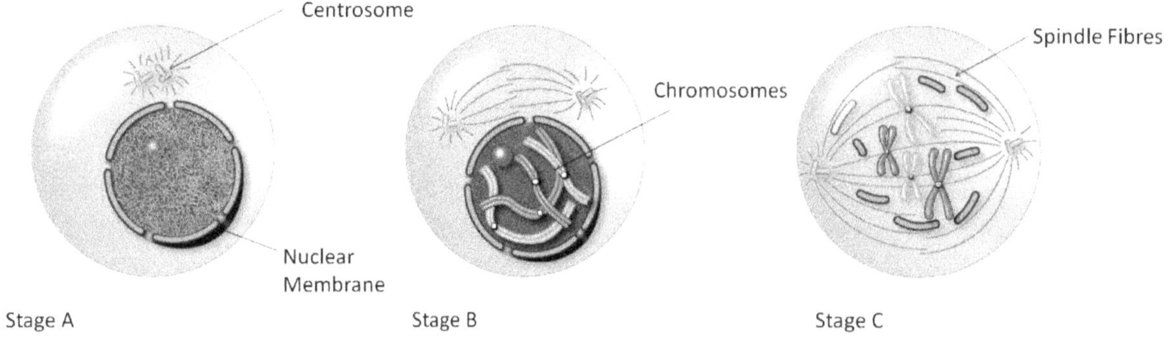

Q 23. Mitosis in plant and animal cells differ by certain points. Work out at least five such differences on the basis of the combined images of cell division in plants and animals is provided.

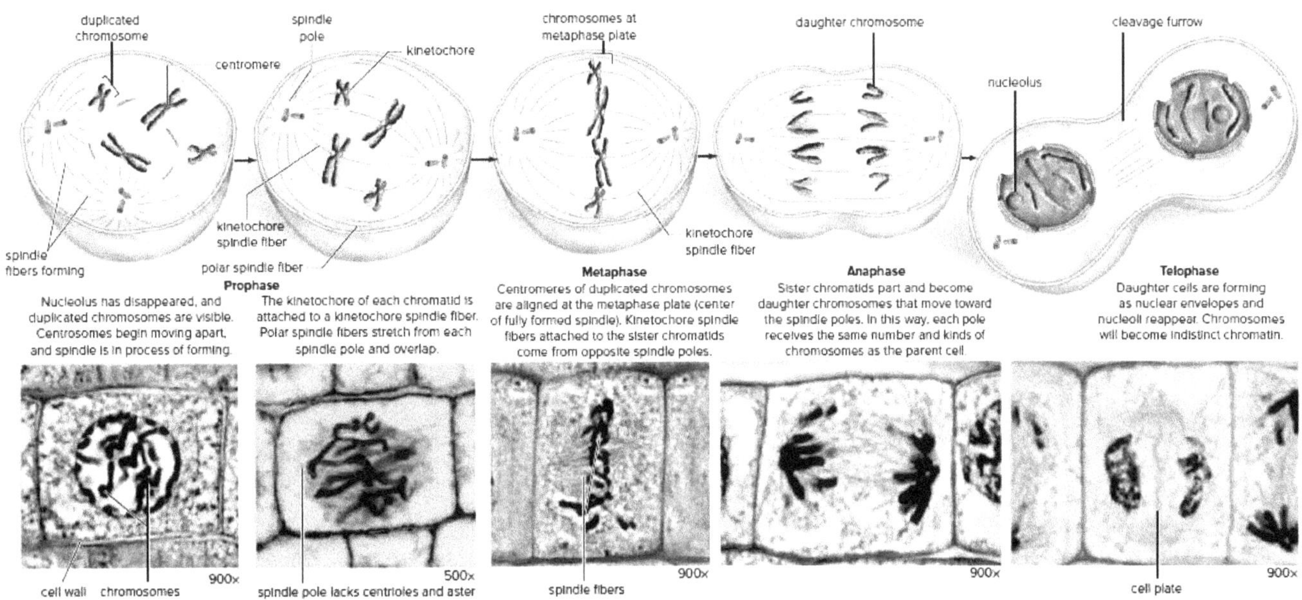

Q 24. Complete the following statement:

The .... is especially significant because, if the cell cycle passes this zone, the cell is committed to divide. If the cell does not pass this ...., it can enter G0, during which it performs its normal functions but does not divide. The proper .... , such as certain .... , must be present for a cell to pass the .... With more perfectness to say, the integrity of the cell's DNA is .... If the DNA is damaged, the protein .... can stop the cycle at this specific point and initiate DNA repair. If .... is not possible, the protein can cause the cell to undergo .... cell death, or ....

Q 25. Is apoptosis the only cause of cell death? Elaborate your answer.

Q 26. Six different stages of un-controlled growth of certain portion of tissue system elaborated through a schematic diagram. Point out these stages of development.

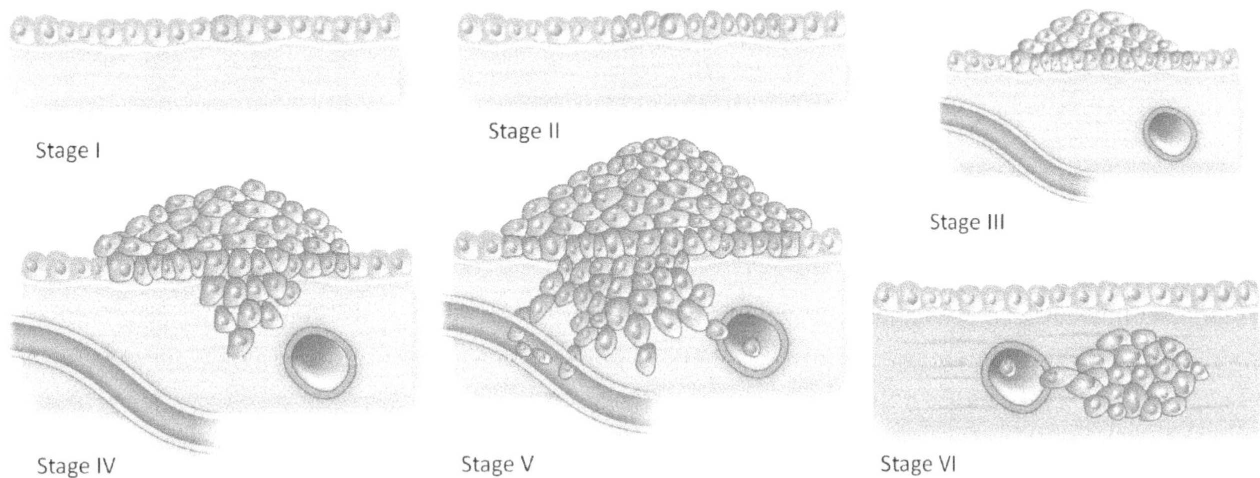

Evaluation 2

1: You picked up two mice (one female and one male) that had escaped from experimental cages in the animal facility. One mouse is yellow in color, and the other is brown agouti. You know that this mouse colony has animals with different alleles at only three coat color genes: the agouti or nonagouti or yellow alleles of the A gene, the black or brown allele of the B gene, and the albino or nonalbino alleles of the C gene. However, you don't know which alleles of these genes are actually present in each of the animals that you've captured. To determine the genotypes, you breed them together. The first litter has only three pups. One is albino, one is brown (nonagouti), and the third is black agouti. a. What alleles of the A, B, and C genes are present in the two mice you caught? b. After raising several litters from these two parents, you have many offspring. How many different coat color phenotypes (in total) do you expect to see expressed in the population of offspring? What are the phenotypes and corresponding genotypes?

2. A married man and woman, both of whom are deaf, carry some recessive mutant alleles in three different "hearing genes": d1 is recessive to D1, d2 is recessive to D2, and d3 is recessive to D3. Homozygosity for a mutant allele at any one of these three genes causes deafness. In addition, homozygosity for any two of the three genes together in the same genome will cause prenatal lethality (and spontaneous abortion) with a penetrance of 25%. Furthermore, homozygosity for the mutant alleles of all three genes will cause prenatal lethality with a penetrance of 75%. If the genotypes of the mother and father are as indicated here, what is the likelihood that a live-born child will be deaf?

Mother: D1 d1, D2 d2, d3 d3

Father: d1 d1, D2 d2, D3 d3

3. In humans, chromosome 16 sometimes has a heavily stained area in the long arm near the centromere. This feature can be seen through the microscope but has no effect on the phenotype of the person carrying it. When such a "blob" exists on a particular copy of chromosome 16, it is a constant feature of that chromosome and is inherited. A couple conceived a child, but the fetus had multiple abnormalities and was miscarried. When the chromosomes of the fetus were studied, it was discovered that it was trisomic for chromosome 16, and that two of the three chromosome 16s had large blobs. Both chromosome 16 homologs in the mother lacked blobs, but the father was heterozygous for blobs. Which parent experienced nondisjunction, and in which meiotic division did it occur?

Answer

This problem requires an understanding of nondisjunction during meiosis. When individual chromosomes contain some distinguishing feature that allows one homolog to be distinguished from another, it is possible to follow the path of the two homologs through meiosis. In this case, because the fetus had two chromosome 16s with the blob, we can conclude that the extra chromosome came from the father (the only parent with a blobbed chromosome). In which meiotic division did the nondisjunction occur? When nondisjunction occurs during meiosis I, homologs fail to segregate to opposite poles. If this occurred in the father, the chromosome with the blob and the normal chromosome 16 would segregate into the same cell (a secondary spermatocyte). After meiosis II, the gametes resulting from this cell would carry both types of chromosomes. If such sperm fertilized a normal egg, the zygote would have two copies of the normal chromosome 16 and one of the chromosome with a blob. On the other hand, if nondisjunction occurred during meiosis II in the father in a secondary spermatocyte containing the blobbed chromosome 16, sperm with two copies of the blob-marked chromosome would be produced. After fertilization with a normal egg, the result would be a zygote of the type seen in this spontaneous abortion. Therefore, the nondisjunction occurred in meiosis II in the father.

4. II. (a) What sex ratio would you expect among the offspring of a cross between a normal male mouse and a female mouse heterozygous for a recessive X-linked lethal gene? (b) What would be the expected sex ratio among the offspring of a cross between a normal hen and a rooster heterozygous for a recessive Z-linked lethal allele?

Answer: This problem deals with sex-linked inheritance and sex determination. a. Mice have a sex determination system of XX 5 female and XY 5 male. A normal male mouse (X R Y) 3 a heterozygous female mouse (X R X r) would result in X R X R , X R X r , X R Y, and X r Y mice. The X r Y mice would die, so there would be a 2:1 ratio of females to males.

b. The sex determination system in birds is ZZ 5 male and ZW 5 female. A normal hen (Z R W) 3 a heterozygous rooster (Z R Z r) would result in Z R Z R , Z R Z r , Z R W, and Z r W chickens. Because the Z r W offspring do not live, the ratio of females to males would be 1:2.

5. A woman with normal color vision whose father was color-blind mates with a man with normal color vision. a. What do you expect to see among their offspring? b. What would you expect if it was the normal man's father who was color-blind?

Answer: This problem involves sex-linked inheritance. a. The woman's father has a genotype of X cb Y. Because the woman had to inherit an X from her father, she must have an X cb chromosome, but because she has normal color vision, her other X chromosome must be X CB . The man she mates with has normal color vision and therefore has an X CB Y genotype. Their children could with equal probability be X CB X CB (normal female), X CB X cb (carrier female), X CB Y (normal male), or X cb Y (color-blind male). b. If the man with normal color vision had a colorblind father, the X cb chromosome would not have been passed on to him, because a male does not inherit an X chromosome from his father. The man has the genotype X CB Y and cannot pass on the color-blind allele.

<u>Solution : Worksheet 1</u>

Ans 1: tri-carboxylic acid cycle; mitochondrion; inorganic phosphate (Pi); energy currency; cytoplasm ; nicotinamide adenine dinucleotide (NAD+);

Ans 2: three; two ; Ans 3: 38 ATP ; 34; 100 percent ; 29 to 30 ; Ans 4: internal; Homeostasis;

5: metabolism; autotrophic metabolism; 6: insulin; receptors; insulin; insulin; 7: Statement IV;

8: Statement I is not correct. ;

Correct statement: The cycle for a myosin II head that is part of a thick filament accommodated in cells of muscle bands, but other myosins that attach to other cargo (e.g., the membrane of a vesicle) are thought to operate according to the same cyclical mechanism. In the absence of bound nucleotide, a myosin head binds actin tightly in a "rigor" state.

9: hydrolytic; phospholipid; selective traffic ; lamins; lamins; filaments; lamins; polypeptide ; lamina;

10: polar; channels; eukaryotic; Translation; synthesis; cytoplasm; aqueous; selectively transported ; regulated channels ; selectively imported ; exported;

11: electron microscopy ; nuclear export signals; cytoplasm; cytoplasm; nuclear export signals ; ribosomal subunits ; transported; nucleus appears; nuclear export remain ;

12: rough ER → Golgi → secretory vesicles → cell exterior; proteins; Plasma membrane and lysosomal proteins; eukaryotic cells; ER, Golgi apparatus, lysosomes, or plasma membrane; membrane-bound ribosomes; nucleus, mitochondria, chloroplasts, peroxisomes etc.; free ribosomes ; cytosol ;

13: A = inserted into the ER membrane ; B = ER→ Golgi→ plasma membrane or lysosomes; C = hydrophobic; D= 20 to 25 hydrophobic amino; E = hydrogen bonding; F =peptide bonds ; G =fatty acid tails; H = amino; I = carboxy terminus; J = ER, Golgi, lysosomal, and plasma membranes;

14: A = correct three-dimensional conformations; B = multisubunit proteins; C =translocation across the ER membrane; D = proteolytic cleavage ; E = translocated across the ER membrane; F = stages of glycosylation; G =glycolipid anchors;

15: oligosaccharide;

Solution: Worksheet 2

Ans : 1: Statement II is not correct. 2: Blood, plasma, blood cells; 3: A = protein; B = cholesterol; C= a lipid molecule; D = lipid bilayer;

4: bone marrow ; erythropoietin; erythropoiesis; Hypoxia (deficient oxygen supply to body cells); haemorrhage; excessive erythrocyte breakdown (haemolysis) ; Hypoxia; erythropoietin; proerythroblasts; reticulocyte; oxygen-carrying capacity , reverse tissue hypoxia; erythropoietin; hypoxia; anaemia (the inability of the blood to carry adequate oxygen for body needs)

5: A = Ribosome; B = Chloroplastid; C = Mitochondria; D = Golgi body; 6: Statement 6 requires modification;

7: Both the statements are true and support each other;

8: heme; porphyrin ring ; oxygen-binding components ; conformational; additional oxygen; sigmoidal oxygen-binding curve ; peripheral tissues; oxygen concentrations ;

9: Option A and B are correct; 10: secretory and membrane; membrane lipids; hydrophobic; cytosol; Smooth; site of synthesis; vesicles;

11: Statement VII requires modification. The corrected statement: The glycerol phospholipids, cholesterol, and ceramide are synthesized in the Endoplasmic Reticulum. Sphingomyelin and glycol-lipids are then synthesized specifically from ceramide present in the Golgi apparatus.

12: 1 = Q; 2 = R; 3 = S; 4 = P; 13: A = ; hydrogen bond between Guanine and Thymine; B = associations between larger purine and smaller pyrimidines;

14: RNA molecules ; ribozymes; ribozyme structure ; ribozymes; internal RNA; ligated; functional mRNA; bacteria and archaea ; self-splicing; catalytic activity ;

15: P = cisterna [plural = cisternae]; Q = dictyosome; R = Golgi complex;

16: Zymogen of exocrine pancreatic cells; Mucus (=a glycoprotein) secretion by goblet cells of the intestine ; Lactoprotein (casein) secretion by mammary gland cells (Merocrine secretion) ; Secretion of compounds (thyroglobulins) of thyroxine hormone by thyroid cells; tropocollagen and collagen ; melanin granules and other pigments; and yolk and vitelline membrane of growing primary oocytes.

17: It is also involved in the formation of certain cellular organelles such as parts of plasma membrane, lysosomes, acrosome of spermatozoa and cortical granules of a variety of oocytes; the transport of lipid molecules around the cell; production of proteoglycans (molecules that are present in the extracellular matrix of the animal cells); synthesis of carbohydrates; synthesis of glycosaminoglycans; formation of proteoglycans.

18: mainly involved in the secretion of materials to be incorporated in the primary and secondary cell walls (e.g., formation and export of glycoproteins, lipids, pectins and monomers for hemicellulose, cellulose, lignin, etc.)

19: To perform this function, the Golgi vesicles contain different sets of enzymes in different types of vesicles (cis, middle and trans cisternae) that react with molecules and modify normal chain of proteins passing through the Golgi lumen to manufacture secondary and tertiary structures or membrane proteins and glycoproteins that are transiently incorporated in the Golgi membranes as they are en route to their final destinations.

<u>Solution: Worksheet 3....</u>

Ans 1: Messenger RNA (mRNA) ; . Transfer RNA (tRNA) ; Ribosomal RNA (rRNA)

Ans 3: P stands for dominant and Q stands for recessive; Ans 4:

Solution Worksheet 4...

Ans 1: Statement VIII requires modification;

Ans 2: Autosomal recessive type and autosomal dominant type;

Solution Worksheet 5 ...

Ans 4: Many gene products are essential to an organism's survival. Mutations resulting in the synthesis of a gene product that is non-functional can often be tolerated in the heterozygous state; one wild-type allele may be sufficient to produce enough of the essential product to allow organism to survive. Such type of mutation behaves as a <u>recessive lethal allele</u>, and homozygous recessive individuals in this case will not survive.

Ans 7. Diverse microbial populations were widespread on Earth for billions of years before plants and animals appeared. Microbes are abundant in the biosphere and their activities greatly affect the chemical and physical properties of their habitats. It is also evident from studies of evolutionary records that during primitive stage of organic evolution Bacteria were widely distributed in the entire globe and were constituted the majority of population. In modern times Bacteria, Archaea, and Eukarya are the major phylogenetic lineages (domains) of cells.

Ans 8. An inherent limitation of bright-field microscopy is the lack of contrast between cells and their surroundings. This problem can be overcome by the use of stains or by using alternative forms of light microscopy, such as phase contrast or dark field.

Ans 9. *Carl Woese* discovered that ribosomal RNA (rRNA) sequences can be used to determine the evolutionary history of microorganisms, and he also diagrammed the tree of life and discovered the domain Archaea. Analysis of rRNA sequences from the environment reveals that microbial diversity is exceptional and that the majority of microorganisms have not yet been cultivated. It was also proved experimentally that the template responsible for incorporating amino acids in a polypeptide chain are transcribed primarily from a definite segment of DNA present in the genome of the organism.

Ans 10: Suitable keywords:

a: Aseptic technique ; b: Cell wall ; c: Chemolithotrophy; d: Colony; e: Culture; f: Cytoplasm; g: Cytoplasmic; h: Differentiation; i: Domain; j: DNA replication ; k: Enzyme ; l: Eukaryotic ; m: Evolution; n: Extremophiles;

Ans 11: A stands for Peptidoglycan;

<u>Solution to Worksheet 6</u>

Ans 1: All features display Illustrated correlation between the Mendelian postulates of (I) unit factors in pairs, (II) segregation, and (III) independent assortment, showing the presence of genes located on homologous chromosomes and their behavior during meiosis.

Ans 2: a) Genome; b) Gram-negative ; c) Gram-positive ; d) Gram stain ; e) Growth; f) Gut microbiome ; g) Horizontal gene;

Ans 3:

<u>Solution to Worksheet 7</u>

Ans 1: P = lipoteichoic acid; S = Plasma membrane; Q = wall associated protein ; R = peptidoglycan;

Ans 2: Statement k requires modification;

Ans 3: A = Bacteria; B = Archaea; C = Eukarya; D = Bacteria; E =Archaea; F =Protists; G =Plants; H =Fungi Animals;

Explanations: Organisms grouped on the same branch of the tree have a common ancestor located at the base of the branch. Organisms grouped on the same branch (e.g., fungi and animals) are more closely related to one another by different means (i.e., have a more recent common ancestor) than organisms on different branches (e.g., animals and plants). The base of the tree itself represents the presence of common ancestor of all living organisms. It also indicates that all the organisms of present day world had originated and gradually evolved from a common ancestral stock.

Ans 5. <u>Cholesterol</u> is a component of an animal cell's plasma membrane, and it also works as the precursor of other steroids, such as the sex hormones testosterone and estrogen. The male sex hormone (testosterone), is formed primarily in the testes, and the female sex hormone (estrogen) in ovaries. Testosterone and estrogen differ only in the functional groups attached to the same chain of carbon skeleton, yet they have a profound effect on the bodies and the sexuality of higher animals like humans.

Anabolic steroids (Example: synthetic testosterone) can be used to increase muscle mass in an organism. The presence of the steroid in the body upsets the normal hormonal balance of living body: The testes atrophy (shrink and weaken), and males may develop breasts; females tend to grow facial hair and start losing hair on their head. Use of this chemical gives athletes an unfair advantage and destroys their health (impact on organs like heart, kidney, liver, and psychological disorders are common).

Ans 6: Lipids ; glycerol; fatty acids ; triglycerides; Trans fats ; fatty acid ;

Ans 7: No modifications needed;

Solution to Worksheet 8

Ans 1: A = Carbohydrate Chain ; B = External layer of membrane showing phospholipid heads ; C = Phospholipid tails (hydrophobic part facing each other to form lipid bilayer ; D = Cholesterols ; E = Embedded Proteins ;

Ans 2: A = Nucleolus; B = Nuclear membrane; C: Chromatin fibre; D= Nucleoplasm; E = Endoplasmic Reticulum (Rough); F = Lumen of Rough E.R. Cisterne;

Solution to Worksheet 8

Ans 1: The gram-negative bacterial cell wall

Ans 2: ! = A = adhesion; II = B = tight; III = C =gap;

Ans 3: Plasmodesmata;

In a plant, adjoining living cells are connected to each other by plasmodesmata (singular: plasmodesma ; numerous narrow, membrane-lined channels that pass through the cell wall.). Cytoplasmic strands within these channels allow the direct exchange of some materials between adjacent plant cells and eventually among all the cells of a plant having series of such kind of linkages. Having some sort of limitations, the plasmodesmata allow only water and other small molecules to pass freely from cell to cell.

Solution to Assignment

Ans 5: In facilitated diffusion, as displayed in the given diagram, a carrier protein in the plasma membrane allows molecules to move from areas of high concentration to areas of low concentration.

Ans 6: P = Isotonic; Q = Hypotonic; R = Hypertonic;

There is no change in isotonic solution; Cell swells up in hypotonic solution; it shrinks in hypertonic solution;

Ans 7: energy (ATP) ; transport protein; sodium-potassium;

Ans 8: Mitochondrial Crest region.

Ans 9: Non-polar molecules and gaseous molecules through simple diffusion;

Ans 10: In facilitated diffusion, molecules diffuse across a plasma membrane through a channel protein (aquaporins are channel proteins for water) or with the assistance of carrier proteins. Both aquaporeins and channel proteins allow movement of water molecules.

Ans 11: a) Inner membrane of thylakoid; b) Stroma; c) Chlorophyll;

Ans 12: Reaction Set I stands for Photo-Phosphorylation; Reaction Set II = Calvin Cycle;

Ans 16: CAM photosynthesis stands for crassulacean-acid metabolism. It gets its name from the Crassulaceae, a family of flowering succulent (water-containing) plants that live in warm, arid regions. Although discovered for the first time in these plants, now it is known to be prevalent among most succulent plants that grow in desert environments, including cacti.

Unlike C4 Plants these plants use partitioning in time to perform photosynthesis. During the night, CAM plants use C3 molecules to fix CO_2, forming C_4 molecules. These molecules are stored in large vacuoles present in mesophyll cells. During the day time, the C_4 molecules release CO_2 to accelerate the Calvin cycle when NADPH and ATP are made available, which were previously synthesized from the light reactions.

Ans 17: A: Glycolysis (2 ATP)   B: Citric Acid Cycle (2 ATP)   C: Electron Transport Chain (34 ATP)

Electron Transport Chain is more efficient in this regard.

Ans 18: About Fermentation

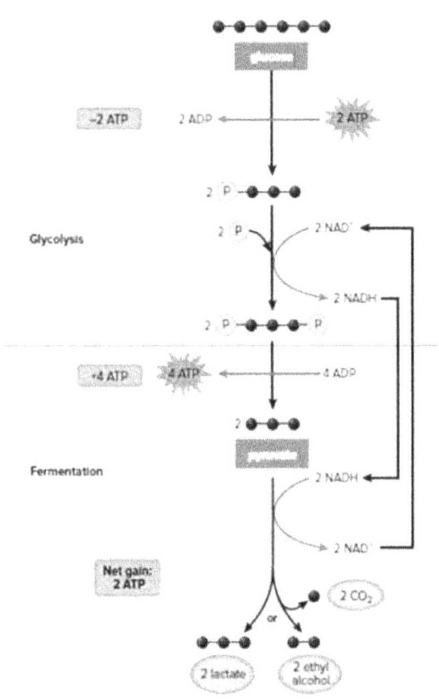

Steps involving Fermentation:
In animals and some bacteria, the pyruvate formed by glycolysis accepts two hydrogen atoms and is reduced to lactate. In the water environment of the cell, this forms lactic acid. Two NADH pass hydrogen atoms to pyruvate, reducing it. Why is it beneficial for pyruvate to be reduced to lactate when oxygen is not available? The answer is that this reaction regenerates NAD+, which can then pick up more electrons during the earlier reactions of glycolysis. This regeneration of NAD+ keeps glycolysis going, during which ATP is produced by substrate-level ATP synthesis.
As was the case with lactic acid fermentation, the electrons needed to reduce the pyruvate are supplied by NADH molecules. In the process, NAD+ molecules are regenerated for use in glycolysis. However, unlike lactic acid fermentation, alcohol fermentation releases small amounts of CO_2.
Yeasts (a type of fungi) are good examples of microorganisms that generate ethyl alcohol and CO_2 when they carry out fermentation. When yeasts are used to leaven bread, the CO_2 makes the bread rise. When yeasts are used to ferment grapes for wine production or to ferment wort—derived from barley—for beer production, ethyl alcohol is the desired product. However, the yeasts are killed by the very product they produce.

Ans 19: TCA Cycle [an Overview]

The citric acid cycle, more popularly called Tri-Carboxylic Acid Cycle, is a cyclical metabolic pathway located in the matrix of mitochondria. [often called the Krebs cycle to honour the scientist who first studied it. At the start of the citric acid cycle, the 2-carbon acetyl group carried by CoA (CoA is released after the successive step and is used again in the preparatory reaction) joins with a 4-carbon molecule, producing a 6-carbon citrate molecule. During the biochemical cycle, which takes place in the mitochondria, the acetyl group is oxidized in the process forming CO_2. Both NAD+ and FAD accept electrons and hydrogen ions, resulting in formation of NADH and FADH2 respectively. Substrate-level ATP synthesis occurs during this process and an ATP results. 2 molecules of ATP will be obtained by consuming 1 molecule of glucose.

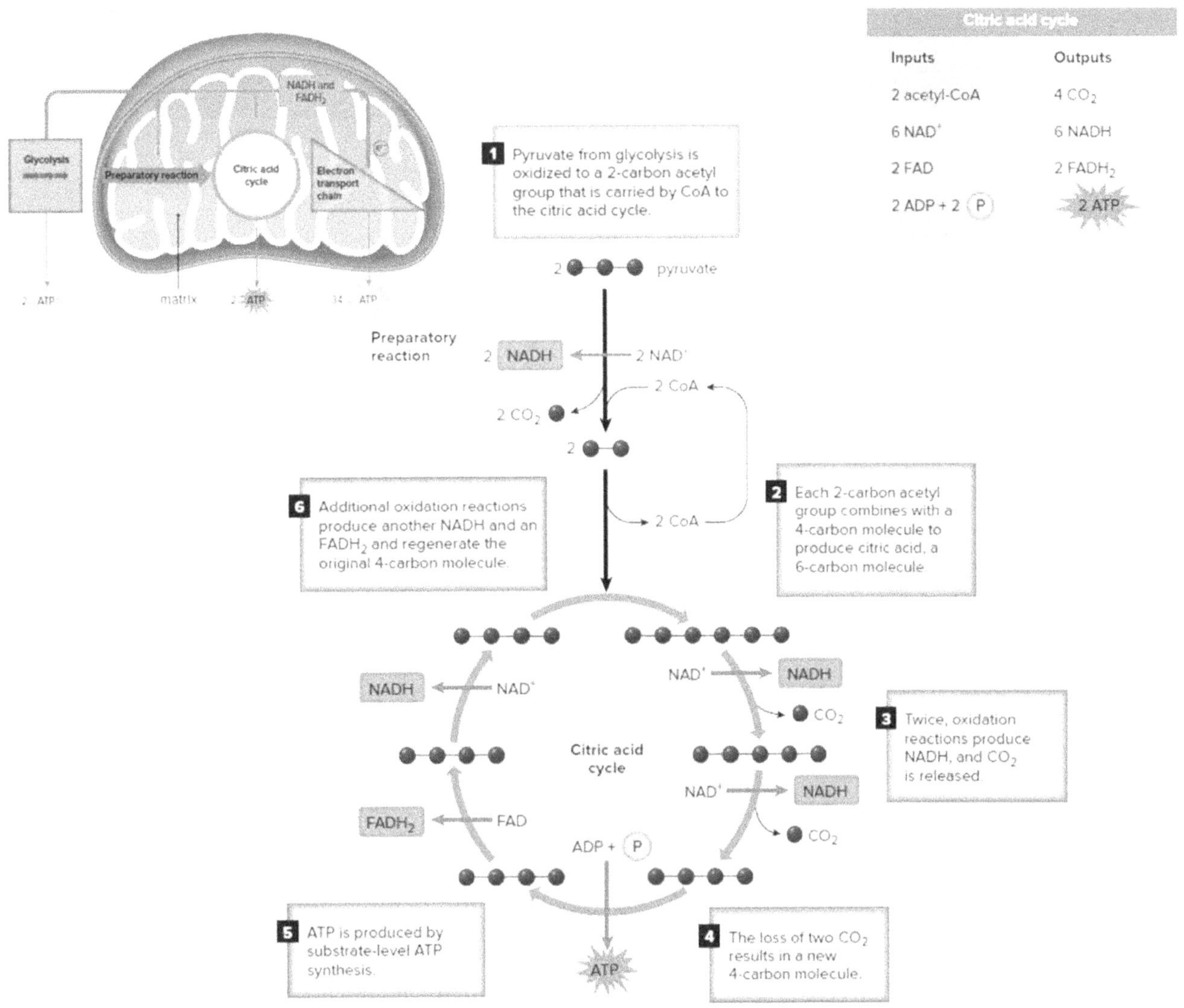

Ans 20. Molecular complexes that contain the electron transport carriers are located in the cristae region of the inner membrane of mitochondria, as are ATP synthase complexes (an enzyme complex responsible for synthesis of ATP during Electron Transport Mechanism). As electrons move from one carrier to the other (floating carrier proteins embedded differently in the lipid bilayer of inter membrane), hydrogen ions (H+) are pumped from the mitochondrial matrix into the inter-membrane space located in between two mitochondrial membrane. As hydrogen ions flow back down a concentration gradient through an ATP synthase complex (in some instances it is also called F_0F_1 Complex or Oxysome), ATP is synthesized by the enzyme ATP synthase. The H^+ gradient contains a large amount of stored energy that is basically used to drive forward ATP synthesis.

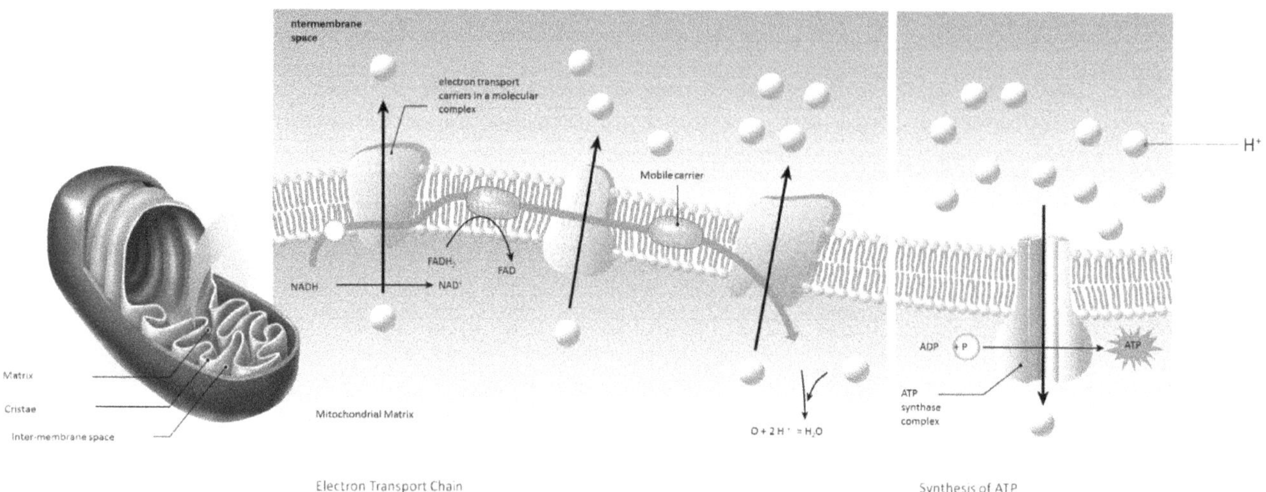

Electron Transport Chain

Synthesis of ATP

Ans 21: I = B; II = D; III= C; IV = F; V = A; VI = E = Nucleosome ;

Ans 22: A = Interphase; B = Prophase; C = Pro-Metaphase;

Ans 24: G1 checkpoint; checkpoint; growth signals; growth factors; G1 checkpoint; checked; p53; repair; programmed; apoptosis;

Ans 25 : Apoptosis, a unique biochemical process, allows an organism to control cell death. It is an important aspect of phases of embryological development. The opposite to stages of apoptosis is necrosis, or unprogrammed cell death (death of cells due to disease or injury; Example, during a heart attack, the cells of the heart are deprived of oxygen and nutrients; leading finally towards getting collapsed.) During shortage of nutrients and oxygen cells burst and die, causing inflammation of the surrounding tissues, which can cause the death of nearby cells; a phenomenon similar to autolysis facilitated by hydrolytic enzymes possessed by lysosomes. On the other hand, apoptosis does not cause inflammation and does not spread to surrounding cells.

Ans 26.
Stage I : A particular cell acquires a mutation for repeated cell division.
Stage II: New mutant cell arises and one cell found capable of starting tumor.
Stage III: Cells gained ability to develop tumor.
Stage IV: Cells have gained the ability to invade underlying tissues by producing a proteinase enzyme.
Stage V: Cancer cells are capable enough to invade underlying tissues and blood vessels.
Stage VI: Metastatic tumors are found at certain distance from the original tumor.

Evaluation 3

MULTIPLE CHOICE QUESTIONS

1. Holoenzyme is made of

a. Apoenzyme and Zymogen b. Apoenzyme and Co-enzyme

c. Co-enzyme and Prosthetic group d. Prosthetic group and Co-factor

2. Which of the following organelle is called ‘Suicidal Bag’

a. Mitochondria b. Endoplasmic reticulum

c. Lysosome d. Ribosome

3. Most abundant blood cells in the human body are

a. WBCs b. RBCs

c. Platelets d. Plasma Cells

4. Number of iron atoms in one haemoglobin molecule are

a. 1 b. 3

c. 4 d. 8

5. Which of the following is not a co-enzymea. NAD b. NADP

c. FAD d. Mn++

6. Activity of allosteric enzymes are influenced by

a. Allosteric modulators b. Allosteric site

c. Catalytic site d. None of the above

7. In competitive inhibition, inhibitors bears a close structural similarity with the

a. Co-enzyme b. Co-factor

c. Prosthetic group d. Substrate

8. Enzyme acts best at a particular temperature called

a. Catalytic Temperature b. At normal Body temperature

c. Optimum temperature d. None of the above

9. Lock and Key model is also known as

a. Template model b. Induced fit model

c. Khosland's Model d. Enzyme-substrate interaction

model

10. Which bond is not associated with Enzyme-substrate interaction -

a. Hydrogen bonds b. Ionic bonds

c. Di-sulfide bonds d. Van deer Waal's force of attraction

11. Which of the following statement is incorrect

a. Enzymes are protein in nature b. Enzymes are colloidal in nature

c. Enzymes are thermolabile d. Enzymes are inorganic catalyst

12. Apoenzymes dissociates from co-enzymes due to

a. Change in pH b. Change in temperature

c. Change in substrate concentration d. Change in inhibitor concentration

13. Which of the following enzyme inhibitions shows decreased Km Value ?

a. Competitive inhibition b. Un-competitive inhibition

c. Non-competitive inhibition d. Feed back inhibition

14. Amount of total blood volume in an individual is approximatelya. 50 ml/Kg body weight b. 60 ml/Kg body weight

c. 90 ml/Kg body weight d. 80 ml/Kg body weight

15. Normal blood pH is

a. 7.3 b. 7.2

c. 7.4 d. 8.4

16. Haematocrit value is the ratio of

a. WBC to plasma b. Platelets to plasma

c. RBCs to plasma d. Total blood cells to plasma

17. Plasma represents _______ percent of total blood volume

a. 35 b. 45

c. 55 d. 5

18. Normal amount of plasma protein ranges from

a. 2.2-4.3 gm% b. 4.4-6.3 gm%

c. 6.4-8.3 gm% d. 8.4-10.2 gm%

19. Which component of protein contribute to maximum percentage to total plasma protein

a. Albumin b. Globulin

c. Fibrinogen d. Prothrombin

20. Serum does not contain

a. Calcium b. Prothrombin

c. Factor VIII d. Factor-X

21. Combination of heam with O2 is called

a. Oxyhaemoglobin b. Oxidation

c. Oxygenation d. Oxidized haem

22. Adult haemoglobin contains _______polypeptide chains

a. 2α,2γ b. 2α,2β

c. 2α,2δ d. 2β,2γ

23. Each haemoglobin molecules carries___________ number of O2 molecules

a. 2 b. 4

c. 1 d. 8

24. Each gram% of haemoglobin, when fully saturated, can carry___________ ml of O2

a. 1.34 ml b. 3.14 ml

c. 4.13 ml d. 5ml

25. In Sickle cell anaemia, the defect lies in which polypeptide

a. Alpha chain b. Beta chain

c. Gamma chain d. Delta chain

26. Average mean corpuscular diameter is __________ µm

a. 5.1 b.6.3

c. 7.3 d. 8.5

27. Increase in RBC count beyond 10 million per cu mm is known as

a. Anisocytosis b. Poikilocytosis

c. Polycythemia d. Leucocytosis

28. During erythropoiesis haemoglobin first appears in

a. Early normoblast b. Intermediate normoblast

c. Late normoblast d. Pronormoblast

29. During hypoxia Kidney releases

a. Renin b. Renal Erythopoietic factor

c. Erythropoietin d. None of the above

30. Intrinsic factor is secreted by

a. Liver b. Chief cells of stomach

c. Parietal cells of stomach d. Beta cells of pancreas

31. Which of the following extrinsic factor is required for maturation of RBCs

a. Vit B12 b. Folic acid

c. Iron d. Both (a) and (b)

32. Largest WBCs in peripheral blood is

a. Neutrophil b. Large lymphocyte

c. Monocyte d. Eosinophil

33. The process by which WBCs squeeze through pores in capillary wall is

a. Chemotaxis b. Pinocytosis

c. Opsonization d. Diapedesis

34. Smallest blood cell is

a. Small lymphocyte b. Platelet

c. RBC d. Neutrophil

35. Commonest anaemia in India is

a. Pernicious anaemia b. Sickle cell anaemia

c. Iron deficiency anaemia d. None of the above

36. The term ER was coined by

a. Camillo Golgi b. Porter

c. Robert Brown d. Benda

37. Which of the following organelle has a continuous connection with nuclear membrane

a. Golgi apparatus b. Lysosome

c. RER d. SER

38. In RER, ribosomes are located on

a. the cytoplasmic side b. on the luminal side

c. both (a) and (b) d. all throughout

39. Which of the following statements were true regarding ER

a. ER provides structural framework to the cell

b. ER acts as intra cellular transporting system

c. SER is involved in the synthesis of lipid

d. All of the above

40. Which of the following statements are correct regarding Golgi apparatus

a. sorting and packaging b. exocytosis of melanin granules

c. exocytosis of thyroxine hormone d. all of the above

41. The term Golgi apparatus was coined by

a. Camillo Golgi b. Robert Brown

c. Robert Hook d. Benda

42. F0-F1 Particles are located on

a. Thylakoids b. inner mitochondrial membrane

c. Golgian vacuoles d. None of the above

43. In mitochondria cristae act as sites for

a. protein synthesis

b. phosphorylation of flavoproteins

c. breakdown of macromolecules

d. Oxidation–reduction reaction

44. Mitochondrial inner membrane is rich in which phospholipid

a. Phosphatidyl inositol b. Phosphatidyl serine

c. Cardiolipin d. Phosphatidyl choline

45. Which of the following is NOT a function of mitochondrion

a. electron transport and associated ATP production

b. Fatty acid breakdown

c. non-shivering thermogenesis

d. glycolysis and associated ATP production

46. Who coined the term mitochondria

a. Kolliker b. Benda

c. Fleenming d. Robert Brown

47. Nucleus was first discovered by

a. Robert Hook b. Strasburger

c. Robert Brown d. None of the above

48. Nuclear membrane is in continuous connection with

a. SER b. RER

c. Golgi apparatus d. Lysosomes

49. The number of nuclear pores depends on

a. Size of cells b. Transcriptional activity of the cell

c. DNA content of the cell d. all of the above

50. The DNA Protein ratio in chromatin is

a. 3:1 b. 2:1

c. 1:1 d. 4:1

51. The function of nucleolus is

a. RNA synthesis b. DNA synthesis

c. Histone synthesis d. Ribosomal subunit synthesis

52. The basic protein of the nucleus are

a. nucleohistones b. nuceoprotamines

c. both (a) and (b) d. none of these

53. Lysosomes are present in all except

a. muscle cells b. acinar cells

c. erythrocytes d. hepatocytes

54. Which of the following is the function of lysosomes

a. autophagy b. autolysis

c. digestion d. all of the above

55. Lysosomes are involved in

a. Extracellular digestion b. Intracellular digestion

c. both (a) and (b) d. none of the above

56. Who identified lysosome

a. Novikoff b. Claude

c. Palade d. none of the above

57. All the following has ribosomes except

a. nucleus b. mitochondrion

c. chloroplast d. cytoplasm

58. In 70S ribosome 'S' stands for

a. S.I unit b. Solubility factor

c. Svedberg unit d. None of the above

59. 80S ribosomes are found in

a. Eukaryotes b. Prokaryotes

c. Both eukaryotes and Prokaryotes d. Eukaryotic plant cells

60. The subunits of 80S ribosomes include

a. 40S and 50S b. 30S and 50S

c. 40S and 60S d. 20S and 60S

61. The subunits of 70S ribosomes include

a. 40S and 50S b. 30S and 40S

c. 30S and 50S d. 20S and 50S

62. 70S ribosomes occur in

a. Viruses b. prokaryotes

c. eukaryotic plant cells d. eukaryotic animal cells

63. Ribosomes are made up of

a. RNA only b. RNA and Proteins

c. RNA,DNA and Proteins d. nucleic acids, proteins and lipids

64. The rough ER is specially well developed in cells actively engaged in

a. Protein synthesis b. Nucleotide synthesis

c. Lipid synthesis d. Secretory functions

65. The nucleus contains

a. Mitochondria b. Golgi apparatus

c. Chromosomes d. Lysosomes

66. Plasma membrane is

a. Permeable b. Selectively permeable

c. Impermeable d. Semi-permeable

67. Most accepted structural model of plasma membrane is

a. Sandwitch model b. Unit membrane model

c. Lamellar model d. Fluid-mosaic model

68. Plasma membrane is composed of

a. Glycoproteins b. Lipoproteins

c. Chromoproteins d. Lipids

69. Ribosomes contain maximum amount of

a. Steriods b. Lipids

c. RNA d. DNA

70. Which structure is present in animal cell but is absent from plant cell ?

a. Centrioles b. Golgi apparatus

c. Mitochondria d. Endoplasmic reticulum

71. A unit membrane is about :

a. 50-60 Å thick b. 60-75 Å thick

c. 75-100 Å thick d. 100-120 Å thick

72. The enzymes which break up starch into sugar are called

a. Hydrolases b. Amylases

c. Lipases d. Nucleases

73. Apoenzyme is a

a. Protein b. Carbohydrate

c. Vitamin d. Amino acid

74. Coenzyme is :

a. Always a protein b. Often a metal

c. Always an inorganic compound d. Often a vitamin

75. Enzymes are named after their substrates by adding suffix :

a. -in b. -ase

c. -ose d. -sin

76. Enzyme exist in the cells asa. Solid b. Crystals

c. Colloid d. None of the above

77. An enzyme brings about :

a. Reduction in activation energy b. Increase in reaction time

c. Increase in activation energy d. All the above

78. Which of the following statement is “NOT’ correct

a. All enzymes are thermolabile b. All enzymes are biocatalysts

c. All enzymes are proteins d. All proteins are enzymes

79. Who discovered blood groups

a. F. Galton b. Carl Linnaeus

c. Edward Jenner d. C. Landsteiner

80. Enzymes bringing about hydrolysis of esters and peptides are :

a. Transferases b. Lyases

c. Hydrolases d. All of the above

81. Aerobic respiration is performed by :

a. Glyoxisomes b. Mitochondria

c. Lysosomes d. Chloroplast

82. Bile reduces the surface tension and causes

a. Emulsification of fat b. Digestion of fat

c. Absorption of fat d. All of the above

83. Dialysis causes

a. Separation of colloids from crystalloids b. Purification of colloids

c. Precipitation of colloids d. None of the above

84. Ultrafiltration helps in

a. Formation of Glomerular filtrate b. Formation of urine

c. Accumulation of proteins d. Separation of vitamins

85. pH of RBC is lower due to

a. Na+-K+ Pump action b. Gibb's Donnan Effect

c. Efflux of OH- from RBC d. None of the above

86. Gibb's Donnan effect creates

a. Diffusion b. Surface tension

c. Osmotic pressure d. None of the above

87. Transmembrane potential results due to

a. Donnan Effect b. Influx and efflux of oppositely charged ions

c. Retention of anions inside the membrane d. All the above

88. Rate of diffusion of a substance depends on

a. Presence of semi-permeable membrane b. Concentration gradient of solute

c. Concentration of solvent d. Concentration of ions

89. Homeostasis means

a. Control of internal environment of the body b. Adaptation with the environment

c. Constant environment of the body d. All of the above

90. Diffusion is more rapid in

a. Solid b. Liquid

c. Gas d. Mixture of liquid and gas

91. In Osmosis, movement of __________ occurs through the semi-permeable membrane

a. Solvent b. Solute

c. Both (a) and (b) d. All the above

92. Viscosity of blood increases with rise in

a. Albumin b. Globulin

c. Fibrinogen d. Prothrombin

93. Osmotic pressure across the capillary wall is exerted by

a. Size of the molecule b. Shape of the molecule

c. Concentration of the molecule d. All the above

94. Effect of change of temperature on viscosity involves

a. Increase in viscosity b. Decrease in viscosity

c. No change d. Both (a) and (b)

95. pH means

a. –log [H+] b. –log10 [H+]

c. –log [H] d. log [H+]

96. Microcytic anaemia develops in

a. Vit B12 deficiency b. Folic acid deficiency

c. Both (a) and (b) d. None of the above

97. Extrinsic system of blood clotting is initiated by

a. Factor-III b. Factor-VIII

c. Factor-II d. Factor-I

98. One of the following is NOT an anticoagulant

1a. Heparin b. Protein-C

c. Antithrombin-III d. Thrombin

99. Following are the membrane bound cell organelles except

a. Endoplasmic reticulum b. Lysosome

c. Ribosomes d. Peroxisome

100. The intrinsic protein present in the cell membrane mainly functions as

a. Enzymes b. Carrier

c. Pores d. Channels

ANSWERS

1.(b) 2.(c) 3.(b) 4.(c) 5.(d) 6.(a) 7.(d) 8.(c)9.(a) 10.(c) 11.(d) 12.(a)13.(a) 14.(d) 15.(c) 16.(c)

17.(c) 18.(a) 19.(a) 20.(a) 21.(a) 22.(b) 23.(d) 24.(b) 25.(b) 26.(c) 27.(c) 28.(b) 29.(b)

30.(c) 31. (d) 32.(c) 33.(d) 34.(b) 35.(c) 36.(b) 37.(c) 38.(a) 39.(d) 40.(d) 41.(a) 42.(b)

43.(d) 44.(c) 45.(d) 46. (b) 47.(c) 48.(b) 49.(b) 50.(c) 51.(d) 52.(c) 53.(c) 54.(d) 55.(c)

56.(a) 57.(a) 58.(c) 59.(a) 60.(c) 61.(c) 62.(b) 63.(b) 64.(a) 65.(c) 66.(b) 67.(d)

68.(b) 69.(c) 70.(a) 71.(c) 72.(b) 73.(a) 74.(d) 75.(b) 76.(c) 77.(a) 78.(d) 79.(d) 80.(c) 81.(b)

82.(d) 83.(a) 84.(a) 85.(b) 86.(c) 87.(a) 88.(b) 89.(c) 90.(c) 91.(a) 92.(a) 93.(c) 94.(d) 95.(b)

96.(c) 97.(a) 98.(d) 99.(c) 100.(a)

Evaluation 4

1. Which is a function of the cell wall?

A. To maintain turgor pressure

B. To provide support to the cell

C. To control what molecules enter and exit the cell

D. All of the above

Answer to Question #1

D is correct. All of these are functions of the cell wall.

2. The cells of which group of organisms lack a cell wall?

A. Archaea

B. Bacteria

C. Animals

D. Fungi

Answer to Question #2

C is correct. Animal cells do not have cell walls; they only have a cell membrane that is semipermeable. Animal cells are able to move more easily without a cell wall.

3. Which organism has a cell wall containing chitin?

A. Plants

B. Algae

C. Fungi

D. Bacteria

Answer to Question #3

C is correct. The cell walls of fungi contain chitin, which makes them strong and tough. Chitin is a polysaccharide that also forms the exoskeletons of some insects and crustaceans.

4. Which of the following is a component of peptidoglycan?

A. N-acetylglucosamine

B. N-acetylmuramic acid

C. Peptide chain of amino acids

D. All of the above

Answer to Question #4

D is correct. Peptidoglycan is made up of two repeating amino sugars, N-acetylglucosamine (NAG) and N-acetylmuramic acid (NAM), and a peptide of multiple amino acids is attached to each NAM unit.

5. Which substance is NOT a component of Gram staining?

A. Crystal violet dye

B. Safranin

C. Iodine

D. These are all components of Gram staining

Answer to Question #5

D is correct. All of these are components of Gram staining. Crystal violet dye forms a complex with iodine, which becomes trapped in the peptidoglycan cell wall structure of bacterial cells with thick cell walls (gram-positive bacteria). Safranin is the counterstain, and appears in bacteria with thin cell walls that do not hold the crystal violet-iodine staining (gram-negative bacteria).

6. What color will a gram-negative bacterium appear on a slide that has undergone Gram staining?

A. Red

B. Violet

C. Blue

D. Green

Answer to Question #6

A is correct. A gram-negative bacterium, such as a cyanobacterium, will appear red due to the safranin counter-stain used during Gram staining. Its peptidoglycan cell walls are too thin for the crystal violet-iodine complex to adhere to, so the violet color that is characteristic of gram-positive bacteria washes away and the red color from safranin remains.

www.ingramcontent.com/pod-product-compliance
Lightning Source LLC
Chambersburg PA
CBHW041830110726
48006CB00020B/2572

* 9 7 9 8 8 8 6 6 7 6 5 8 7 *